Property Law Handbook

putyourknowledgeintopractice

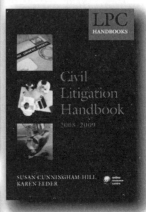

Property
Law
Handbook

ROBERT ABBEY

MARK RICHARDS

OXFORD
UNIVERSITY PRESS

OXFORD
UNIVERSITY PRESS

Great Clarendon Street, Oxford OX2 6DP

Oxford University Press is a department of the University of Oxford.
It furthers the University's objective of excellence in research, scholarship,
and education by publishing worldwide in

Oxford New York

Auckland Cape Town Dar es Salaam Hong Kong Karachi
Kuala Lumpur Madrid Melbourne Mexico City Nairobi
New Delhi Shanghai Taipei Toronto

With offices in

Argentina Austria Brazil Chile Czech Republic France Greece
Guatemala Hungary Italy Japan Poland Portugal Singapore
South Korea Switzerland Thailand Turkey Ukraine Vietnam

Oxford is a registered trade mark of Oxford University Press
in the UK and in certain other countries

Published in the United States
by Oxford University Press Inc., New York

British Library Cataloguing in Publication Data

Data available

Library of Congress Cataloging in Publication Data

Abbey, Robert M.
  Property law handbook / Robert Abbey, Mark Richards.
    p. cm.
  ISBN 978–0–19–923389–2
  1. Real property—England. I. Richards, Mark B. II. Title.
  KD829.A73 2008
    346.4204'3—dc22   2008021779

Typeset by Newgen Imaging Systems (P) Ltd., Chennai, India
Printed in Great Britain
on acid-free paper by
Ashford Colour Press Ltd, Gosport, Hampshire

ISBN 978–0–19–923389–2

10 9 8 7 6 5 4 3 2 1

DEDICATION

For Alison and Lesley

ACKNOWLEDGEMENTS

Grateful acknowledgment is made to the publishers of copyright material which appears in this book.

Crown copyright is reproduced under Class License C2006010631 with the permission of the Controller of HMSO and HM Land Registry.

Reproduced for educational purposes only by kind permission of the Solicitors' Law Stationery Society Limited and the Law Society of England and Wales are the Standard Conditions of Sale (fourth edition) and the Standard Commercial Property Conditions (second edition).

The Law Society of England and Wales for kind permission to reproduce the Law Society's Code for Completion by Post (1998 edition), Property Information Form TA6, and Part II of the Law Society's National Conveyancing Protocol.

OUTLINE CONTENTS

DETAILED CONTENTS

PREFACE

In our experience, students on the Legal Practice Course often have difficulty in translating their knowledge into distinction or commendation level examination answers. All too often we hear a student say, 'I worked hard, I thought I knew my subject but I underperformed in the exam'. We think that part of the problem lies in the fact that Property Law and Practice is an inherently practical subject. As such, a study of it differs in approach to other areas of previously studied substantive law.

In this book we have endeavoured to set out a concise but comprehensive coverage of Property Law and Practice. We have included key points summaries and checklists to aid study, as well as end-of-chapter self test and revision questions to assist learning and provide areas for discussion. The Online Resource Centre linked to the book contains, we hope, useful case studies to enable students to see practical examples of realistic conveyancing transactions. It also contains longer problem-style questions with commentary and suggested answers.

The technical rules of Property Law and Practice are often complex and intimidating and of course have to be mastered; but that is not enough to succeed. The key to excellence is the ability to apply those rules in a practical and often commercial context. We hope this book will help towards achieving that aim.

Along with Cheryl Cheasley and Lucy Read at Oxford University Press, we would also like to thank the following people who gave advice and reviewed various draft chapters of this book:

Margaret Arrand, Birmingham City University

Ian C Brookfield, Centre for Professional Legal Studies, Cardiff Law School

Shan Cole, University of Glamorgan

Lucy Crompton, Staffordshire University

Klearchos Kyriakides, University of Hertfordshire

Angela Latham, Nottingham Law School

Amanda Rees, University of Swansea

Louise Seymour, formerly Oxford Institute of Legal Practice

Mark Richards
Robert Abbey
London
August 2008

GUIDED TOUR OF THE BOOK

Abbey & Richards' *Property Law Handbook* contains numerous features which have been specifically designed to facilitate your learning and understanding of property law and practice. To help you get the most out of your text, this 'Guided Tour of the Book' highlights the features used by the authors to explain the complex processes involved, and their application to a range of conveyancing transactions.

WITHIN EACH CHAPTER

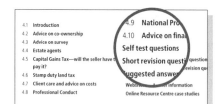

CHAPTER CONTENTS

Use the detailed contents list, contained at the beginning of each chapter, to quickly and clearly identify the key topics to be covered, and locate where each topic appears in the wider subject area.

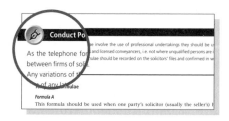

'CONDUCT POINT' BOXES

Look for the conduct point icon, featured throughout the book, to identify situations in which an awareness of best practice and professional conduct is essential, and to find practical advice and guidance on how to act should you encounter such situations in practice.

'KEY POINTS' SUMMARIES

Use the key points summaries, featured at the end of important topics, as a useful checklist, both throughout study and during revision, to ensure that you have fully covered and understood the essential points of each topic.

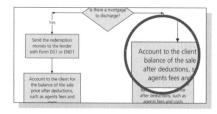

FIGURES

Diagrams and flowcharts are featured throughout the book and are designed to clearly explain, and provide a visual representation of, complex legal processes.

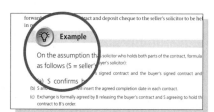

EXAMPLES

Look for the example icon to find practical examples of how the law should be applied, or operates, in a realistic practice situation providing you with a valuable insight into how the legal principles covered in the book are used in practice.

ONLINE RESOURCE CENTRE ICON

Look out for this icon in the margins of the book. Wherever it appears further information is available on the Online Resource Centre which accompanies the *Handbook*.
Please visit
www.oxfordtextbooks.co.uk/orc/lpcpropertyhandbook08_09
to see the full range of supporting resources to accompany this book.

END OF CHAPTER FEATURES

SELF-TEST QUESTIONS

Use these questions, either following your reading of a chapter or as a revision tool, to ensure that you have fully understood the topics covered and to identify gaps in your knowledge where further study may be required. You can check your own answers against the suggested answers provided at the end of chapters.

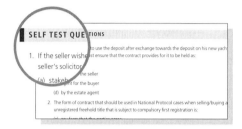

SHORT REVISION QUESTIONS

Following your reading of a chapter or during your revision, use these questions to practise applying your subject knowledge to practical scenarios. You can check your own answers against the suggested answers provided at the end of chapters.

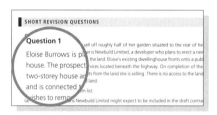

WIDER READING

Build on your existing knowledge of the subject area by consulting the books, articles and further materials identified in the wider reading sections.

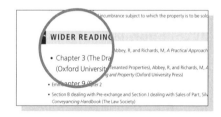

WEBSITES FOR FURTHER INFORMATION

Use the annotated web links to guide you to relevant further sources of information online, and to identify and explore those websites which will be most useful to you in practice.

ONLINE RESOURCE CENTRE CASE STUDIES

For an insight into the operation of the law in a realistic practice setting, refer to the fictional case studies featured throughout the book. Full documentation relating to these case studies is available on the Online Resource Centre accompanying the *Handbook* at:
www.oxfordtextbooks.co.uk/orc/lpcpropertyhandbook08_09.

GUIDED TOUR OF THE WEBSITE

Online Resource Centres offer a valuable range of additional, free to use, online learning and teaching resources for both lecturers and students which have been specifically designed to complement the text they accompany. All resources can be downloaded and are fully customisable allowing them to be easily incorporated into your institution's existing virtual learning environment.

To view the resources available to accompany the *Property Law Handbook*, please visit www.oxfordtextbooks.co.uk/orc/lpcproperty handbook08_09

Resources featured in this section of the site are freely accessible but are password protected. To access the resources simply visit the site at:
www.oxfordtextbooks.co.uk/orc/lpcpropertyhandbook08_09
and enter the following username and password:

Username: property08
Password: rainbow

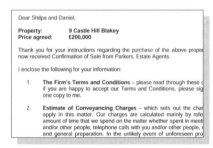

CASE STUDY DOCUMENTATION

Accompanying the fictional case studies in the book, this area of the site contains documentation you would expect to see in a real transaction, ensuring that you are fully prepared for practice by highlighting the documents which a typical solicitor's file might contain.

PROBLEM QUESTIONS AND ANSWER GUIDANCE

These problem based questions offer you the opportunity to practise applying your knowledge of the subject to realistic scenarios ensuring that you are fully prepared for the type of questions you may encounter in exams. All questions are accompanied by full answer guidance.

LECTURER RESOURCES

Resources featured in this section of the site are available solely to adopting lecturers and are accessed with the use of a free password. To obtain a password, follow the links on the main site at: **www.oxfordtextbooks.co.uk/lpcpropertyhandbook08_09**. Our web team will contact you with a password within three working days. For ease of use, all resources in this part of the site can be easily downloaded into your institution's virtual learning environment.

TEST BANK OF QUESTIONS

A bank of questions covering all aspects of the book is available to download into your virtual learning environment (VLE). Also available in Word format, the multiple choice questions give you the ability to provide a resource which your students can use to test themselves, or which you can use to assess their learning. Once included in your VLE, the questions are entirely customisable, enabling you to remove questions which are less relevant to your course, or to change the order of the questions to match the order in which topics are taught at your institution.

Each question is accompanied by feedback which highlights why the selected answer is correct or incorrect. Students are also directed to the relevant page of the textbook should they need to re-read or clarify a particular point.

FIGURES

All flowcharts and diagrams featured in the book are available in electronic format enabling you to make full use of the figures in your lectures or course handouts.

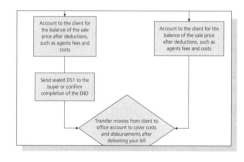

TABLE OF CASES

TABLE OF STATUTES

TABLE OF STATUTORY INSTRUMENTS

1 INTRODUCTION

1.1 Introduction to property law and practice

1.1 INTRODUCTION TO PROPERTY LAW AND PRACTICE

Property Law and Practice (PLP) covers all aspects of the subject matter of conveyancing. This book has been written to assist you in the study of the process that enables the transfer of legal title to property. To become a solicitor, you now need to apply your PLP knowledge to questions that you may encounter in your examinations that on the Legal Practice Course (LPC) are usually called subject assessments. Again, this book is here to help you in that endeavour.

1.1.1 THE SOURCES OF PROPERTY LAW AND PRACTICE

It is likely that you will benefit from a reminder of the foundations upon which PLP has been built. You should therefore reflect upon how PLP rests upon the three foundations of land law, contract law, and equity and trusts. When you are faced with examinations you will have gone through your course and will perhaps be over-concerned with detail. It is therefore of benefit to just stand back a moment and consider the broader view, to give you the kind of holistic understanding of the subject that will help with your examination answers. Remember also that PLP concerns itself with several other areas of the law such as company and partnership law, succession, planning law, and especially several parts of revenue law. It is this diversity that makes PLP a tricky subject to grasp. However, a brief look at the three main supports will help you get to grips with the full perspective of this broad subject.

1.1.2 LAND LAW

As you might expect a strong understanding of land law is critical for success in PLP. If you are still unsure of some fundamentals of land law you will surely have trouble with PLP. If you are still in doubt about such matters as easements or restrictive covenants then we firmly suggest that you go back to your land law notes and refresh your memory of the salient points. Please also look at the subsequent chapter in this book that gives you an overview of land law in general. If you still need further detail then *A Textbook on Land Law* by Mackenzie and Phillips (Oxford University Press) is a clear and direct guide to the fundamentals of this important buttress to PLP.

In the context of assessment a clear understanding of land law is a fundamental prerequisite of PLP. Indeed, The Law Society, in their original written standards for the LPC, specifically stated that the course is based on the assumption that students will have prior knowledge and understanding of the nature of legal estates and interests, equitable interests, easements, covenants and mortgages, joint ownership, and unregistered and registered title (including the registration of charges). It is assumed further that students will have prior knowledge and understanding of formation of contract, formalities of written contracts, misrepresentation, and remedies for breach of contract. Accordingly you will appreciate that there will inevitably be questions in examinations that will test not just your knowledge of the conveyancing process, but also these foundations of land law upon which PLP is built.

1.1.3 CONTRACT LAW

Contract law is considered to be just as important for students of PLP as land law. When you consider that conveyancing is about the transfer of title and these transfers are in the main made by contract then you will appreciate why contract law plays such an important part. Should you end up being a property practitioner you will do well to actively maintain your knowledge of the fundamentals of contract law as you will regularly encounter transactions concerned with it. As you now know, each conveyance on sale will involve the actual preparation of a written contract. Indeed your land law will tell you that without a written contract containing all the terms of the agreement there is no deal! (If this information comes as a surprise to you then we suggest that you look again at the Law of Property (Miscellaneous Provisions) Act 1989 for clarification.)

So, in these circumstances it is not difficult to anticipate questions in PLP that will examine your understanding of contract law as well as its application in conveyancing. However, it goes further than just the formation of valid contracts. You will also need to know about misrepresentation and in particular remedies for breach of contract. It is clear that these areas are of particular interest to examiners and a thorough grounding in both topics is advisable if you wish to do well in your subject assessment.

1.1.4 EQUITY AND TRUSTS

Then there is the potentially opaque foundation subject of equity and trusts. This important stanchion to PLP is not so obviously relevant as land law and contract law, but it is nevertheless a pervasive element in PLP and certainly as far as assessment is concerned. Why is this? Frankly, it is because this complex area provides challenging questions that are just ripe for a subject assessment/examination question. For example, the whole topic of third party rights is a fertile and attractive location for your examiner to find questions that will concern equity and trusts in the context of the conveyancing process. Co-ownership however, is the topic for the kind of challenging question set by examiners. You will therefore need to be absolutely clear on the law relating to trusts and in particular trusts of land. You will need to understand the differences between tenants in common and joint tenants and their relevance to joint ownership in PLP. Finally you will need to remind yourself about the equitable remedies that are available. It is one thing to understand their availability in theory but it is another to actually apply them to a practical situation. Property Law will in practice be an area that will give rise to the application of those equitable remedies. This being the case they will often end up in subject assessment questions.

1.1.5 BLENDING YOUR KNOWLEDGE

So, the key to understanding the nature of PLP in the context of assessment is to appreciate how it calls upon these various strands of the law. In doing so it brings together other parts of the law that you should have encountered and which you will now need to apply on a practical basis. You will need to be able to integrate these other areas into your knowledge and understanding of the conveyancing process. It means that you must abandon a discrete approach to learning and applying the law. PLP requires you to blend your knowledge and this will need to be displayed in your answers. Moreover, many elements of the above apply to both domestic and commercial properties. As such you need to understand the fundamentals of both items to enable you to be prepared for exams and practice.

2 IMPORTANT PRINCIPLES OF LAND LAW

2.1 INTRODUCTION

Land Law is an important foundation for the study of Property Law and Practice (PLP) and this chapter will, we hope, provide a useful summary of the fundamental principles that you should have studied at the academic stage of training. Please be aware that our commentary is not exhaustive and for more substantive coverage of the law you should consult a specialist text (see Wider reading below).

2.2 ESTATES AND INTERESTS IN LAND

2.2.1 LEGAL ESTATES AND INTERESTS

An estate is a right to own and enjoy land for a particular length of time (although in the case of a freehold estate the time can last indefinitely). An interest is a right affecting someone else's land. The Law of Property Act 1925 (LPA 1925) reduced the number of legal *estates* to two—freehold and leasehold; and the number of legal *interests* to five, the three most important of which are:

- legal easements and profits;
- a legal rentcharge; and
- a charge by way of legal mortgage.

2.2.2 EQUITABLE INTERESTS

Any interest in land which is not classified as a legal estate or legal interest is known as an equitable interest (LPA 1925, section 1(3)). Equitable interests include:

- the benefit of a restrictive covenant or contract;
- the interest of a beneficiary under a trust.

Only legal estates and interests are capable of being registered under the Land Registration Act 2002 (LRA 2002). Equitable interests are not capable of substantive registration at Land Registry but may be protected on the register by notice or registration (see 2.8 below).

2.3 **TRUSTS AND CO-OWNERSHIP**

2.3.1 **INTRODUCTION**

Where two or more persons are entitled to possession of land at the same time there is a trust of land governed by the Trusts of Land and Appointment of Trustees Act 1996. The legal estate is vested in the trustees, and the persons with co-ownership rights are known as the beneficiaries. The trustees hold the legal estate but the beneficiaries as owners in equity are effectively the 'real' owners. Very often the trustees and beneficiaries are one and the same, e.g. husband and wife. Trusts can be created expressly or may be implied by law.

2.3.2 **IMPLIED TRUSTS**

Co-ownership may arise in favour of someone even though that person's name does not appear on the register of title or in the deeds. This is known as an implied trust. It arises where someone acquires an interest in land, e.g. by contributing to the purchase price or paying for improvements to the property. There are essentially two types of implied trust—the resulting trust and the constructive trust.

2.3.3 **RESULTING TRUSTS**

A resulting trust occurs typically where the legal estate is transferred into the name of one person following the payment of some or all of the purchase price by another person. For example, in *Bull v Bull* [1955] 1 QB 234 property was conveyed into Mr Bull's name but the purchase price for the property was provided by both Mr Bull and his mother. Mr Bull therefore held the legal estate on resulting trust for himself and his mother.

2.3.4 **CONSTRUCTIVE TRUSTS**

A constructive trust arises where it would be unconscionable for the legal owner of the land to deny the equitable interest of another. There needs to be evidence of a common intention between the parties that the property would be jointly owned and that the non-legal owner relied on this agreement to his or her detriment (see *Lloyds Bank v Rosset* [1991] 1 AC 107).

2.3.5 **OVERREACHING**

Payment of capital money to at least two trustees will overreach the interests of the beneficiaries under the trust. This means that a buyer or mortgagee making the payment will not be bound by the interests of the beneficiaries as those interests will attach to the proceeds of sale (see *Williams & Glyn's Bank v Boland* [1981] AC 487 and *City of London Building Society v Flegg* [1988] AC 54).

Once overreaching has occurred the beneficiaries will no longer be entitled to remain in possession of the land. Instead they will obtain an interest in the proceeds of sale which will be held on trust for them by the trustees, e.g. the sellers of the legal estate.

2.3.6 **CO-OWNERSHIP**

There are two types of co-ownership—joint tenancy and tenancy in common. The legal estate can be held under a joint tenancy but not a tenancy in common. The beneficiaries holding the equitable estate can hold either under a joint tenancy or a tenancy in common.

The crucial distinction between these two types of co-ownership is that the survivorship principle applies to a joint tenancy but not a tenancy in common. This means that on the death of a joint tenant the land immediately passes to the surviving joint tenant(s); it does not pass under the deceased's will or intestacy. Conversely under a tenancy in common the survivorship principle does not apply and the deceased's share passes under his will or intestacy.

2.3.7 JOINT TENANCY

Under a joint tenancy the co-owners own the whole of the land together and all joint tenants have the same interest in the land irrespective of their respective contributions to the purchase price. Four unities must be present as between the co-owners:

1. Unity of possession, i.e. all joint tenants are entitled to possess every part of the land.
2. Unity of interest, e.g. the land is all freehold or all leasehold.
3. Unity of title, i.e. title acquired under the same document or transaction.
4. Unity of time, i.e. all co-owners acquired their interest at the same time.

2.3.8 TENANCY IN COMMON

As mentioned above, only the equitable estate can be held as a tenancy in common, not the legal estate. Each co-owner owns specific shares in the land, either equally or unequally. Only unity of possession is necessary for a tenancy in common. Where co-owners of registered land hold as tenants in common, Land Registry will enter the following restriction in the proprietorship register of the title:

> No disposition by a sole proprietor of the registered estate (except a trust corporation) under which capital money arises is to be registered unless authorised by an order of the court.

2.3.9 SEVERANCE OF A JOINT TENANCY

A joint tenancy in equity can be severed and thereby converted into a tenancy in common. In this case the right of survivorship no longer applies. If there are more than two joint tenants, severance operates only on the share of the party effecting the severance. The other parties remain as joint tenants as between themselves.

The different methods of severance are:

- written notice under LPA 1925, section 36(2) given by one or more joint tenants to all the other joint tenants;
- selling or charging the beneficial interest (including a charging order made by a court);
- bankruptcy—the bankrupt's severed beneficial interest vests in the trustee in bankruptcy.

Remember that a legal estate cannot be held as a tenancy in common so notwithstanding severance of an equitable joint tenancy the legal estate will remain as a joint tenancy.

The maximum number of trustees of the legal estate permitted by statute is four (Trustee Act 1925, section 34(2)). Where more than four are named in the deed, the property vests in the first four who are of full age.

2.4 EASEMENTS

2.4.1 INTRODUCTION

An easement is a right attached to one piece of land (the dominant tenement) which gives the owner of that land a right to use another person's land (the servient tenement). The owners of the dominant and servient tenements must both have estates in the land. Examples of easements are rights of way or drainage, and the rights of tenants to use common parts in a block of flats.

2.4.2 CHARACTERISTICS OF AN EASEMENT

A right can only be capable of being an easement if it satisfies the four characteristics laid down in *Re Ellenborough Park* [1956] Ch 131:

1. There must be a dominant and a servient tenement. Note that a public right of way is not an easement because it does not benefit specific land, i.e. there is no dominant tenement.

2. The dominant and servient tenements must be owned or occupied by different persons.

3. The right must benefit the dominant tenement, i.e. it cannot be purely a personal right in favour of the occupier.

4. The right must be capable of forming the subject matter of a grant, i.e. granted by deed and sufficiently definite. In addition no exclusive possession must be conferred.

2.4.3 CREATION OF AN EASEMENT

If the right satisfies the *Re Ellenborough Park* test it does not become an easement unless it is created either through a grant or a reservation. A grant is where an easement is given to a buyer over land that is retained by a seller, e.g. right of way or drainage. A reservation occurs where an easement is retained by a seller over land which is sold to a buyer.

A grant may be either express (i.e. by deed), or be implied by various methods (see below), or it may be presumed (i.e. by prescription). A reservation may be either express, or implied by necessity or common intention only (see section 2.4.4 below).

An express easement may be legal (if it is created by deed) or equitable (if it complies with section 2 of the Law of Property (Miscellaneous Provisions) Act 1989, i.e. it is in writing, contains all the agreed terms, and is signed by the parties).

An easement created impliedly or by prescription is a legal easement.

2.4.4 IMPLIED GRANTS

An implied grant may be created by the following:

1. Necessity, e.g. where land is land-locked (see *Nickerson v Barraclough* [1981] Ch 426). Mere inconvenience is insufficient to create an easement of necessity.

2. Common intention of the parties (see *Liverpool City Council v Irwin* [1977] AC 239).

3. On a sale of part, i.e. where some land is sold off, the rule in *Wheeldon v Burrows* [1879] 12 ChD 31 if the following conditions are met:
   • one person owned and occupied the whole of the land;
   • the owner previously exercised a quasi-easement over the land;
   • the right is continuous and apparent, i.e. obvious;
   • the right is necessary for the reasonable enjoyment of the land.

4. Section 62 of the LPA 1925. This converts mere permissions into easements if the following conditions are met:
   • there is diversity of ownership and occupation, e.g. landlord and tenant;
   • there was a 'conveyance', i.e. a transfer of legal title to the occupier, e.g. a lease (see *Wright v Macadam* [1949] 2 KB 744).

To avoid uncertainty it is standard conveyancing practice for the parties to agree to exclude the operation of the implied grant rules. If any easements are required by the buyer then they should be granted expressly in the transfer deed.

2.4.5 **IMPLIED RESERVATIONS**

If an easement is not expressly reserved it can only be implied by necessity or common intention, i.e. not by the rule in *Wheeldon v Burrows* or section 62 of the LPA 1925.

2.4.6 **PRESUMED OR PRESCRIPTIVE EASEMENTS**

This is the grant of an easement through long usage. It applies only to freehold land, except for easements of light. It can be acquired in three ways: at common law; through the fiction of 'lost modern grant'; or under the Prescription Act 1832.

In addition a claimant must satisfy the following criteria:

- The easement must have been exercised as of right, i.e. not by force, not in secret and not with permission.
- There must have been continuous and unbroken use of the easement for the prescribed period.
- The use was by a freehold owner of the dominant tenement against a freehold owner of the servient tenement.

> **Grant of easements (in favour of buyer)—methods of creation**
>
> Express
>
> Implied (necessity, common intention, the rule in *Wheeldon v Burrows* or LPA 1925, section 62)
>
> Presumed (i.e. prescription)
>
> **Reservation of easements (in favour of seller)—methods of creation**
>
> Express
>
> Implied (necessity or common intention only)

2.4.7 **EASEMENTS IN REGISTERED LAND**

Registration of title includes the benefit of any appurtenant easements whether or not expressly referred to on the register.

Section 27(2) (d) of the LRA 2002 provides that an express easement over registered land must be completed by registration. This applies even in respect of estates not capable of substantive registration, e.g. a lease for a term not exceeding seven years. In this case the easement must be registered even though the lease itself cannot be registered. The easement is not a legal easement until it has been registered, i.e. it takes effect only in equity.

2.4.8 **EASEMENTS THAT ARE OVERRIDING INTERESTS**

Under Schedule 3 of the LRA 2002, since 13 October 2006 any legal easement arising through implied grant or reservation or prescription is an overriding interest binding on a buyer, only if:

- it is known to the buyer; or
- it would have been obvious to the buyer on a reasonably careful inspection; or
- it has been exercised in the 12 months prior to the disposition.

In registered land equitable easements can be protected by the entry of a notice under section 34 of the LRA 2002. In unregistered land equitable easements can be protected by registering a D(iii) land charge against the name of the estate owner.

2.4.9 PROFITS A PRENDRE

A profit a prendre is different from an easement in that it is a right for one person to remove something from land belonging to another person, e.g. wood, grass, or fish. The person enjoying the profit does not need to own land that is benefited by the profit. This is known as a profit 'in gross'.

Profits can be created in the same way as easements except that they cannot be acquired by implied grant or reservation. The benefit of a profit in gross is capable of substantive registration under the LRA 2002.

2.5 FREEHOLD COVENANTS

2.5.1 INTRODUCTION

Covenants affecting freehold land can be either restrictive or positive in nature. A restrictive covenant restricts a person's use of land, e.g. not to build or not to run a business. A positive covenant imposes an obligation to perform a specific act and normally involves doing work or spending money, e.g. erecting and maintaining a boundary wall. Courts will consider the substance of the covenant in determining whether it is positive or negative. So 'not to allow land to become infested with rabbits' requires positive action e.g. shooting the rabbits, and is therefore a positive covenant.

The person with the benefit of the covenant is known as the covenantee and the person with the burden of the covenant is known as the covenantor. The benefit and burden of restrictive covenants can run with the land. The benefit of positive covenants can run with the land but the burden of positive covenants cannot run with the land either at common law or in equity. This is now explained.

2.5.2 ENFORCING COVENANTS

A covenant is always enforceable between the original parties because of privity of contract (X and Y in Figure 2.1). But if either piece of land is sold there is no longer privity of contract between the current owners of the two pieces of land. Whether the covenant can be enforced will now depend on whether the benefit of the covenant has passed to the buyer of the benefiting land (A in Figure 2.1) and the burden of the covenant has passed to the buyer of the burdened land (B in Figure 2.1).

FIGURE 2.1

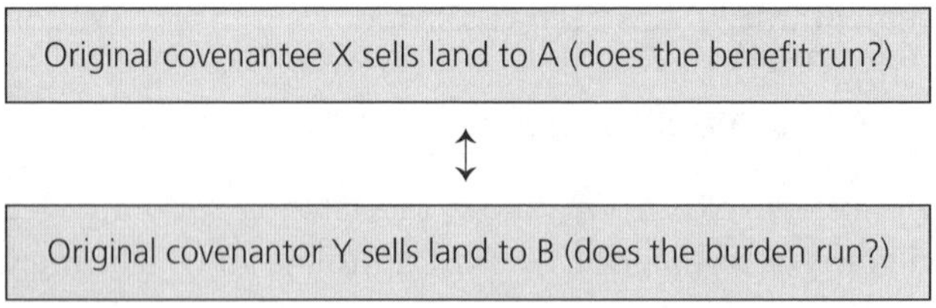

Original covenantee X sells land to A (does the benefit run?)

↕

Original covenantor Y sells land to B (does the burden run?)

2.5.3 THE BENEFIT AT COMMON LAW

The benefit of the covenant will run at common law if the following requirements are satisfied:

1. the covenant 'touches and concerns' the land of the covenantee, i.e. it benefits the land and is not purely personal;

2. the covenantee owns the legal estate in the land to be benefited when the covenant is made so that the benefit can attach to it;

3. the original parties intended that the covenant should run;

4. the assignee derives title from the original covenantee.

2.5.4 THE BURDEN AT COMMON LAW

The burden of the covenant will not run at common law (*Rhone v Stephens* [1994] 2 AC 310). However this rule can be circumvented by:

- a chain of indemnity covenants in which each successive buyer agrees to indemnify his predecessor in title (see 5.9);
- the conveyance containing the covenant reserves a rentcharge with a right of entry to make good any breach of covenant;
- the rule in *Halsall v Brizell* [1957] Ch 169 which says a person cannot take a benefit unless they observe a related obligation (e.g. to use a road provided they contribute towards its maintenance);
- creating commonhold land (see Chapter 17).

2.5.5 THE BENEFIT IN EQUITY

The benefit of the covenant may run in equity in one of three ways:

- annexation of the covenant to the land. This is implied by LPA 1925, section 78;
- express assignment of the covenant to the buyer of the benefiting land;
- through a building scheme (see *Elliston v Reacher* [1908] 2 Ch 374).

2.5.6 THE BURDEN IN EQUITY

The burden of the covenant will run in equity if the rules derived from *Tulk v Moxhay* (1848) 2 Ph 774 are satisfied:

- the covenant is restrictive in nature (see 2.5.1 above);
- the original parties intended that the burden should run. This is implied by LPA 1925, section 79;
- the covenantee owned land capable of benefiting from the covenant at the time it was created;
- the party to be bound has notice of it, i.e. if created after 1925, the covenant has been protected by registration either as a notice in registered land (LRA 2002, section 34) or a D(ii) land charge in unregistered land.

Importantly, where the burden passes in equity a buyer of the benefiting land must show that the benefit has also passed in equity as well. In these circumstances it is not enough to show that the benefit passes merely at common law.

2.5.7 DISCHARGE OR VARIATION OF COVENANTS

A covenant may be discharged or changed in one of the following ways:

1. Lands Tribunal Order (LPA 1925, section 84(1)) if the covenant has become obsolete or impedes the reasonable use of the land.

2. Deed of release or variation entered into by the parties entitled to the benefit and burden of the covenant.

3. Where both the benefited and burdened land has come into common ownership (unless the covenant remains enforceable under a building scheme).

4. Where the covenant is void for non-registration as a D(ii) land charge.

2.6 LEASES

2.6.1 INTRODUCTION

A lease (or tenancy) is a right for a person to occupy and use land for a term with a fixed commencement date and a fixed maximum duration. This includes fixed term leases and periodic tenancies which automatically renew themselves at the end of each period of the tenancy.

2.6.2 FORMALITIES

A legal lease must be made by deed. However a legal lease may be created orally or in writing if it is for a term of three years or less and takes effect immediately, reserving the best rent reasonably obtainable (LPA 1925, section 54(2)). If not legal, the tenant will have an equitable interest provided the lease complies with section 2 of the Law of Property (Miscellaneous Provisions) Act 1989, i.e. it is in writing, contains all the agreed terms, and is signed by the parties.

The tenant (or lessee) must hold a term which is shorter than that held by the landlord (or lessor). Although quite normal, payment of rent is not an essential element of a lease.

The tenant must have exclusive possession, i.e. the right to use the premises to the exclusion of all others including the landlord (*Street v Mountford* [1985 2 All ER 289]). If not, the agreement will not create a legal interest in land and be merely a licence.

A lease for a term of more than seven years is compulsorily registrable at Land Registry. If such a lease is granted on or after 19 June 2006 it must contain prescribed clauses (see 16.2.1 for further details).

2.6.3 LEASEHOLD COVENANTS

Leasehold covenants are the obligations of the landlord and tenant under the lease. Typical landlord covenants are to allow the tenant quiet enjoyment of the premises and to repair and maintain the exterior of a building where part of it is let. Typical tenant covenants include payment of rent, not to assign the lease without the landlord's consent and not to use the premises except as authorized by the lease.

There is privity of contract between the original parties to the lease (L1 and T1 in Figure 2.2) so there is little problem with enforcement if the lease or reversion has not been assigned.

FIGURE 2.2

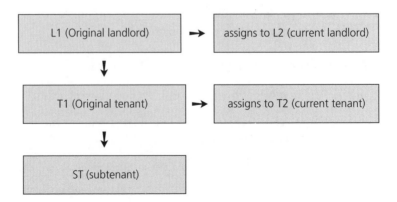

However if assignment of the lease or reversion has taken place then one set of rules applies to 'old' leases granted before 1 January 1996 (LPA 1925) and another set of rules applies to 'new' leases granted on or after that date (Landlord and Tenant (Covenants) Act 1995).

2.6.4 RULES FOR 'OLD LEASES'

An assignee of an old lease (T2) is liable for breaches of covenant under the principle of 'privity of estate', i.e. the relationship between the current landlord and the current tenant. For the burden to run, however, the covenant must 'touch and concern' the land, i.e. relate to the land itself (*Spencer's Case* [1583]). This applies to most tenants' covenants in leases.

The original tenant (T1) will remain liable throughout the term of the lease for any breach of covenant by his successor (T2). Thus the original tenant can still be sued by the landlord even after the original tenant has assigned his lease. If the current tenant has disappeared or been made bankrupt the landlord can therefore pursue the original tenant.

The original landlord (L1) after assigning its reversion also continues to remain liable under the landlord's covenants.

2.6.5 RULES FOR 'NEW LEASES'

Under privity of estate rules for new leases the 'touch and concern' test no longer applies. The burden of all covenants will pass to the assignee of the lease (T2) unless in the lease the covenants are expressed to be personal only.

The key difference for new leases is that once the original tenant (or assignee) has assigned his lease he is released from the tenant's covenants and cannot be sued by the landlord. However the landlord may, where the landlord's consent to the assignment is required, require the tenant to enter into an Authorised Guarantee Agreement (AGA) under section 16 of the 1995 Act. Under an AGA the tenant agrees to guarantee his immediate assignee's performance of the covenants.

Unlike tenants of new leases, landlords are not released automatically from their covenants when they assign their reversion. However they can apply to their tenant to be released or, failing that, to the court.

2.6.6 SUB-LEASES

There is no privity of contract or privity of estate between a head landlord (L1) and a subtenant (ST) so on the face of it neither can sue the other directly. However restrictive covenants in a head-lease may be enforced against a subtenant if the subtenant has notice of them. This is based on the old doctrine of notice (*Tulk v Moxhay* (1848) 2 Ph 774).

2.6.7 TERMINATION OF LEASES

Leases can be brought to an end by forfeiture, expiry, notice, surrender, merger, disclaimer, repudiation, and frustration. The detail of the law in this area goes beyond the scope of this text. Do remember, however, that the landlord's right to forfeit a lease is not implied at common law. The lease should contain an express clause providing for forfeiture on breach of a tenant's covenant.

2.7 MORTGAGES

2.7.1 INTRODUCTION

A mortgage is a right of a lender (mortgagee) over land which guarantees the payment of a debt. The borrower is known as the mortgagor. Mortgages can be created expressly or arise under statute. They can be either legal or equitable. A legal mortgage must be by deed. An equitable mortgage will normally arise inadvertently due to some defect in a legal mortgage, e.g. where the document has not been executed as a deed. Equitable mortgages are quite rare so we shall confine ourselves to the law relating to legal mortgages.

2.7.2 REGISTERED LAND

A legal mortgage of registered land must be completed by registration if the mortgagee wishes to exercise its statutory powers including the power of sale. Once registered, it has priority over other interests unless they are protected on the register or are overriding interests.

2.7.3 UNREGISTERED LAND

A mortgagee with a first mortgage will hold the title deeds as security. A first mortgage protected in this way has priority over all other mortgages. Second and subsequent mortgagees should protect their mortgages by registering them as C(i) land charges.

2.7.4 COMPANY MORTGAGOR

Mortgages by companies must be registered at the Companies Registry within 21 days of creation of the mortgage. If not, the mortgage will not bind the liquidator or creditors if the company subsequently goes into liquidation.

2.7.5 RIGHTS OF THE MORTGAGOR

The mortgagor has the following important protections:

1. Undue influence. The court can set aside a mortgage which has been obtained through undue influence on the mortgagor. The principal ground for setting aside a transaction is the notice which the mortgagee had or ought to have had of the undue influence (see *Barclays Bank plc v O'Brien* [1994] 1 AC and *CIBC Mortgages plc v Pitt* [1994] 1 AC 200). In *Royal Bank of Scotland v Etridge (No 2)* [2002] 2 AC 773 the House of Lords gave guidance to lenders as to the steps they should take to guard against the risk of being affected with notice of undue influence (see 9.10).

2. The Consumer Credit Act 2006 allows the court to reopen a credit agreement to do justice between the parties, e.g. if the interest rate is extortionate.

3. There must be no clog or fetter on the mortgagor's right to redeem the mortgage. Thus any provision in the mortgage which prevents the mortgagor from redeeming is ignored by equity and is void (see *Jones v Morgan* [2002] 1 EGLR 125).

4. There must be no postponement of the right to redeem that would effectively make it impossible to redeem the mortgage (see *Fairclough v Swan Brewery Co Ltd* [1912] AC 565).

5. There must be no collateral advantage to the mortgagee, e.g. where an owner of a public house agrees to buy all his beer from a brewery mortgagee. See generally *Noakes & Co Ltd v Rice* [1902] AC 24 and *Kreglinger v New Patagonia Meat & Cold Storage Co Ltd* [1914] AC 25.

2.7.6 RIGHTS OF THE MORTGAGEE

The mortgagee has the following rights against the mortgagor:

1. To sue for the debt.

2. To take possession of the property.

3. Foreclosure. This is the judicial procedure by which the mortgagee acquires the land free from the interests of the mortgagor. It is now rarely used.

4. To appoint a receiver to manage or sell the property. This is more common in commercial mortgages. The receiver acts as the agent of the mortgagor.

5. To sell the property, i.e. the mortgagee's power of sale. This is the right most frequently used by a mortgagee. It may sell if:

  - the power of sale exists. This is implied in a mortgage made by deed unless, unusually, the deed expressly excludes it;
  - the power of sale has arisen. This occurs once the contractual date for redemption of the mortgage has passed (usually about six months after creation of the mortgage);
  - the power of sale has become exercisable. Under LPA 1925, section 103 this occurs when:
    - interest payments are more than two months in arrears; or
    - there has been a written request for repayment of the capital and three months have elapsed without payment; or
    - there has been a breach of some other term of the mortgage.

The mortgagee can choose when to sell and the mode of sale but must obtain the best price reasonably obtainable (*Cuckmere Brick Co v Mutual Finance Ltd* [1971] Ch 949). This is why sales by mortgagees are often held at auction, i.e. to demonstrate that they are getting the best price.

A sale by mortgagee is subject to any prior mortgages but will be free of the mortgagor's interests and of any estates or interests over which the mortgagee has priority (LPA 1925, section 104(1)), e.g. subsequent mortgages.

2.7.7 APPLICATION OF SALE PROCEEDS

Under section 105 of the LPA 1925, after paying off any prior mortgages the money received from the buyer must be held on trust by the selling mortgagee to pay:

- all expenses incidental to the sale;
- itself the principal sum, interest, and costs due under its mortgage;
- any surplus to the next mortgagee in line or, if none, to the mortgagor.

2.8 THIRD PARTY RIGHTS, OVERRIDING INTERESTS, AND THE REGISTER OF TITLE

2.8.1 INTRODUCTION

In registered land a registrable disposition for valuable consideration, e.g. a transfer on sale, has priority over any third party right which is not protected in one of the ways prescribed by the LRA 2002.

The means of protection of third party rights are either by an entry on the register (e.g. notice or restriction) or by virtue of the right's status as an overriding interest. An overriding interest will not appear on the register but will bind a buyer irrespective of notice (see 2.8.4 below).

2.8.2 NOTICES

A notice is the appropriate way to protect rights that are intended to bind third parties (LRA 2002, section 32). It may be either an agreed notice (i.e. with the consent of the registered proprietor) or a unilateral notice. Examples of interests that may be protected by notice are:

- a restrictive covenant;
- an easement;
- a right of occupation under the Family Law Act 1996;
- a lease affecting a reversionary title;
- charging orders made against a sole registered proprietor.

2.8.3 RESTRICTIONS

A restriction regulates the circumstances in which a disposition of a registered estate or charge may be the subject of an entry in the register (LRA 2002, section 40(1)). Examples of situations in which restrictions may be used are:

- to ensure that purchase monies are paid to at least two trustees or a trust corporation in order to overreach interests under the trust. Such a restriction will be entered where co-owners hold the beneficial estate as tenants in common (see 2.3.8 above);
- to show any limitation on the powers of a corporation or other body;
- to ensure that any necessary consents to a disposition are obtained.

2.8.4 OVERRIDING INTERESTS

Overriding interests are those interests which bind a purchaser of a legal estate despite not being protected by an entry on the register. The LRA 2002 distinguishes between interests which override first registration (set out in Schedule 1 of the LRA 2002) and those which override registered dispositions (set out in Schedule 3 of the LRA 2002). There is, however, much overlap between the two.

In relation to PLP the most important overriding interests are:

- leases for a term of seven years or less;
- the interest of a person in actual occupation of the land, unless enquiry was made of that person who failed to disclose the interest. Such an interest will not be overriding in registered land where the buyer of the land had actual knowledge of the interest or the occupation was apparent on a reasonably careful inspection of the land;
- legal easements and profits (subject to limitations, see 2.4.8 above).

2.8.5 THE REGISTER OF TITLE

The register of title is the official record of ownership of a piece of registered land and the other interests that are registrable under the LRA 2002. A new edition of the register is prepared whenever a register entry is created or removed. Section 66 of the LRA 2002 allows anyone to inspect or make copies of the register and title plan and any document kept by the Registrar which is either referred to in the register or relates to an application. Anyone may apply for official copies of the register (LRA 2002, section 67) which are of course commonly used in conveyancing.

An example of a registered title appears in Appendix 1. There are three parts to the register:

1. Property Register. This provides a description of the property including a statement of estate, i.e. whether it is a freehold or leasehold. If leasehold, the statement of estate will also include the date of the registered lease, its term, parties, and start date. Rights of way and all other easements for the benefit of the property can also be detailed in this register. For all properties reference will also be made to the title plan of the registered property. The title plan shows the location of the property together with adjoining property. The title plan shows general boundaries only unless the exact line of the boundary has been determined (which is rare).

2. Proprietorship Register. This includes the class of title followed by the name and address of the registered proprietor. Notices and restrictions will appear within this register.

3. Charges Register. This lists the registered charges affecting the property and these are listed in order of priority. The charges register also includes adverse interests, such as restrictive covenants, to which the property may be subject. Leases that do not comprise overriding interests will also be noted on the charges register of the superior title.

WIDER READING

- MacKenzie, J-A, and Phillips, M, *Textbook on Land Law* (Oxford University Press, 2008)

- Thompson, M, *Land Law* (Oxford University Press, 2006)

- Green, K, and Cursley, J, *Land Law* (Palgrave Macmillan, 2004)

- Gray, K, and Gray, S, *Elements of Land Law* (Oxford University Press, 2008)

- Smith, RJ, *Property Law* (Longman, 2005)

- Abbey, R, and Richards, M, *Blackstone's Guide to the Land Registration Act 2002* (Oxford University Press, 2002)

- Murphy, W, and Roberts, S, *Understanding Property Law* (Sweet & Maxwell, 2003)

WEBSITES FOR FURTHER INFORMATION

- House of Lords judgments, **<http://www.parliament.the-stationery-office.co.uk/pa/ld199697/ ldjudgmt/ldjudgmt.htm**>. Keep up to date with important new cases on land law.

- Acts of Parliament, **<http://www.hmso.gov.uk/acts.htm**>. Keep up to date with statutory developments.

- Law Commission, **<http://www.lawcom.gov.uk/projects.htm**>. Keep up to date on proposals for law reform.

- Land Registry practice and procedure, **<http://www.landreg.gov.uk**>.

- Lands Tribunal On-Line, **<http://www.landstribunal.gov.uk/index.htm**>. The Lands Tribunal considers applications to discharge or modify restrictive covenants.

3 AN OUTLINE OF A CONVEYANCING TRANSACTION

3.1 INTRODUCTION

Property law and practice (and that label includes conveyancing) is not just about the transfer of title; it is the process as a whole that enables that transfer to take place. We have, in the subsequent chapters considered each part of the process. We have deconstructed the procedure to reveal its constituent parts. However, in this chapter we look at the process as a whole through an outline of a conveyancing transaction. In all the following chapters we provide tests to assess your progress. As a result there are some self test questions to test your knowledge of the outline of a conveyancing transaction as a whole. You will find tests on the several elements of the conveyancing transaction at the end of each of the following chapters.

3.2 A TRANSACTION IN OUTLINE

So, Table 3.1 is an overview of the conveyancing process that applies in most residential cases and many commercial transactions:

TABLE 3.1 GENERAL CONVEYANCING: OUTLINE OF A SIMPLE CONVEYANCING TRANSACTION

SELLER	BUYER
Take instructions	Take instructions
Prepare and issue draft contract	Make pre-contract searches and enquiries
Deduce title	Investigate title
	Approve draft contract
Exchange contracts	Exchange contracts
	Prepare purchase deed
Approve purchase deed	Make pre-completion searches
Prepare for completion	Prepare for completion
Completion	Completion
Post-completion procedures	Post-completion procedures

Table 3.1 makes several assumptions, the most important of which will be readily obvious, and that is that there may not be any borrowings involved for either party. However,

the principles are sound and set out a clear overview. You will find chapters on these various steps following this one. In the same vein you could prepare an overview of the differences in the process between registered and unregistered titles. It could look something like Table 3.2.

TABLE 3.2 OUTLINE OF MAIN DIFFERENCES BETWEEN REGISTERED AND UNREGISTERED CONVEYANCING

STEPS TAKEN	UNREGISTERED	REGISTERED
Taking instructions	No real difference	No real difference
Draft contract	No real difference	No real difference
Pre-contract searches	Preliminary enquiries of seller	Same
	Local land charges search	Same
	Water and drainage search	Same
	Inspection of the property	Same
	Search of Public Index Map	Not needed
	Search in Central Land Charges Department	Not needed
Deduce title	By abstract or copies of title deeds, and production of originals at or shortly before completion	By official copies of the registered title
Investigate title	By perusing abstract or copies of title deeds and checking them against the originals	By checking official copies and any overriding interests
Exchange of contracts	No basic difference	No basic difference
Preparation and approval of purchase deed	To be drafted by buyer's solicitor	To be prepared by buyer's solicitor on basis of prescribed forms of transfer
Pre-completion search	Central Land Charges Department	Land Registry Office
Prepare for completion	No basic difference	No basic difference
Complete	Title deeds and transfer handed to buyer. Legal estate passes	Only the transfer handed to buyer. Legal estate does not pass yet
Post-completion matters	Buyer registered as proprietor on first registration	Buyer registered as proprietor. Legal estate passes

In both cases what these charts show you is that you need to have a holistic approach to your understanding of property law and practice. By this we mean that you need to appreciate the complete picture to enable you to successfully deconstruct the process. In this way you will understand the mechanics of the conveyancing process more clearly by understanding the way they all come together to make property law and practice.

3.3 HOME INFORMATION PACKS

There is one recent important change to the process of residential conveyancing, brought about by the introduction of a new element to the earliest stage of the process. The Home Information Pack (HIP) is mandatory from 1 August 2007 for properties with four or more bedrooms, and from 10 September 2007 for three-bedroomed properties. From 14 December 2007 it is now the case that all properties about to be marketed for sale in England and Wales will first require a HIP before the marketing commences. The legislation requires homeowners or their selling agents to have a HIP in existence before marketing homes for sale, and to make a copy of the pack available to prospective buyers on request. The person marketing the property will be responsible for ensuring that the pack is available.

3.3.1 CONTENTS OF THE HOME INFORMATION PACK

The documents that are required (i.e. are mandatory contents) are an energy performance certificate, a sale statement, searches, evidence of title, leasehold and commonhold documents, and a HIP Index. A HIP may also contain authorized documents (i.e. contents that *may* be included) e.g. a home condition report.

In the case of leasehold properties the required documents are:

- a copy of the lease;
- any regulations or rules that apply to the property that are not mentioned in the lease and any proposed amendments to same;
- statements or summaries of service charges covering the previous 36 months;
- where appropriate, the most recent requests for payment of service charges, ground rent, insurance against damage for the building in which the property is situated, and insurance in respect of personal injury caused by or within the building during the 12-month period before marketing began;
- the name and address of the current or proposed lessor, and details of any managing agent that has been appointed or proposed by the lessor to manage the property;
- a summary of any works being undertaken or proposed that will affect the property or the building in which it is situated.

3.3.2 MANDATORY HOME INFORMATION PACK

The Government believes that the HIP must be made compulsory to ensure that anyone selling a residential property uses it. The enforcement regime is based on civil sanctions. Local weights and measures authorities have primary responsibility for enforcing the HIP obligations. Trading Standards Officers have been given discretion to determine appropriate action in each case—whether to provide information and assistance, issue a warning, or a civil fixed penalty notice. The penalty is set at a rate determined by the Secretary of State in the regulations at £200. In addition, a person who has breached the HIP obligations is liable to be sued by prospective buyers for recovery of the costs of obtaining documents that should have been provided in the pack.

As was stated in *The Independent* on 31 July 2007, a view we endorse:

> The packs fail to make it cheaper and easier to buy a home and add more bureaucracy and expense to the process of selling a property. The Government would be better withdrawing them altogether, rather than wasting any more time on this embarrassing and sorry fiasco.

 Conduct Point

- Do not market a property for a client without first having prepared a HIP. Failure to do so could incur you in a fixed penalty charge of £200 and your breach of duty under part 5 of the Housing Act 2004 (Home Information Packs) will amount to a breach of the Solicitors' Code of Conduct

FIGURE 3.1 A HOME INFORMATION PACK QUICK REFERENCE GUIDE

> **Home Information Packs**
> **Quick reference guide**

> **What is a HIP?**
> - A Home Information Pack (HIP) must include:
> - Terms of sale
> - Evidence of title
> - Local searches
> - Water and drainage search
> - Fixtures and fittings list
> - Energy Performance Certificate (EPC)
> - If leasehold, a copy of the lease

> **What is an EPC?**
> - An EPC is carried out by a domestic energy assessor to rate the property's energy efficiency
> - Each property is rated from A to G
> - A is the most energy efficient, G the least efficient

> **Who needs a HIP?**
> - From 14 December 2007 anyone selling/marketing any house or flat in England or Wales with any number of bedrooms needs a HIP

> **How does a seller get one?**
> - Sellers can get a HIP from:
> - A specialist pack provider, e.g. Law Society, or
> - Buy one through their estate agent, or
> - Do one themselves
> - NB—A sale to a family member without marketing means no HIP is required

> **What if you sell your house without a HIP?**
> - If you do not obtain a HIP you risk a fixed penalty fine of £200
> - This is cheaper than the cost of a HIP! (£300–£600)

SELF TEST QUESTIONS

1. Acting for a buyer you only have to carry out searches once in a standard conveyancing transaction. Is this statement TRUE/FALSE? Please delete the incorrect choice.

2. In a standard conveyancing transaction the seller normally prepares (drafts) the purchase deed. Is this statement TRUE/FALSE? Please delete the incorrect choice.

3. In a standard conveyancing transaction the buyer normally prepares (drafts) the contract. Is this statement TRUE/FALSE? Please delete the incorrect choice.

4. Which of the following documents is not a required (mandatory) document in a standard Home Information Pack

   (a) An energy performance certificate

   (b) A lease

   (c) A local authority search

   (d) A home condition report

5. The following list of searches includes one that is a required document in a Home Information Pack; which is it

   (a) A water and drainage search

   (b) A Land Registry search

   (c) A land charges search

   (d) A commons registration search

SUGGESTED ANSWERS TO SELF TEST QUESTIONS

1. The correct answer is false. The buyer must carry out searches on behalf of the purchaser on two separate occasions, first before exchanging contracts and secondly just before completion. The pre-contract searches are completely different to the pre-completion searches and both are necessary to protect the interests of the buyer. These differing searches will be explained in detail in subsequent chapters.

2. The correct answer is false. In a standard conveyancing transaction the solicitor for the buyer is expected to prepare the purchase deed. The drafting of the deed is the job of the practitioner acting for the purchaser, but the seller's solicitor will approve the draft deed and in doing so, make such amendments as are thought appropriate given the circumstances of the transaction.

3. The correct answer is false. In almost all conveyancing transactions the seller will prepare the draft contract. The reason for this is that the seller will have the details of the sale (and the deeds, if there are any) and will want to ensure that the contract contains all the terms. See section 2 of the Law of Property (Miscellaneous Provisions) Act 1989 for more on this requirement.

4. The correct answer is d. A home condition report is not required in a HIP but is considered an optional item that is authorized for inclusion. A home condition report contains information about the physical condition of a property. The report can be included by sellers on a voluntary basis. When HIPs were first proposed these reports were going to be mandatory but the Government changed its mind and made them optional.

5. The correct answer is a. There are only two searches that must be in a HIP: a local authority search, and a water and drainage search. Any other search included in a HIP is done so on an optional basis.

WIDER READING

- Abbey, R, and Richards, M, *A Practical Approach to Conveyancing* (Oxford University Press, 2008)

- Silverman, F, *Conveyancing Handbook* (The Law Society, 2006)

- The Solicitors' Code of Conduct 2007 (Solicitors Regulation Authority at **<http://www.sra.org.uk/code-of-conduct.page**>)

WEBSITES FOR FURTHER INFORMATION

- Acts of Parliament, **<http://www.hmso.gov.uk/acts.htm**>. Keep up to date with statutory developments.

- Council of Mortgage Lenders, **<http://www.cml.org.uk**>. This is the website serving most of the main mortgage lenders in the UK domestic conveyancing market.

- Financial Services Authority, **<http://www.fsa.gov.uk/**>. Obtain information on all aspects of financial regulation in the UK and how it relates to conveyancing.

- Land Registry, **<http://www.landreg.gov.uk/**>. Further information on the Land Registration Act 2002 and the Land Registration Rules 2003 and how these relate to conveyancing in England and Wales.

- Law Society, **<http://www.lawsoc.org.uk/**>. Details of the representative body for all solicitors in England and Wales.

- National Association of Estate Agents, **<http://www.naea.co.uk**>. Details of the representative body for many estate agents in England and Wales.

- Solicitors' Regulation Authority, **<http://www.sra.org.uk**>. The regulatory arm of the Law Society that deals with conduct issues affecting conveyancing practitioners who are solicitors.

ONLINE RESOURCE CENTRE CASE STUDIES

RESIDENTIAL TRANSACTION CASE STUDY

Our clients:
Shilpa Jennings—sale of 19 Minster Yard Blakey
Shilpa Jennings and Daniel Rodriguez—purchase of 9 Castle Hill Blakey

We act for Shilpa Jennings who is selling 19 Minster Yard Blakey for £100,000 and Shilpa Jennings and Daniel Rodriguez who are buying 9 Castle Hill Blakey for £200,000. See the Online Resource Centre for further details of the two conveyancing transactions.

COMMERCIAL TRANSACTION CASE STUDY

Our client: Cambo Ltd—acquisition of 18 Clover Street London W2

Timothy Wainwright and his family have run a successful wholesale clothing business for many years. Timothy has decided to sell the business and enter the world of property investment. He has formed a company called Cambo Ltd in which he, his wife, and their three sons are all shareholders. Cambo Ltd has agreed to buy 18 Clover Street London W2 for £700,000 subject to and with the benefit of two occupational business leases. The property was built 70 years ago. A commercial mortgage has already been arranged in principle. See the Online Resource Centre for further details of the conveyancing transaction.

---

4 TAKING INSTRUCTIONS AND OTHER INITIAL MATTERS

4.1 INTRODUCTION

The first interview will enable you to gather essential facts, but it should also be used, where necessary, to furnish the client with important advice on how to proceed. It gives you the opportunity to instil confidence in the client of your abilities as a conveyancer. To this end always try to see the client in person. Too many firms cut corners by relying solely on the telephone for obtaining instructions, but in the long run this may be a false economy, for clients will normally prefer to meet their solicitor at an early stage. It is our view that, ultimately, it is still the high level of service that impresses clients more, not the low level of fees; and a satisfied client is one who will return to you with future instructions. If a personal interview is impossible, at least ensure that the instructions received and advice given over the telephone are clear, and backed up with a letter of confirmation to the client.

In our experience students often make silly mistakes when conducting or explaining a first interview with a client. Always remember to note down basic information such as the client's name, address, and contact telephone numbers—this is sometimes overlooked. Other errors include forgetting who pays stamp duty (the buyer), who pays the estate agent's commission account (the seller), and who pays any capital gains tax (the seller). Remember that giving survey advice to a buyer is essential and the type of survey you recommend will depend primarily on the age of the property. Regarding mortgage advice, these days, endowment mortgages should generally be avoided at all costs with the usual recommendation being a repayment mortgage, especially for first time buyers who are looking for the cheapest option in terms of monthly outlay.

4.2 ADVICE ON CO-OWNERSHIP

When giving advice to joint buyers on co-ownership explain the differences between a joint tenancy and a tenancy in common simply, clearly, and without using legal jargon.

4.2.1 JOINT TENANCY

Under a joint tenancy, the purchasers own collectively the whole of the equitable estate with each other—they do not own individual shares. Accordingly, a 'share' in the property cannot be left by will, because upon death the deceased's 'share' passes automatically to the survivor(s). This is known as the right of survivorship. A joint tenancy is normally suitable for a married couple or cohabitees in a stable relationship, but not for those who have children from a previous relationship (see the next paragraph).

4.2.2 TENANCY IN COMMON

A tenancy in common is the opposite to a joint tenancy in that the buyers do own separate shares which may be left by will, or pass on intestacy in the event of no will, or may even be disposed of *inter vivos*. A tenancy in common should be recommended where the buyers are neither married nor in a stable relationship, where they have contributed in unequal proportions to the purchase price, or where they are business partners. It would also be appropriate for couples where one or both have children from a previous relationship, so that those children (and possibly any grandchildren) can be provided for.

4.2.3 TRUST DECLARATION AND MAKING WILLS

Where purchasers buy as tenants in common you should, on or before completion of the purchase, prepare a declaration of trust, signed by the parties, setting out their respective financial contributions and agreeing their share of the beneficial interest in the property. The declaration can also deal with other matters, such as the proportions each will pay towards the mortgage (if any) and other household expenditure, and the procedures for a later sale if one wishes to sell and the other does not.

The declaration of trust should be kept safely and referred to in the event of any later dispute. Without a trust declaration uncertainty may arise in the event of a later dispute between the co-owners over the distribution of future sale proceeds. The court has a wide discretion to assess their shares in the property having regard to the conduct and contributions of each party (*Oxley v Hiscock* [2004] EWCA Civ 546) but a purchase of domestic property in the joint names of cohabitants will establish a *prime facie* case of joint and equal beneficial interests until the contrary is proved (see *Stack v Dowden* [2007] UKHL 17). Because the survivorship rule does not apply to a tenancy in common, tenants in common should also be advised to make wills.

Failure to give proper advice in this area may result in a negligence claim against the solicitor if a client suffers loss as a result. The classic mistake is for a conveyancer to advise a joint tenancy where a tenancy in common is clearly appropriate; for instance, where unmarried co-purchasers contribute in unequal shares to the purchase price (see *Ahmed v Kendrick* (1988) 56 P & CR 120).

4.2.4 ESTABLISHING WHETHER OWNERS ARE JOINT TENANTS OR TENANTS IN COMMON

You may need to know whether clients who already own property are joint tenants or tenants in common, for instance, if one owner dies, or if the property is to be sold and the proceeds split. You can find out as follows.

Registered land

If the title is registered you should consult the proprietorship register of the title to see whether a joint proprietorship restriction has been entered in the following terms: 'No disposition by a sole proprietor of the registered estate (except a trust corporation) under which capital money arises is to be registered unless authorised by an order of the court' (you may come across earlier versions). The presence of such a restriction tells you that the owners are tenants in common. The absence of such a restriction tells you that they are joint tenants.

Unregistered land

If the title is unregistered, you should consult the most recent conveyance to the present owners, which should state whether they (i.e. the purchasers in the conveyance) are joint tenants or tenants in common.

 Key Points Co-ownership

- Explain to prospective co-buyers the differences between a joint tenancy (where the buyers collectively own all the property) and a tenancy in common (where the buyers own separate shares in it).

- Explain the principle of survivorship in a joint tenancy.

- Failure to give correct co-ownership advice may result in negligence.

- If buying as tenants in common the buyers should make a declaration of trust and consider making wills.

- For tenants in common the Land Registry will enter a co-ownership restriction in the proprietorship register to prevent a sole survivor from disposing of the land.

- If the above restriction is absent from the register you know that the owners are joint tenants.

4.3 ADVICE ON SURVEY

4.3.1 GENERAL CONSIDERATIONS

A buyer should always be advised to have a survey of the property carried out before exchange of contracts because of the *caveat emptor* principle ('let the buyer beware'). It is for the buyer to discover any physical defects in the property and these may not be apparent from the client's own inspection. A client is sometimes reluctant to incur the additional expense of a survey fee so it is your job to reassure the client that this is money well spent. Failure on your part to give this advice could amount to negligence.

A physically defective property may of course be unsafe to occupy, but there are financial implications for the purchaser as well. The market value of a property will be reduced if it is in poor condition and so the purchaser may be paying more than he should for it. It may also adversely affect the purchaser's ability to mortgage the property or sell it at a later date. These are all considerations that must be drawn to the client's attention.

4.3.2 DIFFERENT TYPES OF SURVEY

There are currently three types of survey widely available.

Basic valuation

This is the simplest and cheapest form of survey but it does no more than establish the property's value on the open market. A prospective mortgagee will normally commission this type of survey in order to verify whether the property being charged is adequate security for the proposed loan. The mortgagee's surveyor owes a duty of care not only to the lender but also to the borrower who relies on the report (*Smith v Eric S Bush* [1990] 1 AC 831). A copy of the report should be made available to the borrower.

Unless the property has been built within the last ten years and has the benefit of a National House Building Council (NHBC) guarantee, clients should be advised to seek a survey which is more detailed than the basic valuation. Even for new properties a basic survey should be recommended.

Home buyer's valuation and survey report

This is more detailed than the basic valuation but not as comprehensive as the full structural survey. It is popular amongst house buyers who, reluctant to incur the costs of a full structural survey, seek a compromise which gives more information than a basic valuation. The small print should be read carefully though; the conditions will often reveal just how superficial the report can be. Invariably, the surveyor will not inspect unexposed or inaccessible areas, for instance, the roof space or below floorboards.

A buyer who opts for this type of survey should be advised to contact the buyer's mortgagee to request that the mortgagee's surveyor carries it out instead of—not in addition to—the basic valuation. This will generally be acceptable to the mortgagee and means that the client will avoid incurring two survey fees.

Full structural survey

A full survey ought in theory to reveal the true state and condition of the property, but this is not always the case and the small print of the conditions of survey should be checked for exclusions. You would generally advise the client to have a full structural survey if the property is old (say, more than 80 years), or is of high value, or if the client has plans to alter the property structurally. The survey fee is obviously more (usually in excess of £500), but for this the client should at least get peace of mind (as long as the survey is favourable). If physical defects are revealed then the client should be advised either to withdraw from the transaction, or to seek from the seller a reduction in the purchase price.

4.3.3 SPECIAL CONSIDERATIONS

Neighbouring property

There will be occasions when a survey of neighbouring property will be necessary, e.g. on the purchase of a flat or property which is structurally attached to neighbouring property. In this case the surveyor should be instructed to inspect the main structure of the building and the adjoining property (if possible), as well as the subject property. The poor physical condition of the building of which a flat forms part will inevitably lead to increased levels of service charge payable by the occupiers of the flats (see Chapter 16 regarding service charges in leases).

Drainage

You should consider whether the subject property is served by mains drainage, maintainable at the public expense (this will be revealed by the water search, see 6.5). If not, and the drainage system is privately owned, it would be prudent to commission an expert's report on its condition, because your client buyer may incur future costs of maintenance.

Electric wiring

If the electric wiring in the property has not been checked for many years then an inspection by an expert should be considered.

Commercial premises

The acquisition of commercial premises will usually necessitate a thorough inspection and survey, the extent of which will depend on the nature and location of the property and the terms of any relevant lease. This is considered again in Chapter 19. One particular area of concern today is the potential liability for expensive 'clean-up costs' under the Environmental Protection Act 1990 and the Environment Act 1995. The detail of these statutes is outside the scope of this book, but the point must be stressed that any purchaser (and mortgagee) of land for development should consider the desirability of an environmental survey to check for contamination by hazardous substances (e.g. industrial waste).

Under the Environment Act 1995, local authorities are required to identify contaminated land within their areas and to serve a remediation notice requiring clean-up works to be carried out where necessary. The 'appropriate person' upon whom the notice is served is the original polluter, but if that person cannot be found then the appropriate person will be the 'owner or occupier' of the land.

For further information concerning the important topic of contaminated land, please refer to Abbey, R. and Richards, M., *A Practical Approach to Commercial Conveyancing and Property* (Oxford University Press).

 Key Points Advice on survey

- For residential property advise on the three different types of survey: Basic valuation; Home buyers; Full structural.
- Full structural is preferable for older or high value properties.
- Commercial premises may require a more comprehensive survey.
- When buying a flat consider a survey of the whole building because of service charge liability etc.

4.4 ESTATE AGENTS

Most sellers will use an estate agent to market their properties and to negotiate on the sale price. The agent normally charges the seller a percentage of the selling price as commission. This becomes due on exchange of contracts but is paid out of the sale proceeds on completion. By the time the seller first contacts the conveyancer, the seller usually will have secured a buyer at an agreed price.

4.5 CAPITAL GAINS TAX—WILL THE SELLER HAVE TO PAY IT?

4.5.1 PRINCIPAL PRIVATE DWELLINGHOUSE EXEMPTION

Capital gains tax (CGT) is *prima facie* payable on the disposal of an interest in land. The disposal for tax purposes occurs at exchange of contracts (when the beneficial interest passes to the buyer), not on completion. Nevertheless, CGT is rarely payable in the context of residential conveyancing because of the availability of the principal private dwellinghouse (PPD) exemption. The disposal (i.e. sale) of an individual's PPD, including grounds of up to 0.5 hectare, is exempt from CGT. Although this will apply in most domestic transactions, the practitioner should always check the client's situation carefully to ensure that the exemption does in fact apply in each case.

Only or main residence

In the first place, one should establish whether the seller has lived anywhere else since the subject property was acquired, because the exemption states that the seller must have lived in the house as his or her only or main residence throughout the period of ownership. Certain periods of absence are disregarded, in particular, the following cumulative periods:

(a) non-residence during the last 36 months of ownership;

(b) the first 12 months of ownership;

(c) any period of absence in employment overseas;

(d) up to four years' absence if a condition of employment;

(e) any period up to three years in total throughout the period of ownership.

Exclusive business use

Secondly, one should obtain the client's confirmation that no part of the PPD has been used exclusively for business purposes; otherwise a proportion of the exemption may be lost in respect of the business use area. The word 'exclusively' is emphasized because if the business room (or rooms) is shared with other members of the household, this should qualify as 'duality of user', enabling the full exemption to apply.

Half a hectare limit

The practitioner should establish how much land is being sold along with the PPD. If the grounds exceed half a hectare (5,000 square metres or 1.235 acres) there could be a tax liability on the excess unless the excess is proved to be necessary for the reasonable enjoyment of the house, e.g. if a large house with a large garden is being sold. Where ownership of the house is retained but land alone is sold, the land enjoys the benefit of the PPD exemption provided the land sold does not exceed half a hectare.

Other matters

Check whether the client owns another house. Married couples are only entitled to one PPD exemption. If a married couple own more than one house then they should elect which house is to take the benefit of the exemption. This election is revocable if they wish to change their mind. Finally, check that the client's house was not originally purchased in the name of a company, otherwise the PPD exemption will not apply.

Losses and allowances

Even if the PPD does not apply, either in full or in part, any chargeable gain on the sale of the property could be reduced or possibly wiped out altogether if certain allowable deductions are available and taken into account. For example, losses from previous assessment years can be carried forward and set off against gains. Also, each individual has an annual allowance for CGT, which is £9,600 for tax year 2008/09. If tax is actually payable, it will usually be charged at a flat rate of 18 per cent.

Advising buyers

Advice on CGT is of course primarily of importance to a client who is selling a property. However, a client who is intending to buy a property which will not be a PPD should be advised of any potential liability for CGT on a subsequent disposal.

 Key Points Capital Gains Tax

- The principal private dwelling (PPD) exemption means that clients selling their only or main home will usually be exempt from CGT.

- The seller must have lived in the house as his only or main residence throughout the period of ownership, although certain periods of absence are disregarded.

- A part of the exemption may be lost for large gardens over 0.5 hectares or if part of the house is used exclusively for business purposes.

- The PPD exemption does not apply to second homes although an election can be made, i.e. the client can choose which home is exempted.

- Advise buyers of potential CGT in the future if they are not buying a PPD.

4.6 STAMP DUTY LAND TAX—WILL THE BUYER HAVE TO PAY IT?

Where the price for the property exceeds a certain figure (known as the stamp duty land tax threshold; currently £125,000 for residential properties and £150,000 for non-residential or mixed-use properties) the buyer is required to pay a government tax called stamp duty land tax. The duty is calculated at 1 per cent of the total consideration for the property (or 3 per cent over £250,000, or 4 per cent over £500,000). If the consideration is just over £125,000, £250,000, or £500,000, you should consider apportioning the price between the land and any chattels included in the sale (e.g. carpets and curtains). This could reduce the price for the land below the threshold and thus reduce or avoid stamp duty land tax altogether. However, you should take care that the price for the chattels is a proper reflection of their value. Any overvaluation in these circumstances may constitute a fraud against HM Revenue and Customs (by both you and the client) and could also make the contract for sale unenforceable by action (see *Saunders v Edwards* [1987] 1 WLR 1116).

HM Revenue and Customs has issued guidance as to items it regards as chattels where apportionment is allowable, and items it regards as fixtures where apportionment is not allowable:

- *Chattels:* carpets, curtains, light shades, pot plants, free-standing kitchen white goods, and portable electric or gas fires.
- *Fixtures:* fitted bathroom sanitary ware, central heating systems, plants growing in the soil, and gas fires connected to a piped gas supply.

Any reduction in the purchase price of the property should also be reported to and first approved by the client's prospective mortgagee (if any). The mortgagee may possibly decide to reduce the amount it is prepared to lend.

There is a stamp duty exemption for property acquired in certain designated disadvantaged areas of the country. In these areas, where the consideration does not exceed £150,000 no stamp duty land tax will be payable. A list of the qualifying areas can be found at <http://www.hmrc.gov.uk/so/dar/index.htm>.

To assist you in filling out the stamp duty land tax return ask the buyer for his national insurance number when taking instructions and keep it on file.

 Key Points Stamp duty land tax

- Over £125,000 = 1% (NB for disadvantaged areas and non residential properties this first threshold is £150,000).
- Over £250,000 = 3%.
- Over £500,000 = 4%.
- If the price is just above one of the thresholds consider apportioning price between the land and any chattels included. Do, however, report any reduction in price to your client's mortgagee.
- Ask the client for their NI number which is needed for the SDLT return.

4.7 CLIENT CARE AND ADVICE ON COSTS

Client care procedures are a formal requirement of the Solicitors' Code of Conduct 2007 (the Code). Full details of the Code can be found on the Solicitors' Regulation Authority website at <http://www.sra.org.uk/code-of-conduct>.

4.7.1 COSTS

The Code requires solicitors to give the client the best information possible about costs including a breakdown between fees, VAT, and disbursements. At the start of a conveyancing transaction it should be possible to agree an estimate for the whole transaction. Remember that this will also have to include your fee for acting for the client's lender (if any). You should also advise the client of VAT payable on top of your profit costs together with other expenses such as possible stamp duty, Land Registry fees, search fees, and bank transfer fees. If you forget to mention VAT, the client may assume that the quoted figure is inclusive of it (Value Added Tax Act 1994, section 89).

Once you have settled an estimated figure it is sensible to inform the client that you reserve the right to increase your charges should the transaction prove to be unduly complicated or protracted. In this way you are not binding yourself to a fixed, unalterable fee. You may reassure the client, however, by saying that in the vast majority of cases, no increase is usually necessary. You should also discuss how and when the costs are to be met (normally at the conclusion of the transaction). You should confirm the estimate to the client in writing, and you must also advise the client immediately in writing if the figure is to be revised. Care is needed here because if you go further than giving an estimate—by committing yourself to a fixed (or 'agreed') fee—then you will not be permitted to charge more even if circumstances change.

4.7.2 COMPLAINTS HANDLING PROCEDURE, AND CLIENT CARE GENERALLY

Solicitors are required to operate a complaints handling procedure. It should be in writing and all staff made aware of it. You must inform the client of the name and status of the person dealing with the matter, the name of the principal responsible for its overall supervision, and who the client should contact if there is a problem with the service. You must also ensure that the client is informed about the likely timescale of the transaction.

Rule 2 of the Code is clear and self-explanatory, and breach of it will raise a question of professional conduct to be investigated by the Solicitors Regulation Authority. However, Rule 2 indicates that it may be inappropriate to give full information in certain cases, e.g. when acting for a regular client for whom repetitive work is done where the client has already been provided with the relevant information. It follows that Rule 2 is of particular importance when taking instructions from a new or non-established client.

At some stage during the first interview, you should advise the client of the future action to be taken to progress the matter, the likely timescale of the transaction, and when you will next contact the client. If the client is unfamiliar with the conveyancing process it is always good practice to offer a brief explanation of the procedures involved and to estimate when exchange of contracts and completion are likely to take place. All relevant client care information, including advice on costs, must be confirmed to the client in writing.

 Key Points Client care and advice on costs

- Give the client a costs estimate and remember to include VAT, disbursements, and any stamp duty land tax.
- Advise the client of your firm's complaints procedure, who will have the day to day running of the file, and the name of the partner in overall charge.
- Advise the client of the future action to be taken and the likely timescale of the transaction.
- Confirm everything in writing to the client.
- Generally become familiar with the Code of Conduct, Rule 2 (client relations).

4.8 PROFESSIONAL CONDUCT

4.8.1 GENERAL CONSIDERATIONS

The purpose of the professional conduct rules is to protect the public whose affairs are entrusted to solicitors, and to maintain the good reputation and integrity of the solicitors' profession. The rules provide a platform for safe and efficient practice and breach of them is a serious matter which may lead to disciplinary proceedings. Many conduct issues may arise during the course of a conveyancing transaction. On exchange of contracts and completion professional undertakings will be given; there are rules governing practitioners' handling of clients' money; there are special provisions regarding contract races (see 5.4). In this chapter we will consider client confidentiality, money laundering, and acting for more than one party in a property transaction.

4.8.2 CLIENT CONFIDENTIALITY AND MONEY LAUNDERING

Confidentiality

The general rule is that client affairs are confidential and must never be disclosed to a third party without the client's consent, even where the practitioner is no longer acting for the client. Suppose you act for borrower and lender and your borrower's client tells you that he intends to run a business from the premises, in breach of a mortgage condition. You cannot continue to act because there is a conflict of interest, but neither can you tell the lender the reasons why you can no longer act—this would be a breach of confidentiality to the borrower.

Money laundering

One exception to the confidentiality rule which is of importance in the context of conveyancing concerns money laundering. The National Criminal Intelligence Service (NCIS) has highlighted the prevalence of property transactions as a means of laundering criminal funds, and the high risk of exposure of professionals offering conveyancing services to the public. The Criminal Justice Act 1993 and the Proceeds of Crime Act 2002 introduced criminal offences for *failing to disclose* to the authorities (i.e. the NCIS) knowledge or suspicion of others who are involved in laundering the proceeds of a crime, drug trafficking, or terrorism. Thus, if you have such knowledge or suspicion, you must report it to your firm's Nominated Officer (see below) as soon as practically possible prior to the transaction taking place (subject to any legal professional privilege, see below).

The Law Society has issued a 'blue card warning' to solicitors alerting them to likely circumstances which could amount to assisting in money laundering. These include:

(a) clients who ask you to hold large sums of cash and who then ask for a cheque from your firm;

(b) secretive clients who will not disclose their identity;

(c) unusual instructions, e.g. clients instructing you from the other end of the country when they could be using a local firm;

(d) unusual settlement requests, e.g. paying for a property with large sums of cash.

'Tipping off'

It is an offence to 'tip off' the client that you have made a disclosure to the authorities, or that the authorities are investigating a possible laundering offence. This rule is also contrary to the normal solicitor–client relationship of confidentiality. The duty of disclosure extends to any party (not just your client) suspected of being involved, so this covers the other side's client as much as suspicion about your own client.

Legal professional privilege

The case of *Bowman v Fells* (2005) EWCA Civ 226 has altered how conveyancers should approach reporting issues, and careful attention should be paid to The Law Society guidance on its website about the implications of this decision. Essentially, if a conveyancer forms knowledge or suspicion of money laundering he should first consider whether the information on which that knowledge or suspicion is based was received in legally privileged circumstances. If it was, he cannot make a report to NCIS without the client's authority. In these circumstances conveyancers should consider whether they would prefer not to act for the client. Advice on a case-by-case basis can be obtained from The Law Society's Professional Ethics helpline (0870 606 2577).

Money Laundering Regulations

The Money Laundering Regulations 2007 apply to all legal professionals acting in any real property transaction and extend to the proceeds of any criminal activity. The following matters should be noted:

(a) All staff who handle investment business must be trained to recognize and deal with suspicious transactions (e.g. a large cash sum received from a client for a deposit on a purchase should be treated as suspicious).

(b) Each firm must appoint a reporting officer (known as a Nominated Officer) and establish internal reporting procedures.

(c) There must be procedures for obtaining satisfactory evidence of the client's identity where necessary.

(d) A record of each transaction must be maintained for at least five years.

(e) Evidence of clients' identity obtained must be kept for at least five years after the relationship with the client has ended.

4.8.3 ACTING FOR SELLER AND BUYER

The Solicitors' Code of Conduct 2007 (the Code) contains important rules that apply to the transfer of land for value, and the grant or assignment of a lease or some other interest in land for value. Both commercial and residential conveyancing transactions are covered. The terms 'seller' and 'buyer' include a lessor and lessee. Important provisions of the Code as they affect conveyancers can be accessed at www.sra.org.uk/code-of-conduct.

Subject to certain exceptions (see below), acting for both parties in a conveyancing transaction at arm's length is generally prohibited by Rule 3.07 of the Code. This applies to seller and buyer and also lessor and lessee.

For conveyancing transactions not at arm's length (e.g. between connected persons such as those related by blood, adoption, or marriage or living together), provided there is no contract race (see 5.4), you may act for seller and buyer as long as there is no conflict or significant risk of conflict. When judging whether or not a transaction is 'at arm's length', you need to look at the relationship between the parties and the context of the transaction.

For conveyancing transactions at arm's length (e.g. where parties are not connected and where full value is given), provided there is no contract race (see 5.4), you may act for seller and buyer if the conditions set out below are satisfied and one of the following applies:

(a) both parties are established clients;

(b) the consideration is £10,000 or less and the transaction is not the grant of a lease; or

(c) seller and buyer are represented by two separate offices in different localities.

Conditions for acting above

In order to act for seller and buyer above, the following conditions must be met:

(a) the written consent of both parties must be obtained;

(b) no conflict of interests must exist or arise;

(c) the seller must not be selling or leasing as a builder or developer; and

(d) when the seller and buyer are represented by two separate offices in different localities:

    (i) different individuals who normally work at each office, conduct or supervise the transaction for seller and buyer; and

    (ii) no office of the firm (or an associated firm) referred either client to the office conducting the transactions.

If when taking instructions you are in any doubt as to whether a particular situation falls within an exception or whether a conflict of interest may arise, the best practice is to err on the side of caution and refuse to act for more than one party.

Meaning of 'established client'

In practice the most common exception to the rule prohibiting acting for seller and buyer is the established client exception. However, careful consideration should be given to whether the exception properly applies in each case. Ask yourself, 'Would a reasonable solicitor regard this person as an established client?' The answer would be 'No' if that person is instructing your firm for the first time, and may also be 'No' if your firm has acted only two or three times for that person. There needs to be a degree of permanence in the solicitor–client relationship as exemplified by some continuity of instruction over time and the likelihood of future instruction. You may act if the person is related by blood, adoption, or marriage to an established client, or who is living with an established client. Furthermore, if only one of two joint sellers or buyers is an established client, you may act as if both were established clients.

4.8.4 ACTING FOR JOINT BUYERS OR JOINT SELLERS

You can act for joint buyers or joint sellers provided no conflict of interest exists or is likely to arise between them. In most cases, the interests of the joint buyers or sellers are the same, so there is rarely a problem. You should obtain instructions (or verification of instructions) directly from each client, not simply rely on the word of the other(s). This allows you to clarify the client's exact requirements and to ensure that the instructions are not tainted by undue influence or duress.

4.8.5 ACTING FOR LENDER AND BORROWER

This is considered in Chapter 9 dealing with mortgages.

 Conduct Points

- Do not act for buyer and seller in the same arm's length transaction unless it falls within one of the exceptions e.g. both parties are established clients.
- Keep your client's affairs confidential.
- Be aware of potential money laundering. Verify your client's identity and do not accept large sums of cash.
- You can normally act for joint sellers or joint buyers.
- You can normally act for buyer and lender.

4.9 NATIONAL PROTOCOL

4.9.1 GENERAL CONSIDERATIONS

The Law Society introduced the National Conveyancing Protocol in 1990 to help speed up the process of residential conveyancing. There is no compulsion to use the Protocol, just an obligation on solicitors to agree whether or not it will be used. In practice, the decision is usually taken by the seller's solicitor and the buyer's solicitor normally goes along with it. If the Protocol is to be used in a varied form, the variations ideally should be recorded in writing between the conveyancers. Likewise, if, during the course of the transaction, one party departs from the Protocol procedures, the other side must be informed. The Council of the

Law Society recommends that conveyancers follow the Protocol procedures in all domestic conveyancing transactions.

Reference will be made to the Protocol throughout this book as the various stages in the conveyancing process unfold. Part II of the latest edition of the Protocol is set out in Appendix 6. It is worth consulting at regular intervals during the transaction to refresh one's memory of what exactly is required under the Protocol.

4.9.2 ADVISING THE CLIENT ABOUT THE PROTOCOL

You should explain the use and purpose of the Protocol to the client when taking instructions. Its use will generally be beneficial to the client but there is one area which may cause difficulty—the requirement to keep the other side informed of the client's situation in any related sale or purchase. This should be discussed with the client because it could be contrary to the client's best interests to disclose this information. For instance, if you tell the client's seller that your client has not found a buyer for his own property, the seller may decide to sell to someone else who is in a better position to proceed (e.g. buyer found, or no property to sell). If the client declines to offer information about a related sale or purchase, the practitioner must of course respect this wish in accordance with the duty of confidentiality to the client. The Law Society has confirmed that non-disclosure in these circumstances would not constitute a departure from the terms of the Protocol.

Seller's Property Information Form

If your client is selling and you have decided to use the Protocol, you can save time by asking the client to complete the Property Information Form during the first interview. This Form raises standard questions about the property such as whether the owner is aware of any boundary disputes, or whether the owner has received any notices concerning the property from the local authority. The Property Information Form is discussed in more detail in Chapter 6. There is also the seller's Home Information Pack which contains important information about the property (see 3.3).

4.9.3 COMMERCIAL TRANSACTIONS

The full terms of the Protocol are generally not appropriate in the context of commercial conveyancing for the simple reason that the standard forms adopted by the Protocol contemplate the sale of a dwelling. Nevertheless, the spirit behind the Protocol is usually adopted in that the seller will provide the buyer with a pre-contract package which will include a draft contract, replies to pre-contract enquiries, and evidence of title (see Chapter 19 regarding commercial conveyancing).

A commercial developer selling new houses on an estate should also provide a comprehensive pre-contract package to the individual purchaser's solicitors. Although the properties are dwellings, the full terms of the Protocol are, as above, generally inappropriate because the properties very often have not been physically completed before contracts are exchanged (see Chapter 18 regarding new properties).

4.10 ADVICE ON FINANCE

4.10.1 GENERAL CONSIDERATIONS

You should ensure that sufficient funds will be available both to complete the purchase and to pay for the costs and disbursements, including Land Registry fees and stamp duty land tax. The funding would be achieved either directly from the client's own resources or, more usually, through a combination of the client's own resources, a mortgage loan, and the proceeds of any related sale (unless of course the client is a first-time buyer).

It is helpful for the client if, while taking instructions, you can prepare a brief financial statement, showing the expected payments and receipts on the sale and/or purchase. In this way, you can calculate how much extra money the client may need to find, either from the client's own resources or by mortgage loan, in order to complete the transaction(s).

Before proceeding with the conveyancing process, it is obviously important to check that:

(a) the client understands all the financial implications and can afford to go ahead; and

(b) sufficient funds are or will be available to finance the total expenditure.

If the client has a related sale and purchase, the net proceeds of sale will normally be used to assist the funding of the purchase price:

(a) *Calculating the net sale proceeds.* You can calculate roughly how much will be available from the sale by deducting from the total sale price the following:

(i) amount to be repaid under any existing mortgage(s) on the sale property (the client should be able to guide you on this, and you can verify the exact figure direct with the mortgagee);

(ii) if estate agents are involved, their commission fee including VAT;

(iii) your costs on the sale, plus VAT and disbursements;

(iv) rarely, any capital gains tax payable on the sale.

You should also consider whether any person other than your client has a claim to any part of the sale proceeds which would reduce the amount available to your client, e.g. someone who contributed towards the purchase price when the property was bought.

(b) *Calculating the full cost of purchase.* You will add to the purchase price:

(i) the price agreed for any chattels or other extras included in the purchase;

(ii) any stamp duty land tax payable;

(iii) your costs on the purchase, plus VAT and disbursements (including search fees).

To calculate how much the client must find either from the client's own resources or by mortgage loan, simply deduct the net sale proceeds ((a) above) from the full cost of purchase ((b) above). Examples of completion statements are set out in the Online Resource Centre and are more fully explained in 12.9.

If the client is only selling (without a related purchase), you should confirm to the client calculation (a) above. If the client is just buying (without a related sale) you should confirm to the client calculation (b) above.

It is also prudent to remind the client of other possible expenditure which the client will have to settle personally before completion, for example, the surveyor's fee on a purchase (see 4.3), and furniture removal costs.

Advice may be required on potential liability to capital gains tax (see 4.5).

4.10.2 DEPOSIT PAYABLE ON EXCHANGE OF CONTRACTS

A buyer will normally be required to pay a deposit on exchange of contracts. The deposit acts as part payment as well as a guarantee, which the seller can forfeit if the buyer defaults on the contract. The deposit is usually 10 per cent of the purchase price, although sometimes the parties agree less. Your client buyer will need to place you in funds for the deposit before exchange and you should advise the client of this now. Many clients believe mistakenly that their mortgage advance will cover the deposit but the advance is of course not available until shortly before completion (i.e. after exchange).

Financing the deposit

If the client does not have funds available, you will need to explore other ways of financing the deposit. If the client has a related sale, it may be possible to utilize the deposit you receive on the sale towards the purchase deposit. This will depend on the terms of the contract. Alternatively, the deposit guarantee scheme could be considered, or, if the client has a related sale, short-term bridging finance (see 10.2.2). The last two methods will incur cost for the client and these should be explained.

4.10.3 MORTGAGES

Mortgages are considered in Chapter 9.

 Key Points Advising on finance

- Ensure that sufficient funds will be available both to complete the purchase and to pay for the costs and disbursements, including Land Registry fees and stamp duty land tax.
- Prepare a brief financial statement showing the expected payments and receipts on the sale and/or purchase.
- Remind the client of other expenditure which the client will need to settle personally before completion, e.g. the surveyor's fee on a purchase and furniture removal costs.
- Consider how the purchaser client will be financing the deposit payable on exchange of contracts.
- It may be necessary to give generic advice on mortgages (see Chapter 9).

 Key Points Taking instructions generally (seller and buyer)

- Obtain client's full names, address and contact telephone numbers.
- Has your firm acted for the client before (relevant to client care advice)?
- Is it necessary to check client's identity (relevant to money laundering and mortgage fraud)?
- Confirm address of property and tenure.
- Is it a residential or commercial property?
- Details of any estate agents involved. Obtain copy of agent's particulars. Any preliminary deposit paid to agents?
- If it is a commercial transaction, have the parties agreed heads of terms? If so, what are they?
- Details of solicitors acting for other side.
- Price agreed.
- Other terms agreed, e.g. sale of chattels, likely completion date?
- Which fixtures will remain or be removed?
- Does client have a related sale or purchase, which has to be synchronized with this transaction?
- Who occupies the property (relevant to third party rights and vacant possession)?
- If it is a commercial lease are there any sub-leases?
- Is property near river or railway or in unusual location (relevant to searches and enquiries)?
- Advise on costs and prepare brief financial statement. Remind client about other expenses, e.g. removal fees.
- How much deposit will be paid or received on exchange?
- If you are dealing with a lease, is it the grant of a new lease or the assignment of an existing one?
- Is there anything additional you need to know from the client or upon which the client requires your advice, which may be relevant to this particular transaction?
- Advise the client how long it should all take and what the next steps will be.

Key Points Additional matters when acting for a buyer

- How will purchase price be financed? If client requires a mortgage, consider mortgage advice.
- How will deposit payable on exchange be financed?
- Advise on survey.
- If more than one buyer, advise on co-ownership.
- Confirm proposed use of property (relevant to planning and any restrictions in the title).
- Advise the client whether stamp duty is payable. Can you apportion the price between land and chattels to reduce or eradicate stamp duty?
- If client presently in rented accommodation, advise on giving landlord notice to end tenancy.

 Key Points Additional matters when acting for a seller

- Where are the title deeds? If property is mortgaged, obtain full name and address of first mortgagee plus mortgage account number, so you can write to mortgagee requesting deeds on loan.
- Are there any second or subsequent mortgages? Obtain details of *all* outstanding mortgages on property including names and addresses of lenders and amounts outstanding.
- Did you act for the client when the property was bought? If yes, it may be helpful to get the old file from store.
- What are client's instructions regarding sale proceeds?
- If Protocol being used, client to complete Property Information Form.
- Advise client not to stop mortgage repayments or cancel building insurance until completion.
- Will Capital Gains Tax be payable on sale proceeds? Confirm whether principal private dwellinghouse exemption applies.
- On an assignment of a commercial lease has the client approached the lessor for consent to assign (if required)?

SELF TEST QUESTIONS

1. When taking instructions on an intended sale of a commercial freehold property that is mortgaged, on which of the following matters would you generally NOT be required to advise your client

    (a) Stamp duty land tax

    (b) Capital Gains Tax

    (c) Mortgage redemption

    (d) The contract

2. You have a client who owns and lives in a large house and garden extending to 1.5 hectares. It has been his family home for the last seven years. He wishes to sell off one half, being the bottom of the garden, to a company developer for a small high-class housing estate. Which of the following will apply for tax purposes

    (a) The sale is exempt from capital gains tax

    (b) The sale is not exempt from capital gains tax

    (c) The sale is subject to income tax

    (d) The sale is subject to corporation tax

3. A young married couple wishing to buy their first home instruct you to act for them. They are each contributing £5,000 and a mortgage advance will fund the rest of the purchase price. Generally, how will you advise them to hold the beneficial ownership in the property

   (a) As legal and equitable co-owners

   (b) As tenants in common

   (c) As licensees

   (d) As joint tenants

4. You act for the purchaser of a 200-year-old cottage. Your client is buying with the aid of a building society mortgage. The survey you will recommend is

   (a) The one suggested by the building society as being appropriate for this type of property

   (b) A full structural survey

   (c) A valuation report

   (d) A home buyer's valuation and survey report

5. In registered land the appropriate method of protecting a beneficial interest under an implied trust is to register a

   (a) Caution

   (b) Charge

   (c) Notice

   (d) Restriction

SHORT REVISION QUESTIONS

Question 1

Mrs Olena Yeltsin is an established client of your firm and has made an appointment to see you regarding her proposed sale and a related purchase. You note from the official copies of the sale property that she and her husband Yuri are registered as joint proprietors. She has told your secretary that she and her husband are divorcing and has asked whether it would be acceptable for us to act for them both on the sale. She has already received a mortgage offer on her purchase and so does not require any mortgage advice.

What key matters will you discuss with her in the interview?

Question 2

Your firm has recently been instructed to act for Stuart Rush and his wife Harriet Rush in the sale of 'Saxifrage' and the related purchase of 'Bentley Lodge'. Your principal has passed you the two files from which you note the following:

(a) The sale price of Saxifrage is £175,000.

(b) The purchase price of Bentley Lodge is £185,000.

(c) The clients have an endowment mortgage on Saxifrage securing a loan of £120,000.

(d) The clients have received a mortgage offer on Bentley Lodge of £130,000. There is a retention of £30,000 on the mortgage advance until essential repairs have been carried out to the roof and chimney stacks.

(e) The clients wish to complete the purchase before the sale as Harriet's mother lives with them and they wish to carry out the repairs before they all move.

(f) The clients' bank has offered them a bridging loan of £30,000 to enable them to complete the purchase before the sale.

(g) The bank will only release the bridging loan upon receipt of a solicitor's undertaking to pay the net sale proceeds of Saxifrage to the bank.

(h) The estate agents' particulars relating to Saxifrage have arrived in this morning's post.

What advice will you give your clients in respect of their proposed financial arrangements and what factors should you consider before you give any undertaking to the bank?

SUGGESTED ANSWERS TO SELF TEST QUESTIONS

1. The correct answer is (a). Stamp Duty Land Tax is payable by a buyer and so is of no concern to your client seller. As far as the other options are concerned: You are told in the question that the property is mortgaged and so you should advise your client of the need to redeem the mortgage on completion. It may well be the case that on a disposal of a commercial property a seller will require your advice as to whether any capital gains tax liability arises. Finally you should always advise your client on the terms of the contract. This applies to both buyer and seller clients.

2. The correct answer is (b). The principal private dwelling exemption for CGT does not apply here because the grounds being sold exceed half a hectare. Do not be drawn towards corporation tax simply because you see the word 'company' in option (d). Remember that it is the seller who *prima facie* pays CGT on the disposal of an interest in land.

3. The correct answer is (d). Only options (b) or (d) are relevant on these facts. As the couple are married and are contributing in equal shares, a joint tenancy is appropriate. You will, however, have explained to them the differences between a joint tenancy and a tenancy in common and have taken their instructions on the matter. Note the word 'generally' in the question. Occasionally married couples prefer to hold as tenants in common but generally this is not the case.

4. The correct answer is (b). This is a very straightforward question. The fact that the property is over 100 years old means you must recommend a full structural survey notwithstanding the extra cost involved. Note that the question asks for your recommendation—ultimately it will be up to the client to choose what to do. Be careful not to be drawn to option (a). Remember that the mortgagee is only interested in establishing that the value of the property is adequate security for the proposed loan.

5. The correct answer is (d). Remember that cautions against dealings have been abolished under the Land Registration Act 2002 and it is not possible to protect a beneficial interest by notice. The appropriate entry is a restriction in the proprietorship register. Before the Land Registration Act 2002 it was possible to lodge a caution to protect such an interest.

SUGGESTED ANSWERS TO SHORT REVISION QUESTIONS

Question 1

This is a fairly straightforward question on taking instructions but you need to tailor your answer carefully to the facts. Do not write everything you know about the subject but confine your answer to relevant matters. One complication here is the client's impending divorce. Do not be put off by this, as you are not being tested on family law! However you will need to think through the conveyancing ramifications.

To begin with you are told that Olena is an established client so there is no need for you to give full client care advice or to verify her identity. However, inform her that you will have the day-to-day running of the files and give her the name of the partner with overall responsibility. Note down her contact details, e.g. telephone number, and details of the estate agents involved. Ask her to confirm the agreed sale and purchase price, whether she has paid any preliminary deposit, and whether other terms have been agreed, e.g. sale of chattels. Inform her of your firm's fees plus VAT and any other relevant expenses, such as stamp duty. Ask whether anyone else, apart from her and her husband, occupies the sale property. You could give her the Property Information Form for her to complete and return.

Explain that as her husband is joint proprietor you would need him to confirm that he wishes to proceed with the sale (remember the conduct rule that you must not receive instructions through a third party, in this case Olena). There appears to be no conflict of interest in acting for Yuri on the sale provided both husband and wife are in agreement. He will no doubt be instructing his own solicitors in connection with the divorce and you will be in touch with his divorce solicitors regarding the distribution of his agreed share of the sale proceeds. His firm may indeed confirm on his behalf that he is happy for you to act on the sale.

As Olena has a related purchase you will ensure that the sale and purchase are synchronized so that exchange of contracts and completion occur simultaneously. In particular you will ensure that Olena's financial arrangements are in order. She must have sufficient funds from her share of the proceeds and her new mortgage to finance the purchase (including costs, stamp duty, etc.). However this may be difficult given that her share of the sale proceeds will be determined only once the divorce settlement has been agreed. Prepare a brief financial statement for her in respect of both sale and purchase and give her an indication of any likely shortfall she must find in order to complete.

Tell her you will write to her existing mortgagee, requesting the deeds and asking for confirmation of the loan currently outstanding. Ask her for the mortgage account or roll number, which you will need to mention in your letter. On the purchase, establish the age of the property and give appropriate advice on survey. On the sale, check that the principal private dwelling exemption applies for CGT purposes.

Conclude the interview by informing her of the next steps and that you will be writing to confirm your advice. Give her some indication of how long the whole conveyancing process is likely to take (on average about two months).

Question 2

Before considering our advice, it may be helpful to prepare a brief financial statement:

Sale price	175,000
less mortgage redemption	120,000
sale proceeds	55,000
Purchase price	185,000
less net mortgage advance	100,000
	85,000
sale proceeds	55,000
add bridging loan	30,000
	85,000

At first glance the calculations appear to be correct, but a careful analysis of the clients' instructions will reveal that they have overlooked the following matters:

(a) The amount required to redeem the Saxifrage mortgage will not be exactly £120,000. This is the initial loan and does not take into account any outstanding interest charges, administration fees, or redemption penalties. We must obtain an up-to-date redemption figure. (As the mortgage is an endowment rather than a repayment, the principal sum will not have been reduced).

(b) We are told there are estate agents on the sale so the clients will be liable to pay their commission + VAT.

(c) They must pay 1 per cent stamp duty on the purchase (£1,850).

(d) They must pay legal fees on the sale and purchase, plus VAT and disbursements (e.g. Land Registry and search fees). They must also pay their surveyor's fee.

(e) The bridging loan will incur interest charges and probably an arrangement fee.

In the light of the above, the clients should be advised that the net sale proceeds of Saxifrage will be insufficient to repay the bridging loan. We cannot advise them to proceed unless they can increase their bridging loan or find additional funds. An alternative solution would be to try and negotiate a reduction in the purchase price of Bentley Lodge.

We would advise the clients that they will need to fund the 10 per cent deposit on the purchase, payable on exchange of contracts. We could seek to utilize the deposit we receive on the sale (this is permitted under a contract incorporating the Standard Conditions of sale), but this would still leave a shortfall of £1,000. The clients would have to find this from their own resources or seek a further bridging loan. Alternatively, the owners of Bentley Lodge could be asked to accept a reduced deposit.

Saxifrage appears to be the clients' principal private dwelling house but if this is not the case then they must be advised of their potential liability to CGT.

Undertaking

In the event of the bridging loan proceeding we must consider several matters before giving an undertaking to the bank. Breach of a solicitor's undertaking is professional misconduct and will result in disciplinary action.

(a) Can we trust the clients and are they creditworthy?

(b) The clients must give us an express and irrevocable authority in writing to give the undertaking.

(c) Our undertaking should be in writing and signed by a partner.

(d) We must be sure that we can comply absolutely with the terms of the undertaking. To this end, the wording must be clear, unambiguous, and wholly capable of performance by our firm.

(e) Are we satisfied that the anticipated net sale proceeds will be sufficient to discharge the bridging finance plus interest?

(f) In our undertaking we would state the sale price and itemize the anticipated deductions (e.g. mortgage redemption, agent's commission, legal fees, etc.) to calculate the approximate net proceeds of sale.

(g) As the undertaking is one to pay money, we would make it clear in the wording that payment by us of the net sale proceeds of Saxifrage will be made only if and when the sale proceeds are received by our firm. This safeguards against the possibility of us never receiving the proceeds of sale (e.g. because of client bankruptcy), but still being obliged to repay the bank.

(h) Ideally, the undertaking should not be given until after exchange of contracts. However as the clients will require a synchronized exchange we would in practice give it shortly before the point of exchange provided there are no unresolved problems.

WIDER READING

- Chapter 2 (Taking Instructions and other initial matters) Abbey, R, and Richards, M, *A Practical Approach to Conveyancing* (Oxford University Press, 2008)

- Section A dealing with preliminary conveyancing matters, Silverman, F, *Conveyancing Handbook* (The Law Society, 2006)

- The Solicitors' Code of Conduct 2007 (Solicitors Regulation Authority at **<http://www.sra.org.uk/code-of-conduct.page>**)

WEBSITES FOR FURTHER INFORMATION

- Acts of Parliament, **<http://www.hmso.gov.uk/acts.htm>**. Keep up to date with statutory developments.

- Council of Mortgage Lenders, **<http://www.cml.org.uk>**. There is an on-line version of the CML Lenders' Handbook available at this site and it should be referred to in cases of doubt about lenders' requirements.

- Financial Services Authority, **<http://www.fsa.gov.uk/>**. Obtain information on all aspects of financial regulation in the UK.

- Stamp duty disadvantaged areas, **<http://www.hmrc.gov.uk/so/disadvantaged.htm>**.

- Land Registry, **<http://www.landreg.gov.uk/>**. Further information on the Land Registration Act 2002 and the Land Registration Rules 2003.

- Law Society, **<http://www.lawsoc.org.uk/>**.

- National Association of Estate Agents, **<http://www.naea.co.uk>**.

- Solicitors' Regulation Authority, **<http://www.sra.org.uk>**.

online
resource
centre

ONLINE RESOURCE CENTRE CASE STUDIES

RESIDENTIAL TRANSACTION CASE STUDY—TAKING INSTRUCTIONS AND GIVING ADVICE

Our clients:
Shilpa Jennings—sale of 19 Minster Yard Blakey
Shilpa Jennings and Daniel Rodriguez—purchase of 9 Castle Hill Blakey

We act for Shilpa Jennings who is selling 19 Minster Yard Blakey for £100,000 and Shilpa and Daniel Rodriguez who are buying 9 Castle Hill Blakey for £200,000. See the Online Resource Centre for further details on taking instructions and giving initial advice.

COMMERCIAL TRANSACTION CASE STUDY—TAKING INSTRUCTIONS AND GIVING ADVICE

Our client: Cambo Ltd—acquisition of 18 Clover Street London W2

Timothy Wainwright and his family have run a successful wholesale clothing business for many years. Timothy has decided to sell the business and enter the world of property investment. He has formed a company called Cambo Ltd in which he, his wife and their three sons are all shareholders. Cambo Ltd has agreed to buy 18 Clover Street London W2 for £700,000 subject to and with the benefit of two occupational business leases. The property was built 70 years ago. A commercial mortgage has already been arranged in principle. See the Online Resource Centre for further details on taking instructions and giving initial advice.

5

THE DRAFT CONTRACT

5.1   INTRODUCTION

Acting for the seller you will draft the contract and send it in duplicate to the buyer's practitioner. Before drafting the contract you should obtain the seller's title deeds and, if the title is registered, apply for official copies from the Land Registry. If the property is leasehold you will need the original lease too. The title to the property should be checked carefully. This is to ensure primarily that the seller's duty of disclosure is satisfied because you have to disclose any encumbrances in the contract. In addition, you must also check that the seller actually owns the legal estate and/or is otherwise entitled to sell it. You can also check for any discrepancies on the title plan, e.g. if any land is missing from it. Investigating your own client's title will enable you to identify any defects in the title and to anticipate (and hopefully remedy) the questions (or requisitions) which the buyer's practitioner is likely to raise.

5.2   OCCUPIERS AND TENANCIES

Be careful to check with the seller who occupies the property. This is important because, to fulfil a contractual obligation to give vacant possession, the seller must be satisfied before contracts are exchanged that all occupiers will vacate the property on or before the contractual completion date. In respect of a non-owning spouse, civil partner, or other adult occupier, always obtain a written release of any rights in the property together with an agreement to vacate.

 Conduct Point

- The occupier(s) must be informed that their rights may be affected by giving such consent and that they should obtain independent advice from another practitioner before signing the release.

If the property is to be sold subject to tenancies, full details of these must be disclosed in the contract. Standard Condition (SC) 3.3 deals with leases affecting the property. It says that the seller is obliged to provide full particulars of lettings with copies of any documents relating thereto so as to ensure the buyer enters into the contract 'knowing and fully accepting those terms'. To give effect to this provision the seller should supply, with the draft contract, a copy of any relevant lease or tenancy agreement along with any deeds or documents that are supplementary to them, such as a deed of variation. The seller must inform the buyer of any lease or tenancy termination after exchange but before completion, as well as to act as the buyer reasonably directs, with the buyer indemnifying the seller against any consequent loss or damage. Similarly, the conditions prohibit the seller from agreeing any changes to the lease terms and require the seller to advise the buyer of any proposed or agreed changes. If there are tenants but the property is to be sold with vacant possession then the seller must take steps to terminate the tenancies and ensure that the tenants vacate.

5.3 SELLER'S DUTY OF DISCLOSURE

The seller is obliged to disclose in the contract all latent encumbrances and defects in title (see *Faruqi v English Real Estates Ltd* [1979] 1 WLR 963 and SC 3.1). This duty does not extend to physical defects in the property to which *caveat emptor* (let the buyer beware) applies. However, wilful concealment of a physical defect may give rise to a claim in the tort of deceit (*Gordon v Selico Co Ltd* [1986] 1 EGLR 71, which concerned the covering up of dry rot). A breach of the seller's duty of disclosure will normally permit the buyer to rescind the contract and claim damages.

A latent encumbrance is one which is not apparent from an inspection of the property (a restrictive covenant is an example of a latent encumbrance). However, there is some doubt about the precise meaning of 'latent'. In *Yandle and Sons v Sutton* [1922] 2 Ch 199 a right of way across land was held to be a latent encumbrance that the seller should have disclosed. The seller's conveyancer will therefore ensure that all non-physical defects and encumbrances which are known to the seller are disclosed in the contract. This includes matters apparent from an inspection of the title deeds, thus underlining the importance of a full title investigation by the seller's conveyancer.

 Key Points Before drafting the contract

- If property has registered title, apply to Land Registry for official copies of title plus copies of other documents referred to on the title.
- Obtain deeds from mortgagee or seller. Mortgagee will require your undertaking to hold deeds to order pending redemption.
- If the property is leasehold obtain the original lease from the mortgagee or seller.
- Investigate the seller's title and if title is unregistered carry out necessary land charges searches against previous estate owners (unless valid searches are already with the deeds).
- Contract implies that seller is selling free from encumbrances. Important to disclose in the draft contract all latent incumbrances and defects in title.
- Obtain details of occupiers of property. In particular, is there a non-owning spouse or civil partner? Contract will imply that Home Rights are released. Obtain from occupiers release of any rights of occupation and agreement to vacate on completion.
- Check seller's capacity to sell. What conditions, if any, need to be satisfied before seller can deal with the property?

5.4 **FORMALITIES**

Section 2 of the Law of Property (Miscellaneous Provisions) Act 1989 lays down the requirements for the creation of land contracts created on or after 27 September 1989. It provides that the contract must be in writing and incorporate all the agreed terms, either in one document or by reference to another document. The written contract must be signed by or on behalf of each party to the contract, although where contracts are to be exchanged, both sides need sign only their respective parts, not both parts.

 Conduct Point Contract races

- A contract race arises when a seller decides to deal with more than one prospective buyer, thus creating a 'race' by the buyers to see who can secure the property by being first to exchange contracts. A contract race raises an issue of professional conduct for the seller's practitioner, who must comply with the Solicitors' Code of Conduct rule 10.06. This rule states that, provided your client consents, you must immediately inform the practitioners acting for each buyer (or the buyer direct if acting in person) of your client's decision. Telephone conversations should be confirmed by letter or fax. If the seller refuses to consent to the disclosure, you must immediately cease to act for the seller.

5.5 **CONTENTS OF THE CONTRACT**

As well as the formal parts, i.e. names and addresses of the parties, the contract will comprise the particulars of sale and the conditions of sale. The particulars describe the physical extent of the property being sold and its tenure, i.e. freehold or leasehold. The property may be described using a simple postal address, provided the land is easily identifiable from it. If not, a more detailed description is necessary, referring to a scale plan and/or measurements. This applies particularly on a sale of part of an existing title where a new description will be required. For registered land the description in the property register of the title can be used and the title number quoted, together with the class of title (absolute, good leasehold, etc.). For unregistered land the description in the previous conveyance to the seller can usually be used, although its accuracy should always be verified. A misdescription may of course entitle the buyer to rescind the contract or seek an abatement in the purchase price.

Due to the complexity of the common law rules concerning land contracts (known as the 'open contract rules'), property lawyers have devised their own standardized general conditions of sale. These are periodically updated, and the current edition is the 4th edition of the Standard Conditions of Sale, which is reproduced in Appendix 2. There is also a set of conditions for commercial property known as the Standard Commercial Property Conditions (2nd edition). The general conditions cover a variety of areas, such as time limits for submission and approval of the draft purchase deed, proof of title and remedies. The standard commercial conditions (2nd edition) are reproduced in Appendix 3 and are examined in detail in chapter 19, Section 19.3.1.

In addition, there are special conditions that are specific to the transaction in question. If the parties agree to delete or modify a general condition, this is done by an appropriate special condition (e.g., 'Standard Condition 5.1 shall not apply'). Some special conditions almost invariably apply in every transaction, and for convenience they are printed on the last page of the Law Society standard form of contract (see Appendix 2). It should be noted that one of the alternatives in special condition 4 must be deleted depending on whether the property is to be sold with vacant possession or subject to tenancies.

In every transaction the practitioner must consider whether any additional special conditions are necessary, over and above those on the printed form. This is particularly so in sales of part of an existing title where the parties often agree to create new easements and covenants, the precise terms of which should properly be expressed in the special conditions (see below).

5.6 **DEPOSIT**

The deposit, payable on exchange of contracts, is normally 10 per cent of the purchase price, (although the parties sometimes agree less). The Standard Conditions provide for the deposit to be held as stakeholder except where the seller before completion agrees to buy another property in England or Wales for his residence (i.e. the seller has a related purchase). In this situation the seller may use all or any part of the sale deposit as a deposit on the related purchase provided it is used only for this purpose (SC 2.2.5.). Effectively this permits a deposit to be passed along a chain of transactions and assists the operation of a telephonic exchange under Law Society Formula C (see Chapter 10).

The buyer should be wary of allowing the deposit to be held as agent for the seller. This would mean that once exchange has taken place the seller's practitioner is free to release the deposit to the seller. But if this release occurs, there is inherent risk for the buyer if the seller defaults. This is because although the buyer will be legally entitled to the return of the deposit if the seller defaults, the buyer may have practical difficulty in actually recovering the deposit from the seller (for instance because the seller is bankrupt or cannot be traced).

5.7 **COMPLETION**

Where your client has a related sale and purchase you should seek to ensure that the agreed completion dates for both transactions are the same. If synchronization is not possible the client must be advised before exchange in writing of the implications, financial or otherwise. By completing the sale first the client may have to move into temporary accommodation and incur other expenses such as furniture storage fees. By completing the purchase first the client will almost certainly require a bridging loan and the consent of the buyer's mortgagee.

If the seller has met all deadlines during the transaction and the buyer fails to pay the balance of the purchase price on the contractual completion date, the buyer will be liable to pay the seller interest on the amount outstanding (see SC 7.3.2 and SCPC 9.3.2). Interest is calculated at the 'contract rate' specified in the contract (normally 4 per cent above the base rate of a high street bank). Care must be exercised where the client has a related sale and purchase. The practitioner should ensure that the contract rate in the purchase contract is no higher than the contract rate in the sale contract. Imagine a situation in which the contract rate on the sale is 4 per cent above base while the contract rate on the purchase is 5 per cent above base. If the client is dependent on the sale proceeds to finance the purchase but the client's buyer completes late, the client will as a consequence be forced to complete the purchase late. The compensation the client has to pay under the purchase contract will be 1 per cent more than the compensation receivable under the sale contract; the client will therefore be out of pocket.

5.8 **TITLE GUARANTEE**

The contract should state what title guarantee (if any) the seller is giving to the buyer. The seller must decide whether to give a full title guarantee, a limited title guarantee, or no title guarantee at all. The importance of the title guarantee is that covenants for title on the part of the seller are implied into the purchase deed. By definition, a limited guarantee will imply less extensive covenants for title than a full guarantee, and no guarantee will imply none. A full title guarantee is given normally where the seller owns the whole legal and equitable interest in the property. A limited title guarantee is given normally where the legal owner/seller is a personal representative, or a trustee holding on trust for others. It is usual to give no title guarantee where the seller has little or no knowledge of the property or the title history, or if the disposition is by way of gift.

5.9 INDEMNITY COVENANTS

Under privity of contract, an owner of land may continue to be liable under a covenant affecting the land even after the control of the land has passed to someone else, namely, the buyer or buyer's successor in title. In this situation the seller's practitioner must ensure that the buyer gives the seller an indemnity covenant against any future breaches of the covenant because the seller could in future be sued for breach of contract. As the property continues to change hands a chain of indemnity covenants will be built up between successors in title.

Standard Condition 4.6.4 provides that if, after completion, the seller will remain bound by any obligation affecting the property, the buyer will indemnify the seller against any future breach as well as perform the obligation. The indemnity covenant itself is given in the purchase deed. To determine whether your client seller requires an indemnity from the buyer, you need to ask yourself two questions:

- Did your client previously give any new covenants?
- When your client acquired the land, did he or she give the previous owner an indemnity covenant?

You can discover the answers to these questions as follows: if the land is unregistered, simply read the covenants (if any) given by your client in the most recent conveyance, namely, the one to your client. If the land is registered, inspect the Charges Register for details of any covenants given by the proprietor (i.e. your client) and inspect the Proprietorship Register for evidence of any indemnity covenant given by the proprietor. (If the proprietor is the first registered proprietor, it may be necessary to inspect the last pre-registration conveyance, i.e. the one to the present proprietor.) If the answer to either of the two questions is yes, your client seller will require an indemnity covenant from the current buyer. So when you later approve the draft purchase deed after exchange, you will have to check that the buyer's practitioner has included the indemnity covenant in the draft (see Chapter 7).

 Key Points Drafting the contract

- Ensure that contract contains all agreed terms to satisfy section 2 of the Law of Property (Miscellaneous Provisions) Act 1989.
- Check that description of property is accurate and any plan is to scale.
- Consider which SCs or SCPCs should be amended by special condition.
- Consider special conditions generally.
- Where sale is dependent on a related purchase, ensure that the terms of the two contracts are consistent and protect your client.
- Will deposit be held as agent or stakeholder? Under the SCs, a sale deposit can be utilized towards a related purchase deposit.
- What title guarantee will be given by the seller, if any?
- Check whether seller will need an indemnity covenant from the buyer.

5.10 **SALES OF PART**

Sales of part are generally more complex transactions than sales of whole and special considerations apply when dealing with the draft contract. First it will be necessary to draft an entirely new description of the land being sold off, and for this purpose reference to a scaled plan is essential. The plan should be of sufficient size and scale to enable the boundaries to be easily identified. Convention dictates that the land being sold should be edged red on the plan, while the land being retained by the seller (normally defined in the contract as 'the retained land') should be edged blue. Other features should also be clearly marked so that, for instance, if a right of way is being granted or reserved, the route would be shown by a broken line of a different colour or, if appropriate, by hatching.

On a sale of part the buyer may acquire certain rights over the seller's retained land by virtue of section 62 of the Law of Property Act 1925 and the rule in *Wheeldon v Burrows* (1879) 12 ChD 31. As the nature and extent of these implied rights is not always clear, it is prudent for the seller's practitioner to exclude the effect of the rules and set out expressly the rights and reservations required by the parties. If implied rights of light or air were granted to the buyer, this could hinder any future plans of the seller to develop the retained land. SC 3.4 provides on a sale of part for the exclusion of implied rights of light or air in favour of the buyer. The Condition also provides for the mutual grant of easements and reservations on a sale of part, but the condition is not exact and should be relied upon only as a fallback, i.e. if express easements are overlooked. Ideally the special conditions in the contract should deal with these matters expressly.

The seller's practitioner should always consider the covenants, if any, that the seller may wish to impose on the buyer, for instance, regarding the future use of the land being sold off. The buyer's practitioner in turn must determine whether the seller should enter into any new covenants, e.g., not to obstruct access to the property being sold or possibly a fencing obligation.

 Key Points Sales of part

- Draft new accurate description of part being sold by reference to a scale plan; define seller's retained land.
- Draft any new easements and covenants expressly as special conditions (do not rely on SCs, SCPCs or implied rights under common law or statute).
- What express easements will the buyer wish to be granted over the land being retained by the seller? (Seller should negate any implied rights in favour of buyer.)
- What express easements will the seller wish to reserve over the land being sold to the buyer? (Remember that unlike for buyers, no implied rights are reserved in favour of the seller.)

 Example Sale of part

You act for the owner of 151 Langley Way, Torquay registered with title absolute under title number BT12345. Your client is selling part of the garden as a building plot with planning permission to a property developer and has given you the following instructions:

(a) Access to the building plot will be along the client's driveway which runs along the side of the garden. The client will share the use of the driveway with the buyer.

(b) The buyer can lay new drains and sewers and connect them into the client's existing drains and sewers ('the existing services'). The existing services in turn connect into the mains drainage and sewage systems in Langley Way.

(c) Once the buyer's connection is made, the buyer can share the use of the existing services and come on to the seller's retained land to carry out any necessary maintenance or repairs to the services.

(d) There is a greenhouse on the building plot. Once the sale is legally binding on the buyer, the seller will relocate it in the part of the garden he is keeping.

(e) The client does not want to be overlooked, so the new building must be no more than one storey high. The seller will also want to see and approve the plans for the new property before it is built.

(f) The buyer will put up a suitable fence along the boundary between the plot and the land the seller is keeping, and the buyer will maintain the fence.

Recommended clauses for the draft contract (with commentary)

The following 'new' description of the land being sold is suggested:

> All that freehold land ('the Property') more particularly delineated and shown edged red on the plan annexed ('the Plan') forming part of 151 Langley Way Torquay registered at HM Land Registry with Title Absolute under title number BT12345. The land being retained by the Seller is more particularly delineated and shown edged blue on the Plan ('the Retained Land').

The following special condition is suggested regarding the grant of easements:

> The Transfer to the Buyer shall contain the following rights in favour of the Buyer and the Buyer's successors in title:
>
> (a) A free and uninterrupted right of way at all times and for all purposes with or without vehicles over the accessway shown hatched black on the Plan ('the Accessway') leading across the Retained Land subject to the Buyer paying a fair proportion according to user of the cost of maintaining repairing and renewing the Accessway;
>
> (b) A right to lay maintain and use for all proper purposes connected with the Property a new drain and sewer ('the New Services') to be laid within a period of eighty years from the date hereof under the Retained Land along the route marked with a broken orange line on the Plan;
>
> (c) A right to connect into the Seller's existing drain and sewer ('the Existing Services') on the Retained Land and to use the Existing Services in common with the Seller subject to the Buyer paying a fair proportion of the cost of maintaining repairing and renewing the Existing Services and making good any damage caused to the satisfaction of the Seller;
>
> (d) A right on giving reasonable notice and at reasonable times (except in the case of emergencies) to enter the Retained Land for the purpose of inspecting maintaining and repairing the New Services and the Existing Services the person exercising such right causing as little damage as possible and making good any such damage caused.

The period of 80 years referred to in (b) above is necessary because if new easements are to be created in the future their grant must be limited to the 80-year perpetuity period (see the Perpetuities and Accumulations Act 1964).

The seller has been protected by the provision for the buyer to make good any damage caused to the seller's retained land and for repairs to be carried out only upon prior notice, save in the case of an emergency. The route of the new services has also been specified so as to avoid any unnecessary intrusion on to the seller's retained land.

A special condition highlighting the negation of implied grants of easements would also be appropriate and the following clause can be used for this purpose:

> The Transfer to the Buyer shall contain an agreement and declaration that the Buyer shall not by implication or otherwise become entitled to any rights of light or air which would restrict or interfere with the free use of the Retained Land for building or other purposes.

From the instructions, it appears that the only reservation the seller will require is the right to remove the greenhouse. The following special condition would cover the point:

> The Seller reserves the right to remove the greenhouse on the Property provided that the Seller shall exercise this right before completion and shall cause no unnecessary damage to the Property.

The right to remove the greenhouse could be taken care of by mentioning it on the Fixtures, Fittings and Contents Form.

The seller has imposed some specific conditions and each one will be the subject of a new covenant imposed on the buyer. Although not mentioned in our instructions, it would be prudent in addition to:

(a) restrict the use of the new property to residential only (this is probably a condition of the planning permission anyway);

(b) prohibit the buyer from obstructing the driveway; and

(c) impose a general covenant against causing a nuisance or annoyance to the owners and occupiers of the seller's retained land.

The following special condition is suggested:

> The Buyer shall in the Transfer enter into a covenant with the Seller to the intent that the burden of such covenant shall run with and bind the Property and every part thereof and that the benefit of such covenant shall be annexed to and run with the Retained Land and every part thereof to observe and perform the following:
>
> (a) Not to erect on the Property any building or other structure other than one bungalow and garage for residential use and occupation by one family in accordance with plans previously approved in writing by the Seller or the Seller's successors in title;
>
> (b) Within three months from the date of completion to erect and forever thereafter maintain a close-boarded fence not less than two metres in height along the boundary between the Retained Land and the Property between the points marked A and B on the Plan;
>
> (c) Not to park vehicles on or otherwise obstruct or cause or permit to be obstructed the Accessway;
>
> (d) Not to do or permit to be done on the Property anything which may be or grow to be a nuisance or annoyance to the owners or occupiers of the Retained Land.

5.11 OPTION AGREEMENTS

A typical option agreement is a contract in which the grantee of the option (the buyer) is able, within a fixed period, to serve notice on the owner requiring the latter to transfer the land to the buyer. The option is a particularly useful tool for developers wishing to acquire several pieces of land from different owners in order to develop a larger site. Once the developer has secured options over all the pieces of land, it has effectively gained control of the development site and can safely apply for planning permission. Then once planning permission is obtained the developer can exercise all the options to ensure that it owns every part of the proposed development site.

The option agreement should state that title having been deduced the grantee shall not raise any requisition or objection to it. The agreement should provide for a completion date for the purchase, e.g., ten working days after service of the buyer's notice exercising the option. The method of service of the notice should also be made clear, e.g. 'notice in writing served on the grantor on or before...' As with ordinary contracts, the agreement should also provide for the incorporation of general conditions of sale, e.g. the latest Standard Commercial Property Conditions. The grantee may require a warranty from the owner that it will not encumber the land without the grantee's consent.

Owners who grant options must of course appreciate that the land will be tied up for the length of the option period and any sale of the land by the owner will be subject to the rights under the option (provided the option is registered). Consequently, an option is an estate contract and as such the grantee must protect it by registration. This is done either by lodging an agreed or unilateral notice in registered land or, in unregistered land, registering a class C (iv) land charge. Only registration of the option will make it binding on any subsequent purchaser of the land; actual notice of the option by a subsequent purchaser will be irrelevant (*Midland Bank Trust Co Ltd v Green* [1981] AC 513).

Key Points Option agreements

- Permits the grantee of the option to serve notice on the owner requiring a transfer of the land to the grantee.
- Useful for a developer when buying several pieces of land from different owners.
- The option agreement should provide for a completion date for the purchase when the option is exercised.
- As an estate contract the grantee should protect the option by registration.

SELF TEST QUESTIONS

1. If the seller wishes to use the deposit after exchange towards the deposit on his new yacht, the seller's solicitor must ensure that the contract provides for it to be held as

   (a) Stakeholder

   (b) Agent for the seller

   (c) Agent for the buyer

   (d) By the estate agent

2. The form of contract that should be used in National Protocol cases when selling/buying an unregistered freehold title that is subject to compulsory first registration is

   (a) Any form that the parties agree

   (b) The unregistered freehold title form

   (c) The Law Society form incorporating the Standard Conditions of Sale

   (d) The National Protocol form incorporating the National Conditions of Sale

3. In a transaction where the seller owns the whole legal and equitable interest in the subject property the draft contract should normally provide that the seller will give the buyer a limited title guarantee

   Is this statement TRUE/FALSE? Please delete the incorrect choice.

4. Acting for a client who is selling his home 'Sunnylands' and buying a new home 'Green Willows', which of the following would you NOT normally include in the draft contract for Sunnylands (both properties have registered titles)

   (a) A special condition ensuring that on the day of completion the latest time for completion of the sale is earlier than the corresponding provision in the purchase contract

   (b) A reference to Sunnylands' registered title number

   (c) That the purchaser of Sunnylands will be responsible for any stamp duty land tax that is properly payable

   (d) That Sunnylands is sold with vacant possession

5. If your client instructs you to submit a draft contract to another prospective buyer without informing the original buyer's conveyancer of this fact, you should

   (a) Refuse your client's instructions and cease to act

   (b) Carry out your client's instructions with reasonable promptness

   (c) Inform the original buyer's conveyancer in any event

   (d) Advise both buyers' conveyancers that there is a contract race

SHORT REVISION QUESTIONS

Question 1

Eloise Burrows is planning to sell off roughly half of her garden situated to the rear of her dwelling-house. The prospective purchaser is Newbuild Limited, a developer who plans to erect a new detached two-storey house and garage on the land. Eloise's existing dwellinghouse fronts onto a public highway and is connected to all mains services located beneath the highway. On completion of the sale Eloise wishes to remove some rare plants from the land she is selling. There is no access to the land she is selling other than over her retained land.

Without actually drafting them list:

(a) any special conditions Newbuild Limited might expect to be included in the draft contract, and

(b) any special conditions Eloise might expect to be included in the draft contract.

Limit your answer to those special conditions that are specific and relevant to the facts of the question.

Question 2

Patel Panesar is selling a registered freehold property known as High Trees to Beryl Meyers and has instructed you to act for him. In respect of each of the following matters affecting the property, state whether or not you should disclose them in the contract, giving a brief explanation of your answer:

(a) the property has several missing roof tiles

(b) entry number one in the charges register refers to a right of way over High Trees which benefits an adjacent property

(c) the property is subject to a registered charge in favour of Barclays Bank plc

(d) a tenant is in occupation under a lease for a fixed term of 5 years granted by deed by Patel last year

(e) entry number two in the charges register refers to a fencing covenant along the rear boundary of High Trees which benefits a property to the rear

SUGGESTED ANSWERS TO SELF TEST QUESTIONS

1. The correct answer is (b). If the deposit is held as agent for the seller then following exchange the seller is free to do what he likes with it (including buying a yacht!)

2. The correct answer is (c). The reference to unregistered freehold title subject to compulsory registration is a red herring. In *any* transaction in which the conveyancers agree to adopt the National Protocol unamended, the parties should use the Law Society contract incorporating the Standard Conditions of Sale.

3. The statement is false. If the seller owns the whole legal and equitable interest in the subject property then the buyer would expect to receive a *full* title guarantee. This implies more comprehensive implied covenants for title than would be the case with a limited title guarantee.

4. The correct answer is (c). Although the buyer of Sunnylands will be responsible for any stamp duty land tax, this is not something that need concern the seller and so no mention of it will be made in the contract.

5. The correct answer is (a). If you carry out any of the other alternatives in the question you will be in breach of rule 10.06 of the Solicitors Code of Conduct. You may only inform the buyers' conveyancers of the contract race if your client consents to it. If, however, your client refuses to consent to the disclosure you must cease to act.

SUGGESTED ANSWERS TO SHORT REVISION QUESTIONS

Question 1

Before writing your answer, note how the question asks you to limit your special conditions to those that are specific and relevant to the facts of the question. You should therefore avoid referring to special conditions of a more general nature, such as those listed on the back of the Law Society contract or those which are commonly used to amend the Standard Conditions, e.g. the latest time for completion.

(a) On these facts the special conditions Newbuild Limited might expect to be included in the draft contract are as follows:

- As the land being sold comprises land to the rear of Eloise's existing property, the developer will require a right of way with or without vehicles over Eloise's retained land to enable it to gain access to and from the public highway.

- The developer will also require a right to lay, maintain, and use new services which will no doubt pass through Eloise's retained land and connect into the mains services beneath the public highway fronting the property.

- A further right may be needed to connect into Eloise's existing services that currently serve her dwellinghouse and to use them in common with Eloise.

- Finally the developer will require a right to enter Eloise's retained land (on reasonable notice and at reasonable times, except for emergencies) to inspect, maintain, and repair the new and existing services as and when necessary.

(b) The special conditions Eloise might expect to be included in the draft contract are as follows:

- Eloise should reserve the right to remove her rare plants from the land being sold.

- Eloise should consider imposing a covenant on Newbuild Limited restricting development on the land to one two-storey dwellinghouse and garage for residential use only. The design and construction should be in accordance with plans previously approved in writing by Eloise.

- Eloise should consider imposing a covenant on Newbuild Limited to erect and maintain a fence along the boundary between the land being sold and Eloise's retained land. Ideally the fence should be close-boarded and not less than two metres in height.

- There should be negated any implied grant of easements in favour of the developer (e.g. under section 62 of the Law of Property Act 1925 or the rule in *Wheeldon v Burrows* (1879) 12 ChD 31). Although mention of this is made in SC 3.4, in practice, the point is often highlighted by special condition as well. The grant of any new easements should be dealt with expressly as special conditions (see (a) above).

Question 2

(a) There is no need for the seller to volunteer information concerning the missing roof tiles and no reference should be made to it in the draft contract. The Latin maxim *caveat emptor* (let the buyer beware) applies and the purchaser should rely on her survey. However, if the purchaser raises a pre-contract enquiry regarding the condition of the roof the seller should ensure that no misrepresentation is made.

(b) Yes, the right of way is clearly a latent incumbrance, which is noted on the charges register, and should be disclosed in the contract as a specified incumbrance subject to which the property is to be sold.

(c) Although the registered charge is an incumbrance noted on the charges register, it will be discharged on completion out of the proceeds of sale. It is therefore not an incumbrance subject to which the property is sold and there is no need to disclose it in the contract. The purchaser will of course seek an assurance from the seller that it will be discharged on or before completion.

(d) The legal lease is an unregistered interest which overrides a registered disposition under the Land Registration Act 2002, Schedule 3, paragraph 1. As the tenant is in actual occupation, the tenant's interest will also be overriding under Schedule 3, paragraph 2 of the same Act. The lease should be disclosed as an incumbrance subject to which the property is sold.

(e) The positive fencing covenant is another latent incumbrance, which should be disclosed in the contract as a specified incumbrance subject to which the property is to be sold.

WIDER READING

- Chapter 3 (The Draft Contract), Abbey, R, and Richards, M, *A Practical Approach to Conveyancing* (Oxford University Press, 2008)

- Chapter 9 (Selling and Buying Tenanted Properties), Abbey, R, and Richards, M, *A Practical Approach to Commercial Conveyancing and Property* (Oxford University Press, 2006)

- Emmet on Title, chapter 2

- Section B dealing with Pre-exchange and Section J dealing with Sales of Part, Silverman, F, *Conveyancing Handbook* (The Law Society, 2006)

- Ruoff, Theodore, BF and Roper, RB, *The Law and Practice of Registered Conveyancing* (Sweet & Maxwell, 2007)

- Chapters 3 (The Contract) 17 and 18 (Resulting and constructive trusts and proprietary estoppel), MacKenzie, J-A, and Phillips, M, *Textbook on Land Law* (Oxford University Press, 2008)

WEBSITES FOR FURTHER INFORMATION

- Council of Mortgage Lenders, **<http://www.cml.org.uk>**. There is an on-line version of the CML Lenders' Handbook available at this site and should be referred to in cases of doubt about the requirements of the lender in relation to the contract.

- House of Lords judgments, **<http://www.parliament.the-stationery-office.co.uk/pa/ld199697/ldjudgmt/ldjudgmt.htm>**. Keep up to date with any important new cases on conveyancing contracts.

- HM Revenue and customs, **<http://www.hmrc.gov.uk>**. The site for information on any problems about the possible payment of stamp duty land tax (in particular the apportionment of price in the contract between land and chattels).

- Land Registry Internet register access, **<http://www.landregistrydirect.gov.uk>**. The location for on-line applications for official copies of registered title.

- Law Commission, **<http://www.lawcom.gov.uk/review.htm>**. Keep up to date on proposals for law reform.

- Law Society, **<http://www.lawsoc.org.uk/>**. Information about the Law Society standard form of contracts.

- Location statistics, **<http://www.upmystreet.com/>**.

- Ordnance Survey, **<http://www.ordnancesurvey.co.uk>**. It might be useful to consult a detailed Ordnance Survey map when drafting descriptions of land in the draft contract (e.g. sales of part)

- A street map anywhere in the UK, **<http://www.streetmap.co.uk>**.

online
resource
centre

ONLINE RESOURCE CENTRE CASE STUDIES

RESIDENTIAL TRANSACTION CASE STUDY—THE DRAFT CONTRACT

Our clients:
Shilpa Jennings—sale of 19 Minster Yard Blakey
Shilpa Jennings and Daniel Rodriguez—purchase of 9 Castle Hill Blakey

We act for Shilpa Jennings ('Shilpa') who is selling 19 Minster Yard Blakey for £100,000 and Shilpa and Daniel Rodriguez ('Daniel') who are buying 9 Castle Hill Blakey for £200,000.

Sale of 19 Minster Yard

We have drafted the contract for the sale of 19 Minster Yard, using the Law Society form of contract incorporating the Standard Conditions of sale. See the Online Resource Centre for details.

Purchase of 9 Castle Hill

The purchase price of £200,000 includes carpets, curtains, and some items of furniture. The seller of 9 Castle Hill is the Reverend Doyle. He shares the house with his aged aunt, Constance Shorey.

See the Online Resource Centre for the draft contract received from our clients' seller's solicitors, together with our suggested amendments to it.

COMMERCIAL TRANSACTION CASE STUDY—THE DRAFT CONTRACT

Our client: Cambo Ltd—acquisition of 18 Clover Street

We act for Cambo Ltd who is acquiring the freehold reversion of 18 Clover Street London W2 for £700,000 subject to and with the benefit of two occupational business leases.

Lease of the ground floor is dated 19 October 1994 and is made between (1) Satelite Property Company Ltd and (2) Webmaster Communications Ltd.

Lease of the first and second floors is dated 29 March 1994 and is made between (i) Satelite Property Company Ltd and (2) Lifestyle Mortgage and Insurance Brokers Ltd.

See the Online Resource Centre for the draft contract using the Standard Commercial Property Conditions.

6.1 INTRODUCTION

The topics covered by this chapter seem on the face of it to be straightforward. However, as is usually the case with conveyancing, topics that seem simple generally turn out to be quite complex. The main difficulty for you will be the broad variety of problems that solicitors can expect to encounter in search results and replies to enquiries. This chapter will first look at pre-contract searches and then enquiries. These are interesting and important topics within the conveyancing process and cover a lot of points that can be of considerable consequence to a buyer. So far as enquiries are concerned, they have been greatly affected by changes brought in by the Law Society's National Conveyancing Protocol. You should acquaint yourself with the contents of the old style pre-printed traditional forms of enquiries before contract as well as the newer property information forms introduced by the Protocol. You will also need to be aware of the different enquiries required in commercial transactions. By doing this you will come to appreciate the ways in which the forms differ and how the residential system has been streamlined with the adoption of the Protocol approach. Finally, there is some overlap between enquiries and planning in that there should always be planning enquiries in most transactions. You should be aware of this and be able to demonstrate your knowledge of this possible combination of topics. Planning matters are covered in Chapter 11. Furthermore, all three items, searches, enquiries, and planning, are all items that will be important to both sides of property practice, i.e. commercial and residential.

Finally we set out below a decision tree that covers all of the topics considered in this chapter but in diagrammatic format. This should help you to understand the topics from the perspective of an overview and enable you to make selections according to the nature of a particular transaction, be it commercial or residential.

6.2 PRE-CONTRACT SEARCHES

Caveat emptor (let the buyer beware) remains a cornerstone of conveyancing in England and Wales. As such a buyer will need to find out as much as possible about the subject property before contracts are exchanged. This being so it will inevitably lead to a buyer's practitioner making all appropriate pre-contract searches and detailed pre-contract enquiries.

6.2.1 THE NATIONAL LAND INFORMATION SERVICE

The modernization of the process of applying for pre-contract searches has been ushered in with the creation of the National Land Information Service (NLIS). The idea behind the NLIS is to create an environment over the internet that will allow speedy and simple access to a wide range of land and property information, held on the databases of many different public and private sector groups. The aim of the service is that this wide range of data will be available from a single point of enquiry. This is because it brings together in one point of enquiry almost all the different agencies involved in a conveyance, such as the local authority, the Land Registry, the local water companies, Companies House, the Environmental Agency, and the Coal Authority. The NLIS is now operative (having gone live in February 2001) in all of England and Wales through three NLIS licensed channels. Practitioners can set up facilities to carry out searches via these companies, whose website addresses are set out in the websites section below. Eventually the NLIS will use Britain's first comprehensive gazetteer of addressable properties: *The National Land and Property Gazetteer*. All addresses will be given a unique identifier, called a 'Unique Property Reference Number' (UPRN), which will be used to cross-reference data for conveyancing searches. Indeed, there is already a section in the latest edition of the local authority search form for practitioners to insert the NLPG UPRN to assist in identifying a subject property.

6.3 WHY DO SEARCHES?

A seller has a common law duty to disclose latent defects, defects in title and land charges affecting the property (Land Charges Act 1969, section 24). Technically, local land charges also fall within this duty of disclosure. Under the terms of the Standard Conditions of Sale (4th edition) a property is sold subject to incumbrances specified in the contract, or discoverable by inspection of the property, or which the seller does not reasonably know about, as well as entries in public registers (except those at HM Land Registry, the Land Charges Registry, and Companies House) and public requirements. Many sellers put a special condition in the contract that the subject property is sold subject to all matters that would have been revealed by searches and enquiries that a prudent buyer would make before entering into the contract, (subject to the exclusion of monetary charges or incumbrances.) The effect of this is to allocate to the buyer the responsibility of making all appropriate searches.

A seller's duty of disclosure and the documentation arising from this duty will not satisfy a buyer's needs regarding the investigation of the title and other relevant factors about a possible purchase of a property. A buyer needs to know all the matters that affect the property, either positively or negatively, before exchanging contracts for the purchase. Because the buyer needs to be fully aware of all of these matters before committing himself to a purchase the buyer must carry out all pre-contract searches.

6.4 THE SELLER'S HOME INFORMATION PACK

The Home Information Pack (HIP) is mandatory from 1 August 2007 for properties with four or more bedrooms and for three-bedroom properties from the 10 September 2007. From 14 December 2007 it is now the case that all properties about to be marketed for sale in England and Wales will first require a HIP before the marketing commences.

The HIP legislation requires homeowners or their selling agents to have a HIP in existence before marketing homes for sale, and to make a copy of the pack available to prospective buyers on request. The person marketing the property will be responsible for ensuring that the pack is available. The pack must include standard documents and information for prospective buyers (see below).

A HIP will contain required documents defined in the Home Information Pack Regulations 2007 (SI 2007/992) as being documents that must be included. Just two searches are required: the local authority search, and the water and drainage search. Therefore, the HIP *must* contain replies to local authority searches and water and drainage searches or contain evidence that the searches have been applied for. The HIP must include the local land charges register relating to the subject property. If the search is carried out by the local authority, an official search certificate will be provided. Alternatively a personal search company can be used. The HIP must also include other records held by the local authority on matters of interest to buyers, such as planning decisions and road building proposals. These are referred to as local enquiries in the HIP regulations. A local authority or a personal search company can be used.

For the standard drainage and water search for the subject property, the local water company or a personal search company can be used. It should be noted that searches are not initially required in the HIP as long as they have been applied for. This is as a result of rule 15 which says that only certain documents must be in the HIP at the first point of marketing the property, while the remaining documents must be included within 28 days of the first point of marketing. The documents that must be in at the start are the index, the energy performance certificate, the sale statement evidence of title, and, if unregistered, the index map search result.

Although not compulsory the HIP may contain other authorized documents such as all other types of searches, e.g. coal mining searches or environmental searches. In practice we cannot see that sellers will go to the expense of including other types of searches if they are not required to do so. This is a patent systemic weakness of the HIP.

As a result of these provisions, practitioners should be aware that the HIP will transfer responsibility for obtaining local and drainage searches from the buyer to the seller and, as such, the seller will bear the costs of these additional requirements. One other problem is in relation to time limited components of the HIP. For example, local authority searches that are more than three months old are generally not acceptable to solicitors acting for a buyer, and many would not accept a search that was more than two months old. It is possible under the regulations to continue to market a property with searches that are older than this and yet meet with the requirements of the HIP regulations. This is clearly another patent defect in the system.

6.5 WHAT SEARCHES SHOULD YOU DO AND WHEN?

In the context of pre-contract searches, the first concern for a practitioner is—have I completed all the searches I need to for a particular property? Figure 6.1 should assist.

online resource centre

As to when the searches should be completed, the answer is as soon as possible following confirmation that a buyer's offer has been accepted and full details of the property have been provided including a sample scale plan. In addition to appropriate enquiries of the seller's solicitors, and an inspection of the property the following searches should be considered, all or some of which maybe required prior to an exchange of contracts:

(a) *Local authority search incorporating a commons registration search*. This is of such importance that no conveyancing matter be it commercial or residential should proceed without one. A practitioner will need to carefully review both the results of the search on the local land charges register (form LLC1) as well as the replies to standard enquiries completed by the local authority (form CON29). The two items together are accepted in practice as constituting the local authority search result. With regard to the Commons registration search question in the optional enquiries that may be sent to the local authority, this is of particular relevance when buying a new property. This search now forms part of the local authority search as an additional optional question that can be asked of the local authority in part 2 of the enquiries section.

FIGURE 6.1 SEARCHES DECISION TREE

Q.1 Is the property registered	
Yes Go to Q.2	No Do a map index search and if you have title details a land charges search
Q.2 Is the property in an urban area?	
Yes Go to Q.3	No If it is rural or on the edge of town or a recent development do a commons registration search question
Q.3 Have you checked the location in the Coal Mining Directory and is it affected?	
Yes Complete a coal mining search	No Go to Q.4
Q.4 Are you buying from a company?	
Yes Complete a company search	No Go to Q.5
Q.5 Have you completed an environmental search?	
Yes Go to Q.6	No Check your client's instructions and always advise that one is necessary
Q.6 Have you completed a local authority search, a water company search?	
Yes Go to Q.7	No Do them now. Both searches should be made in all transactions
Q.7 Have you advised your client to inspect the property prior to exchange?	
Yes Go to Q.8	No This should be done to check the state of the property, whether there any unlawful occupiers etc.
Q.8 Have you checked for other location-dependant searches	
Yes Go and do something else.	No Complete all other such searches, e.g. Tin mining in Cornwall, Brine extraction in Cheshire etc.

Regarding the first part of the search, the burdens in the register are set out in the search in 12 parts of the register. They are:

1. General financial charges.

2. Specific financial charges.

3. Planning charges.

4. Miscellaneous charges.

5. Fenland ways maintenance charges.

6. Land compensation charges.

7. New towns charges.

8. Civil aviation charges.

9. Open-cast coal mining charges.

10. Listed buildings charges.

11. Light obstruction notices.

12. Drainage scheme charges.

The list highlights the kind of information that will be disclosed in the search result. This includes various financial charges that will affect the property, planning consents concerning the property, and compulsory purchase orders, as well as tree preservation orders. Additionally, other registrations of consequence will be revealed such as whether or not the property is within a conservation area or smoke control zone. In the case of this last kind of restriction the client will need to be advised of the restrictive nature of the registration and how it might affect the property and its neighbourhood. Once the search result is issued, it should be appreciated that there is no priority period for the result, or indeed any other form of protection given by the search.

In relation to the second part of the search, form CON 29 should always accompany the local land charge search request. The questions in themselves are straightforward. However, in the main all that is sent to the applicant by the local authority is a rather confusing list of 'Yes' and 'No' answers adjacent to the number of the question concerned. This therefore means that practitioners must either memorize the questions or, more practically, have a reminder list to hand when looking at the usually dislocated answers. Caution should be exercised, as familiarity with the form may induce a cursory look at the answers that might result in an important answer being overlooked. Answers in the positive must always be investigated.

(b) *Water company search and enquiries.* This provides details about water and drainage services to the subject property. Once again this will be of relevance to all types of conveyancing cases. Commercial property searches should be specifically marked as such on the search form to gain the benefit of extra insurance cover against mistakes by the issuing water company.

(c) *Coal mining search.* This affects all types of conveyancing cases when they are located in an area currently or previously affected by coal mining. The subject property might be a victim of subsidence or could be a potential victim. A buyer needs to know this before deciding on the merits of the proposed purchase.

(d) *Index map search.* This is used particularly to see if the title to the subject property is partially or completely registered and if so what tenures are registered.

(e) *Land charges search.* This is of use in unregistered land when you have seen all the title before exchange and you are taking the prudent step of checking for undisclosed encumbrances at an early stage in the transaction.

(f) *Company search.* This search is relevant if you are buying from a company and want to make sure that it is properly registered at Companies House and is not subject to any winding up or liquidation proceedings. This will also be required where the property is leasehold and there is a management company involved in the leasehold relationship.

(g) *Other searches dependent upon the location of the property.* See the section on extra searches at 6.5.1 below.

(h) *Physical search or inspection of the property.* This is to check the condition of the property just before exchange and to make sure that any contents or fixtures and fittings mentioned in the contract are where they should be at the time the contract becomes binding. Accordingly, when considering searches it is always appropriate for domestic conveyancing and probably for many types of commercial conveyancing matters to advise the buyer to inspect the subject property prior to exchange. In detail the reasons for the inspection are fivefold and are to check:

- the state and condition of the property;
- who is in actual occupation of the property;
- the boundaries;
- any rights and easements affecting or benefiting the property; and
- that the fixtures and fittings contracted to be sold are in the subject property just prior to exchange.

(i) *Environmental searches (including flooding).* The need for this search has arisen out of recent legislation making land owners responsible for contamination remediation of land that they own. Similarly, the recent increase in the frequency of the flooding of property has affected the insurability of some premises located near to or adjacent to sources of flooding. Accordingly, in every transaction, a conveyancer must consider whether contamination or flooding might be a relevant issue. Searches and enquiries should be made about these environmental concerns in all transactions, both domestic and commercial, hence the need for environmental searches including enquiries about flooding.

6.5.1 EXTRA PRE-CONTRACT SEARCHES

In addition, you should also appreciate that other searches may be necessary and you can only decide on what others are required by looking closely at the address and location of the subject property. England and Wales can be viewed as a patchwork of exclusive localities. Consequently each exclusive locality can have a speciality, a peculiarity, all to itself. This being so, searches can be specialized or localized depending on the location of the subject property. An examiner could quite easily place a subject property in the Greater Manchester area and ask about pre-contract searches. In doing so you would be expected to know that coal mining and brine extraction might affect the property, and consequently searches would be required to address these potential concerns. Examples of some of these less common localized searches are:

(a) *Limestone mining searches.* If the property is located in Dudley, Sandwell, Walsall, or Wolverhampton a search should be sent to the local council asking about limestone mining. The result will reveal the presence, or indeed absence, of disused underground workings that could cause subsidence.

(b) *Clay mining searches.* If the property is located in Devon or Cornwall a search should be sent to English China Clay Company asking about clay mining. The result will reveal the presence or absence of any operations that could cause subsidence.

(c) *Brine extraction searches.* If the property is located in Cheshire or Greater Manchester a search should be sent to the Coal Authority who deal now with brine extraction searches. This search asks about brine extraction works in the locality. The result will reveal the presence or absence of old workings that could cause subsidence.

(d) *Tin mining searches.* If the property is located in Devon or Cornwall a search should be sent to the Cornish Chamber of Mines asking about tin mining. The search result will reveal the presence or absence of disused mines that could cause subsidence.

Key Points Pre-Contract Searches

- Unless otherwise agreed the conveyancer acting for the buyer should always make a local search and a water search or ensure up-to-date results are in a Home Information Pack (HIP).
- Reflect on the location of the subject property to enable you to decide which other searches are relevant to this particular property.
- Location is also crucial when considering the necessity for a coal-mining search and other unusual searches.
- On receipt of the local authority search always check the result. Scan the land charges disclosed in the result and then check all answers provided by the local authority.
- In unregistered land always carry out an index map search.
- Always advise clients of any onerous or unusual replies or results to any of the searches and request their written instructions in response.
- Consider an environmental search and make such a search in all cases both residential and commercial. On receipt of the result always check to see if the subject property might be affected by flooding and if it is report the findings to the client and check the position regarding the availability of insurance

 Conduct Point Home Information Packs (HIPs)

- Do not market a property for a client without first having prepared a HIP that should always include a local authority search as well as a water and drainage search. Failure to do so could incur you in a fixed penalty charge of £200 and your breach of duty under part 5 of the Housing Act 2004 (Home Information Packs) will amount to a breach of the Code of Conduct for solicitors.

6.6 PRE-CONTRACT ENQUIRIES

This topic covers questions asked by the buyer or the seller to find out as much as possible about the subject property. It will span questions raised in Protocol cases as well as those where traditional conveyancing procedures are used. In Protocol cases this involves Property Information Forms and in traditional cases forms called enquiries before contract. Consideration is then given to specific enquiries that are preferred for commercial transactions, namely the Commercial Property Standard Enquiries.

6.7 WHY RAISE PRE-CONTRACT ENQUIRIES?

The buyer must carry out all appropriate enquiries before entering into a binding contract to purchase the subject property. If a buyer does make all necessary enquiries of the seller, and gets sensible answers, an informed decision can then be taken about the nature and suitability of the property based on all the information obtained prior to exchange. So a buyer will need to find out as much as possible about the subject property before contracts are exchanged. The simple yet compelling reason for this is that the buyer must take the property in whatever condition it is in, at the point when there is a binding contract for the purchase. Consequently, the law imposes a clear obligation upon the buyer to find out as much about the property because the common law recognizes that the seller has only a limited duty of disclosure.

6.8 **WHAT ENQUIRIES SHOULD YOU RAISE AND WHEN?**

Pre-contract enquiries, otherwise called preliminary enquiries, can, in domestic transactions, take two different forms. The first type is the orthodox traditional form in the style of a list of far-reaching questions aimed at the seller and intended to seek out as much detail via the seller's solicitor. In commercial transactions traditional lists of questions are always used, as specific questions are always required for non-domestic transactions, because commercial properties will usually be more complicated than a house or flat and in many cases will involve leaseholds that require particular enquiries about the nature of the tenancy.

The second more modern style of form emanates from changes made by the Law Society. Preliminary enquiries have been greatly affected by procedural changes ushered in by the Law Society's National Conveyancing Protocol. Practitioners should acquaint themselves with the contents of the old-style printed traditional forms of enquiries before contract as well as with the new Protocol Property Information Forms. By doing this you will come to appreciate the ways in which the forms differ and how the conveyancing process has been, to a limited extent, streamlined with the adoption of the Protocol approach.

The old style preliminary enquiry forms have been replaced by client questionnaires that form an integral part of the Protocol. The latest edition of the Protocol brought with it a revision of these questionnaires. The fifth edition forms have been revised to take account of Home Information Packs and they are listed below with their form reference number. The forms that appear underlined are intended exclusively for use with the preparation of a HIP:

- TA1 Home Information Pack Index
- TA2 Sale Statement
- TA3 Required leasehold information
- TA4 Required commonhold information
- TA5 Proof of requests for missing documents and information
- TA6 Property information form
- TA7 Leasehold information form
- TA8 New home information form
- TA9 Commonhold information form
- TA10 Fittings and contents form
- TA11 Additional property information
- TA12 Buyer Information
- TA13 Completion information and requisitions on title
- TA14 Leasehold information request
- TA15 Commonhold information request

Many conveyancing practitioners have adopted the Protocol 'enquiry' Forms even when they are not actually using the full Protocol process. They will also use the Protocol forms specifically dedicated to leaseholds. However, others remain traditionally minded and use pre-printed forms, or their own in-house preliminary enquiry forms. These questions, sometimes actually entitled preliminary enquiries and sometimes enquiries before contract, are listed in duplicate and submitted to the seller. (Two copies are issued as a convenient and helpful practice, enabling the seller's practitioner to retain a copy of the questions with replies as a file copy.) Whatever form is used, the intention remains the same: to seek out answers from the seller about any matters that affect or could affect the subject property.

The problem that has arisen with the introduction of Home Information Packs is that enquiry type forms are not required, they are merely authorized. This means that completed questionnaires can be in a HIP but do not have to be. The likelihood is that they will be ignored and that enquiries will be dealt with after the HIP has been compiled.

When using Protocol forms, there still remains the difficulty of reconciling the professional obligation on the buyer's conveyancing practitioner to make all proper and reasonable enquiries on behalf of their client with the aim of the Protocol, that of streamlining the enquiry process. The difference between this aspect of the Protocol procedures and the buyer's conveyancing practitioner's overriding duty to the client now appears to be very slender. It seems inevitable that either the printed Protocol forms will continue to expand, or they will be accompanied by copious extra enquiries raised by anxious or perhaps prudent conveyancing practitioners. It is only natural for them to incline towards more rather than fewer questions. This is of course in the perhaps vain hope that, notwithstanding the Property Information Forms, by asking as many questions as possible, practitioners might be able to avoid negligence claims by dissatisfied clients.

It is clear that when a conveyancer is involved in the buying or selling of tenanted properties, the heavier burden rests with the buyer's practitioner. This is because the buyer will want to have full details of the title approved, as well as details of the tenancy or tenancies affecting the subject property. A buyer will expect a good and marketable title to the subject property, as well as a letting that is upon terms that the buyer deems acceptable. This will of course centre on the rental due, but will also cover other terms of the tenancy or letting. Therefore, this form of conveyancing transaction in particular requires extra care when raising preliminary enquiries. This is also the case when looking at the title and when raising requisitions.

In summary, the following matters should always form the subject of preliminary enquiries:

(a) *Disputes*. No buyer would willingly buy a property that is subject to an on-going dispute. Furthermore it is incumbent upon a seller to advise a buyer of any dispute, particularly one that involves a neighbour.

(b) *Notices*. A buyer will want to know about notices served upon the seller from, say, the local authority or central government of the landlord of the subject premises.

(c) *Boundaries and fences*. Where adjoining properties meet should be clearly delineated, to avoid subsequent disputes.

(d) *Services and conducting media*. Does the property have the benefit of all the main services such as gas and electricity? Is there main drainage or does the property have a private drainage arrangement?

(e) *Exclusive facilities*.

(f) *Shared facilities*.

(g) *Occupiers*. This might cover both tenants as well as licencees.

(h) *Use and planning*.

(i) *Service charges*. This can cover both leaseholds as well as freeholds paying an estate rentcharge and will therefore cover both commercial and residential properties.

(j) *Insurance arrangements*.

(k) *Covenants*. On the title and possibly in a lease.

(l) *Flooding and general environmental concerns*.

There will be a need for additional core topics for leasehold matters. For example, it is a great help for the buyer and the buyer's conveyancer if the seller can accurately confirm the names and addresses of the lessor, any superior lessor, the superior lessor's managing agent, if any, and the superior lessor's solicitors. If there is a management company mentioned in any of the leases of the subject property, full details of the management company, its officers, agents, and solicitors should be requested. Finally, with leasehold properties full details of insurance arrangements will be necessary along with similar details for service charges.

6.9 COMMERCIAL PROPERTY ENQUIRIES

The Commercial Property Standard Enquiries (CPSEs) are a set of documents that have been drafted by members of the London Property Support Lawyers Group under the sponsorship of the British Property Federation (BPF). Contributions were also made by a number of other firms and individuals. The CPSEs are endorsed by the BPF and it is anticipated that they might become industry standard pre-contract enquiries for commercial property conveyancing. Form CPSE.1 is designed to cover all commercial property transactions and will (together with any additional enquiries relevant to the particular transaction) be sufficient if the transaction deals only with a freehold sold with vacant possession. The supplemental enquiries forms listed below are intended to be used in conjunction with CPSE.1. Which particular additional form or forms will be required will depend upon the individual circumstances of each transaction. The following supplemental forms are available:

- CPSE.2: where the property is sold subject to existing tenancies.
- CPSE.3: where a lease of a property is being granted.
- CPSE.4: where the property being sold is leasehold.

The enquiries set out in CPSE.1 cover the following topics all of which will normally be of concern when buying a commercial property and can therefore be used whether the property is subject to a letting or not:

1. Boundaries and extent.
2. Party walls.
3. Rights benefiting the property.
4. Adverse rights affecting the property.
5. Title policies (by way of indemnity).
6. Access to neighbouring land.
7. Access to and from the property.
8. Physical condition.
9. Contents.
10. Utilities and services.
11. Fire certificates and means of escape.
12. Planning and building regulations.
13. Statutory agreements and infrastructure.
14. Statutory and other requirements.
15. Environmental (to include flooding).
16. Occupiers and employees.
17. Insurance.
18. Rates and other outgoings.
19. Capital allowances.
20. Value added tax (vat) registration information.
21. Transfer of a business as a going concern (TOGC).
22. Other vat treatment.

23. Standard-rated supplies.

24. Exempt supplies.

25. Zero-rated supplies.

26. Transactions outside the scope of vat (other than TOGCs).

27. Notices.

28. Disputes.

29. Stamp duty land tax on assignment of a lease.

30. Deferred payments of stamp duty land tax.

Finally as a general word of warning, the seller and the seller's solicitor should be aware of the risks of qualifying a reply to an enquiry with words like 'not so far as the seller is aware' or 'not to our knowledge but no warranty can be given'. These and similar phrases are treated by the courts as an implied representation that the seller and the seller's solicitors have no actual knowledge of a matter and that they have made all the investigations that a prudent conveyancer would be expected to have made (*William Sindall PLC v Cambridgeshire County Council* [1994] 1 WLR 1016). Clearly, an answer of this type is intended to avoid making the effort to research the true answer. The decision makes it clear that the answer will infer that the work was done even if in reality it was not.

6.10 A PRE-CONTRACT DECISION TREE

Please see Figure 6.2 for the different branch-decisions and selections you need to make for pre-contract searches and enquiries. There are two clear strands to the diagram and each represents the approach you will need to consider for each part covered by this chapter. The decision tree can apply equally to commercial as well as domestic property transactions.

 Key Points Pre-contract enquiries

- Which forms should you use—Protocol or not, pre-printed or not, core and/or additional?

- What extra questions need to be asked that are specific to the subject property?

- Always advise your client of any onerous or unusual replies to any of the preliminary enquiries and request written instructions in response.

- In commercial transactions can you utilise the Commercial Property Standard Enquiries?

- Remember the effect of the decision in *William Sindall PLC v Cambridgeshire County Council* [1994] 1 WLR 1016 and never give vague evasive and generalised type answers

SELF TEST QUESTIONS

1. You are buying for a client a commercial unit in Holborn in the Centre of London. Which of the following pre-contract searches would you not complete

   (a) Local authority search

   (b) Coal mining search

   (c) Water and drainage search

   (d) Environmental search

FIGURE 6.2 PRE-CONTRACT SEARCHES AND ENQUIRIES

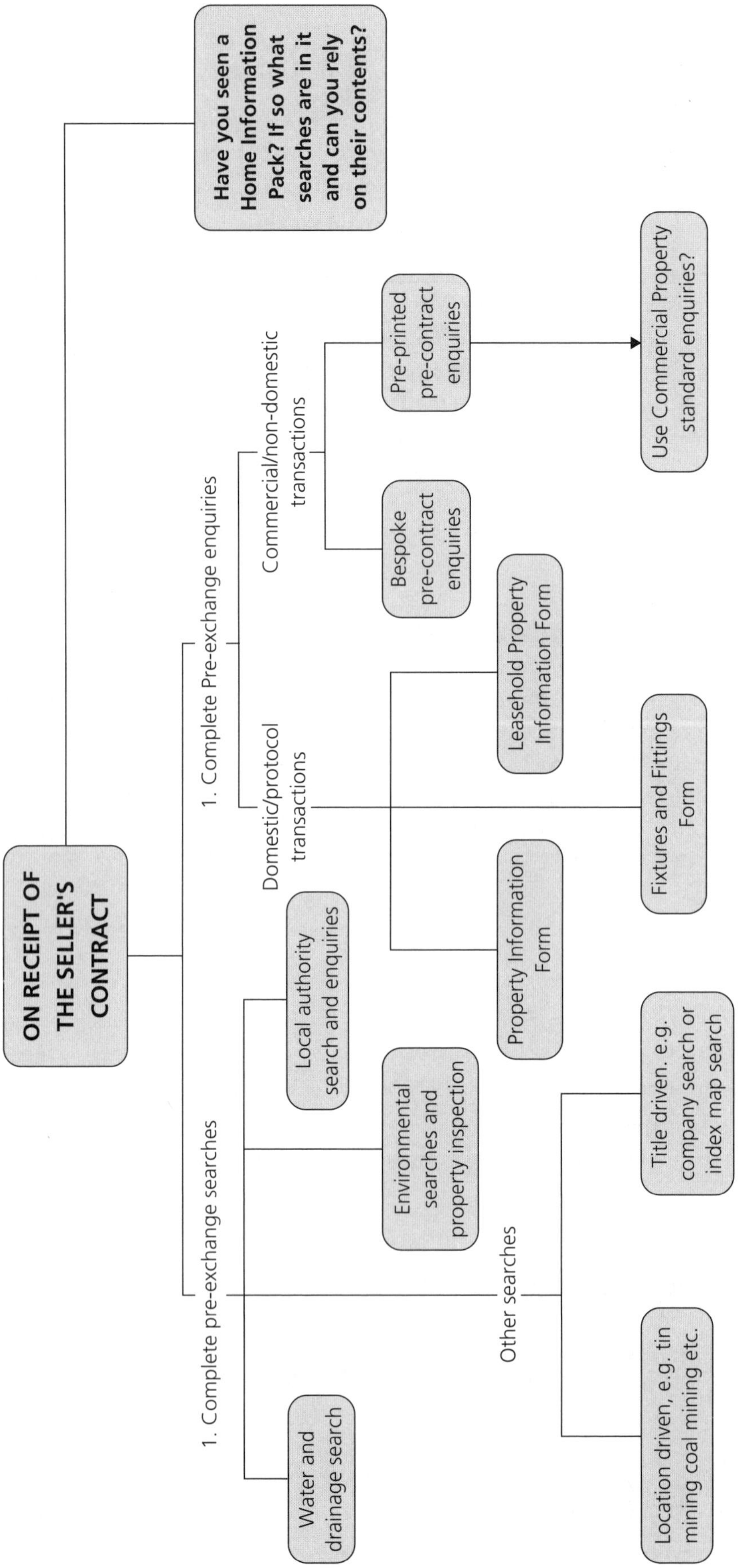

ON RECEIPT OF THE SELLER'S CONTRACT

Have you seen a Home Information Pack? If so what searches are in it and can you rely on their contents?

1. Complete pre-exchange searches

1. Complete Pre-exchange enquiries

Water and drainage search

Local authority search and enquiries

Environmental searches and property inspection

Other searches

Title driven. e.g. company search or index map search

Location driven, e.g. tin mining coal mining etc.

Domestic/protocol transactions

Property Information Form

Fixtures and Fittings Form

Leasehold Property Information Form

Commercial/non-domestic transactions

Bespoke pre-contract enquiries

Pre-printed pre-contract enquiries

Use Commercial Property standard enquiries?

2. When applying for a local authority search which registry deals with the application and issues the result of the search

   (a) The land charges registry

   (b) The Land Registry

   (c) The local land charges registry

   (d) The district Land Registry

3. The National Land Information Service allows conveyancing practitioners to apply over the internet for pre-contract searches. Which of the following pre-contract searches cannot be obtained through this service

   (a) A coal mining search report

   (b) A drainage and water search

   (c) The local land charge or local authority search

   (d) The Land Registry index map search

4. A buyer should always be advised to inspect a subject property prior to exchange. The reasons for the inspection are listed below. Please indicate which is not relevant

   (a) To arrange for contracts to be signed in readiness for exchange

   (b) To check who is in actual occupation of the property

   (c) To check on rights and easements affecting or benefiting the property

   (d) To check that the fixtures and fittings contracted to be sold are in the subject property just prior to exchange

5. Question 3.12 of a local authority search covers contaminated land. There is sufficient information in the answers for a buyer of residential property. Is this statement TRUE/FALSE? Please delete the incorrect choice.

SHORT REVISION QUESTIONS

Question 1

You act for Darren and Anna Bent, the proposed purchasers of a residential property called 38 Moorcroft Road Ringtown Hull. You have completed your local authority search and there is nothing onerous or unusual in the result of the search made of the local land charges registry. The replies to the accompanying enquiries are attached with the actual questions. Where necessary please comment upon the replies given to the standard questions. (NB Replies to enquiries are in Figure 6.3.)

Question 2

You act for Bazlur Rashid in connection with his purchase of a freehold property in Leicester. It is a three-bedroom terraced house with both small front and rear gardens. The seller is Leslie King. The Protocol has been adopted. You have received the seller's replies to the Property Information Form although the solicitors for the seller have not completed Part II saying that it is not their policy to do so. The replies to Part I are available in Appendix 5. Where necessary please comment upon the replies given to the standard questions.

SUGGESTED ANSWERS TO SELF TEST QUESTIONS

1. The correct selection is (b). The reason for this is that there is no coal mining in London, nor has there ever been and it is a reasonable assumption to make that this is common knowledge enabling

FIGURE 6.3 REPLIES TO ENQUIRIES OF LOCAL AUTHORITY

**STANDARD ENQUIRIES OF LOCAL AUTHORITY
(2007 Edition)**

Re: 38 Moorcroft Road Ringtown Hull

1.1
    (a) none
    (b) none
    (c) Property in Ringtown Conservation Area made 2.1.92
    (d) none
    (e) none
    (f) none
    (g) none
    (h) none

1.2 Copies from Planning Dept. Civic Centre Hull HS1 2HS

2
    (a) Moorcroft Road
    (b) none
    (c) none
    (d) none
    (f) Side passage and rear alleyway is private.

---

3 See below, copies from the Civic Centre Hull HS1 2HS
    3.1   None
    3.2   None
    3.3   None
    3.4   Kingston Underpass improvement scheme 175 metres away
    3.5   Kinston City tramway scheme proposed 2010, not in this road
    3.6   Cycle way proposed for Moorcroft Road, 2007
    3.7   None
    3.8   None
    3.9   None
    3.10 Property in Ringtown Conservation Area made 2.1.92
    3.11 None
    3.12 None
    3.13 None

---

the correct answer to be made on this basis. Clearly all the other searches listed will be relevant to a transaction of the kind described in the question.

2. The correct answer is (c). Students always get confused about which registry is which and who does what. Remember the local searches are of the local land charges registry while the land charges registry deals with land charge searches as well as bankruptcy searches. Just to confuse you further the land charges service operates under the umbrella of the Land Registry!

3. The correct answer is in fact that none of the selections apply. This is a difficult question in that all of these searches can be applied for through the National Land Information Service. Indeed, there are very few searches that cannot be obtained through this electronic facility.

4. The correct answer is (a). The other three selections are all highly relevant reasons why a buyer should always be advised to inspect a subject property prior to exchange. Selection (a) has little or no relevance as this will normally be dealt with between a solicitor and client.

5. The correct answer is that the statement is false. Practitioners should not merely rely upon any contaminated land information obtained from the local authority in the reply to question 3.12 of the enquiries in the local authority search. This is because the detail supplied is likely to be insufficient, being limited to land identified by the local authority as contaminated or potentially affected by nearby contaminated land. A detailed environmental search report should be obtained both for the buyer and if necessary the buyer's surveyor.

SUGGESTED ANSWERS TO THE SHORT REVISION QUESTIONS

Question 1

This question requires you to do what any conveyancer must do for each transaction: check the replies to a local search questionnaire and consider what steps must be taken to deal with various entries. Where a search result discloses an entry you need to review the disclosure and decide upon the gravity of it. You will then have to consider the need to refer the information to the client. Clearly anything that might affect the use or enjoyment of the property should be mentioned to the buyer.

The first reply of concern relates to question 1.1 (c). This concern also links to the answer given by the Council to question 3.10. In both answers the Council have indicated that the property is in a conservation area. In the case of this kind of disclosure, the client will need to be advised of the restrictive nature of the registration and how it might affect the property and its neighbourhood. Question 3.10 will confirm if a conservation area not disclosed in the official certificate of search affects the subject property. This will cover all such areas that were designated before 31 August 1974. The reason for this is that after that date conservation areas became land charges and are disclosed in searches of the local land charges registry. A buyer will want to know if the property is in a conservation area as there will, as a result, be limitations on development. Even minor alterations can be disallowed in a conservation area and consequently this information may be critical to a buyer intending to alter, demolish, or improve the property.

The answer to question 2(f) should be referred to the client as the buyer may be under a duty to maintain or pay for the maintenance of the alleyway. You will need to check the title for possible details.

The answers to questions 3.4, 3.5, and 3.6 should all be referred to the client as they might all adversely affect the property. The first disclosure mentions a nearby traffic improvement, the second a future travel proposal, and the third an imminent scheme for the road that could mean the banning of cars and lorries. The buyer needs to consider if this is likely to be adverse. You should write to the Council for full details of all these matters for onward transmission to the buyer.

Question 2

This question requires you to do what any conveyancer must do for each transaction: check the replies to a property information form or questionnaire and consider what steps must be taken to deal with various entries. The same will be true for pre-contract enquiries where the Protocol does not apply. Where a reply discloses a matter of concern, you need to review the disclosure and decide upon the gravity of it. You will then have to consider the need to refer the information to the client. Clearly anything that might affect the use or enjoyment of the property should be mentioned to the buyer.

There are not many answers that are problematic. The answer to question 2 needs to be immediately referred to the buyer. The problem might arise again and the reason for them stopping needs to be investigated. Has the noisy neighbour moved? If so, then perhaps the problem has gone as well. In Question 4 work for damp course treatment and rot or infestation has been carried out but there is no mention of a guarantee certificate. You need to ask for the report and estimate and the guarantee so that full copies can be sent to the buyer.

Question 8 is of concern to you as the solicitor for the buyer. You are on notice of a non-owning occupier who may have an equitable interest in the property and who must be required to sign the contract to confirm her willingness to vacate on the day of completion. You need to ensure that the contract is amended to take into account this requirement.

The answer to question 10 makes it clear that the seller has in the past experienced a problem with a blocked drain serving the subject property and that it appears to drain in combination with the neighbouring property. You should copy the full form to the buyer and advise him of the drainage difficulty that has arisen in the past and that because there appears to be a combined drainage system that repairs might need to be dealt with in the same way in the future. The deeds need to be checked to see if there is anything about this in them.

Finally you should ask the seller's solicitors to reconsider their policy and to complete Part II of the form. At the very least they should say if the replies are consistent with the information in their possession and whether there is an indemnity policy with the deeds.

WIDER READING

- Chapter 1 'Matters Before Contract' in Farrand J, *Emmet on Title* (Sweet & Maxwell)

- Chapter 4 in Abbey, R, and Richards, M, *A Practical Approach to Conveyancing* (Oxford University Press, 2008)

- Section B dealing with Pre-exchange and Section J dealing with Sales of Part, Silverman, F, *Conveyancing Handbook* (The Law Society, 2006)

- Chapter 9, Abbey, R, and Richards, M, *A Practical Approach to Commercial Conveyancing and Property* (Oxford University Press, 2006)

WEBSITES FOR FURTHER INFORMATION

- Companies House, **<http://www.companies-house.gov.uk>**. On-line company searches are available from the Companies House website.

- Countrywide Legal Indemnities, **<http://www.helpforconveyancers.com>**. Offers an insurance solution when there are concerns about contamination. The insurance policy on offer is intended to cover homeowners against the potential liability for remediation costs of any contaminants found on their land.

- Environment Agency, **<http://www.environment-agency.gov.uk>**. The Environment Agency has made maps available on the internet that show areas potentially liable to flooding. This is a free service and can be accessed using a property postcode.

- Homecheck, **<http://www.homecheck.co.uk>**. Environmental risk can be checked without cost on this site.

- Homecheck professional, **<http://www.homecheckpro.co.uk>**. On-line environmental searches can be carried out at this site. It will also provide a certificate, where possible, confirming that the subject property is not likely to be described as 'contaminated land' as defined by section 78 of the Environmental Protection Act 1990.

- Land Registry, **<http://www.landreg.gov.uk>**. Details of Land Registry services and the search facilitites available on-line.

- Landmark Information Group, **<http://www.landmark-information.co.uk>**. Environmental searches can be obtained from the Landmark Information Group. They can assist with both residential and commercial properties.

- National Land Information Service, **<http://www.nlis.org.uk>**. Was set up to facilitate on-line searches that can be carried out on its own site. The NLIS, having gone live in February 2001 in all of England and Wales, offers a search service through three NLIS licensed channels. Practitioners can set up facilities to carry out searches via these companies, whose website addresses are:

  (a) **<http://www.transaction-online.co.uk>**

  (b) **<http://www.jordansproperty.co.uk>**

  (c) **<http://www.searchflow.co.uk>**.

- Royal Town Planning Institute, **<http://www.rtpi.org.uk>**.

- Water UK, **<www.water.org.uk>**. Details of the English Water Service Companies can be obtained from Water UK 1 at Queen Anne's Gate, London SW1H 9BT.

ONLINE RESOURCE CENTRE CASE STUDIES

RESIDENTIAL TRANSACTION CASE STUDY—PRE CONTRACT SEARCHES

Our clients:
Shilpa Jennings—sale of 19 Minster Yard Blakey
Shilpa Jennings and Daniel Rodriguez—purchase of 9 Castle Hill Blakey

We act for Shilpa Jennings who is selling 19 Minster Yard Blakey for £100,000 and Shilpa and Daniel Rodriguez who are buying 9 Castle Hill Blakey for £200,000. Search results have been obtained for the property being purchased and these can be seen on the Online Resource Centre. We will need to consider these results and decide if there are any entries in the searches where we need to obtain further details.

COMMERCIAL TRANSACTION CASE STUDY—PRE CONTRACT SEARCHES

Our client: Cambo Ltd—acquisition of 18 Clover Street London W2

Timothy Wainwright and his family have run a successful wholesale clothing business for many years. Timothy has decided to sell the business and enter the world of property investment. He has formed a company called Cambo Ltd in which he, his wife, and their three sons are all shareholders. Cambo Ltd has agreed to buy 18 Clover Street London W2 for £700,000 subject to and with the benefit of two occupational business leases. Search results have been obtained for the property being purchased and these can be seen on the Online Resource Centre. We will need to consider these results and decide if there are any entries in the searches where we need to obtain further details.

7 TOWN AND COUNTRY PLANNING

7.1 INTRODUCTION

Town and country planning legislation seeks to control the development of land and buildings, (see section 57(1) of the Town and Country Planning Act 1990). In particular, this section stipulates that 'planning permission is required for the carrying out of any development of land'.

Development is defined by section 55 as being of two kinds:

1. 'the carrying out of building, engineering, mining or other operations in, on, over or under land'; and

2. 'the making of any material change in the use of any buildings or other land'.

Types of use are defined within the Town and Country Planning (Use Classes) Order 1987, which lists 16 separate classes.

7.2 OBTAINING PLANNING PERMISSION

If a client intends to carry out development in the manner defined by the 1990 Act then planning permission, a planning consent will be required. This can be obtained in one of two ways:

1. by a permission deemed to have been given as a consequence of the effects of the Town and Country Planning (General Permitted Development) Order 1995; or

2. by a formal application for planning permission submitted to the local planning authority. If the Town and Country Planning (General Permitted Development) Order 1995 does not apply then an express application will be needed.

An applicant for express permission has the choice of making an application either for outline planning permission or for full planning permission.

You should also be aware that general permissions for change across different use classes are authorized by the Town and Country Planning (General Permitted Development) Order 1995. Perhaps the most important blanket approval is that for small extensions to an existing dwellinghouse. These small extensions, such as a rear kitchen extension, are subject to restrictions on size and position but otherwise can be made without the necessity for express planning permission.

7.3 **USE CLASSES**

Types of use are defined in the Town and Country Planning (Use Classes) Order 1987, which lists 16 separate classes. From 21 April 2005, there are changes to the use classes that were created by the 1987 Order. That order has been amended by the Town and Country Planning (Use Classes) (Amendment) (England) Order 2005 which substitutes for the former A3 (food and drink) three new use classes mentioned below.

The following classes are of greatest importance. Changes of use *within* a class do not require planning consent, while changes *between* classes do:

(a) *Class A1 shops*: This class includes post offices, travel agencies, internet cafés, hairdressers, dry cleaning agencies, and the retail sale of goods *other than* hot food.

(b) *Class A2 financial and professional services*: This allows property to be used for the provision of financial services or professional services (not being health or medical services), or any other service appropriate to a shopping area where such services are intended for visiting members of the public.

(c) *Class A3 food and drink*: This class has been amended since 21 April 2005, and is now restricted to restaurants and cafés. The class will therefore not cover pubs, takeaways, and bars. Drinking establishments (pubs and bars) are covered by A4, and hot food takeaways is in class A5.

(d) *Class B1 business*: This class covers offices other than those covered by A2 above, for research and development of products or processes, or for any other industrial process.

(e) *Class B2 general industrial*: This is the class that permits any use for the carrying on of an industrial process not covered by B1 above, or by other provisions in the Order covering special industrial processes (e.g. alkaline works and other types of heavy industry that tend to emit noxious fumes or effluent).

(f) *Class C1 hotels and hostels*: This class clearly covers the use of buildings as hotels or hostels, and will include boarding houses and guest houses.

(g) *Class C2 residential institutions*: This class covers buildings used for the provision of personal care or treatment, and residential educational facilities.

(h) *Class C3 dwellinghouses*: This class will allow the use of property for the accommodation of a family, as well as the coming together of up to six individuals as a single household.

7.4 **BREACHES OF PLANNING CONTROL AND ENFORCEMENT**

If the local planning authority becomes aware of a breach of planning control, they have the power to issue and serve an enforcement notice. Failure to comply with an enforcement notice can amount to a criminal offence for which magistrates can impose a fine of up to £20,000.

Where enforcement action is contemplated it must be taken within four years of any operational development (i.e. such as the erection of a new building). The four-year period runs from when the operations were substantially completed. Similarly, a four-year period for enforcement operates for changes of use of any building to use as a single dwellinghouse, running from when the fresh use commenced. In the case of any other breach of planning law, the enforcement action period is ten years from the date of any breach. Any other breach will be all breaches including changes of use other than operational development or a change of use to a single dwellinghouse. The four-year rule therefore applies to the change of use of a building to a single dwellinghouse. The four-year rule also applies to building works such as a flat conversion. If a notice is validly served then the recipient can appeal to the Secretary of State on one or more of the grounds for appeal set out in section 174 of the Town and Country Planning Act 1990. These grounds include indicating that planning permission ought to be granted and that the proposals, if they occur, do not constitute a breach of planning control.

While an enforcement notice is under appeal it has no effect. The consequence of this is that the alleged improper use can continue. If the authority wishes to terminate the use forthwith upon service of an enforcement notice then they must also issue and serve a stop notice. The planning authority can rely upon section 183 of the Town and Country Planning Act 1990, which empowers them to issue stop notices that effectively prohibit any use or activity contained or mentioned in the allied enforcement notice. A stop notice will not prohibit the use of any building as a dwellinghouse (section 183(4) of the Town and Country Planning Act 1990). Accordingly, a stop notice will arise only in the context of an enforcement notice.

 Conduct Point Acting in the client's best interests

- Failure to carry out appropriate planning enquiries on behalf of a client may amount to a breach of the Code of Conduct for solicitors 2007—Rule 1.04 You must act in the best interests of each client; R.1.05 You must provide a good standard of service to your clients.

7.5 TYPICAL PLANNING ENQUIRIES

The following is a list of topics that should prompt pre-contract enquiries of a seller:

(a) *Alterations and additions*: A prudent buyer will want to know if there have been any alterations and/or additions and, if so, when they were made. By obtaining this information a buyer can decide if all appropriate consents are available for these works.

(b) *User*: The seller should be asked to confirm two points: first, the nature of the current use (and when this commenced); and, secondly, that this is the permitted use for planning purposes. This should enable the buyer to decide if the current use is lawful.

(c) *Advertising*: Because section 55(5) of the Town and Country Planning Act 1990 stipulates that the use of an external part of a property for advertising will require planning consent, if there is any advertising on the subject property, questions should be asked about planning consents for the advertising hoarding.

(d) *Building regulations*: Whenever any meaningful building works are carried out to a property they must comply with a range of building regulations. These regulations are in place to ensure adequate standards of building work, and impose minimum standards covering a variety of areas including energy conservation, and health. You need to appreciate that this is an entirely separate requirement from planning matters. There is a requirement for plans to be filed with the local authority which will, on satisfactory completion of the works, issue a final certificate called a certificate of compliance. However, in *Cottingham v Attey Bower & Jones (A firm)* [2000] EGCS Rimmer J held the solicitors for the claimants to have acted negligently by failing to take all reasonable steps to obtain copies of building regulation consents. The judge mentioned in his judgment that injunction proceedings under section 36(6) of the Building Act 1984 enable a local authority to take enforcement proceedings at any time after the works have been carried out. This provision in effect creates an unlimited obligation on conveyancers to seek copy building regulation approvals. Alternatively, Countrywide Legal Indemnities (tel: 01603 617617) has available a 'Lack of Building Regulation Consent' insurance. The policy offers cover up to a tiered number of limits of indemnity at least in respect of any works carried out at the subject property provided they were fully completed 12 months prior to the date cover is taken out.

(e) *Replacement windows*: New building regulations apply from 1 April 2002 to the installation of replacement windows and doors under the Building (Amendment) Regulations 2002 (SI 2002/440). As a result, the conveyancer for a buyer must raise enquiries with the seller covering replacement windows. The latest edition of the Property Information Form now includes question 10.2(c) to cover this topic. In essence, all replacement windows, rooflights, roof windows, and glazed doors will have to comply with the Building Regulations. Confirmatory certificates will be available either from the local authority, or from FENSA (Fenestration Self-Assessment through the Glass and Glazing Federation Self-Assessment Scheme).

Key Points Town and Country Planning

- Does the client want to make any changes to the subject property that will amount to 'development' as defined by the Town and Country Planning Act 1990?

- If so, will the building works or change of use require express planning permission?

- If a change of use is proposed, will it require formal consent, or will it come within a use class, or will it be allowed by the blanket approval available under the General Development Order?

- If the property is newly built, obtain a copy of the Building Regulations approval as well as a copy of the planning permission and place these with the deeds on completion. Consider indemnity insurance if the detail is incomplete.

- Ensure that all the conditions attaching to a planning consent are seen and check that they have all been complied with.

- Obtain copy Building Regulations consent for the last ten years. If the record is incomplete consider indemnity insurance.

- Are there replacement windows in the subject property? If so is there a FENSA certificate?

7.6 TOWN AND COUNTRY PLANNING DECISION TREE

An example of a planning decision tree can be seen on p 76.

FIGURE 7.1 PLANNING DECISION TREE

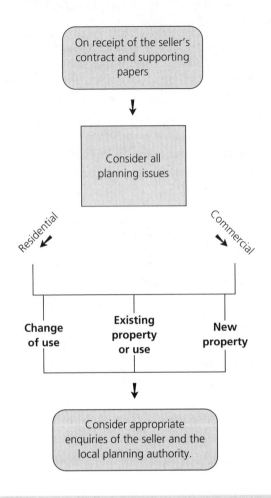

SELF TEST QUESTIONS

1. 'You can build anything anywhere you like on your own land because an Englishman's home is his castle.' Is this statement TRUE/FALSE? Please delete the incorrect choice.

2. With regard to changes of use, changes of use within a class do not require planning consent, while changes between classes do. Is this statement TRUE/FALSE? Please delete the incorrect choice.

3. 'Where planning law enforcement action is contemplated it must be taken within four years of any development.' Is this statement TRUE/FALSE? Please delete the incorrect choice.

4. 'Because section 55(5) of the Town and Country Planning Act 1990 states that the use of an external part of a property for advertising will require planning consent, if there is any advertising on a subject property, then a pre-contract enquiry should be raised about planning consents for any advertising hoarding'. Is this statement TRUE/FALSE? Please delete the incorrect choice.

5. Why is the case of *Cottingham v Attey Bower & Jones (A firm)* [2000] EGCS 48 of importance to conveyancing practitioners? Is it because

   (a) It confirmed that solicitors have a duty to mortgagees as a trustee of the mortgage advance;

   (b) It highlighted the need to register titles before the expiry of a search priority period;

   (c) It confirmed the need for planning consents even when demolishing a property without replacing it with another;

   (d) It confirmed that solicitors would be acting negligently by failing to take all reasonable steps to obtain copies of building regulation consents?

SHORT REVISION QUESTIONS

1. You act for Joan Collingwood who wants to buy a small freehold cottage with a small rear kitchen extension. It is priced at £450,000. It is located in the small Cotswold village of Merrygates. Your local search has come back but it is silent as to building regulations approval for the rear extension. Should you be concerned and if so what then should you do?

2. Your client is Derek O' Fitzpatrick who runs a freehold city centre French restaurant in the middle of Manchester. He has felt for some time that he could make more money if he converted the premises into a bar that also sold bar snack food. He believes there is more profit to be made from the sale of alcohol than from just the sale of food. He therefore wants to change the direction of his business and has asked you if there are any matters of concern that he should have in mind. Please advise him about this business proposal.

3. Four and a half years ago your client Mohammed Ahmed converted a terraced house in Islington into four self-contained flats. He is now selling them off, having first let them out to students. One of the buyers has asked for a planning consent for the conversion of the property into flats at which point your client tells you that he did not obtain consent. What is his planning position in relation to this admission?

SUGGESTED ANSWERS TO SELF TEST QUESTIONS

1. The correct answer is that the statement is false. The reason for this is that town and country planning legislation seeks to control the development of land and buildings, (see section 57(1) of the Town and Country Planning Act 1990). This section stipulates that 'planning permission is required for the carrying out of any development of land'. Development is of two kinds:

    - 'the carrying out of building, engineering, mining or other operations in, on, over or under land'; and

    - 'the making of any material change in the use of any buildings or other land'.

2. The correct answer is that the statement is true. It is a correct account of the law to say changes of use *within* a class do not require planning consent, while changes *between* classes do.

3. The correct answer is that the statement is false. The reason is that, while there is a four-year rule, there is also a ten-year rule, i.e. the four-year rule does not apply to any development but only to specific parts of planning law. The statement is half right and is written in this way to catch the hasty candidate who has not thought through to the correct answer. Always pause and think about an answer to avoid being caught by this all too familiar trap.

4. The correct answer is that the statement is true. If there are adverts on a building then section 55(5) will apply and enquiries should be made about possible planning consents.

5. The correct selection is (d). Regrettably, injunction proceedings under section 36(6) of the Building Act 1984 enable local authorities to take enforcement proceedings at any time after building works have been carried out. This provision in effect creates an unlimited obligation upon conveyancers to seek copy building regulation approvals.

SUGGESTED ANSWERS TO SHORT REVISION QUESTIONS

1. The decision in the case of *Cottingham v Attey Bower & Jones (A firm)* [2000] EGCS 48 has sent a ripple of concern through the conveyancing profession. Rimmer J held the solicitors for the claimants to have acted negligently by failing to take all reasonable steps to obtain copies of building regulation consents. The judge mentioned in his judgment that injunction proceedings under section 36(6) of the Building Act 1984 enable a local authority to take enforcement proceedings at any time after the

works have been carried out. This provision in effect creates an unlimited obligation on conveyancers to seek copy building regulation approvals. There is a need for a commonsense approach to the problem that could be addressed by the adoption of the following procedures:

(a) Raise a specific enquiry of the sellers for copies of all building regulation consents for the last ten years.

(b) If the response is incomplete and copies are not available, or none appears to have been obtained, both the buyer and any lender need to be advised of the problem. They should both be advised to refer the problem to the surveyor for advice as to how best to proceed, if at all.

(c) Ask the client to confirm that you can ask the local authority for copies, with the warning that if there is no building regulation consent the council will be on notice of unauthorized building works where they can take enforcement proceedings.

(d) If the local authority indicates that there is no consent then ask the client to confirm that you can apply to the council for a Regularisation Certificate pursuant to the Building Regulations 2000. The client must appreciate that this will incur extra cost and will delay the exchange of contracts.

(e) Alternatively, indemnity insurance can be arranged.

2. From 21 April 2005, there were changes to the use classes that were created by the Town and Country Planning (Use Classes) Order 1987. That order has been amended by the Town and Country Planning (Use Classes) (Amendment) (England) Order 2005 which substitutes for the former A3 (food and drink) three new use classes:

- restaurants and cafés (A3)

- drinking establishments (pubs and bars) (A4), and

- hot food takeaways (A5).

Accordingly A3 is restricted to restaurants and cafés, and excludes pubs, bars, and takeaways. Pubs and bars have their own use class, A4, and takeaways are given a new use class, A5. Consequently planning consent will not be needed for a change of use from A4 or A5 to A3, but any other change of use will require planning permission. This being so, Derek will have to apply for planning consent for the proposed change of use.

3. If the local planning authority becomes aware of a breach of planning control, it has the power to issue and serve an enforcement notice. Failure to comply with an enforcement notice can amount to a criminal offence for which magistrates can impose a fine of up to £20,000. Accordingly, where development has been carried out without permission the authority can serve such a notice on the owner or occupier, or on anyone else interested in the subject property. Where enforcement action is contemplated, it must be taken within four years of any operational development (i.e. such as the erection of a new building). The four-year period runs from when the operations were substantially completed. Similarly, a four-year period for enforcement operates for changes of use of any building to use as a single dwellinghouse, running from when the fresh use commenced. In the case of any other breach of planning law, the enforcement action period is ten years from the date of any breach. Any other breach will include changes of use other than operational development, or a change of use to a single dwellinghouse. The four-year rule therefore applies to the change of use of a building to a single dwellinghouse. The four-year rule also applies to building works such as a flat conversion.

WIDER READING

- Chapter 1 'Matters Before Contract' in Emmet on Title (Sweet & Maxwell)

- Chapter 4, Abbey, R, and Richards, M, *A Practical Approach to Conveyancing* (Oxford University Press, 2008)

- Section B dealing with Pre-exchange and Section J dealing with Sales of Part, Silverman, F, *Conveyancing Handbook* (The Law Society, 2006)

- Chapter 9, Abbey, R, and Richards, M, *A Practical Approach to Commercial Conveyancing and Property* (Oxford University Press, 2006)

WEBSITES FOR FURTHER INFORMATION

- Royal Town Planning Institute, **<http://www.rtpi.org.uk>**.

- Town and Country Planning Act 1990, **<http://www.opsi.gov.uk/ACTS/acts1990/Ukpga_19900008_ en_1.htm>**.

- Town and Country Planner, **<http://www.vts.intute.ac.uk/tutorial/town?sid=7840192&op=preview &manifestid=129&itemid=12957>**. The tour section of the planner aims to offer internet orientation for town and country planners.

- Town and Country Planning Association, **<http://www.tcpa.org.uk>**. The Town and Country Planning Association campaigns for the reform of the UK's planning system to make it more responsive to people's needs and aspirations and to promote sustainable development.

ONLINE RESOURCE CENTRE CASE STUDIES

online
resource
centre

RESIDENTIAL TRANSACTION CASE STUDY—PLANNING ISSUES

Our clients:
Shilpa Jennings—sale of 19 Minster Yard Blakey
Shilpa Jennings and Daniel Rodriguez—purchase of 9 Castle Hill Blakey

We act for Shilpa Jennings who is selling 19 Minster Yard Blakey for £100,000 and Shilpa and Daniel Rodriguez who are buying 9 Castle Hill Blakey for £200,000. Search results have been obtained for the property being purchased and these can be seen in the Online Resource Centre. We will need to consider these results and decide if there are any entries in the searches where we need to obtain further details, particularly with regard to planning issues disclosed on the search results.

The buyers are also thinking of a loft conversion at the new property. Planning issues may arise and are considered in the online materials.

COMMERCIAL TRANSACTION CASE STUDY—PLANNING ISSUES

Our client: Cambo Ltd—acquisition of 18 Clover Street London W2

Timothy Wainwright and his family have run a successful wholesale clothing business for many years. Timothy has decided to sell the business and enter the world of property investment. He has formed a company called Cambo Ltd in which he, his wife, and their three sons are all shareholders. Cambo Ltd has agreed to buy 18 Clover Street London W2 for £700,000 subject to and with the benefit of two occupational business leases. Search results have been obtained for the property being purchased and these can be seen in the Online Resource Centre. We will need to consider these results and decide if there are any entries relating specifically to planning issues in the searches where we need to obtain further details.

8 DEDUCING AND INVESTIGATING TITLE

8.1 INTRODUCTION

In a modern conveyancing transaction the parties will deduce and investigate title before contracts are exchanged. Put simply, deducing title is the process by which the seller demonstrates to the buyer that the seller owns the property and can convey it. Conversely, the process of investigating title is the means by which the buyer ensures that the seller owns the land and can convey it. This is done by examining the title that the seller has deduced.

If the Protocol is being used, the seller must deduce title at the same time as the draft contract and other pre-contract documents are forwarded to the buyer's solicitor, i.e. the title documents will be part of the 'pre-contract package'. Indeed this is the normal procedure even if the Protocol is not being used. In a Home Information Pack (HIP) one of the required documents is the official copy of a registered title.

8.2 DEDUCING TITLE

8.2.1 DEDUCING TITLE TO REGISTERED LAND

After taking instructions, the seller's solicitor will simply apply to the Land Registry on Form OC1 for an up-to-date official copy of the registered title(s) being sold (and if appropriate on Form OC2 for official copies of documents referred to in the register). These will then be sent to the buyer's solicitor as part of the 'pre-contract package'.

8.2.2 DEDUCING TITLE TO UNREGISTERED LAND

The seller's solicitor will supply the buyer's solicitor with particulars of the deeds, tracing a chain of ownership through to the current seller (or someone whom the seller can compel to convey). This can be done either by a traditional abstract or, the preferred method today, an epitome of title. An epitome involves the preparation of a list or schedule, in chronological order, of all the material title deeds and events which form the chain of title, for example a conveyance, a mortgage, or a death. Photocopies of all the relevant documents are then attached to the schedule. The photocopies must be legible with copy plans correctly coloured.

The buyer should insist that the seller deduces title from at least 15 years before the date of the contract (this applies both at common law and under the Standard Conditions), and the chain of title must commence with a 'good root' (i.e. the starting point for the period of ownership) duly stipulated in the sale contract. A good root must satisfy the following criteria. It should:

(a) deal with or show ownership of the whole legal and equitable interest in the property (the buyer will normally be concerned only with the legal estate; if the proper conveyancing procedures are adopted, any equitable interests should be overreached and thus will not bind the buyer; see *City of London Building Society* v *Flegg* [1988] AC 54);

(b) contain an adequate, identifiable description of the property. A mortgage will fail this test if it lacks a full description of the property (mortgages often refer to a fuller description in the conveyance to the mortgagor). Similarly, an assent will fail if it simply vests the property, 'for all the estate or interest of the deceased';

(c) do nothing to cast doubt on the title. A document will cast doubt if it depends for its effect on an earlier instrument, such as a power of attorney (see *Re Copelin's Contract* [1937] 4 All ER 447), but such doubt can be overcome if the seller can prove that the earlier document still subsisted at the time of its execution;

(d) at the date of the contract be at least 15 years old (section 44 of the Law of Property Act 1925 as amended by section 23 of the Law of Property Act 1969).

online
resource
centre

The best document for the root is a conveyance on sale. This is preferable to a gift of title, such as a voluntary conveyance or an assent, where it is unlikely that any prior title investigation was made before completion of the gift. As a general rule, a buyer should always insist on a conveyance on sale as the root of title (assuming one is available). If unusually a conveyance on sale is not available, the buyer must ensure that the alternative root document does in fact satisfy the good root criteria.

It is courteous and indeed good practice for the seller to supply the buyer with copies of old land charges searches that are present in the deeds. This saves the buyer from having to repeat the searches (provided they are valid).

 Key Points Deducing title

- The process by which the seller 'proves' title to the buyer.

- In registered land the seller applies to Land Registry for official copies of the title including title plan and copy documents.

- In unregistered land the seller prepares an epitome of title and attaches to it copies of the relevant title documents.

- An epitome is simply a list of all the material title deeds and events which form the chain of title, e.g. a conveyance, grant of probate, etc.

- A good root of title (in unregistered land only) must be at least 15 years old.

- The best root is a conveyance on sale.

8.3 INVESTIGATING TITLE

The buyer's solicitor must ensure that the title is good and marketable and free from encumbrances that may adversely affect the use and enjoyment of the property. If you are acting for the buyer's mortgagee as well, it is important to appreciate your duty to your mortgagee client. You should check that the title is acceptable in conformity with the mortgagee's instructions, in particular regarding any special conditions in the mortgage offer. Also check the mortgagee's requirements in the CML *Lenders' Handbook*. The typical lender is seeking an assurance from you that no title deficiencies exist which may reduce the property's value or adversely affect the lender's ability to dispose of its security on the open market.

We now consider separately registered land and unregistered land.

8.3.1 INVESTIGATING TITLE TO REGISTERED LAND

If your client is buying registered land you must check carefully the official copies and other documents referred to on the register and compare them against the information given in the draft contract. Remember that the official copies should be as up to date as possible (ideally just a few weeks old and certainly no more than 12 months old). You should in particular consider the following:

- Confirm whether the estate is freehold or leasehold.
- Is the title number correct?
- Consider the class of title; is it absolute, possessory, good leasehold, or qualified? (Anything less than absolute title will generally be considered as adverse.)
- Does the land being bought correspond with the title description? (Consider the title plan—does it indicate that land has been removed from the title?)
- Is the seller in the contract the same as the registered proprietor?
- Are there any encumbrances in the charges register and how will these affect the buyer?

If there are discrepancies or if other adverse entries are present which protect third party interests, e.g. a unilateral notice, you should raise these as requisitions with the seller's practitioner. Other examples might be the presence of a Family Law Act notice, an apparent breach of covenant, or possibly covenants referred to on the title but details of which were not given to the Land Registry on first registration. Your requisition should identify the defect/problem and require the seller to remedy it (if necessary, at the seller's cost).

In addition to the above, before completion you should carry out a Land Registry search to update the information in the official copies (see Chapter 12 regarding pre-completion searches). You must also check for any overriding interests which are not entered on the register but which will bind the buyer irrespective of notice (e.g. rights of persons in actual occupation, local land charges, etc.).

8.3.2 INVESTIGATING TITLE TO UNREGISTERED LAND

If your client is buying unregistered land, first check that the root of title offered by the seller is a good root and is at least 15 years old at the date of the contract. You must then trace chronologically from the root document, a chain of ownership all the way down to the current seller; a chain which is complete and without missing links. So, if Jones and Clark bought the land previously, make sure it is they who later sell, not Jones and Smith, or even Jones and Clarke (spelling discrepancies should always be raised).

Ensure that you see evidence of any change of name. For example, if a previous owner purchased the property as an unmarried woman using her maiden name, and then after her marriage sold using her married name, you would want to see a certified copy of the marriage certificate. Also make sure that you see evidence of the death of any estate owner. For example, if a joint tenant has died and the survivor(s) has subsequently sold, you would want to see a certified copy of the death certificate.

Having traced the chain of ownership you should now examine carefully each document in the abstract or epitome, checking for any deficiencies or omissions. Examples of defects might be a mortgage taken out by a previous estate owner which has not been discharged, or an improperly executed or stamped document.

Ensure that the description of the property in the most recent conveyance or other document accords with that which the client is buying (this is a fundamental point which will always be thoroughly checked by the Land Registry on first registration). Ensure that the property benefits from all necessary easements. If there has been a sale of part, ensure that an acknowledgement for future production of retained original documents has been given, and that a sale-off memorandum has been endorsed on the previous conveyance. Check that all appropriate documents have been stamped. Lastly, check whether the property should already have been registered—was it in a compulsory area on the date of a previous conveyance?

Any defects should be raised with the seller's practitioner as requisitions on title. You should identify the defects and require the seller to remedy them, if necessary at the seller's cost. For further reading on the often complex area of investigating unregistered title see Abbey R and Richards M, *A Practical Approach to Conveyancing*, Chapter 5 (Oxford University Press).

 online resource centre

FIGURE 8.1 INVESTIGATING AN UNREGISTERED TITLE

> Identify a good root of title—ensure it is at least 15 years old and adequately describes the property

↓

> Trace an unbroken chain of ownership from the root of title down to the current seller. Are there any missing links, changes of name? etc.

↓

> Do any special considerations apply? e.g. has there been a sale of part; sale by mortgagee; sale by PR; sale by surviving co-owner?

↓

> Consider the detail of each document in the title—check for defects, e.g. lack of stamping, incorrect execution

↓

> Do you have clear land charges searches against all previous estate owners?

↓

> In practice—simply raise requisitions of the seller's solicitor But for the LPC—raise requisitions and explain how to remedy them

> **Key Points** Investigating title
>
> • Check that the title is good and marketable, free from adverse encumbrances. Bear in mind your duty to the buyer's mortgagee as well (assuming you are acting).
>
> • If the land is unregistered, ask yourself, will my client obtain absolute title on first registration? Consider referring a difficult title problem to Land Registry for guidance.
>
> • For unregistered title, check that there is a good root and ensure there is an unbroken chain of ownership through to the seller. Check each document in the title for defects, e.g. improper stamping or execution.
>
> • Raise requisitions regarding any problems. Make sure you obtain satisfactory replies to requisitions before exchanging contracts. If there is an unresolved problem, consider indemnity insurance from an insurance company at the seller's expense.
>
> • If the title problem is complex consult a specialist text, e.g. Abbey R and Richards M, *A Practical Approach to Conveyancing*, Chapter 5 (Oxford University Press).

8.4 SOME SPECIAL TITLE SITUATIONS

There are special considerations where the person disposing of the property is not the sole legal and beneficial owner. In unregistered land, these considerations may also be of relevance so far as previous estate owners are concerned.

8.4.1 PERSONAL REPRESENTATIVES

A buyer should not complete a purchase from personal representatives (PRs) until the grant of representation has been issued by the court. It is the grant that confers authority on the PRs to deal with the assets of the deceased's estate. A certified copy of the grant must be given to the buyer's solicitor. You should ensure also that all PRs mentioned in the grant execute the purchase deed.

In most cases the land will already be registered or the transaction will induce first registration (e.g. assent or conveyance). If unusually this is not the case you should ensure that on completion a memorandum of the transaction is endorsed on the grant. Similarly, when investigating an unregistered title which contains an earlier disposition by PRs ensure that a memorandum recording that disposition was endorsed on the grant. Also ensure there are no other endorsements on the grant recording earlier dispositions.

When investigating an unregistered title containing a disposition by a beneficiary as beneficial owner, ensure that the land was properly vested in the beneficiary by an assent. This applies even if the PR and the beneficiary are one and the same person (*Re King's Will Trusts* [1964] Ch 542).

When examining an earlier conveyance of unregistered land by PRs check that it contains a statement under section 36(6) of the Law of Property Act 1925 confirming that no previous disposition of the land was made by the PRs, together with an acknowledgement that the original grant will be produced in future if required.

8.4.2 DISPOSITIONS BY CO-OWNERS

A buyer will not be concerned about beneficial interests behind a trust provided payment is made to at least two trustees (or a trust corporation). It is nevertheless advisable to obtain a release of any rights or interests that may be apparent in respect of the subject property, e.g. rights of an occupier who has a beneficial interest behind a trust.

All surviving trustees should be a party to the transfer or conveyance. If it is necessary to appoint a new trustee, this is done by deed of appointment and all surviving trustees should be a party to that deed.

Registered land

On a sale by a sole surviving co-owner, check whether there is a restriction entered in the proprietorship register protecting beneficial interests. If a restriction is present, the co-owners were tenants in common. To effect overreaching, insist on the appointment of a second trustee to join in selling the legal estate (unless devolution of the deceased's equitable share to the survivor can be proved). If there is no restriction, the co-owners were joint tenants. In this case, a transfer from the survivor alone can safely be accepted, accompanied by the death certificate.

Unregistered land

On a sale by a sole surviving co-owner, establish whether the co-owners were joint tenants or tenants in common. This is done by consulting the conveyance to the co-owners when they purchased. This document should contain an appropriate statement to this effect.

If you are dealing with a surviving tenant in common, you should insist on the appointment of a second trustee to join in selling the legal estate (unless devolution of the deceased's equitable share to the survivor can be proved). If dealing with a surviving joint tenant, then, provided the three conditions in the Law of Property (Joint Tenants) Act 1964 are met, you can assume severance has not occurred and safely accept a conveyance/transfer from the survivor alone, together with the death certificate. The three conditions are:

(a) No bankruptcy petition or order has been registered as a land charge against any of the joint tenants. Thus you should conduct an appropriate land charges search against their full names or, if already made against previous estate owners, check the earlier search.

(b) No memorandum of severance of the joint tenancy has been endorsed on the conveyance to the joint tenants. Thus you should inspect the abstract or epitome and/or raise a requisition for confirmation of this.

(c) The conveyance by the survivor states that the survivor is solely and beneficially entitled to the land (this is normally found in the recitals of the conveyance).

If the above conditions in the Law of Property (Joint Tenants) Act 1964 are not met, insist on the appointment of a second trustee to join in selling the legal estate.

8.4.3 SALE BY MORTGAGEE

A mortgagee may exercise its power of sale and convey the mortgaged property in its own name provided a power of sale exists, has arisen, and has become exercisable. These requirements and the explanations which follow apply equally to registered and unregistered land.

(a) *Power of sale exists.* A power of sale is implied in every mortgage made by deed unless, unusually, the power is expressly excluded in the deed itself (Law of Property Act 1925, section 101(1)(i)). A legal mortgage must be made by deed (Law of Property Act 1925, section 85), and so it follows that a legal mortgagee will always have a power of sale unless the power has been expressly excluded.

(b) *Power of sale has arisen.* The power of sale arises on the legal date for redemption of the mortgage, which is when the mortgage money, in theory, becomes due. This date is normally specified in the deed to be a date within the first six months of the mortgage.

(c) *Power of sale has become exercisable. Prima facie* the power of sale becomes exercisable if one of the events in the Law of Property Act 1925, section 103 occurs, namely a formal demand for payment has not been complied with for three months, interest is unpaid for two months, or the borrower is in breach of some other condition of the mortgage. In practice, however, the modern mortgage deed will generally exclude section 103 and then expressly strengthen the mortgagee's position by enlarging the statutory grounds.

Acting for buyer from mortgagee

When acting for a buyer from a mortgagee, or when investigating an unregistered title which includes an earlier sale by a mortgagee, the buyer's practitioner will only need to be concerned with points (a) and (b) above. There is no need for the buyer to check whether the borrower was or is in default because even if the power is not exercisable, the buyer will still receive a good title (Law of Property Act 1925, section 104(2)). The question of whether the power can be properly exercised is a matter between mortgagor and mortgagee.

Thus the buyer's practitioner, in determining whether a sale by a mortgagee was (or will be) valid, should simply inspect the mortgage deed to verify (a) that the power of sale is not excluded (bear in mind that an exclusion would be exceptional), and (b) that the legal date for redemption has passed. If either of these has not occurred, the mortgagee cannot convey or transfer the legal estate.

Effect of sale by mortgagee

The mortgagee conveys the legal estate free from subsequent mortgages, but subject to any mortgages having priority to the selling mortgagee. The buyer's practitioner should therefore ensure that the selling mortgagee discharges any subsisting prior mortgages from the proceeds of sale in the same way as a mortgagor who is selling would discharge a subsisting mortgage.

On completion of the sale, the mortgage under which the power of sale is exercised is not discharged (allowing the mortgagee to pursue the borrower for any arrears), but the buyer takes free from it.

If you are buying from a receiver appointed by the mortgagee, all mortgages must be cleared off on completion because the receiver acts as agent for the borrower.

Acting for selling mortgagee

The seller's practitioner must ensure that the power of sale has become exercisable; otherwise the mortgagee may be liable in damages to the borrower. In addition, the seller's solicitor should ensure that the mortgagee is able to give vacant possession on completion. Accordingly, it may be necessary to obtain a court order for possession if the property is not already vacant.

The mortgagee should be made aware of its duty to obtain the best price for the property reasonably obtainable on the open market (see *Cuckmere Brick Co Ltd v Mutual Finance Ltd* [1971] Ch 949 CA, and the Building Societies Act 1986, Schedule 4). However, this is not a matter of concern to the buyer. Once the mortgage debt is discharged, if there are any surplus monies, these must be passed by the selling mortgagee to any subsequent mortgagee and, failing that, to the borrower personally. Again this is of no concern to the buyer.

 Key Points Special title situations

- When buying from PRs ensure that the grant has been issued and that all PRs execute the purchase deed.
- When buying from a sole surviving co-owner establish whether he/she is a surviving joint tenant or tenant in common.
- If the survivor is a tenant in common then a second trustee should normally be appointed.
- A mortgagee can sell under its power of sale provided the power exists, has arisen, and has become exercisable.
- A buyer from a mortgagee is only concerned that the power of sale exists and has arisen.
- A buyer from a mortgagee must insist that any prior mortgages are discharged but takes free from any subsequent mortgages.

SELF TEST QUESTIONS

1. Under the Land Registration Act 2002 which of the following is the seller obliged to supply to the buyer when deducing title on the sale of a registered freehold property

   (a) Copy of title plan

   (b) Evidence of overriding interests known to the seller

   (c) Copy of a conveyance containing restrictive covenants noted on the charges register

   (d) Official copies of entries on the register

2. In order to ensure that a buyer obtains a good title from the survivor of joint tenants in relation to registered land, the buyer's solicitor must ensure that

   (a) The terms of any restriction are complied with

   (b) A written assent is used

   (c) The death certificate of the deceased is produced

   (d) There is no memorandum of severance endorsed on the grant

3. You act for a wealthy buyer of a registered freehold property. Your client informs you that following completion she intends to convert the property into a commercial internet café. While investigating the title you discover a covenant from 1910 in the charges register restricting the use of the property to a single private dwelling house. Which of the following are NOT appropriate for you to at least consider

   (a) Arranging restrictive covenant indemnity insurance

   (b) Applying to the Lands Tribunal to have the covenant removed

   (c) Contacting the person who currently has the benefit of the covenant to ask for consent to your client's proposed user

   (d) Discussing with your client the possibility that she may wish to consider buying elsewhere

4. When preparing an epitome of title in unregistered land it is strictly unnecessary to include prior land charges search certificates against previous estate owners. However to assist the buyer's solicitor it is courteous to do so.

   Is this statement TRUE/FALSE? Please delete the incorrect choice.

5. A solicitor acting for a buyer in relation to a sale by a mortgagee in possession should ensure that the mortgagee's power of sale has arisen and become exercisable.

   Is this statement TRUE/FALSE? Please delete the incorrect choice.

SHORT REVISION QUESTIONS

Question 1

Your senior partner has asked you to prepare a briefing paper for the junior property lawyers in your firm. You are required to set out as bullet points the important matters that should be considered by a buyer's solicitor when investigating official copies of a registered title.

Question 2

You act for a prospective buyer of an unregistered title. The seller's solicitor has deduced title specifying the root of title as a deed of gift to the seller dated 12 years ago. What risks or disadvantages are there to your client if you accept this deed of gift as the root of title?

SUGGESTED ANSWERS TO SELF TEST QUESTIONS

1. The correct answer is none. The now repealed Land Registration Act 1925 laid down minimum requirements as to what the seller of registered land should produce to the buyer. The Land Registration Act 2002 is silent on the point; so the seller is not obliged to supply any of these items (although a prudent buyer would insist on seeing them).

2. The correct answer is (c). Note that the question says the land is registered so we need not concern ourselves with the Law of Property (Joint Tenants) Act 1964 which is relevant only to unregistered land. In registered land the buyer from a surviving joint tenant simply needs to see evidence of the deceased co-owner's death to be satisfied that the survivorship principle will apply.

3. The answer is none. You should at least consider all of these matters before advising your client of the best alternative suited to her individual circumstances. There is a good chance that indemnity insurance is appropriate but that is not what the question asks!

4. The statement is true. This is good conveyancing practice and it will assist the buyer's solicitor as it saves him or her having to repeat the searches.

5. The statement is false. To obtain good title it is correct to say that the buyer's solicitor must ensure that the mortgagee's power of sale has arisen i.e. that the legal date of redemption has passed. But it is *not* necessary to check that the power has become exercisable, i.e. that the borrower is in default. This is a matter between the lender and borrower and does not affect the title.

SUGGESTED ANSWERS TO SHORT REVISION QUESTIONS

Question 1

Briefing Paper

To   The Property Department

From   Trainee Solicitor

When acting for a buyer of a registered title the following matters should be considered when inspecting copies of the seller's title:

Generally:

- Check that the copies are *official* copies not mere photocopies.
- Ensure that they are up to date, i.e. the 'search from date' should be within the last 12 months.
- Check that there are no pages missing.

Property register:

- Is the land freehold or leasehold?
- Does the description of the land correspond with the description in the draft contract?
- Is the title number the same as that given in the draft contract?
- What easements (if any) are noted as being enjoyed by the property?
- Has any land been removed from the title? If so, does this affect the land being bought?

Proprietorship register:

- Is the seller in the draft contract the same as the registered proprietor? If not, ask the seller's solicitor who has the ability to transfer the land and obtain evidence of this.
- Are there any entries in the register and, if so, what is their effect? (Examples of such entries might be restrictions, unilateral notices, and old cautions entered prior to 13 October 2003).

- Check that the class of title is Absolute. Any lesser title, e.g. Good Leasehold or Possessory, may be unacceptable to a lender. If appropriate, check the relevant parts of the CML Lenders' Handbook.

Charges register:

- Are there any encumbrances noted on the register (e.g. restrictive covenants, registered charges)?

- If so, how do they affect the buyer? In particular will they adversely affect your client's proposed use and enjoyment of the land?

- Which of the encumbrances will be removed or discharged on completion and how will their removal be achieved?

- Registered charges should be discharged on or before completion—ensure that you receive the seller's solicitors' undertaking to do so.

Title plan:

- Check that the land your client is buying is included within the red edging shown on the title plan.

- Check for any hatchings or colourings, which may show the extent of covenants, rights of way, or land that has been removed from the title (e.g. following a sale of part).

Question 2

There are two aspects to this question: the nature of the proposed root of title, and the age of the document.

Dealing first with the deed of gift (or voluntary conveyance) as the proposed root. It is generally acknowledged that a deed of gift is an inferior root to a conveyance on sale. This is because on completion of a gift it is unlikely that any prior title investigation was made (i.e. the donee just accepts the gift). However with a conveyance on sale there is a perceived 'double guarantee' because of the assumption that the buyer under the root conveyance would have investigated title himself over a 15-year period. This effectively provides the current buyer with certainty of title going back at least 30 years.

Secondly and more importantly, the proposed root will be less than 15 years old at the date of the contract. The Law of Property Act 1925, section 44 (1) as amended by section 23 of the Law of Property Act 1969 provides that the buyer can require the title to be deduced for at least the last 15 years.

There are several risks and disadvantages for a buyer in accepting a short root. Briefly these are as follows:

(a) The buyer will be bound by equitable interests (e.g. restrictive covenants) that would have been discoverable had the buyer investigated for the full 15 years. In accepting a short title the buyer is deemed to have constructive notice of them (see *Re Nisbet and Pott's Contract* [1906] 1 Ch 386, CA).

(b) The buyer will lose any rights to compensation from the State under section 25 of the Law of Property Act 1969. This compensation is for loss arising from undiscovered land charges registered against an estate owner who owned the land before the date of the document which should have been used as the root. This compensation is only available if a prudent buyer who investigated a proper 15-year title would not have discovered such encumbrances.

(c) An important practical issue is that the Land Registry will probably refuse to grant absolute title on the buyer's application for first registration following completion. The registry may also place a 'protective' entry in the Charges Register to cover the possibility of undisclosed restrictive covenants i.e. 'subject to such restrictive covenants as may have been imposed thereon and are still subsisting'.

(d) As a result of the above, the title to the property will become less marketable and unattractive to potential buyers and lenders.

To conclude, the buyer should insist on an earlier root of title (preferably a conveyance on sale) which is at least 15 years old at the date of the contract.

WIDER READING

- Chapter 5, Abbey, R, and Richards, M, *A Practical Approach to Conveyancing* (Oxford University Press, 2008)

- Section D dealing with title, Silverman, F, *Conveyancing Handbook* (The Law Society, 2006)

- Emmet on Title:
  - good root of title—Chapter 5, part 2
  - abstract of title—Chapter 5, part 3
  - mortgagee's power of sale—Chapter 25, part 3
  - co-ownership and sale by surviving joint tenant—Chapter 11
  - execution of deeds—Chapter 20
  - acknowledgements for production—Chapter 12, part 3
  - requisitions on title generally—Chapter 5, part 4

- Theodore, BF and Roper, RB, *The Law and Practice of Registered Conveyancing* (Sweet & Maxwell, 2007)

- For more detail on the changes introduced by the Land Registration Act 2002 see Abbey, R, and Richards, M, *Blackstone's Guide to the Land Registration Act 2002* (Oxford University Press, 2002)

- Chapters 4, 5, 15, and 19, MacKenzie, J-A, and Phillips, M, *Textbook on Land Law* (Oxford University Press, 2008)

WEBSITES FOR FURTHER INFORMATION

- Acts of Parliament, **<http://www.hmso.gov.uk/acts.htm>**. Keep up to date with statutory developments.

- Council of Mortgage Lenders, **<http://www.cml.org.uk>**. There is an on-line version of the CML Lenders' Handbook available at this site and should be referred to in cases of doubt about the requirements of the lender in relation to title matters.

- House of Lords judgments, **<http://www.parliament.the-stationery-office.co.uk/pa/ld199697/ldjudgmt/ldjudgmt.htm>**. Keep up to date with important new cases.

- Land Registry, **<http://www.landreg.gov.uk/>**.

- Lands Tribunal On-Line, **<http://www.landstribunal.gov.uk/index.htm>**. The Lands Tribunal considers applications to discharge or modify restrictive covenants.

- Law Commission, **<http://www.lawcom.gov.uk/projects.htm>**. Keep up to date on proposals for law reform.

- Ordnance Survey, **<http://www.ordnancesurvey.co.uk>**. It might be useful to consult a detailed Ordnance Survey map when considering boundary problems and to compare with title deed plans.

- A street map anywhere in the UK, **<http://www.streetmap.co.uk>**.

ONLINE RESOURCE CENTRE CASE STUDIES

RESIDENTIAL TRANSACTION CASE STUDY—DEDUCING AND INVESTIGATING TITLE

Our clients:
Shilpa Jennings—sale of 19 Minster Yard
Shilpa Jennings and Daniel Rodriguez—purchase of 9 Castle Hill

We act for Shilpa Jennings ('Shilpa') who is selling 19 Minster Yard for £100,000 and Shilpa and Daniel Rodriguez ('Daniel') buying 9 Castle Hill for £200,000. The Standard Conditions of Sale, 4th edn, are adopted in both contracts.

See Online Resource Centre for details of both titles and suggested requisitions that should be raised by us on behalf of our clients in respect of the unregistered title to 9 Castle Hill.

COMMERCIAL TRANSACTION CASE STUDY—DEDUCING AND INVESTIGATING TITLE

Our client: Cambo Ltd—acquisition of 18 Clover Street

We act for Cambo Ltd acquiring the freehold reversion of 18 Clover Street London W2 for £700,000 subject to and with the benefit of two occupational business leases.

See Online Resource Centre for details of the registered freehold title and suggested requisitions that should be raised by us on behalf of our client purchaser.

9 MORTGAGES

9.1 INTRODUCTION

In this chapter we examine the important issues arising in relation to a mortgage taken out by a client to assist in financing the purchase of a property. We will look at the most popular types of mortgage, the impact of the Financial Services and Markets Act 2000 (FSMA), and other matters including important professional conduct issues. We shall also consider briefly mortgages of leasehold property and mortgages of commercial property.

Your client buyer will often inform you that the mortgage has already been arranged, but it is your duty to ensure that the client's arrangements are satisfactory according to their needs and wishes. For example, someone without dependants who wishes to secure the lowest monthly outlay would generally be advised to take out an ordinary repayment mortgage, not a more complicated and expensive mortgage (see 9.2 below). You should also warn clients about the dangers of attractive-looking fixed interest rate mortgages. Although they can be beneficial when interest rates are rising, they may not be as appealing when mortgage rates start to fall, and they often contain hidden penalties for early redemption. Always check the conditions of the mortgage offer carefully. (For a discussion of typical mortgage conditions, including retentions and indemnity guarantee policies, see 9.5 below.)

 Conduct Point Verifying the client's identity

- You must ensure that the Money Laundering Regulations 2007 are complied with. Your firm must have procedures in place for obtaining satisfactory evidence of your client borrower's identity. The most reliable evidence of identification is a passport, and safe practice is to inspect the borrower's full passport to confirm their identity and then keep a copy of it on file for future reference.

9.2 COMMON TYPES OF MORTGAGE

9.2.1 REPAYMENT MORTGAGE

This is generally the cheapest mortgage in terms of monthly outlay. The loan is repaid over the mortgage term (normally 25 years) and each monthly repayment by the borrower to the mortgagee comprises part interest and part capital (in the early years of the mortgage the capital element is very small). The mortgagee will usually insist that a separate mortgage protection term assurance policy is arranged so that if (and only if) the borrower dies during the lifetime of the mortgage, the debt is repaid by the sum assured. The monthly premium on the mortgage protection policy is typically just a few pounds. A client without dependants who is looking for the lowest monthly mortgage cost would be well advised to consider this type of mortgage.

9.2.2 ENDOWMENT MORTGAGE

An endowment mortgage is generally more expensive than an ordinary repayment. The mortgage is linked to a life assurance policy which matures at the end of the mortgage term. None of the capital loan is repaid during the life of the mortgage, the monthly payments to the mortgagee being interest only. In addition, the borrower pays monthly premiums on the life policy to a life company.

The maturity value of the policy should in theory be sufficient to repay the capital loan; there may even be surplus funds available if the investment has performed well. However, returns on endowment policies have suffered over recent years and there is no guarantee that the proceeds will repay the loan (especially for 'low-cost endowments' where initial premium contributions are even lower). Any shortfall on the mortgage debt will ultimately have to be funded by the client, who should be warned of this possibility. The risk of shortfall together with the abolition of tax relief on endowment policy premiums has reduced the attraction of this type of mortgage.

9.2.3 PENSION MORTGAGE

This is similar to an endowment mortgage but, instead of the loan being linked to a life policy, it is linked to a personal pension policy. The proceeds of the policy on maturity are used to discharge the loan. This type of mortgage is likely to suit a self-employed person who has (or should be advised to have) a personal pension. Unlike an endowment policy the contributions to the pension policy are tax deductible, which is attractive, particularly for higher-rate taxpayers.

9.2.4 INTEREST-ONLY MORTGAGE

This is the cheapest for the client in terms of monthly outlay because 'interest only' means exactly that—no capital is repaid and the mortgage is not linked to any life policy, pension, or savings plan. Clients must be advised that they will need to find a method of paying off the loan eventually. Lenders should offer interest-only loans exclusively to borrowers who can demonstrate that they have other arrangements in place for repayment of the loan, e.g. out of an existing pension fund. However this is not always the case and you should make your client aware of the risks involved.

9.2.5 SHARIA-COMPLIANT MORTGAGES

Islamic law—known as sharia—forbids Muslims from paying interest and this excludes many Muslims from the conventional mortgage products which are on offer. Specialist

Muslim lenders such as the Islamic Bank of Britain offer sharia-compliant alternatives. These usually involve the lender initially buying the subject property and then selling it on to the Muslim purchaser at a higher price.

9.3 FINANCIAL SERVICES AND MARKETS ACT 2000

When advising on mortgages you should have regard to the Financial Services and Markets Act 2000 (FSMA). Solicitors who conduct 'mainstream' investment business (e.g. advising on specific investments) must be authorized to do so by the Financial Services Authority (FSA). Only about 300 firms in England and Wales are currently authorized to conduct mainstream investment business. Solicitors who conduct 'non-mainstream' investment business which is incidental to their legal services (e.g. conveyancing) are regulated by the Solicitors Regulation Authority which is a Designated Professional Body (DPB) under the Act. This will cover the overwhelming majority of firms.

9.3.1 THE SCOPE RULES

The Law Society has issued 'Scope Rules' which limit and define the scope of what solicitors can and cannot do as members of the DPB. These are called the Solicitors' Financial Services (Scope) Rules 2001. The aim of the Rules is to ensure that in providing services to clients, solicitors carry on only regulated activities which *arise out of or are complementary to* the provision of services to their clients, e.g. conveyancing, corporate work, matrimonial, probate, and trust work. Essentially, non-mainstream investment business falls within the Scope Rules, but mainstream investment business falls outside the Rules and requires authorization from the FSA.

If firms consider that their activities will go beyond the Scope Rules, i.e. into mainstream investment business, they will need authorization directly from the FSA; otherwise they will be committing a criminal offence.

9.3.2 GENERIC ADVICE ONLY

If you offer the client generic mortgage advice about the different types of mortgage and their suitability for the client (e.g. 'in your circumstances I would recommend a repayment mortgage'), this will fall outside the FSMA as it is not a regulated activity. However, arranging or giving specific advice about different mortgage providers and mortgage products is a regulated activity and would require prior authorization from the FSA. Unless a regulated mortgage is arranged by a person who is authorized under the FSMA or with a (properly authorized) financial institution, it will be unenforceable without the leave of the court. Similarly, offering specific advice on an investment product (e.g. a particular pension company in connection with a pension mortgage) would constitute a regulated activity, for which the firm would require prior authorization. If your client is seeking non-generic (i.e. specific) advice you should refer them to a reputable independent financial adviser who is authorized by the FSA.

9.3.3 MONEY LAUNDERING

As previously discussed, you should be on your guard against possible money laundering (see Chapter 4, section 4.8.2). For example, do not accept large sums of cash from your borrower client.

9.4 **ACTING FOR BORROWER AND LENDER**

In a commercial property transaction the lender will usually instruct its own solicitors (see section 9.13 below). However in most residential transactions the lender will instruct you to act for it as well as the borrower. There are restrictions under the Solicitors' Code of Conduct 2007 (the Code) which are now considered.

Generally, under rule 3.16 you are allowed to act for borrower and lender as long as the lender is an institutional lender which provides mortgages in the normal course of its business and provided no conflicts of interest arise. It is necessary to differentiate between 'standard' mortgages and 'individual' mortgages. A mortgage is a 'standard' mortgage where:

(a) it is provided in the normal course of the lender's activities;

(b) a significant part of the lender's activities consists of lending; and

(c) the mortgage is on standard terms.

Standard mortgages are therefore mortgages from lending institutions such as banks or building societies.

Any mortgage which is not a standard mortgage as defined above will be classified as an 'individual' mortgage, e.g. where the lender is a private individual.

 Conduct Point Acting for borrower and lender

- You must not act for both lender and borrower on the grant of a mortgage of land:

  (a) if a conflict of interests exists or arises;

  (b) on the grant of an individual mortgage of land at arm's length;

  (c) if, in the case of a standard mortgage of property to be used as the borrower's private residence only, the lender's mortgage instructions extend beyond the limitations contained in 3.19 and 3.21 of the Code, or do not permit the use of the certificate of title required by 3.20 of the Code; or

  (d) if, in the case of any other standard mortgage, the lender's mortgage instructions extend beyond the limitations contained in 3.19 and 3.21 of the Code.

See www.sra.org.uk/code-of-conduct page for details of 3.19, 3.20 and 3.21 of the Code. The limitations contained in 3.19 of the Code are important.

9.4.1 **COUNCIL OF MORTGAGE LENDERS' HANDBOOK**

You must acquaint yourself with the Council of Mortgage Lender's Handbook which contains standardized lenders' instructions for solicitors. You can access the handbook via the CML website at <http://www.cml.org.uk>. The handbook is divided into two parts. Part 1 sets out the main instructions and guidance, which must be disclosed by the conveyancers. Part 2 details each lender's specific requirements which arise from those instructions. The instructions from individual lenders will indicate whether the conveyancer is being instructed in accordance with the handbook, in which case the conveyancer should follow the instructions in the handbook.

 Conduct Point Conflict of interest

- Ensure that no conflict of interest arises between borrower and lender. For example, if the solicitor becomes involved in negotiations regarding the conditions of the loan agreement, there will clearly be a conflict of interest. A conflict of interest will also arise if you discover that the borrower intends to breach a condition of the mortgage offer (e.g. to use the property for business purposes when such use is prohibited). In this situation you must explain to the borrower that a conflict has arisen and you can no longer act for the borrower or lender unless the lender permits you to continue to act for the borrower alone. As you can no longer act for the lender, the lender's papers should be returned. However, due to your duty of confidentiality to the borrower (which continues even after termination of the borrower's retainer) you cannot disclose the reason why you can no longer act. You must simply inform the lender that a conflict of interest has arisen and leave it at that.

 Conduct Point Confidentiality

- As a matter of conduct you will need to obtain the borrower's consent before passing on any confidential information to the lender. This is unless the lender can show to your satisfaction that there is a prima facie case of fraud (see Solicitors' Code of Conduct 2007, rule 4.01, paragraph 9(c)). If the borrower refuses consent to disclose, you should send, if requested, only those parts of your file that relate to work done for the lender. Note that some lenders get borrowers to sign a waiver of confidentiality at the time of the mortgage application. In this case you may need to disclose your whole file to the lender, but do check the client's waiver for details of what can be disclosed.

 Key Points Acting for borrower and lender together

- Do not act for a buyer and a private lender unless the transaction is not at arm's length and no conflict of interest arises. If in doubt, do not act for both parties.
- When acting for a buyer and institutional lender check compliance with the Solicitors' Code of Conduct.
- Check the mortgage instructions contained in the CML Lenders' Handbook.

9.5 MORTGAGE OFFER

The typical buyer of a residential property will almost invariably require a mortgage, and it is for the solicitor to ensure before exchanging contracts that an acceptable written offer of mortgage is made and, if necessary, duly accepted. In this regard you should make sure that you receive the written offer yourself. Do not rely merely on the client's word that it has been issued. Moreover, read the mortgage conditions carefully (both general and specific) and, after discussing the terms with your client, establish that the mortgage offer is acceptable.

9.5.1 ADVISING CLIENT ON MORTGAGE OFFER

You should advise the client about the precise terms of the mortgage offer. Be clear in your own mind that the client understands the terms and can comply with them. General conditions (found in the small print or separate booklets) will apply across the board to all mortgages by a particular lender. Common examples are not to make alterations to the property and not to let the property without first obtaining the lender's consent. Many people taking out a mortgage for the first time do not always appreciate that these restrictions exist, so it is important to draw them to their attention. There may also be special conditions relating to the particular mortgage, e.g. a requirement to carry out specified repairs to the property.

9.5.2 SPECIAL CONDITIONS IN MORTGAGE OFFER

You should ensure that any special conditions in the mortgage offer can be met by the client. The following special conditions occur quite often:

(a) *Retention for repairs.* The lender's survey report may recommend that essential repairs are made, e.g. to the roof. As a result, the lender may impose a mortgage condition that a specified sum is held back from the mortgage advance until the repairs have been carried out. If so, the client will of course have to fund the shortfall in order to complete; moreover the client will also have to pay for the cost of the repairs after completion.

(b) *Retention for making up roads and drains.* This may be made in respect of a new property to cover the risks associated with the developer defaulting in making up the roads and drains. The borrower/buyer may in the circumstances of such retention seek to persuade the developer/seller to agree a similar retention from the balance due on completion until the mortgage retention is eventually released. Developers are, however, notoriously reluctant to agree this.

(c) *Mortgage indemnity guarantee.* If the loan exceeds a certain percentage of the lender's valuation of the property, e.g. 75 per cent, the lender may require some additional security. This is to cover a situation in which the borrower defaults and the lender is subsequently forced to sell the property at a loss (i.e. for less than the outstanding debt). The additional security takes the form of a separate indemnity guarantee policy protecting the lender against this risk. The insurance company offering the guarantee charges a single premium (normally several hundred pounds), which the lender pays initially and then either deducts from the mortgage advance or adds to the loan account. Either way the borrower ends up paying the premium and must be made aware of the position.

 Key Points Mortgage offer

- Read the client's mortgage offer carefully, in particular the special conditions.
- Typical special conditions include retentions from advance in respect of repairs or making up roads and drains.
- Ensure that any special conditions can be satisfied.
- Check overall that the mortgage offer is satisfactory to the client.

9.6 LENDER'S INSTRUCTIONS TO SOLICITOR

The lender's instructions to the solicitor will usually be issued at the same time as the mortgage offer and could look like this:

 Example of a typical set of mortgage instructions to a solicitor with client's offer of advance attached

CORNSHIRE BUILDING SOCIETY

Dear Sirs

Please act for the Society in the mortgage in accordance with the latest version of the CML Lender's Handbook for England and Wales. We enclose a copy of the Offer of Advance, the Mortgage Deed for execution by the borrower and a report on title for you to complete and return to us. We certify that these instructions comply with rule 3.16 of the Solicitors' Code of Conduct 2007.

Yours faithfully

Cornshire Building Society

OFFER OF ADVANCE

Date: 3 April 2008

Lender: Cornshire Building Society 5 High Street Blakey Cornshire CL1 3EH

Borrowers' full names and addresses: Colin smith of 20 Sun Street Blakey CL8 2TG

Solicitors: Brown & Co, West Chamber Blakey Cornshire CL1 2EG

Account number: 1234567

Property to be mortgaged:5 Pepperd Road Blakey Cornshire CL8 1LM

Tenure: Freehold

Purchase Price: £90,000

Amount of Loan: £40,000

Repayment Term: 25 years

Interest Rate (variable): 6.95%

Buildings Insurance Cover: £80,000

General Conditions:

1. The General Conditions of the Lender apply which are detailed in the enclosed booklet 'Information about your mortgage'.

2. This Offer of Advance may be varied or withdrawn if the mortgage is not completed within six months or if something occurs which in our view makes it undesirable for the loan or any part of it to be made. You must tell us of any changes in personal circumstances (e.g. loss or change of employment/pay) which occur before the mortgage is completed.

Special Conditions:

1. Lender's solicitors to obtain and place with the title deeds an undertaking signed by the Borrowers to carry out the following repair work to the Property within six months of completion:
   - Replace cracked tiles on roof
   - Repair chimney flashings

2. Lender's solicitors to confirm existence of legal right of way to the Property.

3. Colin Smith's existing mortgage with the Halifax secured on 20 Sun Street to be redeemed on or before completion.

4. Homeguard Insurance will be arranged as requested details of which are as follows: Cornshire Homeguard—Buildings Option A reinstatement value £80,000.

YOUR HOME IS AT RISK IF YOU DO NOT KEEP UP REPAYMENTS ON A MORTGAGE OR OTHER LOAN SECURED ON IT.

9.7 THE MORTGAGE DEED

A legal mortgage must be made by deed (Law of Property Act 1925, section 85). Apart from this requirement, it need take no other prescribed form, although in registered land rule 103 of the Land Registration Rules 2003 provides that a legal charge may be in Form CH1. Although not compulsory at present, Form CH1 is seen as something of a 'stepping-stone' towards a standard compulsory form of charge when e-conveyancing is introduced. Typically the institutional lender will supply its own printed mortgage form, which is sent to the solicitor along with the 'instructions pack'. The solicitor will then simply complete the blanks (name of borrower, property address, etc.) in readiness for execution by the borrower before completion.

9.7.1 ADVISING THE CLIENT

Before your client executes the mortgage deed it is important that you explain to the client its nature and effect, e.g.:

(a) Point out the initial rate of interest and amount of the first monthly repayment; explain that the lender may vary them at any time (unless the mortgage is fixed rate).

(b) Explain the borrower's covenants, such as the covenant to keep the property in good repair, not to make alterations without the lender's consent and any prohibition against letting or sharing possession without the lender's consent (lodgers often help to pay the mortgage).

(c) The borrower must understand that if there is any default on mortgage repayments or breach of covenant, the lender has the right to call in the loan and sell the property.

(d) Any penalty charges for early repayment should be explained (this is often the case in initially attractive looking fixed-rate packages).

(e) If the mortgage secures 'all monies' owed to the lender, a breach of this mortgage would entitle the lender to call in other loans (if any) made to the borrower. Most mortgages are all monies charges. Where there are joint borrowers, this would include sums advanced to them individually on sole mortgages on other properties (see *AIB Group UK plc v Martin* [2002] 1 WLR 94 (HL)).

(f) The lender's right to insure the property and recover the premiums from the borrower should be explained; the mortgage deed normally contains an express power for the lender to insure, extending the statutory power under the Law of Property Act 1925, section 101(1)(ii).

 Conduct Point Guarantors

- Any guarantor of the borrower who is executing the mortgage deed should be told to take independent legal advice before signing. This is because the guarantor may become liable instead of, or as well as, the borrower for all the money owing under the deed.

If the mortgage monies are being used to finance a contemporaneous purchase, the relevant parties must properly execute the mortgage deed before completion of the purchase. A good time for signing is when you see the client to explain the mortgage terms, and you can then act as the client's witness as well. There is no need for the lender to execute the deed unless, unusually, the lender is entering into new covenants.

Ensure that the client executes the mortgage before completion and leave it undated in your file. On completion you will then date the mortgage deed at the same time as you date the purchase deed. You should check the lender's instructions at this stage as some lenders require to be advised as soon as completion takes place.

 Key Points The mortgage deed

- The mortgage deed will normally be in the lender's standard format and you will need to complete the blank parts.
- Advise the client of the nature and effect of the mortgage before they execute the deed.
- Advise the client in particular that their home is at risk if they do not meet the monthly repayments.

- Ensure that the client executes the mortgage deed before completion and leave it undated in your file.
- Date the mortgage deed on completion.

9.8 REPORTING ON TITLE TO THE LENDER

Before the lender is willing to release the mortgage advance it will insist on a written report on title from the solicitor. The report should confirm that the title is good and marketable, free from adverse encumbrances, and can be safely accepted by the lender as security. If the solicitor considers that the title is unacceptable then this must be drawn specifically to the lender's attention.

 Conduct Point Certificate of title

- The Solicitors' Code of Conduct 2007 contains a compulsory common-form certificate of title for all solicitors acting for both lender and borrower in a standard mortgage of property to be used as a private residence.

The use of this certificate of title is not obligatory for mortgage advances secured on commercial property, or for so-called 'buy to let' mortgages of residential property where the owner does not occupy the property. As an alternative to printing the approved certificate for each transaction, you may use a short-form certificate of title which incorporates the approved certificate by reference. The short form must include in the following order:

- the title 'Certificate of Title';
- the contents of the details box in the order set out in the approved certificate (use of two columns is acceptable) but with details not required shaded out or stated not to be required; and
- the wording: 'We, the conveyancers named above, give the Certificate of Title set out in the annex to rule 3 of the Solicitors' Code of Conduct as if the same were set out in full, subject to the limitations contained within it.' Administrative details, such as a request for a cheque, may follow the Certificate of Title.

A solicitor who is in any doubt about whether a particular adverse matter will result in the mortgage offer being withdrawn should refer the matter to the lender *before* contracts are exchanged. Indeed, to avoid delay, all queries should be referred to the lender as soon as they arise, which will normally be at the investigation of title stage, i.e. before exchange.

The report asks you to confirm that no breaches of planning condition or building regulation consent have occurred and, further, that you have complied with all the lender's instructions. Clearly these are matters that must be checked before exchange but it is not always possible for the solicitor to be absolutely clear about certain matters, such as compliance with planning conditions. If in any doubt, you would be wise to qualify your report by adding the words, 'as far as we are aware from our usual searches, enquiries and investigation of title'.

The report on title will include a request to the lender for the mortgage advance. In most cases the lender will agree to send the advance monies by telegraphic transfer, deducting the transfer fee from the advance. The advance monies are regarded as clients' money and as such must be paid into your firm's client account.

Pending completion the solicitor holds the mortgage advance on trust for the lender and must comply with the lender's instructions. Non-compliance will constitute a breach of trust; see *Target Holdings Ltd v Redferns* [1996] AC 421. In particular do not release funds and complete until the borrower has properly executed and you have received the mortgage deed (and any other security documentation). If there is any delay in completion, the lender's instructions may require the advance to be returned, with interest.

In all cases before the advance is drawn down the lender will require confirmation that the borrower is not bankrupt and that there are no insolvency proceedings. The solicitor for the lender should therefore conduct a bankruptcy search against each individual borrower's full name at the Land Charges Department (Form K16 is used for a 'bankruptcy only' search). If the borrower is a company, a company search should also be conducted to ensure that the company is not in liquidation and that there are no winding-up proceedings.

 Key Points Your duties to your lender client

- Refer any queries to the lender before exchange of contracts.
- Always comply with the lender's instructions (refer to CML Lenders' Handbook, parts 1 and 2).
- Check for occupiers' rights (see section 9.9 below)
- Carry out a bankruptcy search against the borrower.
- Carry out a company search against a corporate borrower.
- In a standard mortgage of a private residence when reporting on title use the Solicitors' Code of Conduct standard form Certificate of title.

9.9 POSTPONING OCCUPIERS' RIGHTS

Lenders are naturally cautious about occupiers and will want to know whether any adult will be in occupation of the property after completion in addition to the buyer/borrower. The vigilant lender will require an occupier to sign a declaration postponing any interest behind that of the lender. It is important that the solicitor for the lender/borrower ensures that the occupier obtains independent advice before signing this declaration. This is because of the conflict between the interest of the occupier and that of the lender/borrower and also the possibility of the borrower exerting undue influence on the occupier to sign the declaration.

 Conduct Point Conflict/undue influence

- To avoid a conflict of interest and to counter any suggestion of undue influence the lender must take reasonable steps to ensure that the signatory has an adequate understanding of the nature and effect of the transaction. Effectively this means the solicitor must ensure that the signatory is separately advised (see *Barclays Bank plc v O'Brien* [1994] 1 AC 180). Your recommendation for separate advice and/or representation should be recorded in writing for future reference if necessary.

9.10 THE *ETRIDGE* CASE—GUARANTEEING ANOTHER PERSON'S DEBTS

In *Royal Bank of Scotland v Etridge (No 2)* [2001] 4 All ER 449, the House of Lords laid down guidelines for solicitors advising a spouse being asked to agree to a husband's (or wife's) business debts being secured on the matrimonial home. These guidelines also apply to cases where anyone in a non-commercial relationship has offered to guarantee the debts of another, e.g. a parent and child. Although a solicitor should exercise his own skill and judgement in advising on the merits of each transaction, the 'core minimum' guidelines when advising a spouse are as follows:

- Be satisfied that you have the necessary expertise and time to interpret or advise on what may be very detailed financial information.

- Be satisfied that you can properly act for the wife as well the husband, i.e. that there is no conflict of interest.

- Obtain full financial information concerning the husband's account. This will normally include information on the purpose for the new facility, the indebtedness, the amount and terms of the borrowing, and a copy of any application form.

- Meet the wife face to face in the absence of the husband (telephone calls and letters are not sufficient).

- Confirm the wife's understanding of the transaction, and correct any misapprehension she may have.

- Explain in non-technical language the nature of the documents and their practical consequences, e.g. if the husband's business fails, the risk of losing her home and being made bankrupt.

- Emphasize the seriousness of the risks involved.

- Explain the length of time the security will last.

- Explain that the wife has a choice and that the decision to proceed is hers and hers alone.

- If the wife wishes to proceed there should be clear confirmation from her that this is the case, and she should authorize you to provide written confirmation of this to the lender.

You should also consider the following matters of good professional practice:

- Who will pay your fee for advising the wife? If the wife decides not to guarantee the proposed loan, will your fees get paid at all?

- Open a separate file and send the wife a retainer letter which clearly defines your relationship with her.

- Keep a clear record of your advice, especially if the transaction appears to be to the wife's disadvantage. Consider asking the wife to countersign a copy of that advice.

- The wife's authority for you to provide a 'certificate' to the lender should be given in writing.

9.11 LEASEHOLD MORTGAGES

For mortgages secured on residential leasehold properties, you should check the matters listed below. Refer to Chapter 16 for more information generally on leasehold properties.

(a) Ensure you have a clear receipt for the last ground rent.

(b) Ensure there is no provision for forfeiture on bankruptcy of the tenant or any superior tenant.

(c) Ensure there is a mutual enforceability covenant allowing the tenant to enforce other tenants' covenants in the block.

(d) Check that the lessor's covenants for repair and maintenance of the structure and common parts are adequate.

(e) Check that you have the current name and address of the lessor and any management company and that, if limited companies, neither have been struck off the register.

(f) Are you satisfied with the last three years' accounts of any management company? If not, send them to the lender for clearance.

(g) If the tenants control the Management Company you must keep with the deeds an up-to-date copy of the company's Memorandum and Articles of Association, the borrower's share certificate, and a blank transfer signed by the borrower.

(h) Check that any management company has an interest in land and that the lessees are all members of it. If this is not the case, the lessor should be obliged to carry out the management company's obligations should it fail to do so.

(i) If required, check that the lessor's consent to the proposed lease assignment has been obtained.

9.12 PERFECTING THE MORTGAGE AFTER COMPLETION

Following completion, if the borrower is a company incorporated in, or with an established place of business in, England and Wales, the mortgage must be registered at the Companies Registry within 21 days of completion (Companies Act 1985, sections 395 and 409). If it is not registered, the charge will be void against the company's creditors or a liquidator or administrator. It is important not to delay in registering the charge as an extension of time cannot be given without a court order and such orders are rarely made. You should also note that the Land Registry's practice is not to raise a requisition requiring a charge to be so registered. The Registry will instead simply enter a note in the charges register referring to the relevant section of the Companies Act.

For registered land, you should lodge your application to register the mortgage at Land Registry before the expiry of the priority protection period of your official search (see 12.5.1 for more details on this important pre-completion search). If the land acquired is unregistered, you must apply for first registration (and registration of the mortgage) within two months of completion.

If the mortgaged property is leasehold, you should check the notice requirements in the lease. It will usually be necessary to give notice to the lessor of any mortgage of the leasehold estate within a set time, and to pay a fee. The notice should be given in duplicate with a request that one copy be returned receipted.

After registration at Land Registry when the Title Information Document is returned by Land Registry, remember to check that the lender's mortgage appears properly in the charges register of the title and that the registered title is otherwise in order. Remember that legal mortgages rank in priority according to their order on the charges register; so, for example, do ensure that any intended first mortgage appears first in a list of mortgages on the register.

 Key Points Perfecting the mortgage after completion

- If the borrower is a limited company register the mortgage at the Companies Registry within 21 days of completion.

- For registered land, apply to register the mortgage at Land Registry before the priority period of your pre-completion search expires.

- For unregistered land, within two months of completion apply to Land Registry to register the mortgage at the same time as your application for first registration.

- When you receive the title information document from Land Registry check that the mortgage has been properly registered in the charges register.

9.13 COMMERCIAL PROPERTY MORTGAGES

In relation to a mortgage of commercial property, the lender will normally instruct an independent firm to act for it. In these circumstances the buyer's solicitor must ensure, before committing the buyer to exchange of contracts, that the lender's solicitor is satisfied with the title, the results of searches, and all other matters.

9.13.1 REQUESTING INFORMATION

The borrower's solicitor will be asked to supply copies of all relevant documentation relating to the transaction. Invariably this will include a full abstract or epitome of title or official copies of the registered title, all necessary searches, replies to pre-contract enquiries, planning permissions, details of all occupiers and, assuming the borrower is also buying, the dated and signed contract, replies to requisitions, pre-completion searches, and the approved draft purchase deed.

9.13.2 INVESTIGATION OF TITLE

The lender's solicitor is essentially double-checking the work of the borrower's solicitor. Inevitably this results in duplication of work, but is unavoidable unless the lender is prepared to accept a certificate of title from the borrower's solicitor. If the lender's solicitor has any queries, these should be raised with the borrower's solicitor as formal requisitions. These in turn will be raised by the buyer's solicitor with the seller's solicitor. Although the lender's solicitor will attend to the post-completion work, the borrower's solicitor will normally be expected to supply a completed Land Registry application form.

 Conduct Point Undertaking for costs

- The lender's solicitor will normally insist on an undertaking from the borrower's solicitor to be responsible for the lender's costs whether or not the matter proceeds to completion. This is primarily to cover abortive fees. Such an undertaking should be given up to a maximum specified sum, and only with the borrower's express authority. The borrower's solicitor should always consider the merit of obtaining monies in advance from the client before giving such an undertaking.

9.13.3 PROCEDURE

The lender's solicitor will prepare the security documentation (e.g. mortgage deed) and stipulate that its contents must be properly explained to the borrower. It is normally a requirement that the documentation is executed in the presence of the borrower's solicitor, who will sign as witness. Unless completion occurs at a meeting attended by the lender's solicitor, the latter will normally appoint the borrower's solicitor to act as agent on completion. This is on the basis that the borrower's solicitor holds the mortgage advance to order pending completion and undertakes to supply immediately thereafter the following: all documents of title, the executed security documentation, a Land Registry application form, and, if the borrower is buying as well, the executed purchase deed and Form DS1 (or in unregistered land, the seller's vacated charge). If the matter proceeds to completion, the lender's solicitor's costs and other payments, such as stamp duty, land tax, and Land Registry fees, will be deducted from the mortgage advance.

Key Points Commercial property mortgages

- The lender normally instructs its own solicitors.
- They will 'double check' that the security property is good and marketable and free from adverse matters.
- They will have a standard set of requirements for the borrower's solicitors.
- They will normally request an undertaking for costs from the borrower's solicitors.

9.14 **MORTGAGE FRAUD**

If you become aware that your client is engaging in fraudulent activities of any kind, you are obliged as a matter of professional conduct to discontinue acting for the client. Bear in mind that if you continue to act in these circumstances you risk:

- disciplinary proceedings from the Solicitors' Regulation Authority for breach of the conduct rules;
- civil proceedings for negligence or breach of contract, e.g. by a lender who has suffered loss;
- criminal prosecution for aiding and abetting a fraud or conspiracy to defraud. A guilty verdict invariably means a custodial sentence and being struck off the roll.

 Key Points Mortgage fraud

- Inform your lender client of any price alteration or other information which may be relevant to the lending decision. However, you also have a duty of confidentiality to your borrower client, so the borrower must consent to any disclosure you make to the lender.
- If your instructions are unusual or the transaction is unusual, ask your client for a full explanation. If your client is attempting to commit a fraud or if you are in any doubt about your client's motives, discontinue acting.
- Ensure that all monies are paid through the solicitors' accounts, not between the parties direct.
- Be on your guard against false mortgage applications and inflated property valuations. If in doubt, make further investigations; do not accept the situation and just proceed with the transaction.
- When acting for more than one client (e.g. joint borrowers), take instructions from each client in person. To avoid possible forgery best practice is for all borrowers to sign the mortgage deed in your presence.
- If you become suspicious about any transaction you must take appropriate steps and, if necessary, stop acting for the client.

SELF TEST QUESTIONS

1. It is generally accepted that a solicitor should not give mortgage advice to a client because of the risk of contravening the Financial Services and Markets Act 2000. Is this statement TRUE/FALSE? Please delete the incorrect choice.

2. Under the Solicitors' Code of Conduct which of the following is NOT required to be included in the solicitors' approved certificate on title to the lender (assuming that the subject property will be used as the borrower's private residence)

   (a) mortgage advance

   (b) price stated in transfer

(c) completion date

(d) property description

3. In registered land the form of mortgage that must be used is Form CH1, as prescribed by the Land Registration Rules 2003. Is this statement TRUE/FALSE? Please delete the incorrect choice.

4. Your client has decided to take a fixed rate mortgage with Cornshire Building Society. The interest rate is fixed for five years and there is an early redemption penalty. When advising your client on the contents of the mortgage deed, which of the following would you generally NOT include in your advice

   (a) that the lender has the right to call in the loan and sell the property if the borrower defaults on the mortgage;

   (b) that the initial rate of interest and monthly payments may be varied by the lender;

   (c) that if the client repays the mortgage within the first five years the lender can charge an interest penalty;

   (d) that your client will be unable to let the premises without the lender's prior consent.

5. In registered land, legal mortgages rank in priority according to their order of creation not their order of registration. Is this statement TRUE/FALSE? Please delete the incorrect choice.

SHORT REVISION QUESTIONS

Question 1

To   The Trainee Solicitor

From   The Property Partner

Re our client Javed Miandad: proposed mortgage

We act for Javed Miandad of 14 Willow Way, Drynoch who intends to lend £20,000 to his nephew Younis Khan to help him with his launderette business, which is running into financial difficulties.

Younis Khan and his wife live in a leasehold flat in Drynoch, which they bought with the aid of a mortgage from the local building society. Mr Miandad has told me that Mr Khan is happy to give our client a second charge on the flat to secure the loan.

Mr Khan does not wish to incur the expense of instructing his own solicitor and, in view of their close relationship, says he will gladly rely on our firm's expertise in this area to prepare the necessary paperwork.

He wants us to draw up a mortgage this afternoon, collect it on his way home from work and get his brother-in-law to sign it this evening before he flies to Pakistan tomorrow.

What matters should we consider before advising our client to proceed with these arrangements, if at all?

Question 2

Your firm acts for a new client, Kathleen Johnson in her proposed purchase of freehold shop premises at 21 Marriot Mall, Ipswich at a price of £300,000, subject to contract. You are a trainee solicitor with the firm. Following your general advice when taking instructions, Kathleen has applied for a commercial loan and has told you that the balance of the purchase price will be coming from her savings. This morning your firm's cashier tells you that Kathleen has just handed in £30,000 in cash in respect of the 10 per cent deposit payable on exchange. Discuss.

SUGGESTED ANSWERS TO SELF TEST QUESTIONS

1. The statement is false. A solicitor may give generic mortgage advice provided he or she does not give advice about a specific investment product. So, for example, advising on the merits or otherwise of repayment, endowment, or pension mortgages is fine; but advising a client to take up a mortgage linked to a pension with, say, Standard Life as opposed to Norwich Union is not allowed (unless, unusually, the solicitor is authorized by the Financial Services Authority to give mainstream investment advice).

2. The correct answer is none. Under rule 3.16 of the Solicitors' Code of Conduct 2007 *all* of these facts should be included in the solicitors' certificate on title to the lender.

3. The statement is false. The use of Form CH1 is only optional not compulsory (Land Registration Rules 2003, rule 103).

4. The correct answer is (b). This is an example of where you should read the question carefully. When advising a client on a mortgage you would generally mention (b) but of course in this case you are told that it is a fixed rate mortgage. Accordingly the mortgagee cannot raise the interest rate.

5. The statement is false. Section 48(1) of the Land Registration Act 2002 states that registered charges are 'to be taken to rank as between themselves in the order shown in the register'. Thus following completion, it is essential that the appropriate registration of the charge is made within the priority period of your pre-completion Land Registry search.

SUGGESTED ANSWERS TO SHORT REVISION QUESTIONS

Question 1

The facts in this question are typical of the kind of thing you will come across in practice, especially as far as commercial clients are concerned. Here, the client has already reached agreement and decided in his own mind what he wants from you. However, do not be forced by the client into doing what he wants without first considering carefully all the facts.

There are several areas of concern here, not least how you are going to react to the time-pressure of the client's request for a document to be drafted immediately. Never sacrifice carefully thought out advice in the interests of speed and expediency. The client is not a trained lawyer and is unlikely to have considered the full implications of his proposed course of action. That after all is your job, and you have a professional duty to ensure that vital issues are not overlooked.

Suggested answer

To   The Property Partner

From   The Trainee Solicitor

Re our client Javed Miandad

I refer to your memo regarding the above. I recommend that the following points should be considered before the client can be advised to proceed.

1. Mr Khan must be advised to seek independent legal advice before signing the mortgage. The Solicitors' Code of Conduct 2007 prohibits a solicitor from acting for both lender and borrower in a private mortgage at arm's length. Although it could be argued that this transaction may not be at arm's length given the blood relationship between the borrower and lender, we must in any event be fully satisfied that there is no conflict of interest before we can act for both parties. On the facts of this case I take the view that a conflict would arise if the mortgagor were seen to be relying on our advice and expertise.

2. As this is a proposed second charge we should inspect the first charge to establish whether the consent of the first mortgagee is required to the creation of the second charge.

3. If consent is required this should be obtained in writing before completion of the loan. The first mortgagee may require Mr Miandad to enter into a separate deed of postponement.

4. Importantly, the first mortgagee should also be asked to confirm the current amount outstanding so it can be checked whether there is sufficient equity in the property to cover the proposed advance.

5. The property is leasehold. The lease should be inspected to see if the landlord's consent is required to charge the property. If so, consent must be obtained before completion otherwise the charge will not bind the landlord. Following completion it may be necessary to give notice of the charge to the landlord, and this should also be checked in the lease.

6. We should investigate title and conduct searches and enquiries in the same way as if our client were buying the property. Before we can advise our client to proceed we must be satisfied that the title is good and marketable and free from any unusual encumbrances.

7. We must obtain clear results to pre-completion searches including a bankruptcy search against the full name of Mr Khan.

8. I note that Mr Khan lives in the flat with his wife. We must establish if she is a joint owner, in which case she will also have to join in the mortgage as joint mortgagor.

9. Even if Mr Khan is the sole legal owner, Mrs Khan may have an equitable interest in the property and will have statutory rights of occupation under the Family Law Act 1996. She must give her written consent to the proposed charge and agree to postpone all rights behind our client's charge. Reasonable steps must be taken to ensure that she understands the nature of the transaction and the postponement of her rights (if any). To this end, I recommend we insist that she receives separate independent advice. This should be sufficient to counter any assertion by her at a later date that her husband exerted duress or undue influence on her (see *Barclays Bank plc v O'Brien* [1992] 4 All ER 987).

10. Does Mr Khan own the launderette premises? If so, have the parties considered the alternative possibility of Mr Miandad taking security on these premises? This avenue should be explored as it may prove less complicated.

11. Given the important issues which need to be addressed, we cannot sensibly comply with our client's instructions to draft the mortgage immediately. If Mr Miandad is coming into the office this afternoon I will be happy to see him and explain the position.

Question 2

This question concerns the dangers of possible money laundering when taking instructions and subsequently when acting for a client in a property transaction. It is important that you or your firm do not assist unwittingly in the laundering of proceeds of any crime. The firm should have in place a recognized procedure for obtaining satisfactory evidence of the identity of its clients. As Kathleen is a new client, you should in the first interview have verified her identity by inspecting her passport and keeping a copy for your file.

One sign of possible money laundering is a client who asks you to hold large sums of cash on her behalf and this has occurred here. Your firm will have appointed a partner to whom staff can report suspicions of money laundering. The partner will be responsible for making decisions on whether to report any suspicion to the appropriate authority, the National Criminal Intelligence Unit (NCIS). It is not for you the trainee solicitor personally to make this decision.

It is a criminal offence for a firm to fail to disclose to the authorities knowledge or suspicion of others involved in money laundering. This is an exception to the normal solicitor/client confidentiality rule. It is also an offence to 'tip off' the client by telling her that your suspicions are being reported. You should therefore report the matter to the partner responsible and say nothing to the client at this stage. There may be a perfectly innocent explanation as to why Kathleen has given you the cash but the nominated reporting partner must investigate it further and seek guidance from the NCIS as to whether the cash can be paid into the firm's client account.

WIDER READING

- Chapter 7, Abbey, R, and Richards, M, *A Practical Approach to Conveyancing* (Oxford University Press, 2008)

- Section E dealing with the buyer's mortgage and Section H dealing with lenders generally, Silverman, F, *Conveyancing Handbook* (The Law Society, 2006)

- Emmet on Title, Chapter 25

- Ruoff, Theodore BF and Roper, RB, *The Law and Practice of Registered Conveyancing* (Sweet & Maxwell, 2007)

- Chapter 19 (Mortgages), MacKenzie, J-A, and Phillips, M, *Textbook on Land Law* (Oxford University Press, 2008)

WEBSITES FOR FURTHER INFORMATION

- Acts of Parliament, **<http://www.hmso.gov.uk/acts.htm>**. Keep up to date with statutory developments.

- Council of Mortgage Lenders, **<http://www.cml.org.uk>**. There is an on-line version of the CML Lenders' Handbook available at this site which should be referred to in cases of doubt about the requirements of the lender.

- Financial Services Authority, **<http://www.fsa.gov.uk>**.

- HM Revenue and customs, **<http://www.hmrc.gov.uk/home.htm>**.

- Land Registry, **<http://www.landreg.gov.uk/>**.

- Law Commission, **<http://www.lawcom.gov.uk/projects.htm>**. Keep up to date on proposals for law reform.

- Law Society, **<http://www.lawsoc.org.uk/>**

- Location statistics, **<http://www.upmystreet.com/>**.

- A street map anywhere in the UK, **<http://www.streetmap.co.uk>**.

- Valuation Office, **<http://www.voa.gov.uk>**.

online resource centre

ONLINE RESOURCE CENTRE CASE STUDIES

RESIDENTIAL TRANSACTION CASE STUDY—THE MORTGAGE

Our clients:
Shilpa Jennings—sale of 19 Minster Yard
Shilpa Jennings and Daniel Rodriguez—purchase of 9 Castle Hill

We act for Shilpa Jennings ('Shilpa') who is selling 19 Minster Yard for £100,000 and Shilpa and Daniel Rodriguez ('Daniel') buying 9 Castle Hill for £200,000. The Standard Conditions of Sale, 4th edn, are adopted in both contracts. Our instructions from the lender in respect of the clients' mortgage offer on the purchase are contained on the Online Resource Centre. The Mortgage Deed is also set out there.

COMMERCIAL TRANSACTION CASE STUDY—THE MORTGAGE

Our client: Cambo Ltd—acquisition of 18 Clover Street

We act for Cambo Ltd acquiring the freehold reversion of 9 Clover Street London W2 for £700,000 subject to and with the benefit of two occupational business leases. Our client is obtaining a mortgage and, because this is a commercial transaction, the lender has instructed its own solicitors. Their requirements are set out on the Online Resource Centre accompanying this book, to which we shall need to respond.

10 EXCHANGE OF CONTRACTS

10.1 INTRODUCTION

Exchange of contracts is the most critical stage in the conveyancing process as it represents the point at which the parties become legally bound to proceed. In this chapter we shall examine pre-exchange matters, the process by which contracts are actually exchanged, and matters which should be attended to immediately after exchange has taken place. We shall also consider the risk and responsibility for buildings insurance, and the consequences of the buyer occupying the property before completion.

10.1.1 SYNCHRONIZATION

If your client is selling one property and buying another (assuming the two transactions are dependent upon each other) the importance of synchronizing the two exchanges of contracts cannot be overstated. It is of course routinely the case that many clients selling a house or flat will also be buying another, and *vice versa*. In these cases, the conveyancer must ensure that exchange of contracts on both transactions is synchronized so that the client does not end up with two properties or none at all. Remember that either a seller or buyer in a conveyancing transaction can withdraw without liability at any time prior to exchange of contracts.

10.1.2 COMMERCIAL CONVEYANCING

In a commercial transaction, such as the grant or assignment of a business lease, or the transfer of a freehold property which is tenanted, synchronization is likely to be of less significance. This is because there is usually no chain; only one property is involved and your client is dealing just with one other company or person, e.g. a commercial freehold with seller and buyer, or a landlord granting a business lease to a commercial tenant. Indeed in many commercial leasehold transactions, when the landlord and tenant are ready to proceed, they may simply go straight to completion without exchanging contracts at all. Nevertheless, in each case it is always important to check whether your client has a related transaction in which synchronization is required.

10.2 PRE-EXCHANGE MATTERS

Before committing your client to an exchange of contracts important checks must be made to ensure that your client is ready to proceed. Invariably the buyer's solicitor has more to do because of all the enquiries, searches, and title investigation that have been carried out. We now examine the essential pre-exchange matters when acting for a seller and buyer respectively.

10.2.1 SELLER'S PRE-EXCHANGE CHECKLIST

The contract

When negotiations on the terms of the draft contract have been concluded, the seller's solicitor will prepare two fair copies of the contract: one for signature by the seller and one for signature by the buyer. Both copies of the contract must be identical. The two parts should incorporate all the agreed amendments because otherwise, even if a purported exchange occurs, no contract will come into existence (see the Law of Property (Miscellaneous Provisions) Act 1989, section 2, and *Harrison v Battye* [1975] 1 WLR 58, in which only one part of the contract was amended to reflect an agreed reduced deposit). The date of the contract and the date of completion should not be inserted in the contract until the moment of exchange.

Signing the contract

The seller will of course need to sign the contract before exchange, although the signature need not be witnessed. It is standard conveyancing practice to have two identical contracts, one signed by the seller and the other signed by the buyer, which are then exchanged so that the buyer receives the seller's signed contract, and vice versa. If this practice of exchange is to satisfy section 2 of the Law of Property (Miscellaneous Provisions) Act 1989, the buyer and seller must each sign one of two identical copies.

If you are reporting to the seller in person then this is a good time for the seller to sign the contract in your presence (assuming the terms are agreed). You can then hold the signed but undated contract on file in readiness for exchange. If it is not practicable for you to see the client then the contract can be sent for signature with your written report. Ask the client to return the signed contract as soon as possible and emphasize that the contract should *not* be dated. You will date the contract on exchange.

Signing contract on behalf of another

One trustee or co-owner may sign on behalf of the other trustees or co-owners but the solicitor should ensure that they have all given their authority, not only to sign the contract but also to proceed with the transaction. Similarly, one partner may sign on behalf of the other partners provided the transaction has been authorized by the partnership. A company officer (e.g. director) can sign on behalf of the company provided the company has authorized the transaction. As far as personal representatives are concerned, section 16 of the Law of Property (Miscellaneous Provisions) Act 1994 provides that all proving personal representatives must be parties to the contract (and purchase deed). However one personal representative can sign the contract on behalf of all, provided authorization for signature has been given.

Conduct Point Solicitor signing contract

- It is permitted for the conveyancing solicitor personally to sign the contract on behalf of the client, and in practice this is often done to save time. Strictly speaking, however, you should sign only if you have been formally appointed as the client's attorney (as attorney you can sign in your own name or the client's), or if the client has given you express authority to sign, preferably in writing (see *Suleman v Shahsavari* [1988] 1 WLR 1181, in which a solicitor acting without authority was held liable in damages for breach of warranty of authority). On a sale by auction, an auctioneer has implied authority to sign for both parties.

Non-owning occupiers

In addition, any non-owning occupiers will be expected to sign the contract to release any rights and agree to vacate the property on or before completion. See Chapter 5, section 5.2 for further information on this point.

Seller's mortgage

If the subject property being sold has an existing mortgage secured on it, the buyer will require the mortgage to be repaid and discharged on or before completion (repayment is normally made from the sale proceeds on completion). Accordingly, the seller's solicitor must ensure before exchange that there will be sufficient funds available from the proceeds of sale (and/or other sources) to discharge the mortgage. Failure to do so will amount to negligence if the client suffers loss. Request a redemption statement from the lender for confirmation of the outstanding mortgage debt.

Sale of part

If only part of the seller's property is being sold, it will not be necessary to discharge fully any mortgage on the property (although the seller may choose to do so if sufficient monies are available). The buyer will merely be concerned to ensure that the part of land being bought is released from the mortgage. The seller's solicitor must therefore enquire of the existing mortgagee how much is required for the release of the part being sold, and ensure that at least this sum will be available on completion to forward to the mortgagee.

Synchronization of related purchase

If the seller is expecting to purchase another property at the same time as he is selling a property, then you must synchronize exchange of contracts on both sale and purchase transactions. The ways of achieving synchronization by telephonic exchange are discussed in section 10.3.3. The dangers of not synchronizing become apparent in the following disastrous chain of events:

(a) You exchange on the sale before the purchase.

(b) Your client's seller withdraws before you can exchange on the purchase.

(c) Your client is legally bound to complete the sale and does so.

(d) Your client has no property to move into and will have to find temporary accommodation and arrange furniture storage.

Conduct Point

- If you fail to synchronize exchange of contracts on a related sale and purchase, and the client suffers loss, you will be negligent (see *Buckley v Lane Hrdman and Co.* [1977] CLY 3143).

> **Key Points** Seller's pre-exchange checklist
>
> - Has the sale contract been agreed?
> - Has the seller signed the agreed form of sale contract?
> - Will the net proceeds of sale be sufficient to discharge any mortgage(s) on the property?
> - Agree completion date.
> - Ensure that you synchronize exchange on any related purchase.

10.2.2 BUYER'S PRE-EXCHANGE CHECKLIST

Searches and enquiries

The buyer's solicitor must be satisfied with the results of all relevant pre-contract searches and enquiries, including the enquiries made of the seller's solicitor (see generally Chapter 6). Any outstanding matters must be resolved to the satisfaction of the client and the solicitor before contracts are exchanged.

Survey

As we have seen, *caveat emptor* (let the buyer beware) applies to the purchase of land, and the buyer (and any lender) must be satisfied with the outcome of the survey before proceeding to exchange of contracts. Ensure that the survey carried out is more than a simple valuation. Surveys are examined in more detail in Chapter 4, section 4.3.

Title

As we saw in Chapter 8 the purchaser's solicitor should investigate title before exchange. Many contracts expressly prohibit the raising of requisitions on title after exchange. Accordingly the solicitor acting for the buyer and lender will have to be satisfied that the title is good and marketable, and free from encumbrances that might adversely affect the value of the property or its use and enjoyment. All outstanding requisitions on title should be resolved to your satisfaction before contracts are exchanged.

Buyer's financial arrangements

When taking instructions at the beginning of a transaction we have seen that you should check that the buyer's proposed financial arrangements are in order. See Chapter 9 on mortgages.

Deposit

The deposit paid on exchange is normally 10 per cent of the purchase price, but check the contract to establish how much has been agreed.

Cleared funds

You must ensure that you have cleared funds for the deposit before exchange occurs. This means that not only must you receive the client's cheque for the deposit, but you must also allow time for it to clear through your firm's account. The reason for this is that Standard Condition (SC) 2.2.4 requires the deposit to be paid either by direct credit or by a cheque drawn on a solicitor's or licensed conveyancer's client account.

Utilizing deposit from related sale

If your client has a related sale it may be possible to fund the deposit in other ways. Your client may be able to utilize the deposit receivable on a related sale; your client might consider offering a deposit guarantee instead of a money deposit; a bridging loan might also be a possibility. All of these methods (including the risks of bridging finance) were examined in some detail in Chapter 5, section 5.7, but a further word should be mentioned here about undertakings.

Bridging finance and undertakings

If a bank has offered the client bridging finance, the bank will invariably require your firm's undertaking to repay the bridging loan from the proceeds of the client's related sale (note that a bridging loan will normally only be available where the client has a related sale). Indeed, the *whole* of the net proceeds are normally requested, so that the balance received, after the bridging loan has been repaid, is credited to the client's bank account.

 Conduct Point Undertakings

- Before giving an undertaking to repay a bridging loan you will need to consider its terms very carefully to ensure that you can comply with it. The bank is likely to have a standard form of undertaking but you should always consider whether this is satisfactory both to you and your client. Remember when undertaking to pay money that such payment should be conditional upon your firm actually receiving the funds in the first place. Furthermore, you should obtain from your client prior irrevocable written authority to give the undertaking. The undertaking should not be given until just before exchange once you are satisfied that there are no outstanding matters to be resolved.

Buildings insurance

This is covered in section 10.6 below. If the buyer (or buyer's lender) is to insure the property after exchange, arrangements should be put in place before exchange, so that all that is needed after exchange is, at most, a simple telephone call to put the policy on risk. Some lenders will automatically put insurance in place from exchange.

Reporting to the buyer

 Conduct Point

- You have a duty to use reasonable care and skill in giving such advice as the particular transaction demands, having regard to the level of knowledge and expertise of your client (see *Sykes v Midland Bank Executor and Trustee Co Ltd* [1971] 1 QB 113). So you would generally give fuller advice to a first-time buyer than you would to, say, an experienced property developer (see *Aslan v Clintons* (1984) 134 NLJ 584). Failure to give adequate advice may constitute breach of your duty, entitling the client to damages. Your advice to the client may be given orally or in writing, or by using both methods. For the avoidance of doubt it is best practice, at the very least, to report in writing.

Oral report

Ideally, you should try to report to your client in person, as well as in writing. A sensible approach would be to start by sending your client copies of the relevant documentation, such as replies to pre-contract enquiries, local search, draft contract, and, for registered land, official copies of the title. In your covering letter you could invite the client to read the documents and to arrange an appointment with you to discuss the points arising from them. When subsequently you meet the client you can go through the papers, explaining their significance and highlighting any adverse matters which may be revealed. Here are some examples:

- the replies to enquiries may disclose a neighbour dispute;
- the title may contain covenants prohibiting business use or imposing fencing obligations;
- the local search may show that a flyover is being built within 200 metres of the property.

Your meeting will also give you an opportunity to discuss the terms of your client's mortgage offer (if any), and the result of the survey.

A full attendance note of your advice should be kept on file and your oral advice confirmed in a letter to the client. The letter is helpful for the client for future reference, and the written record of your advice will also protect you against the forgetful client who later complains that certain matters were not brought to his or her attention. Dictate the attendance note and letter immediately after the interview when matters are still fresh in your mind.

Written report

Of course, it may not be practicable to report to the client face to face, in which case you will make a full written report. Write the report in language that the client can understand. It should refer to all matters which may adversely affect the client's use and enjoyment of the property, particularly the following:

online
resource
centre

(a) Advise that the property is being bought in its actual state and condition and that the client must be satisfied with the survey.

(b) Explain the significance of the searches you have carried out (e.g. coal mining, commons, local land charges).

(c) In respect of the local search:
   • advise whether the road fronting the property is publicly maintained;
   • advise whether there are any plans for new roads in the immediate vicinity of the property;
   • report that the search relates only to the subject property, not neighbouring properties.

(d) In respect of the water search:
   • advise whether foul and surface water drainage is connected to the public sewers;
   • advise whether the water supply is connected to the public water system.

(e) In respect of the purchase contract:
   • confirm the property description (if appropriate by reference to a plan);
   • confirm the price and deposit arrangements;
   • advise who will bear the risk of insurance between exchange and completion (see section 10.6 below);
   • explain any special conditions.

(f) In respect of the seller's replies to enquiries (or Property Information Form):
   • highlight any adverse matters;
   • draw the client's attention to the Fixtures Fittings and Contents Form so that the client knows which items the seller is taking and which are being left;
   • advise which boundaries the seller has maintained.

(g) Give the client information about outgoings: In particular:
   • advise the client which band the property is in for council tax purposes;
   • the current annual charge for water rates;
   • if the property is leasehold, the rent and likely level of any service charge the client will have to pay.

(h) In respect of the title:
   • if registered, confirm the class of title (e.g. absolute);
   • advise about any covenants which bind the property and any rights to which the property is subject;
   • advise whether the property has the benefit of any rights or easements (e.g. a right of way along a private accessway).

(i) If the client is obtaining a mortgage, explain the main terms of the mortgage offer and draw the client's attention to the general mortgage conditions and any special conditions. Advise that the property is at risk if repayments are not maintained or if the mortgage conditions are breached. Unless it is a fixed-rate or capped mortgage, advise that the lender is entitled to raise the interest rate. Advise of any retention by the mortgagee.

(j) If the property is leasehold, explain the main terms of the lease, in particular, the tenant's covenants and the landlord's right to forfeit if the covenants are breached (see generally Chapter 16 on leasehold properties).

(k) Lastly, invite the client to telephone you if any matters in the report are unclear, or if the client has any questions or queries.

Approving the draft contract

The buyer's solicitor should consider the terms of the draft contract carefully in the light of the buyer's instructions, the replies to pre-contract enquiries, the results of searches, and the title investigation. If amendments to the contract are necessary, these should be made in red and the contract then returned to the seller's solicitor for consideration. You should retain a copy of the amended contract on your purchase file.

When negotiations on the terms of the draft contract have been concluded, the seller's solicitor will prepare two fair copies of the contract; one for signature by the seller and one for signature by the buyer. Both copies of the contract must be identical. The two parts should incorporate all the agreed amendments because otherwise, even if a purported exchange occurs, no contract will come into existence (see the Law of Property (Miscellaneous Provisions) Act 1989, section 2, and *Harrison v Battye* [1975] 1 WLR 58, in which only one part of the contract was amended to reflect an agreed reduced deposit).

Buyer to sign contract

The buyer will of course need to sign the contract before exchange, although the signature need not be witnessed. See our comments at 10.2.1 above in relation to the seller's signature; the same principles apply when acting for the buyer. The date of the contract and the date of completion should not be inserted in the contract until the moment of exchange.

Synchronization of related sale

If the buyer is relying on money from a related sale in order to assist the finance of the purchase (i.e. the purchase is dependent on the sale) then the solicitor must synchronize exchange of contracts on both sale and purchase transactions. The ways of achieving synchronization by telephonic exchange are discussed at 10.3.3 below. The dangers of not synchronizing become apparent in the following disastrous chain of events:

(a) You exchange on the purchase before the sale.

(b) Your client's purchaser withdraws before you can exchange on the sale.

(c) Your client is legally bound to complete the purchase but is unable financially to do so. Your client is thus in breach of the purchase contract.

(d) Even if your client can secure alternative funds to complete (e.g. bridging loan), your client will end up with two properties.

As previously mentioned, if you fail to synchronize exchange of contracts on a related sale and purchase, and the client suffers loss, you will be negligent (see *Buckley v Lane Herdman and Co.* [1977] CLY 3143).

Key Points Buyer's pre-exchange checklist

- Are results of all searches and enquiries satisfactory?
- Is the result of the survey satisfactory?
- Is the title good and marketable?
- Has the buyer received a mortgage offer (if needed) and are the conditions acceptable?
- Are you in funds for the deposit payable on exchange?
- Is the buyer required to insure the property from exchange? If so, are arrangements in hand?
- Have you reported in writing to the buyer?
- Has the purchase contract been agreed?
- Has the buyer signed the agreed form of purchase contract?
- Agree completion date.
- Ensure that you synchronize exchange on any related sale.

10.3 EXCHANGE OF CONTRACTS

Once the seller and buyer are ready to proceed, the next step is to exchange contracts and thereby bring the contract into force. There are three principal methods by which exchange of contracts can be effected:

- in person, or
- by post (or document exchange), or
- by telephone (the most common method).

10.3.1 IN PERSON

In this method the parties' solicitors meet, normally at the seller's solicitors' office. They physically exchange their respective clients' signed contracts and the buyer's solicitor hands over the client account deposit cheque. The completion date is written in and the contracts are then dated. A personal exchange is recognized as being the safest method because it is an instant exchange and the solicitors can personally check that the contracts are identical. However, exchange in person is very rarely used today unless the two offices are closely situated. Pressures of time and the need for synchronization in chain transactions make personal exchanges largely incompatible with the requirements of modern conveyancing.

10.3.2 BY POST (OR DOCUMENT EXCHANGE)

In this method the buyer's solicitor posts the buyer's signed contract and the cheque for the deposit to the seller's solicitor. Upon receipt, the seller's solicitor posts the seller's signed contract to the buyer's solicitor. It may also happen the other way round by the seller sending his contract first. If the Standard Conditions are being used, SC 2.1 confirms the common law postal rule on acceptance laid down in *Adams v Lindsell* (1818) 1 B & Ald 681, namely, that the contract comes into existence not when the second copy is received but when the second copy is posted (or deposited at the document exchange). Thus even if the contract is lost in the post a binding contract still exists.

We do not recommend postal exchange where either party has a linked transaction, i.e. a dependent sale or purchase. The reason for this is the time lag between the first contract being posted and the second contract being posted, and during this time either party is of course free to change his mind and withdraw.

online resource centre

10.3.3 **BY TELEPHONE**

This is the most common method of exchange used by solicitors today. The moment of exchange occurs at the point in the telephone conversation when the solicitors agree that contracts are actually exchanged. The decision in *Domb v Isoz* [1980] Ch 548 formally endorsed the practice of telephonic exchange and, following a recommendation by Templeman LJ, the Law Society subsequently produced formulae for use by solicitors (see below).

Conduct Point

- As the telephone formulae involve the use of professional undertakings they should be used only between firms of solicitors and licensed conveyancers, i.e. not where unqualified persons are involved. Any variations of the formulae should be recorded on the solicitors' files and confirmed in writing, in case of any later disputes.

Telephone formulae

Formula A

This formula should be used when one party's solicitor (usually the seller's) holds *both* signed parts of the contract, together with the deposit cheque (the buyer's solicitor will have forwarded the buyer's contract and deposit cheque to the seller's solicitor to be held to order in readiness for exchange).

Example

On the assumption that it is the seller's solicitor who holds both parts of the contract, formula A works as follows (S = seller's solicitor, B = buyer's solicitor):

(a) S confirms holding the seller's signed contract and the buyer's signed contract and deposit cheque.

(b) S and B agree that S will insert the agreed completion date in each contract.

(c) Exchange is formally agreed by B releasing the buyer's contract and S agreeing to hold the seller's contract to B's order.

(d) S undertakes to forward the seller's contract to B that day, either by first-class post, personal delivery, or document exchange.

Following exchange, the solicitors must write file memos recording: their own names, the date and time of exchange, the formula used (and any variations to it), the completion date, and the amount of the deposit being paid.

Formula B

This formula should be used when both solicitors hold their own clients' signed contracts (and the buyer's solicitor has cleared funds for the deposit).

Example

The solicitors confirm that they hold the signed contracts, they insert the agreed completion date, each agrees to hold his or her client's contract to the other's order, and they undertake to send the contracts out that day (plus, for the buyer, the deposit cheque). File memos should be made after exchange recording the details of the conversation (see formula A above).

Formula C

This formula should be used where there is a chain of transactions and the deposit monies are to be sent directly to another firm further up the chain.

> ### Example
>
> The solicitor at one end of the chain (X) telephones the solicitor next in line (Y). Both solicitors confirm that they hold their clients' signed contracts. X undertakes that X will definitely exchange with Y if Y rings back X before a specified time later that day requesting X to exchange. The same undertakings are then given to the other solicitors in the chain until the penultimate one in the chain is reached. Now at the end of the chain, a formula B exchange can occur between the penultimate solicitor and the solicitor at the end (assuming they are both ready). Thereafter the other contracts can be exchanged, one by one, back down the chain as the return calls are made. Thus the first call (e.g. by X to Y) activates formula C part 1; the return call (e.g. by Y to X)—when the exchange occurs—activates formula C part 2.

File memos should be made in respect of the conversations in parts 1 and 2 respectively. The part 1 memo will record the date and time of the conversation, the names of the solicitors speaking, any agreed variations to formula C, the final time later in the day for exchange, the completion date, and the name of the solicitor to whom the deposit is to be paid (formula C assumes a 10 per cent deposit). The part 2 memo will record the request to exchange, the time of exchange, and the identities of the speakers.

The following points should also be noted regarding formula C:

(a) Each caller activating part 1 (e.g. X above) must give the name of two other persons in the office who could take the part 2 return call if X is unavailable. X is undertaking that X or one of the other persons will be available up to the final time for exchange.

(b) Formula C cannot be held over to the next day. If exchange does not take place during the day, the whole process must be restarted and part 1 will be reactivated on another day.

(c) The contract must allow the deposit to be passed on up the chain and it must ultimately be held as stakeholder (this is permitted by the Standard Conditions). Consequently, you may well find yourself undertaking that another solicitor will be sending deposit monies. Be aware that this is an undertaking to do something which is outside your direct control.

(d) You should obtain the client's express irrevocable authority (preferably in writing) to exchange using formula C. Unless the client's authority is irrevocable, there is the risk that the client will instruct you to withdraw from the transaction after you have given (in part 1) the undertaking that you will definitely exchange if requested to do so. This would leave you in 'no man's land' because if you now accept your client's instructions and refuse to exchange, you will be in breach of your undertaking. However, if you go ahead and exchange, you will be in breach of your duty to your client by acting contrary to your client's instructions.

> ### Key Points Telephone formulae
>
> | Formula A | Formula B | Formula C |
> |---|---|---|
> | Use where one party's solicitor holds both signed parts of the contract, together with the deposit | Use where both solicitors hold their own clients' signed contracts (and the buyer's solicitor has cleared funds for the deposit) | Use where there is a chain of transactions and the deposit monies are to be sent directly to another firm further up the chain |

Fax and email

An exchange of faxes or emails is not a valid method of exchanging contracts. The common law rule is reinforced by SC 1.3.3, which provides, in effect, that where the delivery of a document is essential (e.g. exchange of contracts), transmission by fax or email is not a valid means of delivery. Faxes or emails may be used, however, to activate the Law Society's formulae for telephonic exchange.

10.4 ACTION TO BE TAKEN IMMEDIATELY AFTER EXCHANGE OF CONTRACTS

- If exchange has taken place by telephone then appropriate memos and letters to the other side must be written in compliance with undertakings that have been given, if necessary accompanied by the signed contracts and deposit cheques.

- Remember to date the contract with the date of exchange and insert the agreed completion date.

- Enter the completion date in your diary so that it is not overlooked.

- Telephone the clients to inform them that you have exchanged and to confirm the completion date. Confirm your telephone conversation in writing (advise them not to open the champagne just yet though—the other side still have to complete).

- The seller's solicitor should write to the seller's mortgagee, if any, requesting a redemption statement calculated to the date of completion with a daily rate of interest thereafter in case completion is delayed.

- If the buyer is to insure the property from exchange of contracts (see section 10.6 below), the buyer's solicitor must ensure that the insurance policy is activated immediately after exchange. In practice the buyer's mortgagee will normally arrange the insurance and this will often occur automatically without any need for you to contact the mortgagee. However, the matter must be checked in each case.

- If necessary the buyer's solicitor should protect the contract by registration (see 10.7 below).

- The seller's solicitor can contact the estate agents (if any) who acted on the sale to advise them of the exchange and completion date. The agents will no doubt send you their commission account for you to discharge out of the proceeds of sale on completion.

10.5 THE EFFECT OF A BINDING CONTRACT

As soon as there is a valid contract, the beneficial ownership in the property passes to the buyer (*Lysaght v Edwards* (1876) 2 ChD 499). Consequently the buyer at common law bears the risk of any loss or damage to the property, subject to the seller's duty to look after the property (see below). The buyer is, however, entitled to any increase in value of the property between exchange and completion. The seller has a lien over the property for the balance of the purchase money.

10.5.1 SELLER'S DUTY AS TRUSTEE

The seller retains ownership of the legal estate as a qualified trustee for the buyer. The trusteeship confers on the seller a duty to exercise reasonable care to keep the property in the same condition as it was at the date of the contract (*Clarke v Ramuz* [1891] 2 QB 456, CA). Accordingly, in winter, the seller should keep the heating on to ensure that the water in the pipes does not freeze (see *Lucie-Smith v Gorman* [1981] CLY 2866). The seller should also replace any slates or windows which may become broken between exchange and completion, and should probably also tend any garden of the property (see *Foster v Deacon* (1818) 3 Madd 394). The seller's duty continues even if the seller vacates before completion (*Lucie-Smith v Gorman*), but the seller's duty will end if the buyer is allowed into occupation before completion (see section 10.8 below).

During the seller's trusteeship the seller is entitled to remain in possession and to receive any rents and profits, but must also discharge the outgoings of the property such as council tax and water rates.

10.6 RISK AND RESPONSIBILITY FOR BUILDINGS INSURANCE

A solicitor will be negligent if proper advice is not given concerning risk and insurance and the client suffers loss as a result. It will be necessary for the solicitor to consider these matters at the draft contract stage because the question of who bears the risk of insurance of the property will depend on whether SC 5.1 is included in the contract, or in commercial transactions whether the Standard Commercial Property Conditions are being used.

10.6.1 IF CONTRACT INCORPORATES STANDARD CONDITION 5.1

Standard Condition 5.1.1 provides that the risk in the property remains with the seller, who must transfer the property in the same physical state as it was at the date of the contract (fair wear and tear excepted). SC 5.1.2 goes on to provide that if at any time before completion the physical state of the property makes it unusable for its purpose at the date of the contract then the buyer may rescind the contract. The seller may also rescind if it is damage against which the seller could not reasonably have insured, or damage which it is not legally possible for the seller to make good. Thus in the case of damage by fire, the seller is unlikely to be entitled to rescind, but there is every possibility that the buyer could rescind if the fire damage is severe.

Standard Condition 5.1.3 states that the seller is under no obligation to insure the property. So if, for example, the property burns down between exchange and completion, the buyer could sue the seller for damages for breach of contract but there is no guarantee that the buyer will recover his loss if the property is not insured for its full reinstatement value. Accordingly, a prudent buyer, before exchange, should consider imposing a special condition in the contract obliging the seller to insure the property to its full reinstatement value and to provide evidence of the insurance.

10.6.2 IF STANDARD CONDITION 5.1 IS EXCLUDED FROM CONTRACT

The seller may impose a special condition in the contract excluding SC 5.1, thus reverting to the open contract position in which the risk passes to the buyer on exchange. This is attractive to the seller because it removes the seller's obligation under SC 5.1.1 and the attendant risk that certain damage, for whatever reason, may not be covered by the seller's insurance policy. The point should also be made that the buyer (or the buyer's mortgagee) will generally prefer to make his or her or its own insurance arrangements anyway, preferring to have a claim against their own insurance company than a claim against the seller for damages for breach of contract.

In this situation, the common law position applies, i.e. the risk passes to the buyer on exchange. It is important for the buyer (or if the buyer requires mortgage finance, the buyer's mortgagee) to arrange adequate insurance of the property from the moment of exchange because if the property is damaged (e.g. by fire), the buyer will still be contractually bound to complete the purchase.

10.6.3 **COMMERCIAL PROPERTY**

The Standard Commercial Property Conditions (SCPC) are discussed more fully in Chapter 19. However, it is worth noting that the SCPC reverse SC 5.1 so that the buyer assumes the risk after exchange (thus reflecting the open contract position).

10.6.4 **INSURANCE AND LEASES**

If the property is leasehold, the lease should stipulate whether it is the lessor or the lessee who insures (if nothing is said about insurance, there is no obligation on either party to insure). If it is the lessee who insures, the same issues apply as above, with the additional consideration that, if the Standard Conditions are being used, SC 8.1.3 provides that the lessee/seller must comply with any lease provisions requiring the lessee to insure. The lessor normally has to approve the policy first, and it is usually simpler for the buyer/assignee to take over the seller/assignor's policy, rather than take out a new one.

If, more commonly, the lessor insures, a claim will be made under the lessor's policy. If any damage was the lessee's fault and, as a result, the lessor's insurance is invalidated, the lessee may, depending on the terms of the lease, be in breach of covenant under the lease.

10.6.5 **EFFECT ON INSURANCE OF BUYER IN OCCUPATION**

If the buyer has moved into occupation between exchange and completion, the terms of the occupation are set out in SC 5.2.2. The buyer is required, *inter alia*, to insure the property in a sum not less than the purchase price against all risks in respect of which comparable premises are normally insured. Condition 5.2.3 provides that SC 5.1 ceases to apply and the buyer assumes the risk until completion.

 Key Points Risk and insurance

- SC 5.1 reverses the open contract position by requiring the seller to transfer the property in the same physical state as it was at the date of the contract (except for fair wear and tear), i.e. the risk is with the seller.

- Under the Standard Commercial Property Conditions the risk passes to the buyer on exchange of contracts.

- Whoever assumes the risk, the seller should maintain his existing insurance until completion just in case damage occurs, the buyer defaults, and completion does not occur.

- After exchange the seller is a qualified trustee of the legal estate and owes a duty to the buyer to exercise reasonable care to keep the property in the same condition as it was at the date of the contract

---

10.7 **PROTECTING THE CONTRACT BY REGISTRATION**

A contract to purchase land is an estate contract and unless the buyer's solicitor protects the contract by registration, it will not bind a bona fide purchaser of the legal estate. If the property has an unregistered title, the appropriate protective registration is a C(iv) land charge against the name of the estate owner at the Central Land Charges Department in Plymouth. If the property has a registered title the appropriate protective entry is a notice against the registered title.

If a solicitor fails to register a contract which subsequently becomes void resulting in loss to the buyer, the solicitor will be liable in professional negligence (see *Midland Bank Trust Co Ltd v Hett, Stubbs and Kemp* [1979] Ch 384 and *Wroth v Tyler* [1974] Ch 30). Despite this it has become standard practice amongst solicitors not to register the contract except in the following situations:

- where a dispute arises between the parties, or
- the buyer becomes suspicious of the seller possibly seeking to dispose of the property to someone else, or
- more commonly, where there is a long period of time between exchange and completion (e.g. in excess of six weeks).

Notwithstanding current practice you should always bear in mind your professional duty to your client and if in any doubt you should register the contract. Note that an option to purchase or a right of pre-emption should always be protected by registration.

10.8 OCCUPATION BY THE BUYER BEFORE COMPLETION

Following exchange of contracts the seller may receive a request from the buyer for access to the property before completion, perhaps to take measurements for carpets or curtains, or to take a final look around before moving in. A request of this nature should not cause any problems for the seller provided the keys are not handed over and the buyer's visit is supervised, perhaps by the estate agent who negotiated the sale.

Occasionally, however, the buyer will want to begin decorating or to carry out alterations, or even actually to move in before completion. The seller should treat such requests with caution for the simple reason that the property does not properly belong to the buyer until the balance of the purchase price has been paid and the title to the legal estate has been transferred. Once in possession, a buyer might easily lose his motivation to complete. Moreover, a residential occupier cannot be compelled to vacate without an eviction order from the court (section 2 of the Protection from Eviction Act 1977). An even worse scenario for the seller would be inadvertently to create a tenancy in which the buyer acquires security of tenure. In this case the seller may be hard-pressed to recover possession at all.

In the light of these dangers, if a buyer in a straightforward transaction requests anything more than a simple inspection, a prudent seller should refuse; after all, the buyer should not have long to wait until completion. Another possibility could be for the parties to agree an earlier completion, if this is convenient. However, you will need to consider the effect of this on any related sale or purchase, because it may be that other parties in the chain do not wish to complete early.

10.8.1 CONDITIONS OF ENTRY

Despite the above advice, there will be times when the seller will consider permitting the buyer into occupation before completion. For instance, there may be a very long period between exchange and completion, or the property may be in need of urgent repairs which the buyer has undertaken to carry out. If this is the case the seller will have to think carefully about the conditions under which the buyer will be allowed to occupy.

If the buyer goes into possession before completion, the position at common law is that the seller's liability to maintain the property ceases, and the buyer is required to pay interest on the balance of the purchase monies. This alone is insufficient to protect the seller from the risks mentioned above but, if the Standard Conditions are used, help is at hand in SC 5.2. The principal protection afforded to the seller under SC 5.2 is that the buyer occupies as licensee not as tenant. The effect of this is that the buyer is conferred no security of tenure.

If occupation is agreed before completion, the solicitors for seller and buyer must each explain the conditions of the occupation agreement to their respective clients, and obtain their confirmatory instructions. The consent of any mortgagee should also be obtained if this is a requirement of the mortgage.

Key Points Occupation by buyer before completion

- Seller try to make the buyer wait until completion, or
- Can completion take place earlier instead?
- Is seller's mortgagee's consent required?
- If occupation is agreed, enter only under licence (e.g. under SC 5.2).
- Both seller and buyer should be advised of the proposed conditions of occupation and their instructions confirmed.

FIGURE 10.1 EXCHANGE OF CONTRACTS DECISION TREE ACTING FOR THE SELLER

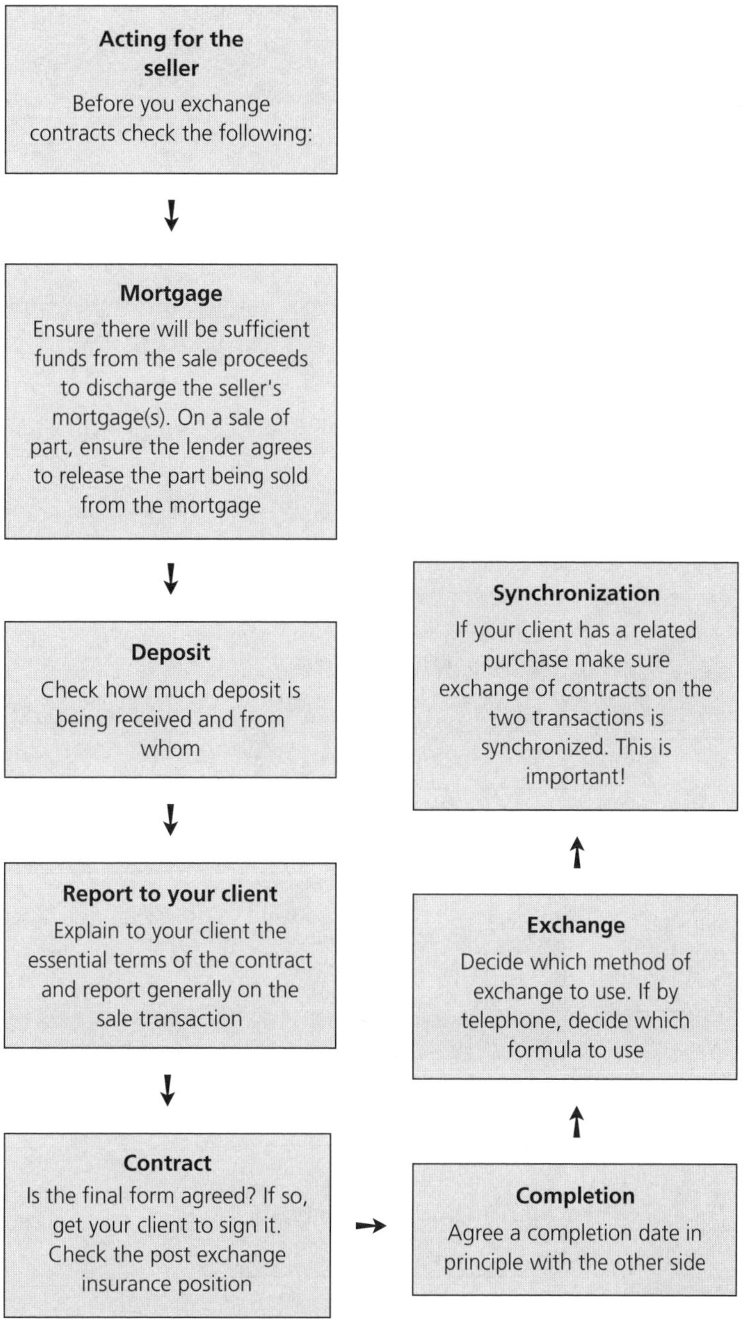

Acting for the seller

Before you exchange contracts check the following:

Mortgage

Ensure there will be sufficient funds from the sale proceeds to discharge the seller's mortgage(s). On a sale of part, ensure the lender agrees to release the part being sold from the mortgage

Synchronization

If your client has a related purchase make sure exchange of contracts on the two transactions is synchronized. This is important!

Deposit

Check how much deposit is being received and from whom

Report to your client

Explain to your client the essential terms of the contract and report generally on the sale transaction

Exchange

Decide which method of exchange to use. If by telephone, decide which formula to use

Contract

Is the final form agreed? If so, get your client to sign it. Check the post exchange insurance position

→

Completion

Agree a completion date in principle with the other side

10.9 **VARIATION OF THE CONTRACT BETWEEN EXCHANGE AND COMPLETION**

A typical variation of the contract might occur where the parties decide after exchange to have a different date for completion. This occurred in *McCausland v Duncan Lawrie Ltd* [1997] 1 WLR 38, where the solicitors exchanged for completion on 26 March but subsequently realized that this was a Sunday, so they exchanged letters agreeing 24 March instead. The Court of Appeal held that the purported variation was unenforceable because any variation of the contract must comply strictly with the provisions of section 2 of the Law of Property (Miscellaneous Provisions) Act 1989. This means that there has to be a further exchange of documents, signed by the parties, referring to the original contract and the subsequent variation.

FIGURE 10.2 EXCHANGE OF CONTRACTS DECISION TREE ACTING FOR THE BUYER

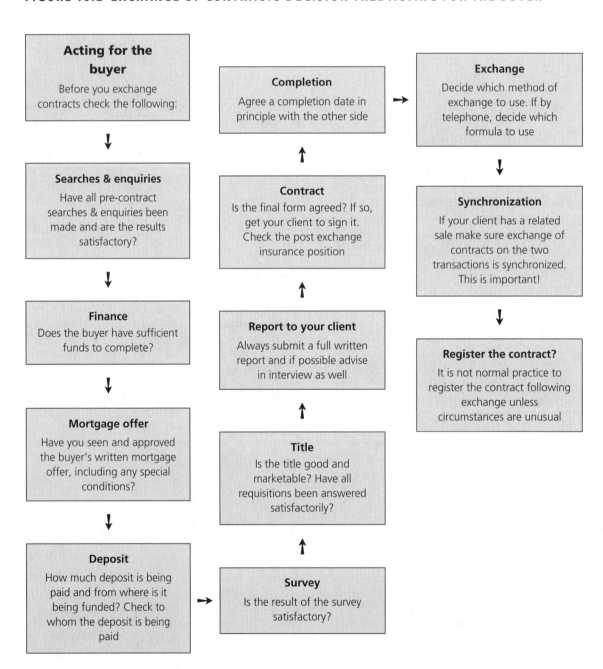

10.10 **DEATH OF SELLER OR BUYER BETWEEN EXCHANGE AND COMPLETION**

Where this unfortunate event occurs the obligations under the contract remain unaffected and the deceased's personal representatives are bound to complete, i.e. they 'step into the shoes' of the deceased. It is important to advise the other party to the contract as soon as possible, as it may be necessary to seek either a termination of the contract (unlikely) or a postponement of the completion date.

If the other side does not agree to this and completion is likely to be delayed you can apply to the Probate Registry for an expedited or limited grant of representation. Ask the Probate Registry to deal with the application quickly so as to avoid the deceased's estate incurring liability for breach of contract.

If one of three or more co-sellers dies the sale can proceed as normal. If one of two co-sellers dies check whether they held as joint tenants or tenants in common. If tenants in common, it will be necessary to appoint a second trustee to act with the survivor. Unless the deceased's share passed by survivorship enabling a surviving co-seller(s) to sell the whole beneficial estate, do not complete until the grant of representation has been issued.

On the death of a sole buyer, any mortgage offer is likely to be withdrawn, so the personal representatives will have to find alternative funding. If you need to serve notice on a deceased estate owner, address it to the deceased and the deceased's personal representatives at the deceased's last known address; also send a copy to the Public Trustee.

10.11 **BANKRUPTCY OF SELLER OR BUYER BETWEEN EXCHANGE AND COMPLETION**

In respect of a registered title a notice on the title will alert the buyer that a petition in bankruptcy has been presented against the registered proprietor. A bankruptcy restriction will alert the buyer that a bankruptcy order has been made. The bankruptcy proceedings will also be registered at the Land Charges Department in Plymouth. The land charges registrations are relevant for buyers of *unregistered* land only—it is not necessary to conduct a land charges search against the seller when buying registered land.

A buyer who has relevant notice of bankruptcy proceedings should wait to take a transfer from the trustee in bankruptcy, not the seller. The buyer's solicitor should ask to see a copy of the bankruptcy order together with documentary proof of the trustee's appointment. Similarly, a buyer from a liquidator or administrative receiver of a company will require written evidence of the appointment.

Any disposition by a bankrupt (including payment of purchase money) after the presentation of the petition is void. The same rule applies on company insolvency. Anyone buying from, or selling to, a company being wound up should deal with the liquidator of the company. A person dealing with a liquidator must ensure that the formalities of the liquidator's appointment have been observed. The appointment of an administrative receiver will normally crystallize a floating charge so that it becomes a fixed charge on the company's property. A buyer must ensure that the property is released from the fixed charge.

A bankruptcy order will sever a beneficial joint tenancy. The bankrupt co-owner's beneficial interest vests in the trustee who must execute the purchase deed with the surviving co-owner(s).

SELF TEST QUESTIONS

1. When exchange of contracts occurs by post the contract becomes legally binding when

   (a) The first contract is posted

   (b) The first contract is received

   (c) The second contract is posted

   (d) The second contract is received

2. The correct Law Society formula to use for telephonic exchange where each solicitor holds his or her own client's signed contract is formula A. Is this statement TRUE/FALSE?

3. In normal conveyancing practice, before exchanging contracts the solicitor for the buyer should ensure that the agreed form of contract held in his or her file is signed by

   (a) The seller

   (b) The buyer

   (c) The seller and the buyer

   (d) The solicitor

4. When exchange of contracts occurs by telephone formula C which of the following is NOT a Law Society requirement

   (a) That the conveyancer expecting to be telephoned back later in the day should give the name of other conveyancers in the office who could take the call if the first solicitor is otherwise engaged;

   (b) That file memos should be made by each conveyancer recording the details of the telephone conversations constituting parts 1 and 2 of formula C;

   (c) That the conveyancer ensures that he or she has the client's express authority to exchange contracts using formula C;

   (d) That if contracts are not exchanged on the day that the conveyancers initiate formula C then the whole process must start again the next working day.

5. You act for the seller of freehold factory premises. Following exchange of contracts but before completion (next week) your client informs you that the managing director of the purchasing company has asked if he can move his company's heavy plant and machinery into the factory a few days before completion. You would advise your client that

   (a) This is normal practice in a commercial conveyancing transaction and your client should allow it;

   (b) This should not be allowed as it may invalidate the contract;

   (c) This is acceptable but you must first draw up a tenancy agreement so that the purchaser's occupation can be formalized;

   (d) The purchaser should be asked to wait until completion.

SHORT REVISION QUESTIONS

Question 1

Harriet Dean acts for John Wainwright, a first time buyer of 19 Bradman Street, a freehold house in Altrincham, Cheshire. Harriet has carried out her pre-contract searches and enquiries, investigated title, and approved her client's mortgage offer. After receiving a full report from Harriet, John has signed the agreed form of contract, which Harriet is currently holding in her file. John has also put Harriet's firm in funds for the 10 per cent deposit.

At 11am today Harriet telephones the seller's solicitor to inform him that she is ready to exchange contracts. The seller's solicitor explains that there is a long chain above him and he wishes to exchange using telephone formula C. Under part 1 of formula C he asks Harriet to agree a time later in the day before which he may ring her back to exchange. Harriet agrees a time of 3pm and releases her client's contract to the other solicitor until that time.

At 2pm today John telephones Harriet to say that he has had a change of heart and no longer wishes to proceed with the purchase. In fact he expressly instructs Harriet not to proceed with the exchange. Five minutes later the seller's solicitor telephones Harriet to say that he has exchanged contracts on his client's related purchase and now wishes to exchange on 19 Bradman Street under formula C part II. When Harriet tells him that her client has pulled out the solicitor angrily informs her that unless she exchanges within the next 15 minutes he will have no hesitation in reporting her to the Law Society.

What can Harriet do and what lessons can she learn from what has happened?

Question 2

You act for Eddie Strang who has exchanged contracts to sell a freehold commercial premises used for the manufacture of kite surfing equipment. The purchaser is Tim Hancock and the contractual completion date is two months today. Eddie has rung you to say that, as Tim has been able to arrange his finance sooner than expected, they have agreed to complete four weeks early. What action should you take, if any?

SUGGESTED ANSWERS TO SELF TEST QUESTIONS

1. The correct answer is (c). The well-established common law rule on acceptance of contracts is that the contract comes into existence when the second copy is posted (*Adams v Lindsell* (1818) 1 B & Ald 681). This is confirmed by SC 2.1.

2. The statement is false. This question is about as straightforward as it gets and tests your basic knowledge of the Law Society telephone formulae. Where each solicitor holds their own client's signed part of the contract the relevant formula is of course B, not A.

3. The correct answer is (b). It is acceptable for a solicitor to sign on the client's behalf with the client's authority, but this is not 'normal conveyancing practice' (read the question carefully). Also, both parties could legitimately sign one contract, but, again, normal practice is to exchange identical contracts.

4. The correct answer is none. This question is quite difficult and requires a thorough knowledge of formula C. In considering each point carefully you will appreciate that *all* of them are formula C requirements!

5. The correct answer is (d). Completion is only a few days' away and in these circumstances it would be most unusual to accede to such a request. The prudent course is simply to wait until completion. Under no circumstances should the buyer be allowed to occupy early under a tenancy agreement as this may confer on the buyer security of tenure.

SUGGESTED ANSWERS TO SHORT REVISION QUESTIONS

Question 1

Although this question is about exchange of contracts, it concerns an important area of professional conduct, namely the solicitor's professional undertaking. It is a classic illustration of the difficulty a solicitor can get into if s/he fails to follow the golden rules before giving an undertaking. Harriet's undertaking was given when she 'released' her client's contract to the other solicitor. In doing so she impliedly undertook that if he rang her back before 3pm she would definitely exchange contracts. Having received this assurance, the seller's solicitor committed his client on his client's related purchase.

Unfortunately Harriet is now stuck in 'no-man's land'. If she goes ahead and exchanges she will be acting contrary to her client's instructions. But if she refuses to exchange she will be in breach of undertaking and may be reported to the Law Society (the chances of the seller's solicitor showing any sympathy with Harriet's predicament are very slim indeed, given that the other contracts in the long chain are now exchanged). Harriet's only sensible option would appear to be to persuade her client to go ahead with the purchase after all (she might indicate to John that in signing the contract he has given a clear indication of his intent upon which she has relied).

What lessons can Harriet learn? Clearly she should have explained to John the exchange procedure and then, importantly, obtained his prior irrevocable written authority to give the undertaking. If she had done this, John could not have changed his mind at the last minute.

Question 2

This question is concerned with the variation of a contract between exchange and completion. Many conveyancers in this situation would simply do nothing and complete on the earlier date agreed by the clients. Other solicitors might decide to formally record the change of date in correspondence between them. However, there are inherent dangers in this latter approach should the parties fall out and find themselves in a dispute over the terms of the contract (see *McCausland v Duncan Lawrie Ltd* [1997] 1 WLR 38).

In order to satisfy section 2 of the Law of Property (Miscellaneous Provisions) Act 1989 we should ensure that there is a further exchange of documents, signed by Eddie and Tim respectively. This further document would refer to the original contract and the subsequent variation of the completion date. In this way both parties would be protected in the event of any later dispute on the contract.

WIDER READING

- Chapter 6, Abbey, R, and Richards, M, *A Practical Approach to Conveyancing* (Oxford University Press, 2008)

- Section C relating to exchange of contracts in Silverman, F, *Conveyancing Handbook* (The Law Society, 2006)

- Generally—the Solicitors Code of Conduct; in particular professional undertakings

- Ruoff, Theodore, BF and Roper, RB, *The Law and Practice of Registered Conveyancing* (Sweet & Maxwell, 2007)

- Chapter 2 (Buying a house) and Chapter 3 (The Contract), MacKenzie, J-A, and Phillips, M, *Textbook on Land Law* (Oxford University Press, 2008)

WEBSITES FOR FURTHER INFORMATION

- Council of Mortgage Lenders, **<http://www.cml.org.uk>** There is an on-line version of the CML Lenders' Handbook available at this site and it should be referred to in cases of doubt about lenders' requirements.

- House of Lords judgments, **<http://www.parliament.the-stationery-office.co.uk/pa/ld199697/ldjudgmt/ldjudgmt.htm>**. Keep up to date with important new cases.

- Law Commission, **<http://www.lawcom.gov.uk/projects.htm>**. Keep up to date on proposals for law reform.

- Law Society, **<http://www.lawsoc.org.uk/>**.

- Solicitors' Regulation Authority, **<http://www.sra.org.uk>**.

ONLINE RESOURCE CENTRE CASE STUDIES

RESIDENTIAL TRANSACTION CASE STUDY—EXCHANGE OF CONTRACTS

Our clients:
Shilpa Jennings—sale of 19 Minster Yard
Shilpa Jennings and Daniel Rodriguez—purchase of 9 Castle Hill

We act for Shilpa Jennings ('Shilpa') who is selling 19 Minster Yard for £100,000 and Shilpa and Daniel Rodriguez ('Daniel') buying 9 Castle Hill for £200,000. The Standard Conditions of Sale, 4th edn, are adopted in both contracts. We hold on file our sale and purchase contracts duly signed by our clients. We are intending to utilize the deposit on the sale towards the deposit on the purchase. We hold cleared funds from our clients for the balance of the deposit on 9 Castle Hill (£10,000). We are instructed to exchange contracts today.

See the Online Resource Centre for details of the synchronized telephonic exchange.

COMMERCIAL TRANSACTION CASE STUDY—EXCHANGE OF CONTRACTS

Our client: Cambo Ltd—acquisition of 18 Clover Street

We act for Cambo Ltd acquiring the freehold reversion of 18 Clover Street London W2 for £700,000 subject to and with the benefit of two occupational business leases.

Both our client and the seller are ready to proceed. Our client has no related transaction. Each solicitor holds his own client's part of the contract and we have cleared funds for the 10 per cent deposit. Formula B exchange is effected for completion as agreed in one week. We agree to instruct our bank to send a credit transfer of the deposit monies direct to the seller's solicitor's bank.

We prepare appropriate memos for our file recording the details of our conversations and, in our covering letter to the other solicitors, confirm the details of the telephonic exchanges. Please see the Online Resource Centre for details.

11 THE PURCHASE DEED

11.1 INTRODUCTION

The main purpose of the purchase deed is to transfer the legal estate in the property from the seller to the buyer. Whereas the contract sets out what the parties have agreed, the purchase deed actually puts those agreed terms into effect. The transfer of a legal estate is void unless it is made by deed (section 52(1) of the Law of Property Act 1925).

11.2 DRAFTING AND APPROVING THE DEED

The buyer's practitioner will draft the purchase deed once exchange of contracts has taken place. Its contents are governed by the terms of the contract. Sometimes the seller may prefer to draft the purchase deed, e.g. when selling new properties on an estate where uniformity of documentation is important.

The standard procedure is for the buyer's practitioner to submit two copies of the draft purchase deed to the seller's practitioner for approval, and to keep an extra copy on file for reference (in case minor points are raised over the telephone). If the draft is approved as drawn, the top copy can be used as the engrossment. If the seller requires extensive amendments, these should be written clearly in red ink on one copy of the draft, which should be returned to the buyer's practitioner, while a copy of the amended draft is kept on the file for reference. A seller's amendment typically arises where the buyer has overlooked the inclusion of a clause required by the contract, e.g. an indemnity covenant.

11.2.1 TIME LIMITS

If the National Protocol is being used, it provides for the practitioners to submit, approve, and engross the draft purchase deed as soon as possible, and in any event within the time limits laid down by the Standard Conditions. These time limits are set out in Standard Condition (SC) 4.3.2, which of course will apply whenever the contract incorporates the Standard Conditions (even if the Protocol is not being used). A breach of the time limits may be of importance if one of the contracting parties later claims compensation for delay in completion. Under SC 7.3.1 if there is default by the parties in performing their obligations under the contract (e.g. the buyer submits the draft purchase deed out of time) then the party whose total period of default is the greater must pay compensation to the other.

In essence, the time limits are as follows. The draft deed must be submitted at least 12 working days before the completion date; the seller's practitioner then has four working days to approve it; the buyer's practitioner must then send out the engrossment at least five working days before completion. SC 4.3.4 provides that if the period between the date of the contract and the completion date is less than 15 working days, the time limits are reduced pro rata. Fractions of a working day are rounded down (but cannot be less than one working day). For example, if the completion date is 10 working days after exchange, the time limits are reduced by two-thirds (i.e. 10 divided by 15) so that the draft deed must be submitted at least eight working days before the completion date. The Standard Commercial Property Conditions (SCPCs) contain identical time limits (SCPC 6.3).

11.3 FORM OF PURCHASE DEED

For registered land the purchase deed must be in the form prescribed by rule 58 of the Land Registration Rules 2003. For unregistered land there is no prescribed form and the practitioner may use either the traditional form (a conveyance for freeholds; an assignment for leaseholds), or alternatively, where the title is subject to first registration, a Land Registry transfer. The two main Land Registry forms are:

- TR1: Transfer of *whole* of registered land, or *whole* of unregistered land where the title is subject to first registration (see the Online Resource Centre);
- TP1: Transfer of *part* of registered land, or *part* of unregistered land where the title is subject to first registration (see the Online Resource Centre).

Remember that the contents of the purchase deed are governed by the contents of the contract. For example, on a sale of part, if new easements or covenants are to be created, the actual wording of these will have been agreed in the contract and it will simply be a matter of reproducing substantially the same clauses in the purchase deed. Likewise, the description of the property, including reference to any plan, will have been settled at the contract stage and can be copied from the contract.

There may be some clauses in the purchase deed that will not be reproduced word for word from the contract. Reference to them may instead have been made in the Standard Conditions. For example, SC 4.6.5 provides for the seller to give an acknowledgement and undertaking in respect of documents, which the buyer will not receive on completion of an unregistered land transaction. Accordingly the buyer's practitioner will have to draft this clause and best practice would be to consult a precedent. As always, it is important not simply to copy the precedent slavishly; adapt it to suit your needs and make sure it is up to date. Lastly, remember that punctuation is generally not used in the drafting of a deed. The reason for this is to help prevent any fraudulent alteration of the deed (e.g. by inserting a comma) which could change its meaning.

 Key Points Which purchase deed is appropriate?

- If the land being purchased is the whole of a registered title (freehold or leasehold), use Land Registry Form TR1.
- If the land being purchased is part of a registered title (freehold or leasehold), use Land Registry Form TP1.
- If the land being purchased is unregistered, use TR1 (whole) or TP1 (part) (freehold or leasehold).
- If the land being purchased is unregistered and the transaction is complex (e.g. sale of part), it may be easier to use a precedent conveyance (for freehold) or assignment (for leasehold).

- If PRs are transferring land to a beneficiary under a will or intestacy, use an assent (there is a prescribed Form AS1 for registered land (AS3 for part)).
- If PRs are selling land to a third party, use the appropriate Land Registry Form (as above).

11.3.1 PLANS

A plan in a purchase deed is generally only necessary where part of the seller's property is being sold. The plan must be accurate with all colourings and markings correctly made, and it must be tightly bound into the engrossed deed. Metric measurements must be used on the plan (Unit of Measurement Regulations 1995 (SI 1995/1804)). The verbal description of the property in the main body of the document should naturally refer to any plan. The plan should be to a stated scale and must not be merely for identification purposes.

If any discrepancy arises between the plan and the verbal description in the deed, it is a matter of construction as to which should prevail. If the plan is described as being 'for identification purposes only' then the verbal description prevails. If the property is 'more particularly delineated or described' on the plan then the plan will prevail (see *Neilson v Poole* (1969) 20 P & CR 909).

11.4 EXECUTION OF PURCHASE DEED

In order to transfer the legal estate the seller must always execute the purchase deed (section 52(1) of the Law of Property Act 1925). However, the buyer need only execute the deed if the buyer is either making a declaration (e.g. as to co-ownership), or entering into new obligations (e.g. giving the seller an indemnity covenant, or agreeing new covenants on a sale of part).

If the buyer has to execute the deed as well, it is good practice for the buyer to do so first, before sending it across for the seller to execute. This saves time, but the prudent seller will also be disinclined to part with an executed deed before the money is actually received on completion. In these circumstances, the buyer's practitioner should make it clear that the buyer has executed the deed 'in escrow', which means that the deed has no legal effect until it has also been executed by the seller, i.e. this is a condition of the buyer's execution.

As we have seen, the transfer of the legal estate must be by deed and, to be a valid deed, the document must state clearly on its face that it is a deed (Law of Property (Miscellaneous Provisions) Act 1989, section 1). It is no longer necessary for a deed to be sealed (although a company may still use its seal), but it must be signed by the necessary parties in the presence of a witness, and delivered. Although the deed takes effect on delivery, the word 'delivered' is not necessary in the attestation clause. A typical attestation clause for execution by an individual would read as follows:

Signed as a deed by [full name of seller]

in the presence of

[signature, name and address of witness]

A typical attestation clause for execution by a limited company would read as follows:

Executed as a deed by ABC Ltd

[Signature]...Director of the above-named company

[Signature]...Secretary of the above-named company

All parties who execute the deed should also sign any plan. This is an acknowledgement that the plan is an integral part of the document.

Key Points Execution of purchase deed

- The seller always executes the deed.
- The buyer need only execute the deed if it contains new obligations or declarations.
- The buyer often executes the deed first 'in escrow'.
- The parties who execute the deed should also sign any plan attached to the deed.

11.5 ADVISING THE CLIENT

If you send the purchase deed to the client for signature and return, your covering letter should explain the purpose and contents of the document and contain clear instructions as to its execution. Ideally the letter should also specify a date by which the signed document should be returned to you and request that the client leaves the document undated (it is dated on actual completion). Many practitioners write in pencil at the top, 'do not date'.

Inform the client that the witness to the client's signature should be independent from the client (e.g. not the signatory's spouse or another party to the deed). The witness should sign, and then write his or her address and occupation below. If the witness's signature is illegible the full name should also be written in block capitals. If seeing the client in person, it is quite in order for the solicitor to witness the client's signature after explaining the purpose and contents of the deed.

SELF TEST QUESTIONS

1. The traditional form of purchase deed in relation to the acquisition of an unregistered freehold title is

   (a) A transfer

   (b) An assignment

   (c) A conveyance

   (d) An assent

2. A transfer of part of registered land contains new restrictive covenants on the part of the buyer and the grant and reservation of new easements in favour of the buyer and seller respectively. The transfer deed should be executed by

   (a) The seller alone

   (b) The buyer alone

   (c) Both the seller and buyer

   (d) The seller, the buyer, and the buyer's mortgagee

3. When drafting the purchase deed the contents of the draft deed are governed primarily by

   (a) The official copies of the seller's title

   (b) The buyer's instructions

   (c) The correspondence between the seller's and buyer's solicitors

   (d) The contract

4. The correct form of Land Registry transfer to use on a purchase of part of unregistered land from an estate owner is

   (a) TR1

   (b) TP1

(c) TR2

(d) TP2

5. On a transfer of part of registered land the solicitor for the transferee may sign the transfer on behalf of the transferee. Is this statement TRUE/FALSE? Please delete the incorrect choice.

SHORT REVISION QUESTIONS

Question 1

Your firm acts for David Hobbs and Stephen Christopher Ingles both of 7 Brookfield Lane, Basingstoke Hants BR1 7JK in their purchase as tenants in common in equal shares of land to the rear of 10 Ellesmere Close, Hereford for £70,000. The land they are buying forms part of a registered title number KM 74859 comprising the whole of 10 Ellesmere Close. The seller is Ingrid Kirsten Smits. Contracts were exchanged last week for completion three weeks today. The contract provides for the grant of easements to your clients and corresponding reservations in favour of Ms Smits. It also provides for the buyers to enter into restrictive covenants with the seller. The contract provides for a full title guarantee and incorporates the Standard Conditions of Sale. Your principal has asked you to deal with the post-contract conveyancing work and has passed you the file. Identify and explain the contents of the purchase deed that would be acceptable to both buyer and seller.

Question 2

Comment on the validity of the execution of the following purchase deeds (you may assume that the signatures are valid).

(a) *Conveyance of freehold land in 1989*:

SIGNED SEALED and	)	
DELIVERED by	)	James Hart
JAMES HART	)	
in the presence	)	
of:	)	

(b) *Transfer of freehold land in 2008*:

Signed as a deed by	)	
Kay Trew	)	Kay Trew
in the presence of:	)	
Signature of witness	)	William Jones
Name	W. JONES	
Address	188 Langdale Road Norwich NT1 4EG	

SUGGESTED ANSWERS TO SELF TEST QUESTIONS

1. The correct answer is (c). There is very little to be said here—this is probably the easiest question in the whole book so no excuses for getting it wrong!

2. The correct answer is (c). The seller should always execute the deed in order to transfer the legal estate. The buyer should also execute the deed where he or she is entering into new obligations, which is the case here. The buyer's mortgagee does not execute the purchase deed.

3. The correct answer is (d). The contract sets out the terms on which the sale will proceed whereas the purchase deed effectively implements them.

4. The correct answer is (b). A traditional conveyance may be used but of those forms listed only the TP1 may be used. This might appear a little odd given that Form TP1 refers in its body to a transfer

of part of *registered* title. However Land Registry is happy to accept a TP1 on a transfer of part of unregistered land as well, if the land comprises part of the land in the previous conveyance to the transferor. Forms TR2 and TP2 relate to transfers by mortgagees under a power of sale. Form TR1 is used on a transfer of whole (registered or unregistered land), not part.

5. The statement is false. Unless the solicitor has been properly appointed as attorney for the transferee, the transfer should be signed by the transferee personally.

SUGGESTED ANSWERS TO SHORT REVISION QUESTIONS

Question 1

The Law of Property Act 1925, section 52(1) provides that in order to transfer the legal estate to the buyer the transfer document must be in the form of a deed. This deed must implement the terms of the contract and will mirror those terms.

As 10 Ellesmere Close has a registered title the relevant purchase deed is a Land Registry transfer, the form of which is prescribed by the Land Registration Rules 2003. The clients are buying part of the land within the registered title of 10 Ellesmere Close and so the appropriate form of transfer is a transfer of part of registered title, namely Land Registry Form TP1 (see the Online Resource Centre). The form should be completed as follows:

online resource centre

Box 1: This can be left blank as stamp duty on the deed was replaced on 1 December 2003 by stamp duty land tax on the transaction.

Box 2: I would insert title number KM 74859 being the title number out of which the property is transferred.

Box 3: This is left blank as there are no other relevant title numbers.

Box 4: I would insert a description of the land being acquired. The description of the land given in the contract should be adequate for this purpose. I must attach a plan showing the land being acquired edged red and 'check' the first square box. The land retained by the seller should also be defined and identified on the plan, as reference to it will be made later in the document (see Box 13 below). The plan should be securely attached to the engrossed transfer.

Box 5: The date is left blank until completion.

Box 6: I would insert the full name of the seller, Ingrid Kirsten Smits.

Box 7: I would insert the full names of my client purchasers, namely David Hobbs and Stephen Christopher Ingles.

Box 8: I would insert my clients' intended address for service for entry on the register. This should be their home address rather than the subject property address. I would therefore insert 7 Brookfield Lane, Basingstoke Hants BR1 7JK. An email address may also be given.

Box 9: This provides that the transferor transfers the subject property to the transferees.

Box 10: Checking the first square box I would insert the consideration of £70,000 in both words and figures.

Box 11: The question tells me that the contract provides for a full title guarantee and so I would check the full title guarantee box.

Box 12: In accordance with my instructions I would indicate that the transferees are to hold the property on trust for themselves as tenants in common in equal shares.

Box 13: The contract provides for the mutual grant and reservation of easements and these must be expressly repeated in the transfer deed. The same applies to the new restrictive covenants. Reference can be made to the subject property (edged red on the plan) and the retained land (edged blue on the plan). The contract incorporates the Standard Conditions of Sale. SC 3.4 provides that where the seller is retaining land near the property, the buyer will have no right of light or air over the retained land. As this applies here, box 13 should include a declaration by the parties in these terms.

Box 14: The transfer will conclude with the attestation provisions, providing for execution by all parties in the presence of a witness. The reason why the transferees must execute the deed is because they are entering into new obligations. The attestation provisions will read 'signed as a deed' to make it clear on the face of the document that it is deed (The Law of Property (Miscellaneous Provisions) Act 1989, section 1(2)).

Question 2

(a) *Conveyance of freehold land in 1989*: The requirement for execution before 31 July 1990 was that a deed should be signed, sealed, and delivered. The wording here indicates an intention that the deed is delivered, and in the absence of any contrary indication, this can be assumed. We are told to assume that James Hart's signature is valid. Although there is no witness to his signature, a witness is not necessary for validity. The problem with this conveyance is that there is no evidence that it has been sealed. Accordingly the conveyance has been invalidly executed and the document is not a deed. The consequence of this is that the legal estate has not been transferred by this conveyance (Law of Property Act 1925, section 52(1)).

(b) *Transfer of freehold land in 2008*: The requirements for execution of a deed on or after 31 July 1990 are:

- that the document must make it clear on its face that it is a deed;

- it must be signed by the necessary parties in the presence of a witness; and

- it must be delivered by the person executing it (there is no requirement for a seal).

(section 1 of the Law of Property (Miscellaneous Provisions) Act 1989)

In this transfer, Kay Trew's signature has been witnessed and the document clearly indicates on the face of it that it is a deed. Although there is no reference to delivery, this can be assumed in the absence of any indication to the contrary. Accordingly, the transfer appears to be validly executed and will be accepted by Land Registry for registration. The legal estate will be transferred on registration.

WIDER READING

- Chapter 7, Abbey, R, and Richards, M, *A Practical Approach to Conveyancing* (Oxford University Press, 2008)

- Section E dealing with Pre-completion including the purchase deed in Silverman, F, *Conveyancing Handbook* (The Law Society, 2006)

- Emmet on Title: Chapters 13–15, 20, and 25

- Ruoff, Theodore, BF and Roper, RB, *The Law and Practice of Registered Conveyancing* (Sweet & Maxwell, 2007)

WEBSITES FOR FURTHER INFORMATION

- Council of Mortgage Lenders, **<http://www.cml.org.uk>**. There is an on-line version of the CML Lenders' Handbook available at this site and should be referred to in cases of doubt about the requirements of the lender in relation to the subject transaction.

- Land Registry, **<http://www.landreg.gov.uk/>**. You can download purchase deeds, e.g. Form TR1, direct from this website.

- Ordnance Survey, **<http://ordnancesurvey.co.uk>**. It might be useful to consult a detailed Ordnance Survey map when drafting descriptions of land in the purchase deed (e.g. sales of part).

- A street map anywhere in the UK, **<http://www.streetmap.co.uk>**.

ONLINE RESOURCE CENTRE CASE STUDIES

RESIDENTIAL TRANSACTION CASE STUDY—THE PURCHASE DEED

Our clients:
Shilpa Jennings—sale of 19 Minster Yard
Shilpa Jennings and Daniel Rodriguez—purchase of 9 Castle Hill

We act for Shilpa Jennings ('Shilpa') who is selling 19 Minster Yard for £100,000 and Shilpa and Daniel Rodriguez ('Daniel') buying 9 Castle Hill for £200,000. The Standard Conditions of Sale, 4th edn, are adopted in both contracts.

Based on the agreed terms in the contract for 9 Castle Hill we have drafted the purchase deed on Land Registry Form TR1 (see Online Resource Centre). We will send this draft in duplicate to the seller's solicitors together with a Completion Information and Requisitions on Title Form (also in duplicate).

COMMERCIAL TRANSACTION CASE STUDY—THE PURCHASE DEED

Our client: Cambo Ltd—acquisition of 18 Clover Street

We act for Cambo Ltd acquiring the freehold reversion of 18 Clover Street London W2 for £700,000 subject to and with the benefit of two occupational business leases.

Based on the agreed terms in the contract for 18 Clover Street we have drafted the purchase deed on Land Registry Form TR1 (see Online Resource Centre). We will send this draft in duplicate to the seller's solicitors for approval.

12 PRE-COMPLETION PROCEDURES

12.1 INTRODUCTION

To make sure you are in command of the process at this crucial stage in a conveyancing transaction you will need to be fully conversant with all aspects of pre-completion searches. The reason for this is really quite obvious; pre-completion searches are a critical part of any property transaction. Indeed the choice of searches and understanding the results of them can be fraught with all sorts of pitfalls for the unwary practitioner. In the first place there is the obvious but well repeated point that with two land law systems, registered and unregistered, there will always be confusion for the ill-prepared about which searches to make. Secondly, there is also the potential for confusion from the dual role of acting for the buyer and the lender at the same time. Thirdly, there is the variety of different but relevant searches that can confuse. The moral is to know your searches and when to use them.

12.2 PRE-COMPLETION PROCEDURES

The flowchart in Figure 12.1 sets out the steps to be taken after exchange and before completion from the perspective of a practitioner acting for a buyer.

The flowchart in Figure 12.2 sets out the steps to be taken after exchange and before completion from the perspective of a practitioner acting for a seller.

12.3 PRE-COMPLETION WHEN ACTING FOR THE BUYER

This is a busy time for the conveyancing practitioner acting for the buyer. Once exchange has taken place an immediate check is required to see if the contractual terms pass an insurance obligation on to the buyer at the time of the formation of a binding agreement. If they do, then insurance arrangements must be made without delay. Requisitions (usually of just a procedural nature rather than in relation to the title) must be issued to the sellers, along with a draft transfer. If the buyer is utilizing mortgage finance, the mortgage deed must

FIGURE 12.1
BUYER

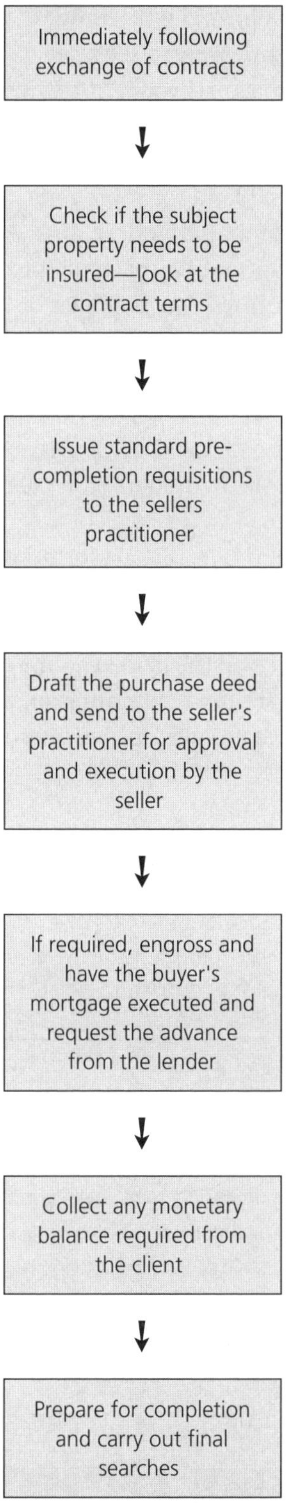

FIGURE 12.2
SELLER

FIGURE 12.1 BUYER	FIGURE 12.2 SELLER
Immediately following exchange of contracts	Immediately following exchange of contracts
↓	↓
Check if the subject property needs to be insured—look at the contract terms	Check if the subject property is mortgaged— if yes obtain redemption figures from all lenders
↓	↓
Issue standard pre-completion requisitions to the sellers practitioner	Reply to standard pre-completion requisitions from the buyers practitioner
↓	↓
Draft the purchase deed and send to the seller's practitioner for approval and execution by the seller	Approve the purchase deed and send to the seller for execution
↓	↓
If required, engross and have the buyer's mortgage executed and request the advance from the lender	Prepare completion statements; one for the seller and one for the buyer's practitioner
↓	↓
Collect any monetary balance required from the client	Prepare for completion and make sure you have the deeds and executed purchase deed
↓	
Prepare for completion and carry out final searches	

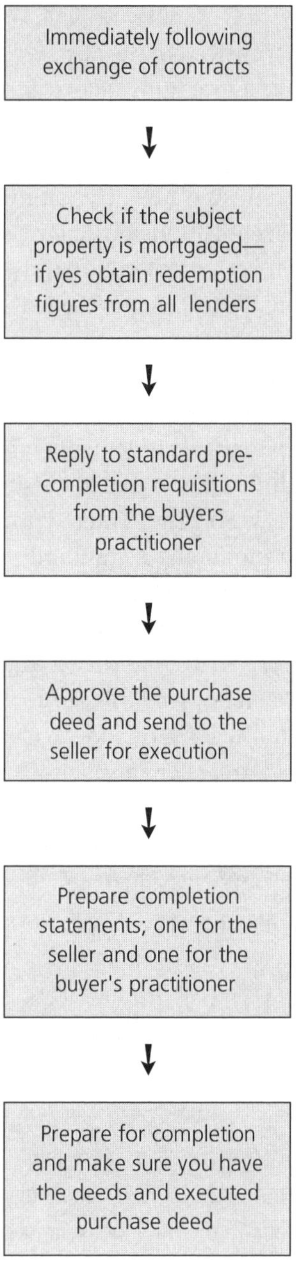

be prepared and executed in readiness for completion. The balance of the purchase price after taking into account the deposit must be calculated and collected from the client in good time for completion. If the buyer is relying on mortgage finance then a clear report on title will be required by the lending institution before it will release the mortgage advance. Lastly, all relevant pre-completion searches must be made and checked to ensure that the buyer is ready to complete by the contractual completion date.

12.3.1 **REQUISITIONS**

A requisition, in the context of conveyancing, is a formal written question that requires a formal written answer. In the past, requisitions on title were raised after exchange because in conveyancing transactions following very traditional pathways, title was not deduced until after exchange. Only encumbrances were disclosed with the draft contract, not the full title. However, modern conveyancing practice has ensured the early disclosure of the full title and certainly this has been the case with registered land for some time. As a consequence the nature of requisitions has changed, and those that are raised after exchange are now standard-form pre-completion requisitions. This format has been adopted in the National Conveyancing Protocol with the use of a form entitled the 'Completion Information and Requisitions on Title' form. Most practitioners have adopted a pre-printed form for requisitions, using either forms pre-printed by themselves, or those issued by law stationers. Alternatively the Protocol Form is used. Whichever form is used, the purpose of it is to sort out completion arrangements rather than raise detailed questions about the title. The Completion Information and Requisitions on Title form used in Protocol cases is a core element of The Law Society's TransAction Scheme.

Apart from producing a standard pre-completion requisitions form, the document was also drawn up to ensure that practitioners remain aware of the danger of giving thoughtless undertakings to discharge mortgages. This kind of trap will arise when an answer is given to a question that is written in such a way so as to place on the person giving the answer a duty beyond that contemplated. Because of this there are many warnings on the form. Indeed, the heading to the form includes a clear warning that replies to two questions (4.2 and 6.2) on the form are treated as a solicitor's undertaking.

 Conduct Point

- Be very careful about how you reply to the Protocol Requisitions form as some answers may amount to enforceable solicitors undertakings. Failure to comply with your answer, e.g. to pay off mortgages, will amount to a breach of the Code of Conduct for solicitors 2007, R.10.05.

 Key Points Acting for the buyer

- When acting for buyer and lender together and if purchasing registered land, apply for a Land Registry search in the name of the lender only; in this way the buyer will also obtain the benefit of the search priority protection.

- When buying from a company consider the necessity of a company search to check on the continuing ability of the vendor company to sell.

- Do not get confused about what search is required:

For registered land:

(a) OS1 (buying the whole title), OS2 (buying part of the title);

(b) K16 land charges bankruptcy search against the buyer, if you are also acting for a lender;

(c) company search if buying from a company.

For unregistered land:

(a) K15 full land charges search against past and present estate owners, post- 1925;

(b) K16 land charges bankruptcy search against the buyer if you are also acting for a lender;

(c) company search if buying from a company.

- If buying unregistered land, try to get pre-root title details for your land charges search or all old land charge search results.

12.4 PRE-COMPLETION WHEN ACTING FOR THE SELLER

When the seller has a mortgage on the title then there is one particularly important pre-completion step, i.e. the necessity to obtain redemption figures for all outstanding mortgages on the title so as to ensure that the property can be sold free of mortgage. (It is also sensible at the same time to ask for a daily rate of interest charged by the lender so that if there is any delay in redeeming the mortgage, fresh figures will not be required for a short delay as the additional interest due can be calculated by reference to the daily rate.)

Furthermore, if the seller is selling through an estate agency, once contracts have been exchanged there is the question of who is to deal with the estate agents' commission account. In many cases the agents will submit their commission account to you on exchange. When you receive it, it is best simply to advise the agents that you will take your client's instructions on the account. In this way the agents will not be in a position to assert that anything you have written should be interpreted as an undertaking to pay their account.

The seller's practitioner must ensure that the purchase deed, which is usually prepared by the buyer, is acceptable and complies with the terms of the contract. He or she must also ensure that it is signed by the seller (and witnessed) in readiness for completion. It is also prudent to prepare Form DS1 (charge release form) in readiness for completion.

 Key Points Acting for the seller

- Where the title is subject to a mortgage, obtain redemption figures immediately after exchange.

- If the title is registered, ensure Form DS1 (or, if applicable, END 1) is prepared before completion, or take a copy of the charges register, to ensure the necessary details of the registered charge can be entered on the form to be sealed by the lender after completion.

- If the title is leasehold, make sure you get all up-to-date receipts and demands relating to ground rent and service charge payments (including buildings insurance premiums) for apportionment, and check that the last receipt for ground rent is clear, i.e. that there are no alleged outstanding breaches of covenant.

12.5 PRE-COMPLETION SEARCHES

Pre-completion searches are made to ensure that the information with regard to the title supplied prior to exchange remains the same up to completion. So in the case of registered land the search will refer to the date of the copy registers supplied by the seller, namely, the issue date of the official copies from the registry, and will disclose any changes since that time. As to unregistered land, the search may disclose many different types of entry such as any mortgages not detailed in the abstract of title and which have been created as a second or subsequent charge since the seller purchased the property. There is another purpose to these searches and that is to obtain a protective period during which completion and registration can take place and during which the buyer will have priority over anyone else seeking to register an entry against the subject property.

The buyer's practitioner will be the person to carry out pre-completion searches. This is because the buyer (and the buyer's lender) will want to ensure that the title is in order and is free from undisclosed encumbrances and is therefore available to be a security for a loan without restraint. (Of course if the lender is separately represented then the lender's practitioner will carry out all searches on behalf of the lender. Sometimes a lender's practitioner will pass on this obligation to the borrower's practitioner.)

The choice of appropriate pre-completion searches can be resolved by reference to the following decision grid:

Q.1 Is the seller a company?	
Yes Complete a search against the company name at Companies House	No Go to Q.2
Q.2 Is the property registered?	
Yes Complete the appropriate Land Registry search—Go to Q.3	No Complete a Land Charges K15 search against all estate owners from at least the root of title and go to Q.4
Q.3 Is this a sale of the whole of the registered title?	
Yes Complete a Land Registry OS1 search	No It is a sale of part so complete a Land Registry OS2 search
Q.4 Is this a residential purchase with a mortgage from a bank or building society?	
Yes Complete a K16 bankruptcy search against the borrowers	No Go to Q.5
Q.5 Have you advised your client to inspect the property prior to completion	
Yes Go and do something else!	No. This should be done to check the state of the property, whether there any unlawful occupiers etc.

12.5.1 **REGISTERED LAND**

A buyer will be supplied with official copies of the registers of the title of the subject property prior to exchange. A binding agreement will have been put in place for the sale and purchase of the property on the basis of the title disclosed in those official copies. These are dated and timed by Land Registry, and the title is therefore accurate only as at the date and time of the official copy entries. It is imperative that a search is carried out from the date of those official copy title details to see if there have been any entries made after the date of the official copies. Because third party protective entries can be made there may be entries made since the date of the official copy entries that even the seller may not know about.

A Land Registry pre-completion search is important not only for the purpose of revealing the state of the title at the time of the search, but also because it will confirm the state of the title at the point of registration. This will be done as a consequence of priority having been given to the search applicant. The effect of this is that any entry due to be made in the registers of the subject property during the priority period will be postponed in favour of the application to register on behalf of the person making the search. The priority period is 30 working days from the search certificate date. The effect of the priority period is, in effect, to freeze the title and the entries in the registers to those disclosed in the official copies as varied, if at all, in the search result, but only until the expiry of the priority period (see section 72 of the Land Registration Act 2002).

The person named on the search application is the person entitled to priority. The position is complicated because most buyers proceed on the basis of a mortgage so that the mortgagee will also require priority protection. To avoid the necessity of making two searches, one for the buyer and the other for the lender, a search is made in the name of the lender, and the buyer takes advantage of the lender's priority period. Accordingly, where a practitioner acts for the buyer and lender, the Land Registry search should always be in the name of the lender (Land Registration Rules 2003 (SI 2003/1417), rule 151).

There are several types of Land Registry search forms, including those described below.

Form OS1, search of the whole of a title

This search is the standard pre-completion search affording the searcher priority when the whole of the registered title is being purchased, mortgaged, or leased. A 'search from date' must be stated, being the date of the official copies supplied by the seller. There is also the option to insert 'FR' instead of a date, and this option will arise for a pending first registration search.

Form OS2, search of part of a title

This search is used when the subject property forms part of a larger title from which it is being sold. In many respects it is the same as an OS1 search save that it does not relate to the whole of the title. Because of this difference, practitioners must remember not only to describe the subject property carefully in the search, but also to describe it in one of two alternative ways. The search of part must describe the subject property either by reference to a plan attached to the search request, or by a plot number shown on an estate plan which has been given prior approval by Land Registry (an estate plan will normally be used on the sale of new properties within a large estate). If the search is to be accompanied by a plan it must be submitted in duplicate, and best practice dictates that the plan should be to scale and should clearly mark the subject property.

Form OS3, non-priority searches

Forms OS1 and OS2 exist for the benefit of a person or company that (for valuable consideration and at arm's length) is buying, leasing, mortgaging, or converting to commonhold all or some of a registered title. The forms cannot be used in other circumstances. Accordingly, an OS3 search should be used in cases other than these. For example, a lender, pursuant to its power of sale, which is selling the mortgaged property, should make an OS3 Land Registry search to ascertain the existence or not of any subsequent mortgages on the title. Similarly, a buyer of an equitable interest in the subject property will also wish to make a final search and, because of the nature of the interest being purchased, Form OS3 must be used as the other searches relate to legal estates (see rule 155 of the Land Registration Rules 2003). In cases where this search is used, the search result will disclose entries subsequent to the official copies in the possession of the searcher, but it will not give any priority to that searcher.

Form HR3, mortgagee search

Where, as a consequence of the default of the borrower, a lender wishes to enforce its rights as a mortgagee of a home, it must first serve notice of the action on any non-owning spouse or a party to a civil partnership union who has registered a protective entry on the title in respect of rights of occupation. The search discloses whether any notice or caution is registered to protect a spouse's or civil partner's right of occupation under the Family Law

Act 1996, the Matrimonial Homes Acts 1967 or 1983, or the Civil Partnership Act 2004. It is possible for entries to have been made of which the lender is unaware (e.g. a notice), and in these circumstances the mortgagee can make a search to update the title utilizing Form HR3, which will disclose homes rights registrations. (A caution would exist to protect entries made before 13 October 2003 under legislation prior to the Land Registration Act 2002.)

12.5.2 **UNREGISTERED LAND**

When dealing with unregistered land, the most critical pre-completion search is made in the Central Land Charges Register (CLCR). Full searches in this register are only necessary when dealing with unregistered land and are completely irrelevant so far as registered land is concerned. The correct search form is Form K15 (not to be confused with a mere bankruptcy search, also sent to this registry, which is K16). Searches can be submitted to the registry either by post, online via Land Registry Direct or the NLIS, or by fax, and they can also be requested over the telephone. The search result confers a priority period of 15 working days on the searcher/applicant. Accordingly, if completion takes place during this period, the searcher/applicant will take free of any entries placed on the register between the date of the search and the completion date, on the proviso that completion did indeed take place within the priority period. (You should note that it is not necessary to apply for first registration of title within the search priority period; the time limit is simply two months from the completion date: see section 6(4) of the Land Registration Act 2002.) Applicants can now ask for search results to be issued electronically. No paper certificate is issued. A result in PDF (electronic form) format is issued instead.

The Central Land Charges Register is a computer database of the names of estate owners and any charges registered against particular estate owners' names. Applicants must therefore list the names of estate owners disclosed in the abstract or epitome of title for land charge search purposes. If the abstract or epitome includes search results against listed names then a fresh search will not normally be required. Land charges are classified into six categories, each of which is labelled by a letter. Some of these categories have sub-categories. For example *Class C* comprises four sub-divisions and contains many of the most important land charges encountered in practice of which the following two appear regularly:

Class C(i) (Land Charges Act 1972, section 2(4)(i)). This is the first of the more commonly-encountered entries and relates to the registration of a *puisne* mortgage. This is a legal charge that does not have protection by the deposit of the title deeds. This situation will arise in unregistered land where this mortgage is a second legal charge.

Class C(iv) (Land Charges Act 1972, section 2(4)(iv)). This is an estate contract. It is commonly encountered in practice as it affords protection in relation to contracts made by estate owners (sellers), or others entitled to take a conveyance (buyers), where the contract relates to the conveying or creation of a legal estate. Accordingly, if a binding contract is made either party can register this protective entry, although in practice it is usually the buyer who will seek protection. This will be the case particularly if completion is delayed or is contractually a long time off, or if the buyer does not trust the seller. Equally, if the seller has cause to mistrust the buyer a protective registration is possible. A conditional contract is registrable even though the condition remains outstanding and unfulfilled at the date of registration of the estate contract (see *Haslemere Estates Limited v Baker* [1982] 1 WLR 1109).

Other classes commonly encountered include:

Class D(ii) (Land Charges Act 1972, section 2(5)(ii)). This registration covers restrictive covenants created after 1925, other than restrictive covenants in a lease or pre-1926 restrictive covenants. Lease covenants are not registrable because their enforceability will depend on the law relating to covenants in landlord and tenant terms. Freehold, pre-1926 restrictive covenants cannot be protected by this registration, as the traditional doctrine of notice will apply.

Class F (Land Charges Act 1972, section 2(7)). This class arose from the provisions of the Family Law Act 1996 relating to a spouse's right of occupation, i.e. matrimonial home rights. Civil partnership unions are now covered by similar legislation with comparable rights of occupation. Where there is a non-owning spouse or partner in occupation, that spouse or partner can register a Class F charge to protect a right of occupation, to protect his or her homes rights. Failure to register will mean that the occupying spouse or partner loses all protection against a buyer for value of the home in question.

12.5.3 NAMES AND SEARCHES

online resource centre

A land charges search should be made against the seller and all estate owners disclosed in the abstract or epitome of title, and diligent practice dictates that the search is made against all estate owners since 1925. The search will also need to mention the period of years of ownership for each estate owner, together with an indication of the county in which the property is located. County names required by the search should be correctly entered, and former county details should be stated: e.g. if a property was formerly in the county of Middlesex, this should be mentioned as well as the 'new' county location. This applies to several 'new' counties, such as Cumbria. With regard to London, parts of Greater London were previously in outlying counties, i.e. not actually part of an administrative area of London such as the London County Council, and became part of the (now defunct) Greater London Council in 1965. These former details should always be mentioned in the search request.

It is possible that there may be an entry on the register against a previous owner not known to the buyer as the period of ownership was before the root of title. If the root of title in the contract is a conveyance to the seller 16 years ago, the buyer will see just one deed, i.e. that conveyance, and can only search against one name, that of the seller.

The unsatisfactory point here is that the buyer will be bound by prior entries against previous owners but will be unable to call for pre-root title details (under section 198 of the Law of Property Act 1925 the buyer is deemed to have notice of all such registrations even though they are undiscoverable). It is possible that compensation may be available for an undiscoverable and adverse land charge under section 25 of the Law of Property Act 1969. If the buyer had no knowledge of the charge, the charge was registered against an owner not disclosed in the abstract or epitome of title (and the root of title was at least 15 years' old), the buyer may seek compensation from public funds. (The buyer may be able to take action against the seller if the seller knew about the encumbrances but did not disclose them; see the seller's duty of disclosure in 3.27.)

To avoid this problem a practitioner should requisition:

1. title from 1925, or

2. names of title owners from 1925, or

3. all previous land charge search results that are with the deeds.

Searches carried out on behalf of previous buyers may be relied on, and it may be possible to construct the preceding chain of ownership for reassurance in this way.

Best practice is to quote the name (or names if more than one version) that appears in the title deed by which the estate owner took the title (see *Standard Property Investment plc v British Plastics Federation* (1985) 53 P & CR 25, and *Diligent Finance Co Ltd v Alleyne* (1972) 23 P & CR 346). Accordingly, great care must be taken as to the accuracy of names, and practitioners should ensure that all former names, if known, are searched against. This will apply to companies and to individuals.

12.5.4 EFFECT OF NON-REGISTRATION

The effect of non-registration varies with the different registers as follows:

A, B, C(i), C(ii), C(iii) and F	Void as against a purchaser/lessee/mortgagee for valuable consideration of the subject property or an interest in it unless registered (Land Charges Act 1925, s 4).
C(iv) and D	Void as against a purchaser *of a legal estate* in the land for money or money's worth unless registered (ibid).
Pending action	Void as against a buyer for valuable consideration if not registered (ibid, s 5).
Writ or order	Void as against a buyer for valuable consideration if not registered (ibid, s 6).
Arrangement deed	Void as against a buyer for valuable consideration if not registered (ibid, s 7).

12.6 ACTING FOR THE LENDER

online resource centre

Title searches for mortgagees are the same as those for a buyer: OS1 and OS2 searches for registered land, and K15 searches for unregistered land, and company searches if appropriate. Lenders will also require a bankruptcy only search against all proposed borrowers. These are made on Form K16. All registered bankruptcy petitions and orders will be disclosed. Clearly, if an entry is disclosed, the lender must be informed without delay, and the mortgage will almost certainly not proceed. It is critical that the full names of the borrowers be stated precisely, and all former names and aliases must also be given. Results can be awkward in that sometimes entries will be disclosed against a surname only. If this happens consideration must be given to supporting information, such as the address, and, if necessary, an office copy (an official copy) should be sought on Form K19. It is appropriate, when you are completely satisfied that the entry does not apply, to certify for the lender on the search result that the entry does not relate to the borrower. In the majority of commercial loans the lender is usually separately represented and as such the lender's solicitors will make their own final searches.

12.7 BUYING FROM A COMPANY

If the seller is a limited company there will be an additional search that will apply to both registered and unregistered land. Where a company is selling, a search of the companies register at Companies House should be carried out. Company information is available online at <http://www.companieshouse.gov.uk>. In large-scale commercial conveyancing transactions, two company searches will be made; one immediately after exchange and the second on the morning of completion.

The Land Registration Act 2002 is quite clear in that it states that the grant of a legal charge is a registrable disposition (section 27(2)(f)). It also states that the effect of non-registration at the registry of a mortgage means that it is void and takes effect as a mere contract made for valuable consideration to create the mortgage (section 7(2)(b)). It is therefore clear that no company charge whatever, be it fixed or floating, will affect a buyer unless it is protected by some form of registration at Land Registry. A company search will still be necessary because a buyer may wish to be sure that the company still subsists and has not been struck off the register, e.g. for failing to file returns. If it has been struck off the companies register then the company ceases to exist in law and cannot therefore enter into a deed, transfer, or conveyance. If the company is subject to winding-up proceedings, these will be shown by a company search.

In the case of unregistered land the company search is very important. The search will reveal subsisting floating charges, specific (or fixed) charges created before 1 January 1970, and the commencement of any winding-up proceedings. All three are of material importance to a buyer and, if disclosed in the search result, would clearly be adverse. No purchaser should proceed until the seller has in the appropriate way shown how and when the adverse entry is to be dealt with. Bearing in mind that any disposition by a company subject to winding-up proceedings is void (Insolvency Act 1986, section 127), it will be appreciated just how important a company search can be.

12.8 PHYSICAL INSPECTION OF THE SUBJECT PROPERTY

Lastly, the subject property should be inspected prior to completion. The reason for this is primarily to check on exactly who is in occupation. The existence of a third-party occupant might amount to an overriding interest to which the purchase would be subject. The contract for sale may include a list of items included in the sale, or there could be items listed in replies to enquiries. In either case the buyer will want to be sure that the listed items actually exist and are within the subject property.

Finally, when the subject property is a new property, just prior to completion it must be examined to list any problems that need to be dealt with by the developer. A 'snagging list' should be compiled by the buyer as soon as the developer asserts that the property is ready for completion. This will be done by revisiting the property with or without a surveyor, and listing all the outstanding defects that need to be remedied by the seller.

 Key Points Pre-completion searching

- Always make sure the following searches are carried our before completion—

For registered land:

(a) OS1 (buying the whole title), OS2 (buying part of the title);

(b) K16 land charges bankruptcy search against the buyer, if you are also acting for a lender;

(c) company search if buying from a company;

(d) physical inspection of the property.

For unregistered land:

(a) K15 full land charges search against past and present estate owners, post-1925;

(b) K16 land charges bankruptcy search against the buyer if you are also acting for a lender;

(c) company search if buying from a company;

(d) physical inspection of the property.

12.9 COMPLETION STATEMENTS

Completion statements are prepared to show a client how much is required to complete or how much will be available on completion or how much is needed on completion. In detail they are as follows:

1. A completion statement prepared by the seller's practitioner for the seller. The purpose of this statement is to show the seller how much will be left over on completion by way of

the net proceeds of sale, either to be applied towards an allied purchase, or as the simple net proceeds of sale.

2. A completion statement prepared by the seller's practitioner for the buyer's practitioner. The purpose of this statement is to show to the buyer how much is required to be paid over at completion. Clearly if this is only the balance of the purchase price after taking into account the deposit then a full-scale statement is unnecessary. These statements can be quite complex and lengthy when the subject property is leasehold. In these circumstances the statement will have to include apportionments of monies paid in advance, or still outstanding and due to be paid. This could include ground rent, insurance payments, and service charges.

online
resource
centre

3. A completion statement prepared by the buyer's practitioner for the buyer. The purpose of this statement is to show the buyer how much will be needed to complete the purchase of the subject property. This will normally be prepared and issued shortly after exchange so that the buyer can put his or her practitioner in funds in good time for completion. If the figures are to be fully comprehensive, a bill of costs should accompany this statement. Failure to use cleared funds is when completion a breach of the Solicitors' Accounts Rules.

SELF TEST QUESTIONS

1. You are buying for a client a commercial unit in Hackney in the Centre of London. It is registered and your client is a company that is a cash buyer. Which of the following searches will you make before completion

   (a) Local land charge search

   (b) Land charges search

   (c) Land Registry search

   (d) Bankruptcy search

2. You client has instructed you to complete a purchase of a new residential flat in a newly erected block in the centre of Liverpool. You have exchanged and completion is next week. The title to the whole block is registered under title number LPL 362638 and our client is a cash buyer. Which of the following searches will you make before completion

   (a) OS1

   (b) K15

   (c) OS2

   (d) K16

3. You act for the buyer of an unregistered title in North Yorkshire. You have just completed your final land charges search and this reveals a c(i) entry affecting the title. Which of the following should you do

   (a) Identify this as a limited owner's charge and ask the seller to make arrangements to pay off the outstanding tax

   (b) recognize this as a general equitable charge and ask the seller to clarify the nature of the charge

   (c) identify this as an estate contract and ask the seller to explain how the entry relates and how it will be removed

   (d) recognize this as a *puisne* mortgage (a second charge) and ask the seller to confirm that it will be discharged on completion

4. If a lease is granted, containing restrictive covenants for the lessee to perform, and the lease is unregistered then you should register them as a D(ii) land charge to ensure their enforceability. Is this statement TRUE/FALSE? Please delete the incorrect choice.

5. The priority period for a Land Registry search result is 30 days. Is this statement TRUE/FALSE? Please delete the incorrect choice.

SHORT REVISION QUESTIONS

Question 1

You are acting for Brian Deepdale on a purchase of registered land from the seller John Smith next Thursday. You have completed your Land Registry OS1 search and the result has just arrived. The search result is attached (see Figure 12.3). Is it acceptable? If not please say why not and what should be done, if anything.

Question 2

You are acting on a purchase of unregistered land being The High Street Wimble Worcestershire DY41 5XH and you are due to complete next Thursday. You have completed your Land Charges K15 search and the result has just arrived. The search result is attached (see Figure 12.4). Is it acceptable? If not please say why not and what should be done, if anything.

Question 3

You are acting on the sale of a commercial property. Completion is due tomorrow. The title is in two parts, both registered freehold, but one part is a part of title sale while the other is a sale of the whole title. The latter title is subject to one mortgage but the former is not subject to any encumbrance other than an occupational 15 year lease with 11 year still unexpired. The buyer is aware of the lease as it was disclosed in the contract and is to take over the receipt of the rent at completion. Your Principal has asked you to list the documents to be handed over at completion. Please list the relevant items.

SUGGESTED ANSWERS TO SELF TEST QUESTIONS

1. The correct selection is (c). As the property is registered and your client is a company the only pre-completion search listed that will apply is a Land Registry search. A local search is carried out before exchange, a land charges search is only necessary for unregistered land and your client is a company so the bankruptcy search is inappropriate.

2. The correct selection is (c). As the property is registered and your client is buying a new flat forming part of the seller's title, the only pre-completion search listed that will apply is an OS2 being a search of part. The remaining searches are inappropriate because an OS1 is a search of whole (and your client is only buying part), a K15 is only relevant to unregistered land, and a K16 is a bankruptcy search (used by lenders to ensure a borrower is solvent) that is not required as your client is a cash buyer.

3. The correct answer is (d). A c(i) entry relates to unregistered title second mortgages that cannot be protected by the deposit of title deeds, the first lender being in possession of them.

4. The statement is false. This registration covers restrictive covenants created after 1925, other than restrictive covenants in a lease (or a pre-1926 restrictive covenant). Lease covenants are not registrable as D(ii)'s because their enforceability depends upon landlord and tenant law and the enforcement of covenants between such parties.

5. This statement is false. The priority period for a registered land search is 30 *working* days. Weekends and bank holidays are therefore excluded from the days counted for priority purposes.

FIGURE 12.3 LAND REGISTRY SEARCH RESULT

Official Certificate of the Result of Search of Whole	HM Land Registry	Form 94D
Official search no. 097—A4-FF	Certificate date [yesterday] Priority Period began at 16:24:45	Priority Period expires on [30 working days time] at midnight but see the note below

Particulars of search as supplied		
Title Number	WCS 1425778	
Applicant(s)	Brian Deepdale	

Result

It is certified that the official search applied for has been made with the following result:

Since 5 August 2007 a new edition of the register has been opened and an official copy dated 12 August 2007 and timed at 15:04:22 showing the entries subsisting then is enclosed. The result is subject to such entries. If further official search applications are made the "search from" date to be quoted must be the date of the official copy.

UNILATERAL NOTICE dated the [seven days ago] in respect of an agreement dated [1 year ago] and made between (1) John Smith and (2) Land Buying Plc

BENEFICIARY: Land Buying Plc of 1 Main Road Bury Lancs.

END OF RESULT		
Note: To be sure to obtain priority for your application you should deliver it to the proper office by 12.00 (noon) on the date when priority expires.		
Your reference: RM505428	Key Number 1028864	Any enquiries concerning this certificate to be addressed to BIRKENHEAD ROSEBRAE DLR
RICHARDS ABBEY &CO DX1212 CHANCERY LANE/LONDON		ROSEBRAE COURT WOODSIDE FERRY APPROACH BIRKENHEAD MERSEYSIDE CH41 6 DU Tel No: (0151) 472 6666

SUGGESTED ANSWERS TO SHORT REVISION QUESTIONS

Question 1

There are two entries disclosed in the search result. The first is really procedural in that a new edition of the register has been opened and a new set of official copies of the title showing the entries subsisting has been disclosed. The result is subject to such entries. An immediate comparison of the new entries

FIGURE 12.4 LAND CHARGES SEARCH RESULT

LAND CHARGES ACT, 1972	FORM K18
CERTIFICATE OF THE RESULT OF SEARCH	
PARTICULARS SEARCHED	
COUNTY	WORCESTERSHIRE, HEREFORDSHIRE AND WORCESTER
CERTIFICATE DATE	PROTECTION ENDS ON
[yesterday]	[15 working days ahead]

NAME(S)	Particulars of charge	PERIOD	Fees £
ALAN JOHN * WILBERFORCE *	NO SUBSISTING ENTRY	1977–1988	1.00
CHRISTINE MARY * WILBERFORCE *	NO SUBSISTING ENTRY	1977–1988	1.00
ANNE * PONSONBY-SMYTHE *	(1) D(ii) NO 10582 DATED 2 JUNE 1988 (2) THE HIGH STREET DY41 5XH WIMBLE WORCESTERSHIRE	1988–1989	1.00
THOMAS ANTHONY * BROWN *	(4) C(i) NO 10452 DATED 7 MAY 2000 (5) 1 THE HIGH STREET DY41 5XH WIMBLE WORCESTERSHIRE	1989–2007	1.00
PAULENE ANN * BROWN *	(1) C(1) NO 10452 DATED 7 MAY 2000 (2) 1 THE HIGH STREET DY41 5XH (3) WIMBLE WORCESTERSHIRE	1989–2007	1.00
- - - - - - - - - - - END OF SEARCH - - - - - - - - - - -			

APPLICANTS REFERENCE	KEY NUMBER	AMOUNT DEBITED
RMA505447	107552	£ 5.00
RICHARDS ABBEY & CO. DX1212 CHANCERYLANE/LONDON	Please address any enquiries to HM LAND REGISTRY Land Charges Department Plumer House Crownhill Plymouth PL6 5HY DX no 8249 Plymouth (3) TEL 01752 636666 or 636601 FAX 01752 636699	

should be made of the old set originally supplied by the seller. If they are the same then nothing more needs to be done. If there are any changes these must be referred to the seller for clarification and if necessary for removal at the seller's expense.

The second entry is more problematic. This appears to be a unilateral or non-consensual notice probably registered by a claimant against the seller as a protective entry, possibly for the protection of a contract involving the seller. The entry should be immediately referred to the seller for clarification and for the immediate removal of the entry at the seller's expense.

Question 2

The result discloses four estate owners. The first two AJ and CM Wilberforce show no subsisting entries and as such may be safely ignored as being of no consequence. However the following three estate owners disclose entries. A Ponsonby-Smythe has a D(ii) restrictive covenants entry affecting the subject property. This registration covers restrictive covenants created after 1925, and not restrictive covenants in a lease or pre-1926 restrictive covenants. You need to check if the entry relates to covenants disclosed in the title on or around the 2nd June 1988. If the entry ties up with disclosed covenants there is nothing more to do. If not you need to require the seller to disclose details and to check that they are not onerous. Immediate reference to the seller of the land charge entry is imperative. The final two entries relate to a Ci entry, and you need to recognize this as a *puisne* mortgage (a second charge of unregistered land). This is a legal charge that does not have protection by the deposit of the title deeds. You will have to ask the seller to confirm that it will be discharged on completion.

Question 3

The documents to be handed over are:

1. Transfer (covering both titles but with a scale plan for the transfer of part).

2. Counterpart lease and any supporting deeds such as licences to assign etc.

3. Authority from the seller to the lessee for the payment of future rents to the buyer.

4. Any old land or charge certificates to be kept with pre-registration deeds and documents.

5. Form DS1 for the mortgage or an undertaking in the Law Society format. If an END is to be employed then an END undertaking is required.

6. Releases for keys and or deposits paid to the agents and or at the time of exchange.

WIDER READING

- Chapter 8, Abbey, R., and Richards, M, *A Practical Approach to Conveyancing* (Oxford University Press, 2008)

- Sections E and F dealing with pre-completion and completion matters, Silverman, F, *Conveyancing Handbook* (The Law Society, 2006)

- Emmet on Title:

  - Searches before completion generally—Chapter 8, part 1;

  - Position Pending Completion—Chapter 6;

- For more detail on the changes introduced by the Land Registration Act 2002 see Abbey, R, and Richards, M, *Blackstone's Guide to the Land Registration Act 2002* (Oxford University Press, 2002)

  - Chapter 2 (buying a house); Chapter 4 (unregistered land); Chapter 5 (registered land), MacKenzie, J-A, and Phillips, M, *Textbook on Land Law* (Oxford University Press, 2008)

WEBSITES FOR FURTHER INFORMATION

- Association of British Insurers, **<http://www.abi.org.uk/>**. Remember insurance may be required from the time of exchange. Look at the contract terms to check.

- Bank of England, **<http://www.bankofengland.co.uk/>**. Details of how the bank operates.

- Companies House, **<http://www.companieshouse.gov.uk/>**. You can make on-line pre-completion searches at Companies House. They will be vital in unregistered transactions when the seller is a corporation.

- Council of Mortgage Lenders, **<http://www.cml.org.uk>**. There is an on-line version of the handbook available at this address and should be referred to in cases of doubt about the requirements of the lender at this stage of the transaction.

- Land Registry, **<http://www.landreg.gov.uk/>**. The location for pre-completion registered land searches.

- Land Registry internet access, **<http://www.landregistrydirect.gov.uk>**. The location for on-line pre-completion registered land searches.

- Location statistics, **<http://www.upmystreet.com/>**.

- National Land Information Service, **<http://www.nlis.org.uk>**. Almost all pre-completion searches can be made on-line through one of the service providers authorized by the NLIS.

- A street map anywhere in the UK, **<http://www.streetmap.co.uk>**.

ONLINE RESOURCE CENTRE CASE STUDIES

RESIDENTIAL TRANSACTION CASE STUDY—PRE COMPLETION SEARCHES

Our clients:
Shilpa Jennings—sale of 19 Minster Yard Blakey
Shilpa Jennings and Daniel Rodriguez—purchase of 9 Castle Hill Blakey

We act for Shilpa Jennings who is selling 19 Minster Yard Blakey for £100,000 and Shilpa and Daniel Rodriguez who are buying 9 Castle Hill Blakey for £200,000. Pre-completion search results have been obtained for the property being purchased and these can be seen on the Online Resource Centre. We will need to consider these results and decide if there are any entries in the searches where we need to obtain further details.

COMMERCIAL TRANSACTION CASE STUDY—PRE COMPLETION SEARCHES

Our client: Cambo Ltd—acquisition of 18 Clover Street London W2

Timothy Wainwright and his family have run a successful wholesale clothing business for many years. Timothy has decided to sell the business and enter the world of property investment. He has formed a company called Cambo Ltd in which he, his wife, and their three sons are all shareholders. Cambo Ltd has agreed to buy 18 Clover Street London W2 for £700,000 subject to and with the benefit of two occupational business leases. Pre-completion search results have been obtained for the property being purchased and these can be seen on the Online Resource Centre. We will need to consider these results and decide if there are any entries in the searches where we need to obtain further details.

13 COMPLETION

13.1 INTRODUCTION

Completion is the point when the buyer pays the balance of the purchase price to the seller in exchange for the deeds, executed purchase deed, keys, and, if the contract so provides, vacant possession. In unregistered land the conveyance or assignment constitutes the passing of title of a legal estate and as such this is effectively completion of the transaction in all respects, see *Killner v France* [1946] 2 All ER 83 (subject of course to the requirement to submit the title to Land Registry for first registration).

This is not the exact position in registered land where the passing of title of a legal estate is only really completed with the registration of the buyer as the registered proprietor at Land Registry. On a practical basis, as the buyer has the obligation to register, completion is, to all intents and purposes, at the time the money is handed over in exchange for the transfer (and any supporting deeds such as the original lease in registered leasehold titles). However, practitioners must always remember to proceed with registration without delay, and to do so within their search priority period.

13.2 THE HOW, WHERE, AND WHEN FOR COMPLETION

When contracts are exchanged it is usual to insert the completion date in the agreement, there having been prior negotiations between the parties to reach the agreed completion date. It is not unusual to see a completion period of just 14 days or less. The period can be of any reasonable length but, if the Standard Conditions are used and no period is stipulated in the contract, or if the date is overlooked at the time of exchange, Standard Condition (SC) 6.1.1 provides that completion is due on the 20th working day after exchange.

13.2.1 WHEN—THE TIME FOR COMPLETION

The latest time for completion on the completion date must also be negotiated and will figure in almost all conveyancing contracts. Certainly SC 6.1.2 now, in effect, sets a final time of 2pm on the day of completion. It does so by providing that if completion does not take place by that time completion is deemed to be overdue and interest will be payable.

Normally completion will take place at the offices of the practitioner acting for the seller. SC 6.2 provides that completion is to be effected somewhere in England and Wales, being either the offices of the seller's solicitor or at some other place which the seller reasonably specifies. SC 6.1 states that both parties to the contract are to cooperate in agreeing arrangements for completing the contract. Rarely will the deeds remain with solicitors acting solely for a lender. This will happen if the lender is separately represented, or possibly if the lender has commenced repossession proceedings. In these circumstances completion may have to take place at the lender's solicitors' offices, although efforts should be made to persuade such solicitors to allow the seller's solicitors to deal with completion and redemption together.

13.2.2 HOW—WHEN YOUR CLIENT IS SELLING AS WELL AS BUYING: SYNCHRONIZATION

It is fundamental to a client who is selling and buying, in the absence of any express instructions to the contrary, that the completion of the two transactions be on the same day. In effect the sale must be synchronized with the purchase to enable the net sale proceeds to be applied towards the purchase price. If there is a whole chain of transactions, of which the client's sale and purchase form part, then for much the same reason, all of the transactions in the chain must fall for completion on the same date, with purchase following sale right along the chain.

13.2.3 HOW—THE MECHANICS OF COMPLETION

Completion can be dealt with in various ways: in person, by appointing an agent to complete on your behalf, or through the post. Until the early 1980s most completions were in person. Postal completions will normally prevail in domestic conveyancing cases. In all forms of completion the practitioner for the buyer should pay close attention to the acquisition deed. It should be checked to make sure that it has been properly executed and can be dated with the date of completion. An individual who is selling should have an independent witness to his or her signature. The witness must also sign and put in his name and address. If a company is executing then care should be taken to ensure that one of the two ways of executing a deed by a company is properly effected. (A company can either seal a deed with the company seal, or the deed can be signed by two directors, a director and the secretary, without the seal—see section 36A of the Companies Act 1985 introduced by the Companies Act 1989.) If an attorney has signed, a check should be made to ensure that the deed has been executed in one of the two permissible ways for an attorney (i.e. AB by his attorney CD or CD as attorney for AB).

13.3 DEEDS AND UNREGISTERED LAND

Where there is a sale of part of a title the seller will, if the property is unregistered, retain the deeds. The buyer will want to examine his or her copy deeds against the originals and mark them up at completion as so examined. (The wording is 'examined at the offices of [insert the name and address of the seller's solicitors]', and this is then followed by a signature of the examining practitioner for the buyer, together with a note of his or her firm's name and address, and the date.) In this way the buyer will acquire an examined abstract or epitome of title which will, with the purchase deed, constitute the title deeds for the part sold off. If completion is to take place in person, the buyer will be able to examine the abstract. If there is an agency completion, the agent can examine the abstract. (This will be so in Protocol cases, as the seller agrees to act as the buyer's agent in these circumstances.)

Completion in person will normally be at the offices of the seller's practitioner. As has been noted, SC 6.2 provides that completion is to be effected somewhere in England and

Wales being either at the offices of the seller's solicitor or at some other place which the seller reasonably specifies. SC 6.7 of the 4th edition now states that 'the buyer is to pay the money due on completion by direct credit and, if appropriate, an unconditional release of a deposit held by a stakeholder'. A 'direct credit' is defined in SC 1.1.1(g) as 'a direct transfer of clear funds to an account nominated by the seller's conveyancer and maintained by a clearing bank'. This means that the only method of payment at completion and authorized by the Standard Conditions is by direct electronic bank transfer. As a result unless SC 6.7 is amended no other method of payment, e.g. by a bankers' draft, can be made.

Lastly, when buying a leasehold property, remember to inspect the last receipt for ground rent to make sure it is an unqualified clear receipt. If there is a clear ground rent receipt, you can assume that in the absence of any other information to the contrary, of which you have had notice, there are no subsisting breaches of covenant affecting the subject property, to which the lessor may refer.

13.4 POSTAL COMPLETIONS—COMPLETION AND THE PROTOCOL

Since 1990 The Law Society has tried to urge practitioners, and in particular solicitors, to adopt all the elements of the National Conveyancing Protocol. One such element is the inclusion of The Law Society's Code for Completion. This inclusion underpins the use of postal completions in residential conveyancing transactions.

13.4.1 THE LAW SOCIETY'S CODE FOR COMPLETION BY POST

This is set out in Appendix 4. It is a set of guidance notes and principles that solicitors can adopt in order to arrange completion by post in an orderly and uniform manner across the profession. If the Code is to be used in non-Protocol conveyances, it must be expressly adopted by both sides (preferably in writing), but for Protocol cases the Code will apply unless otherwise agreed. In all cases, if a practitioner considers that to adopt the Code would create a conflict between the interests of the client and the requirements of the Code, then the Code must not be adopted.

The Main Code Provisions:

(a) The crucial element of the Code is that the buyer's solicitor appoints the seller's solicitor as his or her unpaid agent for completion.

(b) The buyer's solicitor must provide full instructions for the 'agent' relating to the buyer's requirements. These instructions should clearly set out for the seller's solicitor what the buyer's solicitor requires him to do and what is to be sent on from the seller to the buyer, after completion has been effected.

(c) The seller's solicitor must confirm instructions from the seller to receive the sale monies and that he has been appointed the authorized agent of any mortgagee authorizing the receipt of monies required to redeem. This latter section was introduced to the Code as a consequence of the decision in *Edward Wong Finance Co Ltd v Johnson, Stokes and Master* [1984] AC 296, PC. This was a Hong Kong case where monies were handed over against an undertaking regarding the forwarding of the deeds and the discharge of the existing charge. Sadly this was a case where the seller's solicitor unlawfully absconded with the completion monies without having paid anything to the lenders. Even though the buyer's solicitors had acted in accordance with the general practice of the legal community within the colony, it was held that they were negligent in the way they arranged completion. To get around the problem the seller must be appointed the mortgagee's agent. In this way, if the same circumstances arose, the mortgagee could not refuse to complete because of the default of its agent. If there is any doubt then we suggest you ascertain the amount required to redeem and on the day of completion send the redemption amount direct to the mortgagee and the balance to the seller's solicitor.

(d) The buyer's solicitor will send the completion monies by bank telegraphic transfer (a CHAPS payment) and on receipt the completion takes place. Until completion has taken place, the seller's solicitor will hold the purchase monies to the order of the buyer's solicitor. At the point of completion the deeds and documents are held by the seller's solicitor as agent for the buyer's solicitor.

(e) That day (i.e. the day of completion), the deeds and documents must be sent to the buyer's solicitor, and once posted properly they are at the buyer's risk.

(f) Adopting the Code involves the giving of a professional undertaking that will be enforced through The Law Society.

(g) The Code can be used only if there is no obvious conflict, but if such conflict exists, the appointment of an agent would be inappropriate.

(h) Lastly, it should be noted that nothing in the Code shall override any rights and obligations of either the seller or the buyer under the terms of the sale contract or otherwise.

13.5 DEALING WITH THE DISCHARGE OF THE SELLER'S MORTGAGE

Conveyancers for both parties to the contract will normally agree the arrangement to apply at completion for the discharge of the seller's mortgage and will do so after exchange, when dealing with post-exchange standard-form requisitions. Indeed, most pre-printed forms of requisitions include a standard question on the mortgage discharge arrangements. Whatever is agreed, these arrangements should cover all the subsisting mortgages on the title and not just the first and most obvious mortgage. Inevitably, where there is a first mortgage and the seller has received instructions to deal with redemption for the lender, sale proceeds will be applied immediately after completion for the purposes of redemption. This being so, the vacating receipt for unregistered mortgages or Form DS1 for a registered charge will not be available on completion. In these circumstances, practitioners must rely on professional (and enforceable) undertakings. Such undertakings must only be taken from solicitors or licensed conveyancers, and not from an unqualified person whose 'undertaking' will of course be unenforceable. A professional body, such as The Law Society, will ensure that the undertaking is complied with. The Law Society has issued a recommended form of undertaking and we endorse its use by practitioners wherever possible. The wording is:

 online resource centre

> In consideration of you today completing the purchase of [insert subject property postal address or description] we hereby undertake to pay over to [insert identity of the lender] the money required to discharge the mortgage/legal charge dated [insert date of mortgage/legal charge] and to forward the receipted mortgage/legal charge/Form DS1 to you as soon as it is received by us from [insert identity of lender].

Remember that a receipted mortgage or legal charge is appropriate for unregistered land, and Form DS1 (or END1, see 13.6) is appropriate for registered land. Thus, you would not refer in your undertaking to Form DS1 on completion of an unregistered land transaction. Similarly, you would not refer to a receipted mortgage or legal charge in a registered land transaction.

A problem arises when the lender is not a member of the Council of Mortgage Lenders. Members will stand by redemption statements issued by them before completion and relied on at completion and which may ultimately prove to be incorrect. In effect this means that a deed of discharge, forming the subject matter of an undertaking, will be issued even if the lender has issued incorrect figures (and therefore has received incorrect redemption monies). This is not the case for non-members, who can disagree over the amount required to redeem even though completion may have already taken place and undertakings issued. In these circumstances actual redemption may need to take place along with completion, probably at the offices of the lender or the offices of the lender's solicitor. A redemption statement should be read carefully to check assumptions made by the lender about payments to be made by the borrower. It might assume that the next instalment due before completion but after the date of the statement will be made. If it does, the seller must make that payment or a shortfall will arise.

Another problem arises out of the decision in *Patel v Daybells* [2000] EGCS 98 (QBD, 19 July 2000). Gray J held that a solicitor could be held to be negligent in relying on a solicitor's undertaking in the style mentioned above. The judge posed three questions. First, does the acceptance of the undertaking involve foreseeable risk? Secondly, could that risk have been avoided? Thirdly, if so, was there an act of negligence in failing to avoid that risk? The judge considered that there was a risk in the industry standard practice of undertakings and that a different form of completion (probably based on attendance) can avoid the risk. Frankly, the decision may be accurate but it is definitely not practical.

The decision would seem to require practitioners to call for the availability of Form DS1 at completion. However, lenders will not provide the form at that time, as they have not yet been paid.

One way to address the difficulty is to ensure that the seller's practitioner is also the agent of the seller's lender. If then the agent fails to redeem by paying over an incorrect amount, the dispute will be between the agent (the seller's practitioner) and principal (the seller's lender), because with this procedure the lender will be bound to redeem. Express appointment as agent by the lender is required, and the buyer's practitioner should ask for a copy of the letter of appointment as confirmation. In practice this is unlikely to be forthcoming and the risks attendant on industry standard completion undertakings for domestic property particularly will remain.

Lastly, a buyer's practitioner needs to exercise special care where the seller has a high value mortgage. In the *Patel* case it was stated that there could be 'exceptional circumstances' where accepting an undertaking at completion was negligent. This could be where the value of the seller's mortgage exceeds the minimum level required for indemnity insurance for solicitors. This is currently £1 million so, if a buyer's practitioner is aware of this situation prevailing, either the cover must be increased, or the seller's solicitors must warrant that the insurance cover exceeds the amount required to redeem (or Form DS1 must be available at completion).

 Conduct Point Undertakings

- Be very careful about how you reply to the Protocol Requisitions form as some answers may amount to enforceable solicitors undertakings. Failure to comply with your answer, e.g. to pay off mortgages, will amount to a breach of the Code of Conduct for solicitors 2007, R.10.05.

13.6 THE ELECTRONIC NOTIFICATION OF DISCHARGE (END)

Land Registry has been developing a scheme with banks and building societies that will make DS1 forms a rarity. It has been using an Electronic Notification of Discharge (END) to replace the DS1. When the lender is satisfied that their charge has been redeemed in full an END is sent to Land Registry over the Land Registry Direct System (by computer).

Practitioners can check if an END has been received by Land Registry by telephone or Land Registry Direct enquiry. There is no charge for this service at present. Land Registry hopes that all major lenders will use the END system, and current users include the Nationwide Building Society and Halifax plc as well as most leading institutional lenders.

As this system is now in mainstream conveyancing, the DS1 undertaking on completion will have to be replaced and the following wording might be adopted to ensure peace of mind for buyers' practitioners:

> In consideration of your today completing the purchase of [subject property] we hereby undertake to discharge the mortgage/legal charge dated [insert date of mortgage/legal charge] to enable the former lender to forthwith submit an END to Land Registry and to write to you with your confirmation and the existence of the END and that it is not under investigation.

Alternatively, in the guidance notes issued by Land Registry and the Nationwide Building Society, the following undertaking was suggested:

> In consideration of your today completing the purchase of (property) we hereby undertake forthwith to pay over to Nationwide Building Society the money required to discharge the mortgage/legal charge dated (date) and to forward to you a copy of the notice of confirmation from the Society that an Electronic Notice of Discharge has been sent to Land Registry as soon as it is received by us.

It is important to appreciate that an END of itself does not ensure the removal of the registered charge. There must be an application by the buyer's practitioner on Form AP1 (or DS2) seeking removal of the entry in the charges register.

13.7 **THE OUTCOME OF COMPLETION**

The necessary outcome of completion for the seller is to receive the full purchase monies including (especially if leasehold) all apportionments. Never accept cash payments at completion. If the buyer offers to pay in legal tender (here meaning banknotes) you should immediately be concerned about the dangers of money laundering. Where you act for that buyer you need to be sure that the client is not committing a money laundering offence. A practitioner is in danger of committing an offence by not reporting such circumstances. Efforts should therefore be made to investigate the source of these cash funds and the identity of the client.

 Conduct Point Money laundering

- Always be alive to the dangers of money laundering. If a client offers to pay you large amounts in cash or if a buyer makes a similar offer question whether in accepting this money you might be involving yourself in money laundering.

 Key Points Completion

Acting for the seller
- Check you have all the necessary deeds, that you have prepared Form DS1 or, if appropriate, END1, or a vacating receipt for a mortgage of unregistered land, and that you have the executed purchase deed.
- To minimise personal risk and liability, wherever possible only give undertakings about redemption in the form approved by The Law Society.
- Be aware that in Protocol cases (and in non-Protocol cases but where the Code is being adopted) the Code for Completion incorporates professional undertakings.

Acting for the buyer

- Check all searches to ensure they exist and remain in force and ensure the buyer carries out a final inspection immediately before completion.

- Can you accept an undertaking from the seller regarding the mortgage? Preferably not if the lender is not a member of the Council of Mortgage Lenders.

- Seek written confirmation that the seller's practitioner is the agent of the lender at completion.

- Is it cost effective to complete in person? Do you trust the seller's practitioner? If not, complete in person or appoint an agent.

SELF TEST QUESTIONS

1. The priority period in which to complete for a Land Registry search result is thirty days. Is this statement TRUE/FALSE? Please delete the incorrect choice.

2. At completion the seller's practitioner confirms that an END will deal with the seller's mortgage. This means that

   (a) When the lender is satisfied that their charge has been redeemed in full an END is sent to the Land Registry over the Land Registry Direct System

   (b) When the buyer is satisfied that the charge has been redeemed in full an END is sent to the Land Registry over the Land Registry Direct System

   (c) When the borrower is satisfied that the charge has been redeemed in full an END is sent to the Land Registry over the Land Registry Direct System

   (d) When the Land Registry is satisfied that the charge has been redeemed in full an END is issued by the Land Registry via the Land Registry Direct System

3. The Law Society's Code for Completion by Post includes the crucial element that the buyer's solicitor appoints the seller's solicitor as his or her unpaid agent for completion. Is this statement TRUE/FALSE? Please delete the incorrect choice.

4. A contract not relying on the Standard Conditions stipulates that the buyer is to pay over the completion monies in one or more of the following ways

   (a) Legal tender

   (b) A banker's draft

   (c) A direct credit to a bank account nominated by the seller's solicitor

   (d) A solicitor's client account cheque

   Please select the choice that would otherwise be within the Standard Conditions.

5. Acting for a buyer at completion of the purchase of a registered freehold subject to a first charge, which of the following might you never expect to receive in exchange for the purchase monies

   (a) The transfer duly signed and dated

   (b) The charge certificate

   (c) Form DS1

   (d) The keys

   Please select the choice *not* available at completion.

SHORT REVISION QUESTIONS

1. You act for a seller of a registered residential freehold property in Surrey. Your client does not have a mortgage to pay off. The sale contract is based on the Standard Conditions of sale, 4th edition. You are due to complete tomorrow. The buyer is acting for himself, and is a cash buyer. The buyer has just telephoned you to arrange completion. He proposes to complete in person at your offices at noon tomorrow, at which time he will pay over the completion monies in exchange for the transfer. You have the transfer duly signed and witnessed but is there anything else you should consider?

2. You act for a buyer of a large residential property in Mayfair London. The transaction has been difficult because the seller instructed a sole practitioner who always seems to be in court when you try to contact him on the phone. The contractual price is £6.2 million pounds and you have just exchanged and completion is due in two weeks time. You are aware that the seller has a large mortgage on the subject property where the redemption value is going to be in the region of £4 million pounds. Are there any special arrangements you should make to complete this purchase?

3. You are selling a property for a client using the Standard Conditions of sale, 4th edition. There are no special conditions in the contract. Completion is due today. It is now 2.15pm and the buyer has just telephoned to say that the completion monies are on there way to you by bank transfer (the delay having arisen along the previous chain of transactions). What should you do?

SUGGESTED ANSWERS TO SELF TEST QUESTIONS

1. This statement is false. The priority period for a registered land search is 30 *working* days. Weekends and bank holidays are therefore excluded from the days counted for priority purposes.

2. The correct answer is (a). The Land Registry has been developing a scheme with lenders that will make DS1 forms a rarity. It has been using an Electronic Notification of Discharge (END) to replace the DS1. When the lender is satisfied that their charge has been redeemed in full an END is sent to the Land Registry by the lender computer over the Land Registry Direct System.

3. The statement is true. The crucial element of the Code is that the buyer's solicitor appoints the seller's solicitor as his or her unpaid agent for completion. The buyer's solicitor must provide full instructions for the 'agent' relating to the buyer's requirements. These instructions should clearly set out for the seller's solicitor what the buyer's solicitor requires him or her to do and what is to be sent on from the seller to the buyer, after completion has been effected. The seller's solicitor must confirm instructions from the seller to receive the sale monies and that he or she has been appointed the authorized agent of any lender authorizing the receipt of monies required to redeem.

4. The choice covered by the Standard Conditions is (c). Completion monies can only be paid pursuant to SC 6.7 by a direct electronic bank transfer with a release of any deposit held by a stakeholder.

5. The correct answer is none can be selected as they could all be available at completion. Therefore, as none of the selections apply, you should understand why not. Since the 13 October 2003 the land or charge certificate is no longer required when submitting a transfer for registration and need not be handed over at completion. However, best practice dictates that the seller should hand over the certificate especially if it contains other documents such a conveyance containing restrictive covenants. The transfer duly signed and dated must be handed over at completion along with form DS1. Finally the keys can be available at completion, although they are normally held and released by the estate agents.

SUGGESTED ANSWERS TO SHORT REVISION QUESTIONS

1. The obvious point of concern here is in relation to the method of payment at completion. The necessary outcome of completion for the seller is to receive the full purchase monies. However, if the buyer offers to pay in legal tender (here meaning banknotes) you should immediately be concerned about the dangers of money laundering. You need to be sure that your client is not involved in a transaction that might give rise to either party to the contract committing a money laundering offence. A practitioner is in danger of committing an offence by not reporting such circumstances. Efforts should therefore be made to investigate the source of these cash funds and to take the matter further with the appropriate authorities should you be unsatisfied with the buyer's response.

2. This question clearly revolves around the seller's large mortgage. A buyer's practitioner needs to exercise special care where the seller has a high value mortgage. In the case of *Patel v Daybells* [2000] EGCS 98 (QBD, 19 July 2000) it was stated that there could be 'exceptional circumstances' where accepting an undertaking at completion was negligent. This could be where the value of the seller's mortgage exceeds the minimum level required for indemnity insurance for solicitors. This is currently £1 million so, if a buyer's practitioner is aware of this situation prevailing, either the cover must be increased, or the seller's solicitors must warrant that the insurance cover exceeds the amount required to redeem (or Form DS1 must be available at completion). Clearly in this case the amount is well over the limit and therefore the best course of action is to ask for Form DS1 to be available at completion.

3. This question is about the time for completion. Standard Condition 6.1.2 now, in effect, sets a final time of 2pm on the day of completion. It does so by providing that if completion does not take place by that time completion is deemed to be overdue and interest will be payable. This does not mean that completion cannot take place that day. However, if completion cannot take place before 2pm it simply means that interest will be payable (if demanded) for late completion. You must take instructions to see if your client wants you to seek this money. However, in many cases completion will be after this time, and practitioners often take the view that the pragmatic approach is not to call for interest but simply to complete, as the amount of interest involved would be quickly swallowed up by the cost of seeking payment. All these factors should be mentioned to client to allow the client to make an informed decision.

WIDER READING

- Chapter 8, Abbey, R, and Richards, M, *A Practical Approach to Conveyancing* (Oxford University Press, 2008)

- Sections E and F dealing with pre-completion and completion matters, Silverman, F, *Conveyancing Handbook* (The Law Society, 2006)

- Emmet on Title:

  - Searches before completion generally—Chapter 8, part 1;

  - Position Pending Completion—Chapter 6;

- For more detail on the changes introduced by the Land Registration Act 2002 see Abbey, R, and Richards, M, *Blackstone's Guide to the Land Registration Act 2002* (Oxford University Press, 2002)

- Chapter 2 (buying a house); Chapter 4 (unregistered land); Chapter 5 (registered land), MacKenzie, J-A, and Phillips, M, *Textbook on Land Law* (Oxford University Press, 2008)

WEBSITES FOR FURTHER INFORMATION

- Association of British Insurers, **<http://www.abi.org.uk/>**. Remember insurance may be required from the time of exchange. Look at the contract terms to check.

- Bank of England, **<http://www.bankofengland.co.uk/>**. Banking details; relevant to completion arrangements.

- Companies House, **<http://www.companieshouse.gov.uk/>**. You can make on-line pre-completion searches at Companies House. They will be vital in unregistered transactions when the seller is a corporation.

- Council of Mortgage Lenders, **<http://www.cml.org.uk>**. There is an on-line version of the handbook available at this address and should be referred to in cases of doubt about the requirements of the lender at this stage of the transaction.

- Land Registry, **<http://www.landreg.gov.uk/>**. The location for pre-completion registered land searches.

- Land Registry internet access, **<http://www.landregistrydirect.gov.uk>**. The location for on-line pre-completion registered land searches.

- Location statistics, **<http://www.upmystreet.com/>**.

- National House Building Council, **<http://www.nhbc.co.uk>**. Details of new build properties.

- National Land Information Service, **<http://www.nlis.org.uk>**. Almost all pre-completion searches can be made on-line through one of the service providers authorized by the NLIS.

- A street map anywhere in the UK, **<http://www.streetmap.co.uk>**. To assist in the location of a particular property.

online
resource
centre

ONLINE RESOURCE CENTRE CASE STUDIES

RESIDENTIAL TRANSACTION CASE STUDY—COMPLETION

Our clients:
Shilpa Jennings—sale of 19 Minster Yard Blakey
Shilpa Jennings and Daniel Rodriguez—purchase of 9 Castle Hill Blakey

We act for Shilpa Jennings who is selling 19 Minster Yard Blakey for £100,000 and Shilpa and Daniel Rodriguez who are buying 9 Castle Hill Blakey for £200,000. The completion of the transactions is to take place by post. Please consider the documents required by the buyer in exchange for the completion monies. See the action lists for completion for both parties listed within the materials on the Online Resource Centre accompanying this book.

COMMERCIAL TRANSACTION CASE STUDY—COMPLETION

Our client: Cambo Ltd—acquisition of 18 Clover Street London W2

Timothy Wainwright and his family have run a successful wholesale clothing business for many years. Timothy has decided to sell the business and enter the world of property investment. He has formed a company called Cambo Ltd in which he, his wife, and their three sons are all shareholders. Cambo Ltd has agreed to buy 18 Clover Street London W2 for £700,000 subject to and with the benefit of two occupational business leases. As completion has taken place, we need to inform the tenants in occupation of the change of ownership. Please see the authorities as to the future payment of rent on the Online Resource Centre accompanying this book.

---

14 POST-COMPLETION PROCEDURES

14.1 INTRODUCTION

Once completion has taken place conveyancing practitioners still have much to do, whether they are acting for the seller or the buyer. However, the buyer's solicitor will have more to do, as in most transactions acting on behalf of the buyer means after completion dealing with stamp duty land tax and then registration of the title and/or transfer. So far as the seller is concerned, paying off any lender is required, as well as accounting to the client for the net proceeds of sale. All these post-completion procedures will now be considered.

14.2 POST-COMPLETION PROCEDURES IN FLOWCHARTS

The flowchart in Figure 14.1 sets out the steps to be taken after completion from the perspective of a practitioner acting for a buyer.

The flowchart in Figure 14.2 sets out the steps to be taken after completion from the perspective of a practitioner acting for a seller.

14.3 ACTING FOR THE SELLER

If the seller has a mortgage then this must be redeemed and paid off in full (unless there was a sale of part of the mortgaged property when it is possible for a part redemption to occur).

14.3.1 REDEMPTION ARRANGEMENTS

Once completion has taken place, and preferably on the day of completion, the redemption monies must be sent to the lenders in full settlement of the debt due to them. The method of transmission of these monies is dictated by the calculation of the redemption statement. Some lenders issue a statement calculated to a month end. In these circumstances, and on the assumption that completion has not taken place at the end of the month, a payment by a client account cheque sent by post will be acceptable. If, however, the statement is calculated to the day and has a daily rate, the redemption monies can be sent by post, but extra days of interest must be added until the cheque is received and cleared. This would normally add an extra seven days to the total interest. It will probably be more economic for the client if the monies were sent by bank transfer and with the client paying the fee for this, usually in the region of £25. This can normally be accomplished on the day of completion.

FIGURE 14.1 BUYER: POST COMPLETION STEPS

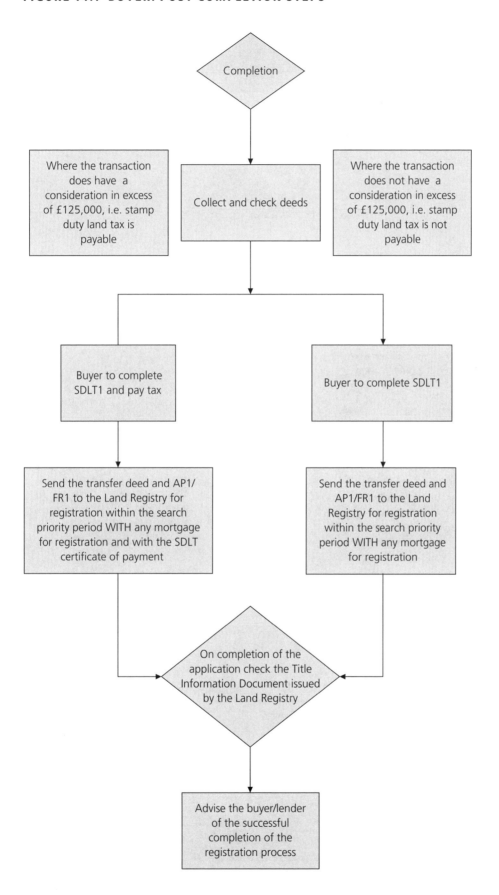

FIGURE 14.2 SELLER: POST COMPLETION STEPS

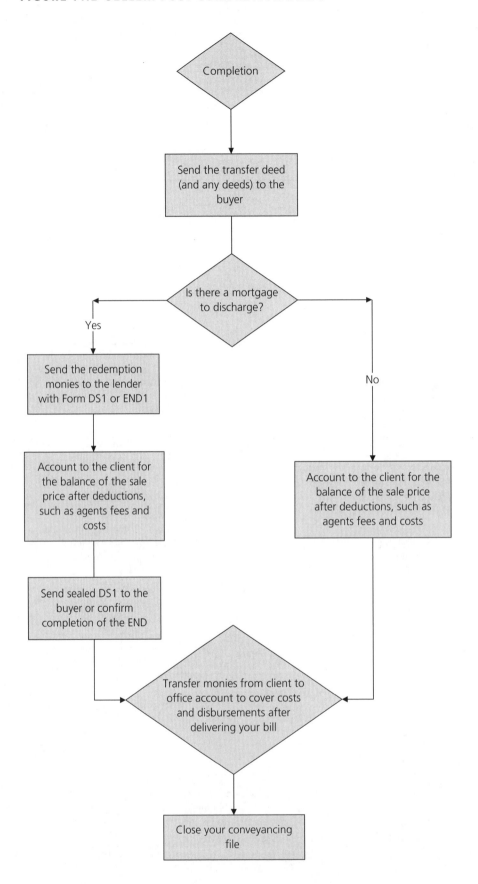

14.3.2 **METHODS FOR PAYING OFF LENDERS**

The methods for paying off lenders are:

(a) *Form DS1.* This is a very simple form that repeats the title details (county, location, title number, and description of property), and in which you must insert the name and address of the registered lender and the dates of the mortgage. The deed must be executed by the lender and dated with the date of completion. You will need to refer to official copies of the registers to complete Form DS1, as you will need to insert the date of the mortgage.

(b) *Mortgage vacating receipt.* The position is a little more complicated and applies to unregistered land only. Mortgages will be released by way of a receipt usually endorsed on the back of the original deed. The receipt, also known as a vacating receipt, must be executed by the lender and dated with the date of completion. In both cases an undertaking will have been given at completion, and the sealed document should therefore be sent to the buyer's practitioner as soon as it is received back from the lender. When sending it on to the buyer a request should be made for the undertaking to be fully discharged, i.e. released.

(c) *Electronic Notification for Discharge (END).* When an END is to be used, the lender will inform the Land Registry of the discharge of their mortgage over whole titles to land by an electronic message, sent through the Land Registry's Direct Access Service. It is intended that ENDs will replace Forms DS1. The form enables the lender to verify the details that they will need to include in their END message to Land Registry. After completion the seller's practitioner will then need to send the redemption monies to the lender in the usual way together with END 1 (and not DS1). If the lender is satisfied about complete repayment, it will transmit the END to Land Registry. Once the buyer's application for registration is received (without the necessity for Form DS1), removal of the registered charge can be made. (In Form AP1, used to register dealings with registered land, all that need be stated on the form in the list of applications to be made is 'Discharge by END', or perhaps 'END'.) Practitioners can check receipt of the electronic message by telephoning HM Land Registry Telephone Services on 0845 308 4545. Many of the main lenders use END.

(d) *Release of part.* In registered land, Form DS3 is required when releasing part of a title from a registered charge. The lender will still require the redundant charge certificate because even though it is not proof of title it will contain the original charge over the retained land. Form DS3 should show the extent of the released land by reference to a scale plan.

(e) *Electronic discharges.* Land Registry have also piloted a new system with selected lenders regarding the electronic discharge of registered mortgages. An Electronic Discharge (ED) is a discharge of a registered charge sent electronically by a lender direct to Land Registry. Land Registry's computer system makes a number of checks and if everything is in order, it cancels the charge entries. In most cases, the charge entries will be cancelled immediately and automatically on receipt of the discharge. An ED is not like an END because an ED cancels the charge entries automatically and, in most cases, immediately. It does not require a separate formal paper application to discharge the charge. It is a computer-to-computer-system driven process. (This compares with an END which is an electronic message to Land Registry authorizing the cancellation of the charge entries. It does not cause the charge to be cancelled. It must be combined with a formal application to Land Registry to discharge the charge.)

Conduct Point Undertakings

- Be very careful about how you handle enforceable solicitor's undertakings. Failure to comply with an undertaking, e.g. to pay off mortgages, will amount to a breach of the Code of Conduct for Solicitors 2007, R.10.05.

14.3.3 ESTATE AGENTS' FEES

If you are instructed to pay the selling agents' fees then you must do so within a reasonable time of completion, and obtain a written form of receipt for the payment. The receipt may be required by the seller if the cost may be a permitted deduction for capital gains tax purposes (as is the case for legal fees in connection with the disposal).

14.4 ACTING FOR THE BUYER

The buyer has much to finalize after the completion of the transaction and in particular must deal with stamp duty land tax and registration matters both at Land Registry as well as Companies House if a client company is involved with a mortgage.

14.4.1 REGISTRATIONS AT COMPANIES HOUSE

In the case of a new mortgage by a company borrower, the mortgage *must* be lodged and accepted for registration by the Registrar of Companies within 21 days of completion (this must be accompanied by Form 395, particulars of mortgage or charge, as required by Part XII of the Companies Act 1985). If you fail to comply with this very strict time limit, you cannot register the mortgage without an order of the court, and such orders are given only in exceptional circumstances. Failure to register is an unanswerable case of professional negligence that would have to be referred to your indemnity insurers. There is a fee payable for the registration of a charge at Companies House. The papers and fee should be sent to Companies House, PO Box 716, Crown Way, Maindy, Cardiff CF14 3UZ. Part 25 of the new Companies Act 2006 repeats this requirement in Part 25 of that Act (sections 860–877).

14.4.2 STAMP DUTY LAND TAX

The Stamp Duty Land Tax (SDLT) regime came into force on 1 December 2003. Section 43 of the Finance Act 2003 defines land transactions as being the focus for land tax and is an extremely wide definition covering dealings in estates and interests including those that are equitable. The starting threshold for the payment of land tax is £125,000 for residential property, but £150,000 for residential properties in a disadvantaged area, and commercial property. The SDLT for land transactions with an effective date on or after 23 March 2006, for transfers of land and buildings (consideration paid) is:

Rate	Land in disadvantaged areas		All other land in the UK	
	Residential	Non-residential	Residential	Non-residential
Zero	£0–£150,000	£0–£150,000	£0–£125,000	£0–£150,000
1%	Over £150,000–£250,000	Over £150,000–£250,000	Over £125,000–£250,000	Over £150,000–£250,000
3%	Over £250,000–£500,000	Over £250,000–£500,000	Over £250,000–£500,000	Over £250,000–£500,000
4%	Over £500,000	Over £500,000	Over £500,000	Over £500,000

In many disadvantaged areas across England and Wales land tax will not be payable on residential transactions where the consideration does not exceed £150,000. This disadvantaged area relief is also available on new residential leases where the premium does not exceed £150,000, and the average annual rent does not exceed £15,000. This relief is not available for commercial property. The areas attracting the relief can be identified from a list available on the Inland Revenue website. The website at <http://www.hmrc.gov.uk/so/> also contains a search engine, which, if you enter the subject property's postcode, will tell you whether it is in a disadvantaged area. You can also phone the Revenue's enquiry line 0845 6030135 for assistance.

The Revenue will require the completion and submission of a land transaction return to their data capture centre in Merseyside within 30 days of completion of the transaction. (Payment is required either on completion or when there is substantial performance of the contract. This will be if the buyer goes into possession or pays a substantial amount, probably 90 per cent of the price.) The centre address is Inland Revenue (Stamp/Taxes MSD), Comben House, Farriers Way, Netherton, Merseyside L30 4RN. If a return is filed late the buyer will be liable to a fixed penalty of £100, or if more than three months' late, £200. The buyer may also be liable to a tax-related penalty, not to exceed the tax payable.

When should a land transaction return be completed?

The land transaction return should be submitted to notify:

1. Any transfer of a freehold or assignment of a lease for consideration, whether or not giving rise to a charge;
2. Any transaction for which relief is being claimed;
3. The grant of a lease for a contractual term of seven years or more or which gives rise to a charge;
4. Any other transaction giving rise to a charge.

The following transactions are not notifiable and as such no land tax return is required. However, a self-certificate will be required to enable the transaction to be registered at Land Registry.

1. The acquisition of a freehold or leasehold interest in land for no chargeable consideration. (Note that there will normally be chargeable consideration where there is a gift of property subject to an existing debt such as a mortgage.)
2. Transactions made in connection with the ending of a marriage.
3. Transactions varying the dispositions made, whether effected by will or laws of intestacy, within two years after the person's death not involving any consideration in money or money's worth.
4. A transaction which effects something other than a major interest in land chargeable with tax at 0 per cent. An example of such a transaction would be an interest, which is not a major interest in land, such as the grant of an easement where the consideration does not exceed £125,000. This would attract Land Tax at 0 per cent, provided it is not linked to any other transaction that would bring the total consideration to more than £125,000. Notification would not be required.

Stamp Duty Land Tax and leases

SDLT is also payable in relation to the rental element of commercial leases. The charge is at a rate of 1 per cent on the net present value (NPV) of the total rent payable over the term of the lease. Future rents will be discounted at 3.5 per cent per annum in order to arrive at the NPV. Leases where the NPV of the rent over the term of the lease does not exceed £125,000 on residential property and £150,000 for commercial property will be exempt. The Revenue have suggested that some 60 per cent of all commercial leases could avoid any SDLT on the rental element. There is on online calculator for SDLT payable in leasehold transactions at <http://www.hmrc.gov.uk/so/new-sdlt-calculators.htm>.

The SDLT5 or certificate of payment

Once the Revenue have received and processed a proper Land Tax return and payment they will issue a certificate of payment. This is called a Land Transaction Return Certificate or SDLT5. The certificate is issued under section 79 of the Finance Act 2003 and evidences that land tax has been accounted on the particular transaction notified to the Revenue. This must be sent to Land Registry to enable an application to register to proceed (alternatively where appropriate a self-certificate will be all that is required, see above for self-certificates). Land Registry will not proceed with a registration application without an SDLT5 certificate being provided.

14.4.3 REGISTRATION OF TITLE

After completion title will not pass to the buyer without registration taking place at the Land Registry. It is therefore vital to ensure that completion is swiftly followed by an application for registration to Land Registry.

The documents that should be sent to Land Registry

All original deeds and documents are sent to Land Registry to ensure that registration of each transaction is properly completed. These original deeds and documents are lodged together with a Land Registry application form, the details of which are set out below. Practitioners who use Land Registry Direct can now lodge applications to change the register electronically. Initially, this covers only simple applications, but Land Registry plans to develop the process to allow more complicated applications. The service is called 'e-lodgement' to differentiate it from 'e-conveyancing'.

online resource centre

Existing registered titles; dealings with whole or part

These applications must be lodged at Land Registry within the priority period given on the pre-completion Land Registry search result. Where the land is registered and the dealing is with the whole of the title, any existing land or charge certificate should not be sent to Land Registry with the dealing application cover AP1 (application to change the register). The application should be accompanied by the transfer deed and all new mortgages. Land Registry will require a certified copy of each mortgage sent for registration with a clear indication of priority. The certification can be in the following form:

> I/We hereby certify this to be a true copy of the original [signed, here signed in the firm name or by the practitioner applying]. In cases where END is not being used, all discharges of previous mortgages on Form DS1 must be lodged with the application.

On a dealing making a transfer of part the appropriate application cover is also the AP1, which now covers both whole-of-title and part-of-title dealings. Otherwise the documents will be the same as for a dealing with the whole of the title. However, it is possible that a mortgage discharge will be of part with the charge remaining on the residue of the seller's title. In this case Form DS3 will be required, but it should have with it a scale plan showing the area to be released from the charge. This will be required from the seller's lender and must accompany the AP1 application form. Where SDLT has been paid SDLT5 must be lodged with the application for registration. (SDLT5 will be required even if no tax was payable. Transactions taxed at 0 per cent will still require an SDLT1 to be submitted.)

The appropriate Land Registry fee must accompany the application. Fees are set out in the Land Registration Fees Order 2006 (SI 2006/1332) and are listed in scales according to the consideration paid for the property.

First registration

Section 6(4) of the Land Registration Act 2002 requires applications for first registration to be made within two months of completion. The application cover required is normally Form FR1 for both freehold and leasehold properties. In both cases the registry requires a list in triplicate of all documents lodged within the cover form, and Form DL is required for this purpose. The registrar will want to see all the documents of title to enable a decision to be taken as to the class of title to be granted. Consequently, practitioners should include and list:

(a) all the documents of title as abstracted including all old land charges search results;

(b) all searches and pre-contract enquiries with replies;

(c) the original contract;

(d) requisitions on title with replies;

(e) the original executed conveyance, or transfer, or deed of assignment with certified copy;

(f) the buyer's mortgage deed, if any, with a certified copy;

(g) all receipted discharged mortgages, including any paid off by the seller; and

(h) if the property is leasehold, the lease (and a certified copy where a new lease is being granted).

Where to send your application

Depending on the location of the subject property, registration applications must be sent to a specific registry. For example, an application affecting a title in Lambeth in London must be sent to the Telford Land Registry office in the Midlands. There is a very helpful online leaflet (Practice Guide 51) indicating which Land Registry office handles which administrative area at <http://www.landreg.gov.uk>. Land Registry will return any application that is not lodged at the proper office. Practitioners can telephone the general enquiry service at any Land Registry office for help with selecting the correct office.

14.4.4 **REGISTRATION WITH THE LESSOR**

Almost all leases include a covenant on the lessee's part requiring the lessee to give notice to the lessor of all transfers, assignments, mortgages, or other dealings affecting the legal title. The purpose of the clause is to ensure that the lessor is aware of who is the lessee and therefore responsible for the performance of all the covenants in the lease and, in particular, the payment of rent. The covenant normally stipulates a time limit for giving notice, usually 28 days from the date of the deed or completion, and calls for copies of the relevant documents (the transfer, mortgage, etc.) to be lodged with the lessor's solicitor. A fee may be required by the terms of the covenant, payable to the lessor's solicitor. (If the fee is stated then that is all that must be paid, as the VAT is deemed to be included in that figure. However, many covenants state the fee and go on to provide that VAT will also be payable on the fee by the lessee.) Notice should be given in duplicate so that a receipted copy can be placed with the deeds. It is quite permissible to give notice by letter.

The following could serve as the basis for a notice of assignment:

> To [lessor] of [address] [insert the date] With regard to the Lease made the [here insert the date of the lease] between (1) [insert the name of the original lessor] and (2) [insert the name of the original lessee] relating to [here insert the postal address or description of premises] ('the Lease') TAKE NOTICE that by a transfer or an assignment dated the [insert the date of the assignment or transfer] the Lease was transferred or assigned by [insert the name and address of the outgoing lessee] to [insert the purchaser, transferee or assignee] of [the incoming lessee's address] ('the Purchaser') for the residue of the term granted by the lease.

Some leases do not state a fee but refer to a 'reasonable fee'. In these circumstances you will need to agree what is reasonable before the lessor's solicitor will receipt the notice.

14.4.5 SHARE TRANSFER REGISTRATION

Particularly when dealing with leasehold properties, it may be that each owner in the block or development is entitled to own a share or shares in a management company. If there is such an arrangement, the share certificate should be obtained on completion along with a stock transfer form completed and signed by the seller. These two documents should then be submitted to the secretary of the company with a request that a new share certificate be issued in the name of the buyer. The new certificate should be kept with the deeds. In many cases these companies are limited by guarantee and therefore do not have or issue share certificates. Where this is the case the change of ownership (and hence guarantee) should be confirmed in writing to the company secretary. A membership certificate may be issued.

 Key Points Post Completion Procedures

- Where you are dealing with a new mortgage granted by a company, you must ensure the mortgage is registered at Companies House within 21 days of completion. (Address all correspondence to 'The Mortgage Section' to hasten delivery.)
- Where SDLT is payable, collect the tax from the client before completion to make sure the tax is paid to the Revenue within the time limit to avoid any penalty fee being charged. Make sure the client has completed and signed the SDLT return and that boxes 58 and 59 on the form have been completed appropriately.
- Alternatively, consider making the SDLT application online (which is preferable).
- Always ensure you submit your registration application for a dealing within the priority period fixed by your Land Registry search result or, if a first registration, within two months of completion.
- Always check the contents of the Title Information Document on its issue from Land Registry and, where there is a mortgage, send to the lender a deeds schedule in duplicate for receipting. Alternatively, retain the deeds where the lender's instructions state they are not required.
- Send a photocopy of the title to the client for information and retention.
- Never overlook transferring your profit costs out of the client account into your office account.
- Make a final check of your file to make sure there are no forgotten points or items still to be dealt with.

SELF TEST QUESTIONS

1. After completion a mortgage discharge will be dealt with by the following

   (a) Form DS1

   (b) END1

   (c) Mortgage vacating receipt

   (d) Promissory note release

   Please select the choice that cannot apply.

2. Your client has completed a freehold purchase for £125,000. The residential property is in a pleasant area of Leeds. What is the stamp duty land tax liability

   (a) £12,500

   (b) £125

(c) £1,250

(d) nil

3. The Land Registry has introduced a new method of lodging applications. Practitioners who use Land Registry Direct can now lodge applications to change the register electronically. The service is called 'e-lodgement' Which of the following cannot be applied for as an e-lodgement

(a) Severance of a joint tenancy by notice

(b) Change of property description

(c) Change of proprietor's address

(d) Change of proprietor's name (by deed poll/marriage).

4. On completion of a registration application from 13 October 2003, which of the following will be issued

(a) A Title Information Document

(b) A land certificate

(c) A charge certificate

(d) A land charges certificate

5. First registration applications must be made within eight weeks of completion, failing which the legal title will not vest in the buyer until the Registry has completed an application. Is this statement TRUE/FALSE? Please delete the incorrect choice.

SHORT REVISION QUESTIONS

1. You act for a buyer of a registered freehold house in Yorkshire who bought for £250,000 with the aid of a mortgage with Barclays Bank. The seller had a mortgage with the Nationwide Building Society and you now have the DS1 for this. Please list the documents needed for your registration application.

2. You act for a buyer of an unregistered freehold house in Suffolk who bought for £250,000 with the aid of a mortgage with HSBC Bank. The root of title was a conveyance to the seller dated 11 June 1988. The seller had a mortgage with Halifax Plc and you now have the vacating receipt for this. Please list the documents needed for your registration application.

3. You act for a buyer of a leasehold flat in London that has been newly granted to your client at a price of £165,000. Your client funded the purchase with the aid of a mortgage with the Principality Building Society. Briefly list what you must do after completion to finalize the transaction in all respects for your client.

SUGGESTED ANSWERS TO SELF TEST QUESTIONS

1. The incorrect selection is (d). A mortgage will be dealt with in registered land either by a form DS1 or if there is an electronic discharge an END1. If the mortgage affects unregistered land then a mortgage vacating receipt will be used. A promissory note release has nothing to do with the redemption of mortgages of land.

2. The correct answer is (d). If the consideration for the subject property is at or under the stamp duty land tax base threshold, currently £125,000, then no stamp duty land tax is payable. Land tax is payable, currently at 1 per cent, up to £250,000; above that other tiers of tax apply. The property being in a 'pleasant' area, it is assumed that the disadvantaged area advantage does not apply.

3. You should appreciate that all of these events can be the subject of e-lodgement. You can also register the death of a joint proprietor of land by the same method. As none of the answers given are right then you should be able to explain why none of the listed answers apply.

4. The correct answer is (a). After the 13 October 2003 a title information document will be issued, in effect a certificate of title registration completion. The title information document will comprise a copy of the register and, where the application has resulted in the preparation of a new or amended title plan, a copy of that title plan. The title information document will not be a document of title as it is issued for information purposes only. There is no requirement to lodge this with any subsequent application affecting the same property.

5. The statement is false. Applications must be made *within two months* of completion, failing which the legal title will not vest in the buyer until an application has been completed by the Registry. Section 6(4) of the Land Registration Act 2002 states that: 'The period for registration is 2 months beginning with the date on which the relevant event occurs, i.e. the dispositions giving rise to first registration.'

SUGGESTED ANSWERS TO SHORT REVISION QUESTIONS

1. You will need to lodge at Land Registry (1) the signed transfer deed (TR1); (2) signed mortgage deed; (3) certified copy mortgage deed; (4) SDLT5 certificate of payment; (5) Form DS1.

2. You will need to lodge at Land Registry (1) the signed transfer deed (TR1); (2) Certified copy transfer; (3) signed mortgage deed; (4) certified copy mortgage deed; (5) SDLT5 certificate of payment; (6) Halifax mortgage with vacating receipt endorsed thereon; (7) Conveyance of 11 June 1988 to the seller; (8) all land charge search results for the title to the subject property; (9) all other searches and pre-contract enquiries with replies; (10) the original contract; (11) requisitions on title with replies; (12) Form DL in triplicate (list of all deeds and documents).

3. The following steps must be taken after completion:

   • Complete SDLT forms and obtain an SDLT5 certificate (make sure rental details are covered).

   • Give notice to the lessor of the charge (there is no assignment, the lease having been granted to the client/first lessee).

   • Apply for first registration of the new leasehold title by sending to Land Registry the lease with a certified copy along with SDLT 5 and any DS3 that might be required or a consent to dealing from any lender registered on the freehold title.

   • Check the completed registration and send a copy of the new title to the client.

   • If the lender requires custody of the lease send it to them otherwise take instruction from the client as to where the lease should be kept.

WIDER READING

• Chapter 9, Abbey, R, and Richards, M, *A Practical Approach to Conveyancing* (Oxford University Press, 2008)

• Sections G and M dealing with post-completion and delays and remedies, Silverman, F, *Conveyancing Handbook* (The Law Society, 2006)

• Emmet on Title:

   • Chapter 7, Remedies for Breach of Contract;

   • Chapters 8 to 10, Completion and Registration;

- For more detail on the changes introduced by the Land Registration Act 2002 see Abbey, R, and Richards, M, *Blackstone's Guide to the Land Registration Act 2002* (Oxford University Press, 2002)

- Chapter 2 (buying a house); Chapter 4 (unregistered land); Chapter 5 (registered land), MacKenzie, J-A, and Phillips, M, *Textbook on Land Law* (Oxford University Press, 2008)

WEBSITES FOR FURTHER INFORMATION

- Council of Mortgage Lenders, **<http://www.cml.org.uk>**. This site will set out post completion requirements of lenders within their CML handbook.

- HM Revenue and Customs, **<http://www.hmrc.gov.uk/>**. This is the site for all stamp duty enquiries as well as any other taxation matters that might arise post-completion.

- Land Registry, **<http://www.landreg.gov.uk/>**. For all post-completion matters relating to registered land.

- Land Registry internet register access, **<http://www.landregistrydirect.gov.uk>**.

- National Association of Estate Agents, **<http://www.naea.co.uk>**. Of benefit should a dispute arise over the payment of the estate agent's account.

- The Royal Institute of British Architects, **<http://www.ribafind.org.uk/>**. After completion the client might want to carry out alterations additions or a complete reconstruction. If so an architect will be needed.

online
resource
centre

ONLINE RESOURCE CENTRE CASE STUDIES

RESIDENTIAL TRANSACTION CASE STUDY—POST COMPLETION PROCEDURES

Our clients:
Shilpa Jennings—sale of 19 Minster Yard Blakey
Shilpa Jennings and Daniel Rodriguez—purchase of 9 Castle Hill Blakey

We act for Shilpa Jennings who is selling 19 Minster Yard Blakey for £100,000 and Shilpa and Daniel Rodriguez who are buying 9 Castle Hill Blakey for £200,000. The purchase deed must be registered. Consider the Land Registry application form that can be seen on the Online Resource Centre. We will need to consider the details required to ensure the property transfer is registered within the search priority period.

COMMERCIAL TRANSACTION CASE STUDY—POST COMPLETION PROCEDURES

Our client: Cambo Ltd—acquisition of 18 Clover Street London W2

Timothy Wainwright and his family have run a successful wholesale clothing business for many years. Timothy has decided to sell the business and enter the world of property investment. He has formed a company called Cambo Ltd in which he, his wife, and their three sons are all shareholders. Cambo Ltd has agreed to buy 18 Clover Street London W2 for £700,000 subject to and with the benefit of two occupational business leases. As completion has taken place, we need to inform the tenants in occupation of the change of ownership. Please see the authorities as to the future payment of rent on the Online Resource Centre.

---

15 DELAYS AND REMEDIES

15.1 INTRODUCTION

This chapter considers what can be done if a conveyancing contract is delayed or denied. The remedies available to a claimant will therefore also be considered. In an agreement for the sale and purchase of a legal estate in land that is regulated by the Standard Conditions the completion date will either be specified on the front page of the contract within the particulars or, more rarely, by Standard Condition (SC) 6.1. This states that completion will be 20 working days after the date of the contract. In this way the normal arrangements for completion are straightforward. However, practitioners need to be aware of the position should completion be delayed.

15.2 LATE COMPLETION

What can be done if one of the parties delays completion? Such a delay will be a breach of contract. It was held in the House of Lords in *Raineri v Miles* [1981] AC 1050 that failure to complete was a breach entitling the innocent party to a claim for damages arising from the delay. When time is of the essence, there is no leeway for delay; completion must be on the date specified, failing which all remedies will be available to the aggrieved party. Section 41 of the Law of Property Act 1925 tried to regulate time clauses in property contracts, but only achieved further confusion: see *Stickney v Keeble* [1915] AC 386 (on a similar provision of previous legislation), and *United Scientific Holdings Ltd v Burnley Borough Council* [1978] AC 904 illustrating how differently the courts have interpreted this statutory provision.

It now seems to be that if a contract states a completion date without qualification, that date is not a strict and binding date that would allow the innocent party to withdraw from the contract on the occasion of the breach. On the other hand, if it is expressly stated that time is of the essence then a strict interpretation arises, and if there is a failure to complete on the stipulated date there will be a breach of contract of such magnitude that the innocent party will be free to pursue all remedies, which can include immediate termination or rescission of the contract.

15.3 **TIME OF THE ESSENCE**

Time will be of the essence for a conveyancing contract:

(a) if the parties agree to it being written into the contract, or

(b) where a notice to complete has been correctly served, or

(c) where time is of the essence by necessary implication from the surrounding circumstances of the case.

In a contract regulated by the Standard Conditions, SC 6.1 specifically states that time is not of the essence unless a notice to complete is served. The parties to the contract can vary this term to make time of the essence but this cannot be achieved unilaterally.

In the absence of an SC 6.1 provision declaring that time is not of the essence, it may become of the essence where the time of completion is clearly expressed to be an essential, almost paramount, term. Examples are *Harold Wood Brick Co Ltd v Ferris* [1935] 1 KB 613 where completion was required 'not later than...', and *Barclay v Messenger* (1874) 43 LJ Ch 449 where if the purchase monies were not paid by a certain date the contract would be null and void. Time of the essence will also arise on the giving of a notice to complete.

What then are the implications where time is not of the essence and yet one party has delayed completion? One element of this predicament is clear; the injured party cannot refuse to complete the contract. If the injured party seeks to establish grounds for terminating the agreement then the appropriate course of action is to make time of the essence, and a notice to complete should be served on the delaying party without further delay.

15.4 **CONSEQUENCES OF DELAY: COMPENSATION**

Where there is delay in completing a transaction that delay, however short, will amount to a breach of contract. If there is delay, even of a matter of hours (or even minutes), the innocent party is entitled to seek damages for any loss occasioned as a result of the delay. In the circumstances of a brief delay of a few hours any loss sustained is unlikely to be such as to justify making a claim in the courts for breach of contract. As a result it has become the norm to include compensation provisions within the express contract terms. These compensatory terms do not preclude a claim in the courts, but where such steps are taken any compensation paid under the contractual terms must be taken into account when computing damages.

The common law has made provision for compensation, but if certainty is required, compensation terms should always be included in a conveyancing contract. The common law position is that where completion is delayed in an open contract, the buyer will be entitled to any income from the property but must bear all outgoings. Furthermore, if the seller remains in the subject property he or she will be required to pay a fee for occupation unless the delay has arisen as a consequence of any default by the buyer. The seller will be entitled to interest on the unpaid purchase monies. The level of interest is likely to be at the level allowed on the court short-term investment account under the Administration of Justice Act 1925 (see *Bartlett v Barclays Bank Trust Co Ltd* [1980] Ch 515). If the seller causes the delay then he must pay the outgoings. Accordingly the position at common law seems to be that the intention is to deal with the parties as if completion had actually taken place even though in reality no such step has been taken. Notwithstanding that the innocent party will be entitled to seek damages, it is clear that to allow open contract provisions to prevail in these circumstances would be unwise.

15.4.1 COMPENSATION AND THE STANDARD CONDITIONS

The Standard Conditions contain clear and precise provisions for compensation for a breach of contract that arises from delayed completion. SC 7.3 states that if a party to the contract defaults and delays completion, the defaulting party must pay compensation to the innocent party. Compensation is quantified as interest at the rate specified in the agreement as the 'contract rate' to the intent that the interest is on the unpaid purchase price. If a deposit has been paid and the buyer is in default, interest is calculated on the unpaid balance of the purchase price, or the total purchase price if the seller is in default. Interest is payable for each day that there is delay. SC 7.3.4 states that if the subject property is tenanted then the seller can elect to take the rent rather than interest. Accordingly, if the rent is likely to exceed the value of the interest, notice should be served on the defaulting buyer to confirm that the rent is to be taken by the seller rather than interest. Of course SC 7.3.4 can be varied in the special conditions to allow the seller to take the interest and the rent should the buyer default and delay completion. SC 7.3 also contemplates the possibility of both parties being in default. In these circumstances the party at greater fault must pay compensation.

The interest rate defined by the Standard Conditions as being the 'contact rate' is 'The Law Society's interest rate from time to time in force'. This is declared each week in the *Law Society's Gazette*. There is space on the front of the contract for an alternative rate to be declared and this could be, for example, 'four per cent above the base rate of Lloyds TSB Bank plc or such other lending rate as the bank shall declare in place thereof'.

Where interest is allowed by the contract it will be payable on completion being delayed even if this is only by a matter of minutes. The Standard Conditions stipulate a time and day for completion, see SC 6.1.2 and SC 6.1.3. If the time limit is breached but completion takes place on the contractual date, completion is deemed to take place the next working day and interest will accrue. The worst time for this to occur is on a Friday when three days' interest will arise for the period over the weekend to the next working day, being the following Monday. All this will be allowed by the contract even though completion actually took place late on the previous Friday.

15.5 NOTICES TO COMPLETE

In a conveyancing contract time is not of the essence if regulated by the Standard Conditions unless the special conditions provide otherwise. As a result an innocent party suffering from a delayed completion cannot consider the agreement as repudiated following the defaulting party's delay. This is an unsatisfactory position because the defaulting party may have no intention whatsoever of completing and yet the contract would in theory subsist. To bring the matter to a head and to terminate the agreement, the innocent party must take steps to precipitate a change, and this will be by way of a notice to complete. The notice will in all cases give a final date for completion failing which there will be no further time for the defaulting party. Time is now of the essence of the contract. The notice can inform the defaulting party that unless completion takes place by the date stated in the notice, the party serving the notice will be entitled to all remedies including a repudiation of the agreement. Because notices to complete deal with timing, practitioners need to reflect on two elements: first, when can the notice be served; and, secondly, how long must the notice be before it expires?

Standard Condition 6.8.1 states that at any time on or after the date fixed for completion, either party who is ready, able, and willing to complete may give the other a notice to complete. SC 1.1.3 goes on to define when a party is ready, able, and willing, i.e. he would have been in a position and ready to complete but for the default of the other party, and in the case of the seller, even though the property remains subject to a mortgage, if the amount to be paid at completion will be enough to pay off the mortgage.

Standard Condition 6.8.2 states that the parties are to complete the agreement within 10 working days of giving the notice to complete. The 10-day period excludes the day on which the notice is given. The condition goes on to state the essential wording, namely, 'for this purpose, time is of the essence of the contract'.

Standard Condition 6.8.3 states that a buyer who delays completion and has paid less than a 10 per cent deposit at exchange must pay the remaining monies required to make up a full 10 per cent deposit, and must pay these monies immediately on receipt of the notice. In practice this is unlikely to happen if the reason for not completing is a lack of finance. However, the seller can claim the full 10 per cent deposit.

If there is still no completion after the service and expiry of a notice to complete, the Standard Condtions which set out what is to be done are SC 7.5 where the buyer is in default and SC 7.6 where the seller defaults. If SC 7.5 comes into operation, the seller may rescind; and if there is rescission, the seller may forfeit the deposit, resell the property, and claim damages. These provisions are not exclusive and the seller therefore retains all other rights and remedies that may also be available. If SC 7.6 is operative, the buyer may rescind; and if there is rescission, the buyer can demand repayment of the deposit with any interest thereon. Again, these provisions are not exclusive and the buyer therefore retains all other rights and remedies that may otherwise be available (see also section 49 of the Law of Property Act 1925). In both cases the conveyancing papers must be returned and any protective registrations cancelled. The notice is binding on both parties and not just the party originally in default (see *Quadrangle Development and Construction Co Ltd v Jenner* [1974] 1 WLR 68, CA). Thus time is of the essence for both the seller and the buyer (see *Oakdown Ltd v Bernstein and Co* (1984) 49 P & CR 282).

15.5.1 **THE FORM OF NOTICE TO COMPLETE**

If you need to serve a notice to complete in connection with a contract incorporating the Standard Conditions, the following is a suitable precedent. It will be addressed to the defaulting party:

online
resource
centre

> On behalf of [insert your client seller/buyer and address] we hereby give you NOTICE that with reference to the contract dated [insert the date of the agreement] and made between [insert the seller's full names and the buyer's full names] for the sale and purchase of [insert the property address or description in the contract] we place on record the fact that the sale/purchase of the property has not been completed on the date fixed in the contract for completion. We further give you NOTICE that the seller/buyer [delete the party not ready] is ready able and willing to complete. We therefore give you NOTICE pursuant to condition 6.8 of the Standard Conditions of Sale (4th edition) and require you to complete the contract in compliance with that condition.

15.6 **REMEDIES**

There will always be cases where completion does not occur or, though it does occur, a dispute over the subject property arises after completion. The following sections cover first, what remedies are available if completion has not taken place and, secondly, what remedies are available if a dispute and potential consequential claim arise after completion. In all cases where a claim is necessary, specialist litigation assistance should be suggested to the client as the best way of advancing it.

15.6.1 WHERE THE CONTRACT HAS NOT BEEN COMPLETED

Where a contract has not been completed, and where a cause of action has arisen, an innocent party to that contract party can consider four available and different remedies. These remedies are:

(a) specific performance;

(b) a claim for compensation by way of damages;

(c) rescission; and

(d) a vendor and purchaser summons.

15.6.2 SPECIFIC PERFORMANCE

Specific performance is an equitable remedy in the form of a discretionary order of the court that is intended to compel the defaulting party to perform and complete the contract for the sale and purchase of land. The remedy is available to both buyer and seller where the other party has committed a breach of contract and where an award of damages would be insufficient compensation for the party suffering loss (this would be the case in most conveyancing matters bearing in mind the unique nature of the subject matter of most conveyancing contracts). If a judgment for that one remedy is granted, it will thereby preclude recourse to the other remedies. SCs 7.5 and 7.6 make it clear that an innocent party's right to apply for an order for specific performance is not precluded by the fact that a notice to complete has been served and not complied with.

Specific performance is an equitable remedy, and the principles of equity will prohibit an award where it would breach equitable principles. So, for example, where there is an element of fraud or illegality, or the award would cause one party exceptional hardship, the court will refrain from granting an order for specific performance. If damages would properly compensate the innocent party for the loss sustained then the court will order damages and not specific performance. Even where an order for specific performance is obtained, damages can still subsequently be ordered if the innocent party cannot enforce the order (see *Johnson v Agnew* [1980] AC 367). An award for damages can be made pursuant to section 50 of the Supreme Court Act 1981. However, it should be remembered that specific performance can be awarded before the contractual date for completion of the transaction, i.e. where a serious breach is likely to occur steps can be taken to seek an order for specific performance even though a breach of contract has yet to arise. See *Manchester Diocesan Council for Education v Commercial and General Investments Ltd* [1970] 1 WLR 241 and *Oakacre Ltd v Clare Cleaners (Holdings) Ltd* [1982] Ch 197 for examples of how the courts will make such decisions.

15.6.3 DAMAGES, INCLUDING FORFEITING OR RETURNING THE DEPOSIT

Where a claim for damages is to be advanced, credit must be given for any deposit forfeited by the seller. (This is also true for any compensation payments made pursuant to SC 7.3.) The Law of Property Act 1925, section 49(2), empowers the court, if it thinks it appropriate, to order the repayment of any deposit where it has refused to make an order for specific performance. It has been held that the court has an unfettered discretion to order the return of the deposit if this is the fairest way of dealing with the dispute (see *Universal Corporation v Five Ways Properties Ltd* [1979] 1 All ER 522, CA). This particular section of the enactment does not seem to allow a partial return of the deposit (see guidance on deposit returns in *Tennero Ltd v Majorarch* Ltd [2003] EGCS 154). The parties cannot agree to exclude section 49(2), see *Aribisala v St James* [2007] EWHC 1694 (ch).

15.6.4 RESCISSION

Rescission has over time gathered two meanings. First, it can mean an order of the court whereby the parties are put back into such a state as would have prevailed had the contract never existed. In effect the court will order the 'undoing' of the conveyancing contract. This may be ordered where there has been a claim arising out of some vitiating factor such as fraud, mistake, or misrepresentation. Secondly, rescission can mean the result of the innocent party accepting the repudiation of the agreement as a consequence of the defaulting party's breach of a major term in the agreement. Rescission can arise by a term in the conveyancing contract, or by agreement, or by an order of the court.

The Standard Conditions refer to rescission in three different circumstances:

(a) *SC 5.1.* This is the insurance clause, under which the risk on the property remains with the seller. Rescission is permitted if, as a consequence of some catastrophic event (e.g. fire), the subject property is unusable for its purpose (e.g. as a residential property), and this event has taken place after exchange but before completion. If the seller wishes to rescind the damage must have been uninsurable or it must be legally impossible to make good the damage.

(b) *SC 7.1.* This condition allows rescission for misrepresentation. SC 7 allows rescission where any statement or plan in the contract or the negotiations leading to it is or was misleading or inaccurate as a consequence of an error or omission. However, SC 7.1.3 limits this provision by allowing rescission only where there is an element of fraud or recklessness, or where, if the innocent party took the property, it would, prejudicially, be substantially different from that which the innocent party expected as a result of the error or omission. This is the one area of conveyancing contracts where an exclusion clause is subject to the reasonableness test within section 11 of the Unfair Contract Terms Act 1977.

(c) *SC 8.3.* Where the subject property is leasehold, and where the lease terms require the landlord's consent or licence to a change of tenant, if that licence to assign is not forthcoming, either party can seek rescission.

To summarize, if there is misrepresentation or mistake, rescission can arise on the fundamental basis of the undoing of the contract. If there is a defective title, failure to complete, or misdescription, rescission can arise for the breach of contract. Lastly, rescission can also arise under the terms of the contract. If this is the case then the contract terms govern when it is exercisable, and the ramifications thereof.

15.6.5 VENDOR AND PURCHASER SUMMONS

Section 49(1) of the Law of Property Act 1925 provides that 'A vendor or purchaser of any interest in land...may apply in a summary way to the court, in respect of any requisitions or objections, or any claim for compensation, or any other question arising out of or connected with the contract', and if such an application is made, the court can 'make such order upon the application as to the court may appear just'. This procedure allows either party to a conveyancing contract to apply to court for its deliberation on a point of dispute without having to apply for specific performance. An example of what could give rise to a summons of this kind is a reference to the court to ascertain if the seller has shown good title and thus complied with the terms in the contract to that effect. If the court did decide that good title had not been shown, the court could order the return of the deposit with interest and costs.

15.7 **AFTER COMPLETION**

Completion of a conveyancing contract narrows down the available remedies. In the main it is the buyer who will commence proceedings as the seller will have the sale proceeds.

At common law, the contract is considered to be at an end as it is deemed to have merged with the purchase deed. The result of this is that the buyer can only sue the seller under covenants for title through title guarantee, contained or referred to in the purchase deed; there is no right to sue under the contractual terms. (Merger takes effect only where the contract and purchase deed cover the same subject matter. If the contract contains ancillary matters then these will not be affected by merger.) However, SC 7.4 provides that 'completion does not cancel liability to perform any outstanding obligation under this contract'. This has the effect of negating the doctrine of merger.

If, unusually, the doctrine of merger effectively puts paid to the terms of the contract the aggrieved buyer can only sue for damages on the covenants for title through title guarantee, implied in the purchase deed.

15.7.1 COVENANTS FOR TITLE—TITLE GUARANTEE

After completion the primary remedy is a claim for breach of title guarantee. Title guarantee is governed by the Law of Property (Miscellaneous Provisions) Act 1994. The title guarantee regime contemplates three possibilities: full title guarantee, limited title guarantee, or no guarantee at all. In the last situation the contract will offer no form of guarantee whatsoever, to the extent that there will be no post-completion remedy arising out of the guarantee available to an innocent party in the event of a dispute arising after completion. The other two possibilities are full and limited guarantee, and are in effect statutory guarantees that will be implied in a purchase deed by the use of the phrases 'with full guarantee' or 'with limited guarantee'. SC 4.6.2 stipulates that the seller is to transfer the property with full title guarantee, but subject to SC 4.6.3 (this refers to SC 3.1.2 and the matters affecting the property, i.e. encumbrances).

Full title guarantee
If the seller sells with full title guarantee, the seller covenants that:

(a) the seller has the right to sell the property;

(b) the seller will at the seller's cost do all things that can be reasonably done to give to the buyer the title the seller purports to give;

(c) if the nature of the title to the subject property is not clear, it is freehold;

(d) if the property is registered, the buyer will receive at least the class of title that prevailed before the transfer;

(e) the seller will provide reasonable assistance to enable the recipient to be registered as proprietor of the registered land;

(f) if the interest is registered, the disposition is of the whole interest;

(g) where the interest passing is leasehold, the disposition is of the whole of the unexpired portion of the term of years created by the lease, the lease still subsists, and there is no subsisting breach that could give rise to forfeiture;

(h) the person making the disposition disposes of it free from all charges and incumbrances and from all other rights exercisable by third parties other than those that the person does not and could not reasonably be expected to know about. (Remember that the contract will include specific reference to encumbrances to which the sale is expressly subject.)

Limited title guarantee

If the seller sells with limited title guarantee, the seller covenants that all the covenants set out above will be complied with save the last covenant, which is replaced by the following:

> the person making the disposition has not since the last disposition for value subjected the property to charges or incumbrances which still exist, or granted third-party rights which still exist.

15.7.2 OTHER POST-COMPLETION REMEDIES

Misrepresentation

A misrepresentation is an untrue factual statement made by one party and relied on by the other, which induces the other party to enter into the contract and, as a consequence, suffer loss. A misrepresentation can be deliberately dishonest and is then termed a fraudulent misrepresentation. Of a lesser degree, the misrepresentation can be simply careless and is then termed a negligent misrepresentation. Alternatively, and of a lesser degree again, the misrepresentation may be made innocently and be a genuine mistake, whereupon it will be termed an innocent misrepresentation. If there is a suggested fraud (see *Derry v Peek* (1889) 14 App Cas 337 for a test of what will amount to fraud), the aggrieved party may sue for damages (by way of the tort of deceit) and rescind the contract. The problem here is that the party alleging fraud must prove it. This is likely to be difficult and costly. Consequently, claims are more usual at the lesser degree of negligent misrepresentation. In this case, the innocent party may take action pursuant to section 2 of the Misrepresentation Act 1967 for either damages or rescission of the contract. If the misrepresentation was innocent the only remedy available is rescission.

Misdescription

A misdescription is an error in the property particulars of the contract. A patent example would be to state incorrectly the tenure as freehold when it is in fact leasehold, or *vice versa*. If the misdescription is sufficiently significant it will entitle the innocent party to seek rescission and damages. A significant misdescription is one that would lead to the innocent party being deprived of what he thought he was going to receive under the terms of the contract (see *Watson v Burton* [1957] 1 WLR 19). Most such cases give rise to a claim under the Misrepresentation Act 1967.

Non-disclosure

This can arise where the seller has not complied with an obligation to disclose matters in the contract or in documents referred to in the contract. Again if the non-disclosure is sufficiently significant to lead to the innocent party being deprived of what he thought he was going to receive under the terms of the contract then that party may seek to rescind the contract.

Rectification

This can arise in different ways. Both the contract and purchase deed can be the subject of rectification. If the contract is involved then an application to the court can be made. If rectification is ordered to correct either an omission or an incorrectly recorded contract term then the court has the discretion to set the date on which the contract is effective. If the purchase deed is involved, again an application to the court can be made to ensure that all the terms in the contract, and which should be in the purchase deed, are incorporated in it. The Land Registration Act 2002, section 65 and Schedule 4 set out the grounds on which an application to correct an entry within a registered title can be made. Rather than rectification, the 2002 Act refers to 'alteration' of the registers. Under the Act, rectification is just one kind of alteration (it is an alteration involving the correction of a mistake which prejudicially affects the title of a registered owner (Schedule 4, paragraph 1)). A right of indemnity will flow from rectification. The order for rectification is discretionary, and the court will not make an order if it would be unjust to the registered proprietor to do so. Section 103 and Schedule 8 permit an indemnity to be claimed from the Chief Land Registrar, *inter alia*, by a person who has suffered loss as a result of any rectification of the register. This indemnity is not available to a claimant who is deemed to have caused or contributed to the loss by fraud or a lack of proper care. Since changes to the Land Registry indemnity rules made with effect from 27 April 1997, indemnity payments will be made whether or not there has been actual rectification.

15.7.3 LIENS

A seller will be entitled to claim a lien (i.e. a right to retain possession of another's property pending discharge of a debt) over the subject property in relation to any unpaid element of the purchase price. The lien is in effect an equitable charge enforceable by the court by way of an order for the sale of the property or for the setting aside of the contract. The lien should always be protected by a notice on the title in registered land and as a C(iii) Land Charge registration for unregistered land.

A buyer is entitled to claim a lien if the deposit is returnable and was paid over originally to the seller's practitioner as agent for the seller. The lien claimed will be in respect of the deposit monies. The lien should be protected by registration.

 Key Points Delays and Remedies

- If the other party is late for completion, remember that under the SCs either party is entitled to claim compensation for delay at the contract rate of interest on a daily basis, until completion takes place.

- If you decide to serve a notice to complete, always do so in a way that enables you to prove service (personal delivery, recorded delivery with advice of receipt, etc.), and remember the period of notice *excludes* the day on which the notice is given.

- Remember that once issued a notice to complete cannot be withdrawn, although the time period set out in the notice can, by mutual agreement, be extended provided both parties acknowledge that time remains of the essence.

- Specific performance can be claimed along with damages and rescission, but the claimant must at the eventual hearing select one remedy in respect of which judgment is to be sought.

- Does the contract include any form of exclusion clause that might limit liability? If it does, is it in any way ambiguous? If it is, remember ambiguity is construed against the person seeking to rely on the exclusion clause.

- Apart from the other party to the contract might there be a claim elsewhere, e.g. against a conveyancing practitioner or surveyor in negligence?

SELF TEST QUESTIONS

1. If a binding land contract states a completion date without qualification, that date is not a strict and binding date that would allow an innocent party to withdraw from such a contract on the occasion of a failure to complete on the contractual completion date. Is this statement TRUE/FALSE? Please delete the incorrect choice.

2. A notice to complete can be served in respect of a contract containing the Standard Conditions

   (a) At any time on or after the date fixed for completion, either party who is ready, able, and willing to complete may give the other a notice to complete

   (b) At any time on the date fixed for completion, either party who is ready, able, and willing to complete may give the other a notice to complete

(c) At any time on or after the date fixed for completion, only the seller who is ready, able, and willing to complete may give the buyer a notice to complete

(d) At any time before the date fixed for completion, either party who is ready, able, and willing to complete may give the other a notice to complete

3. In respect of a contract containing the Standard Conditions, how long should the notice to complete period be

(a) The period within which it would be reasonable to allow completion to take place, when all the outstanding steps are taken into consideration

(b) 10 working days of giving the notice to complete

(c) 10 days of giving the notice to complete

(d) 14 days of giving the notice to complete

4. Where a contract has not been completed, and where a cause of action has arisen, an innocent party to that contract party can consider all available remedies. These remedies are

(a) Specific performance

(b) A claim for compensation by way of damages

(c) Rescission

(d) A summons for possession

Please select the choice that cannot apply.

5. A seller will be entitled to claim a lien (i.e. a right to retain possession of another's property pending discharge of a debt) over the subject property in relation to any unpaid element of the purchase price. Is this statement TRUE/FALSE? Please delete the incorrect choice.

SHORT REVISION QUESTIONS

1. You work for Land and Partners of 1 The High Street Lime Dorset. You act for Mustafa Hadji of 22 The Drive Wembley Middlesex who has contracted to buy the freehold registered property at 11 The Wash Lime Dorset DS1 7QP. He is a cash buyer who has already put you in funds. The transaction was due to complete yesterday pursuant to the terms of a contract exchanged on the 2nd of this month. The seller Bazlur Rashid of 6 The Cut Bethnal Green London E2R 5TY would not complete because there was a delay on his allied purchase. His solicitors are S States & Co. of 69 The High Street Lime Dorset. Please draft a notice to complete.

2. You act for Megalopolis Developers who contracted to buy a plot of land on the edge of Birmingham with a view to developing it into a business park. Being close to the M6 your clients thought there was clear development potential in this land. The sellers were aware of this and as a result were able to inflate the price to take account of this potential. They seem to have now had second thoughts as completion should have taken place some time ago but the sellers are refusing to complete. A notice to complete was served and the time in it has expired. Your client wants to know about compensation that might be claimed against the defaulting sellers. Please advise your client.

3. Consider what might amount to a key points action plan where there is default on a conveyancing contract. Outline the key points in bullet point format taking into account all matters of professional conduct that might be of relevance in these circumstances.

SUGGESTED ANSWERS TO SELF TEST QUESTIONS

1. The statement is true. What can be done if one of the parties delays completion? It is plain that such a delay will be a breach of contract. Can an injured party, immediately upon the happening of

the breach, terminate the contract? It would seem not, because this remedy is only available to the innocent party if time was of the essence in relation to the completion date. When time is of the essence, there is no leeway for delay; completion must be on the date specified, failing which all remedies will be available to the aggrieved party.

2. The correct selection is (a). Standard Condition 6.8 states that at any time on or after the date fixed for completion, either party who is ready, able, and willing to complete may give the other a notice to complete.

3. The correct selection is (b). Standard Condition 6.8.2 states that the parties are to complete the agreement within 10 working days of giving the notice to complete. The 10-day period excludes the day on which the notice is given.

4. The correct selection is (d). Where a contract has not been completed, and where a cause of action has arisen, an innocent party to that contract party can consider four available and different remedies. These remedies are (a) specific performance; (b) a claim for compensation by way of damages; (c) rescission; and (d) a vendor and purchaser summons. Accordingly a summons for possession cannot apply as this will be the order required where a landlord is seeking possession of premises from a defaulting tenant.

5. This statement is true. A seller will be entitled to claim a lien (i.e. a right to retain possession of another's property pending discharge of a debt) over the subject property in relation to any unpaid part of the purchase price. The lien is an equitable charge enforceable by the court by an order for the sale of the property or for the setting aside of the contract. The lien should be protected by a notice in registered land and as a C(iii) registration for unregistered land.

SUGGESTED ANSWERS TO SHORT REVISION QUESTIONS

1. This is a simple matter of applying the facts to Standard Condition 6.8. As such the notice should be in the following format:

Land and Partners
1 The High Street Lime Dorset

S States & Co
69 The High Street
Lime
Dorset
Dear Sirs

11 The Wash Lime Dorset DS1 7QP

On behalf of Mustafa Hadji of 22 The Drive Wembley Middlesex we hereby give you NOTICE that with reference to the contract dated 2nd of this month and made between Bazlur Rashid of the one part and Mustafa Hadji of the other part for the sale and purchase of 11 The Wash Lime Dorset DS1 7QP we place on record the fact that the purchase of the property has not been completed on the date fixed in the contract for completion. We further give you NOTICE that the buyer is ready able and willing to complete. We therefore give you NOTICE pursuant to condition 6.8 of the Standard Conditions of Sale (4th edition) and require you to complete the contract in compliance with that condition.

Yours faithfully

Land and Partners

2. The seller is clearly in breach of contract and indeed a notice to complete has been served and time has expired under the terms of the notice. In *Cottrill v Steyning and Littlehampton Building Society* [1966] 1 WLR 753 a seller knew that the buyer was intending to develop the subject property. The seller failed to complete. Consequently, substantial damages were awarded based on the potential profit the buyer would have made had the transaction been completed properly. Wasted expenses can also be claimed, including wasted legal fees and proper surveying fees. In these circumstances

substantial damages are likely to be awarded once the loss of development potential has been quantified by the client.

3. The action plan is as follows:

- Has the time for completion set out in the contract elapsed?

- If it has, does the client want you to serve a notice to complete, i.e. have you taken instructions approving this step? Make sure the client fully understands the nature and purpose of the notice.

- If you have instructions, have you served a notice using the appropriate wording and in such a way as to enable you to prove service of the notice?

- Has the period set out in the notice expired; and if so does the client want to rescind the agreement, sell the property elsewhere and sue for damages? Make sure you have written confirmatory instructions to that effect.

- Is there some other form of breach of contract? If so, have you obtained a full history of the conveyancing transaction with all supporting papers; and what remedy does the innocent party want?

- Are you able to quantify the client's loss arising from the breach? If so, how much is that loss?

- Is it economic sense to commence proceedings bearing in mind the litigation costs that will be incurred?

- Apart from the other party to the contract might there be a claim elsewhere, e.g. against a conveyancing practitioner or surveyor in negligence?

WIDER READING

- Chapter 9, Abbey, R, and Richards, M, *A Practical Approach to Conveyancing* (Oxford University Press, 2008)

- Sections G and M dealing with post-completion and delays and remedies, Silverman, F, *Conveyancing Handbook* (The Law Society, 2006)

- Emmet on Title:
  - Chapter 7, Remedies for Breach of Contract;
  - Chapters 8 to 10, Completion and Registration;

- For more detail on the changes introduced by the Land Registration Act 2002 see Abbey, R, and Richards, M, *Blackstone's Guide to the Land Registration Act 2002* (Oxford University Press, 2002)

- Chapter 2 (buying a house); Chapter 4 (unregistered land); Chapter 5 (registered land), MacKenzie, J-A, and Phillips, M, *Textbook on Land Law* (Oxford University Press, 2008)

WEBSITES FOR FURTHER INFORMATION

- Council of Mortgage Lenders, **<http://www.cml.org.uk>**. This site will set out post completion requirements of lenders within their CML handbook.

- Land Registry, **<http://www.landreg.gov.uk/>**. For all post-completion matters relating to registered land.

- Land Registry internet register access, **<http://www.landregistrydirect.gov.uk>**.

- National Association of Estate Agents, **<http://www.naea.co.uk>**. Of benefit should a dispute arise over the payment of the estate agent's account.

• The Royal Institute of British Architects, **<http://www.ribafind.org.uk/>**. After completion the client might want to carry out alterations additions or a complete reconstruction. If so an architect will be needed.

ONLINE RESOURCE CENTRE CASE STUDY

> **RESIDENTIAL TRANSACTION CASE STUDY—DELAYS AND REMEDIES**
>
> **Our clients:**
> **Shilpa Jennings—sale of 19 Minster Yard Blakey**
> **Shilpa Jennings and Daniel Rodriguez—purchase of 9 Castle Hill Blakey**
>
> We act for Shilpa Jennings who is selling 19 Minster Yard Blakey for £100,000 and Shilpa and Daniel Rodriguez who are buying 9 Castle Hill Blakey for £200,000. The completion of sale of 19 Minster Yard was due yesterday but the buyers failed to complete on time. Acting for the seller you need to protect her by taking action under the terms of the contract. See the documentation on the Online Resource Centre.

16 LEASEHOLDS

16.1 INTRODUCTION

Leases are a very long established contractual relationship that offers tenants a legal estate in land. The use of leaseholds has really taken off in urban environments with the conversion of large houses into several flats and the development of business leases for commercial properties. However, the relationship between the lessor and lessee can be a troublesome one and the interface between the parties is riddled with litigation. In recent years there has been an increase in demand for the reform of this relationship. This has recently given rise to several statutory attempts at reform.

The present Government has introduced a statute that may make substantial changes to leasehold property law and conveyancing. It is called the Commonhold and Leasehold Reform Act 2002. There is now a new form of holding a freehold estate. It is called commonhold land. It is actually a freehold but held by commonhold across several estate owners in combination. The purpose of the new form of holding is to address the current deficiencies in relation to the enforceability between lessees of covenants and other lease provisions (for the same reason it also addresses the related problems with freehold flats, i.e. flying freeholds). Commonhold is considered in the next chapter. This chapter will focus upon purely leasehold considerations.

A lease is an agreement whereby an estate in land or property is created, but only for a finite term. Different types of leases with differing contents are required to deal with different types of property. No one lease is exactly the same as another. A lessor will require the lease to include clauses and/or covenants that adequately protect the reversionary interest. To that end the lessor will include a long list of obligations, of covenants requiring the lessee to do and not to do various things. However, above all else the lease must contain the most important protection for the lessor, which is a right of re-entry or forfeiture. A lessee will also require essential clauses or covenants, but these are in many cases entirely opposite to those favoured by the lessor. A lessee will seek to limit the number and extent of the lease covenants. Moreover a prudent lessee will also seek covenants from the lessor to perform the obligations resting with the lessor, for example, to keep the main structure of the property, of which the subject property forms part, insured and in good repair.

16.2 **LEASE CONTENTS**

This section contains an examination of the some of the more commonly encountered elements in most leases. In effect it sets out what you might expect to see in a lease of either residential or commercial property. We will start with Land Registry prescribed clauses.

16.2.1 **LAND REGISTRY PRESCRIBED CLAUSES LEASES**

The Land Registry has issued rules requiring certain lease contents to be in a particular position in registrable leases (new leases with a term of more than seven years). As a result they are called prescribed clauses leases. These provisions were contained in the Land Registration (Amendment) (No 2) Rules 2005 (SI 2005/1982). The compulsory requirements have been limited to a set number of 'prescribed clauses' with a requirement that these particular clauses must appear at the start of the lease. New Rule 58A states that '. . . a prescribed clauses lease must begin with the required wording or that wording must appear immediately after any front sheet'. A prescribed clauses lease will cover any lease the term of which triggers compulsory registration and which is granted on or after 19 June 2006. The information that must appear at the lease commencement includes:

online
resource
centre

- lessor's title number;
- the parties to the lease;
- a full description of the property being leased;
- prescribed statements (those required by statute, e.g. involving a charity or pursuant to the Leasehold Reform and Housing and Urban Development Act 1993);
- the term for which the property is leased;
- any premium;
- prohibitions or restrictions on disposing of the lease;
- rights of acquisition such as a contractual right for the tenant to renew the lease (an option to renew);
- easements.

16.2.2 **TYPICAL LEASE COVENANTS AND OTHER PROVISIONS**

The following are typical covenants found in most residential leases and which will form the subject of negotiations between both parties to the intended lease.

To pay rent and other outgoings including service charges
A covenant to pay rent is fundamental and should appear in all leases that include a rental obligation. The lessee will want to introduce another clause that suspends the payment of rent if the property is destroyed or damaged by an insured risk. The lessor should agree this provided the lessor can control the insurance of the whole property and thus include loss of rent as an insurable risk. This leads on to the consideration of the payment of other outgoings such as insurance. This can be by way of an additional rent and the lease can be drafted to give effect to this. Similarly any service charge payable can be made a rent in the same way. (This benefits the lessor because if there are arrears these can be recovered as a rent, rather than as a result of a breach of covenant. As a consequence, a notice pursuant to section 146 of the Law of Property Act 1925 can be avoided. However, statute may limit this power, depending on the nature of the property.) The lease should stipulate that the rents are payable in advance, failing which they will be payable in arrears. If the lease includes a rent review provision allowing the rent to be increased (and/or decreased) at regular intervals, there should also be a specific covenant requiring the lessee to enter into review procedures

and to pay the rent at the reviewed level. Rent reviews are rare in residential leases, which tend to include fixed increases at regular intervals. The lease will also require the lessee to pay all outgoings applicable to the subject property such as council tax and water rates.

Insurance covenants

Insurance can be dealt with in one of two ways. First, the lessee can be made to covenant to insure or, secondly, the lessor can agree to insure. Where the lease is of a whole house or of one of two maisonettes, then it would be sensible to expect the lessee to insure. However, where there is a building in multiple occupation, the converse should apply so as to ensure that there is an appropriate level of cover rather than the patchwork of different policies that would occur if all the lessees insured separately. In this situation the lessor should arrange insurance so that the whole of the building can be covered by one policy, with all the lessees obliged by way of a lease covenant to pay, perhaps as a rent, a proportion of the annual premium. Where the lessor insures, a prudent lessee will want to see the lease include a covenant requiring the lessor to expend any monies claimed and received from the insurance company on reinstating the damaged or destroyed property. This is particularly so where reinstatement will be necessary to all parts of the building to give support to the subject property itself. Some lessees might at this point require the lessor to make up any deficiency in the insurance proceeds from the lessor's own resources. Clearly the lessor will resist such an onerous obligation. The point will have to be negotiated. If the lessor does accept the point, it is an incentive to over-insure the premises, rather than under-insure. A typical lease insurance provision would read:

> to insure and keep insured the building of which the demised premises forms part against loss or damage by the Insured Risks [with the Insured Risks defined elsewhere in the lease, i.e. fire, storm, tempest, flood, etc.] and such other risks as the lessor's surveyor for the time being considers necessary in the full cost of reinstatement together with architects' surveyors' and other fees payable together with the costs of site clearance and the securing of the damaged property and making good any shortfall out of the lessor's own monies.

The lessee will also want a covenant requiring the lessor to supply a copy of the policy on request, as well as details of the existing cover by way of a copy of the current policy cover schedule and the current premium receipt.

An insurance provision should require either the lessor or the lessee, depending on who is covenanting to insure, to arrange insurance cover in the full reinstatement value. The cover should also include all architects' and surveyors' fees incurred in connection with the rebuilding or reinstatement of the property. This will ensure that the property is not under-insured. Damage caused by the action of terrorists is no longer covered in normal buildings policies and separate cover for damage occasioned in this way must be arranged, in particular for property located near potential targets, e.g. in the main cities, near major stations, etc. This needs to be covered in the insurance covenant.

To keep the property in good repair

Where there is a property in multiple occupation, the usual repairing arrangement is for the lessee to be required to keep in good repair the inner skin of the demised property. This would require the lessee to keep properly maintained the plaster, the ceiling, and flooring materials, but not much else. All structural elements of the property, including the floor and ceiling joists, the load-bearing walls, the roof, and foundations, should all be repairable by the lessor with all the lessees paying a service charge to reimburse the lessor for this expense. The rationale for this arrangement is that there is a need for a single consistent approach to the whole question of structural repairs and maintenance.

The precise standard of repair required was set out in *Proudfoot v Hart* (1890) 25 QBD 42. In that case it was held that the standard of repair was to be determined according to several factors, including the subject property's age and character and the environment in which the property was located. In effect this has meant that there is a clear difference in the expected standard of repair between a Victorian property and one that was built in the 1990s. As to the meaning of 'repair', the courts have made it clear this includes renewal (see *Lurcott v Wakeley and Wheeler* [1911] 1 KB 905). A covenant requiring the lessee 'to put and keep the property in good and substantial repair' is particularly onerous. This is way above mere repair and will be interpreted as requiring the lessee to carry out all repairs and renewals, substantial or not, from the start of the lease (see *Elite Investments Ltd v TI Bainbridge Silencers Ltd* [1986] 2 EGLR 43). This kind of covenant is, however, encountered frequently in practice. In addition, a covenant to keep in repair implies a covenant to put and keep in repair.

To ensure compliance with repairing obligations modern leases will always include a covenant allowing the lessor to enter the demised premises, on prior written notice, to view the state of repair. If the repairing covenant is in breach, the lessor will then be able to serve a notice on the lessee calling for work to be carried out to ensure the proper repair of the subject property. Moreover, the lessor, in the case of default by the lessee, will have the benefit of a further covenant enabling the lessor to enter the subject property to carry out the necessary repairs and to charge the lessee for the cost of the work required (*Jervis v Harris* [1996] 1 All ER 303, CA).

User

It is possible for the lease to include a covenant imposing an absolute restriction on the lessee against changing the use from any user precisely stated in the lease. In the case of a residential lease it is desirable that the user clause be such that there can be only one permitted use that cannot be changed. The reason for this is that this form of extremely restrictive covenant will guarantee conformity of use amongst all the lessees and ensure that there is no breach of planning law. Such a clause could read:

> not to use the demised property other than a residential house/flat/maisonette and for no other purpose whatsoever.

Because the covenant is absolute the lessor cannot be compelled to allow a change of use.

The covenant can be qualified requiring the lessor's consent before the use can be changed, and this is more commonly seen in commercial leases. (In such commercial leases an absolute user covenant will mean that the rental on review could be subject to a reduction in valuation. This is because a restriction on user makes the lease less attractive to lessees and will therefore command less as a rental. However, a qualified covenant may avoid this limitation on the rent review.) There is no statutory provision that implies that the lessor's consent cannot be unreasonably withheld as is the case with alienation covenants. Section 19(3) of the Landlord and Tenant Act 1927 provides that if a consent for a change of use is required, then the lessor is not allowed to demand a premium or extra rent for giving that consent. The lessor can require costs to be paid by the applicant including all legal fees. A premium or extra rent can be demanded if alterations to the structure of the property are also proposed.

Alienation

In this context, the term 'alienation' covers covenants against assignments, underlettings, mortgages, and other material dealings with the legal estate. There is no such restriction against alienation unless there is express provision to that effect in the lease. Many leases include a covenant whereby the lessee cannot assign the lease without the prior written consent of the lessor, such consent not to be unreasonably withheld. Some leases extend this provision to include sub-lettings as well as assignments. If the lease states that the lessor's consent is required but does not refer to reasonableness then statute adds this qualification (Landlord and Tenant Act 1927, section 19(1)(a)). The Landlord and Tenant Act 1988 requires the lessor to deal with applications for consent to an assignment within a reasonable time of the making of the application. Should the lessor fail to do so the lessee can, if the lessee has suffered loss as a consequence of the lessor's delay, sue the lessor for damages for breach of statutory duty.

It is now considered inappropriate to fetter a lessee's right to deal freely with a long lease-hold legal estate. The lessee of such an estate should be able to deal with it unchecked, just as any absolute owner would in relation to a fee simple. Therefore the question for a practitioner should be: is there any restriction against alienation; and if so, should there be such a provision in the lease of the subject property? Frankly the answer is in the negative where the lease is a long lease of residential property. However, there can be exceptions. For example, the lease may require an incoming lessee, before being registered with the lessor as the new leaseholder, to enter into a direct covenant with the lessor to observe all the terms and especially the covenants in the lease (the lessor will require this because there is no privity of estate after the assignee sells on). The same arrangement could be predicated upon the incoming lessee applying for licence to assign. The licence would then incorporate an observance covenant in the same format. A typical clause of this kind would read:

> not to assign transfer underlet or part with or share possession of the demised premises or any part thereof without the written consent of the Lessor PROVIDED ALWAYS that it shall be lawful for the Lessor to withhold such consent unless before the assignment transfer or underlease is completed the lessee procures the execution of and delivers to the lessor a deed to be prepared by the Lessor's legal practitioner at the full cost of the lessee and which contains a covenant by the proposed assignee transferee or sub-lessee to perform and observe during the term assigned transferred or granted the covenants by the lessee and the conditions contained in this lease in the same manner as if such covenants and conditions were repeated in full in that deed.

Alterations, additions, and/or improvements

The reversioner will want to ensure that unauthorized alterations do not take place. Additionally, the reversioner will want to be sure that the alterations that do take place are such that the integrity of the structure will not be adversely affected. This will also be the case for additions and improvements. Lessees of long residential leases will argue that they should be free to do what they like with their property. Certainly this would seem to be a tenable argument where the lease is of a house. However, it is less tenable where the lease is of a flat or maisonette. Clearly in these circumstances, alterations, additions, and improvements could very well affect adjacent or adjoining property, and the lessor may therefore feel that there should be controls over what may be done by the lessee in the way of alterations.

A covenant dealing with alterations can include an absolute bar such as 'not to make or allow to be made any alterations additions or improvements to the demised premises'. If this is the prevailing covenant, the lessee cannot carry out any work whatsoever. This could be seen to be unfair to a long leaseholder, and consequently such clauses are sometimes qualified to allow the lessee to carry out non-structural alterations within the demised premises that do not cut or maim any load-bearing walls or timbers.

An absolute bar on alterations or additions must be considered unacceptable in a long lease. If one appears in a draft, the lease should be amended to allow alterations with the lessor's written consent. To the extent that proposed alterations amount to improvements, section 19(2) of Landlord and Tenant Act 1927 will then apply so that consent cannot be unreasonably withheld, and the lessor cannot demand any payment beyond his reasonable legal and other expenses incurred in granting consent (see *Woolworth & Co Ltd v Lambert* [1937] Ch 37). However, to avoid any argument about whether an alteration is or is not an improvement, the clause should be amended to allow alterations or additions with the lessor's consent, such consent not to be unreasonably withheld (this is known as a fully qualified covenant). In this way the lessor will be required to justify any refusal of permission, ultimately in court, and would therefore not be an avenue the landlord would explore without real justification. The statute does not stop the lessor from seeking a reasonable sum should the proposed amendments diminish the value of the premises, or any adjacent premises in the ownership of the same lessor. Similarly, if the alteration or addition does not add to the letting value of the premises the statute does not prevent the lessor from obtaining from the tenant a covenant to reinstate the premises to their former condition at the end (or sooner determination) of the lease.

Quiet enjoyment

A covenant for quiet enjoyment is given by the lessor for the benefit of the lessee and should appear in all leases. If an express covenant is absent, an implied covenant will apply. An express covenant will override an implied one. A typical express covenant should read:

> that the lessee paying all the rents reserved by this lease and performing and observing all the covenants contained in this lease shall peaceably hold and enjoy the demised premises without any interruption by the lessor or any other company or person rightfully claiming under or in trust for the lessor.

The purpose of the covenant is to confirm that the lessee can physically enjoy the complete benefit of the property without the lessor adversely disturbing that enjoyment. The courts have held that this covenant could apply to scaffolding outside the property; see *Owen v Gadd* [1956] 2 QB 99, although this case related to a shop where the scaffolding was outside the shop door and window and consequently affected the lessee's business. In contrast, in *Kenny v Preen* [1963] 1 QB 499 the court held that the lessor's conduct where he banged on the door, sent threatening letters, and shouted abuse at the lessee, amounted to a breach of covenant for quiet enjoyment.

Service charge provisions

Where the lessor is under an obligation to keep in good repair a building of which the subject property forms part, the cost of those repairs will usually be recoverable from the lessee. That cost, along with other expenses incurred by the lessor in providing services (e.g. lighting and heating of common parts) on behalf of all the lessees, will form a service charge. If in the lease it is described as a rent then that enables the lessor to distrain for arrears of a service charge rental.

The following should apply to a lease of part of a residential block, i.e. a flat in a conglomeration of flats all paying a service charge to the one lessor:

(a) The lease may provide for a service charge payable as a rent with payments on account made quarterly at a rate to be decided by the lessor's surveyor (whose decision shall be final, save for manifest error) at the start of each year but having regard to expenditure in the previous year. At the end of the year accounts should be prepared without undue delay to reconcile payments made and received. Excess monies held should go to a sinking fund (see below), while any underpayment should be paid by the lessees within 21 days of the supply of the year-end accounts.

(b) There should also be a sinking fund created for the express purposes of ensuring that there are sufficient monies available to cover major expenses such as lift replacements or external redecoration schemes.

(c) The lessor should be obliged by a covenant to carry out clearly identified obligations listed in a schedule to the lease, including repairs and renovations to the main structure and common parts, and lighting and heating the common parts.

(d) The lessor should be obliged to provide at least two estimates where expenditure is required other than those of a moderate nature.

(e) Different lessees in the block may pay different charges. Consideration should be given to a fair distribution of the burden of payment, e.g. should occupants on the ground floor be required to pay towards the cost of the repair of a lift?

Many of these items are now required by statute (see sections 18–30 of the Landlord and Tenant Act 1985). Section 19 of this Act imposes a requirement of reasonableness as to service charges. Section 20 requires, where the cost of work exceeds £1,000, two estimates to be obtained with notice being given to lessees (provisions within the Commonhold and Leasehold Reform Act 2002 have extended these rights to cover improvements as well as service charges). The best method of avoiding the potential problems in this area is to draft the lease so that the maintenance of the property is carried out by a management or maintenance company with each lessee owning a share in that company. If this arrangement is created then the maintenance of the whole block will be in the control of the lessees, who can control the expenditure in whatever way they wish.

The Commonhold and Leasehold Reform Act 2002 introduces a new requirement that ground rent will not be payable unless it has been demanded. The demand is to be made by giving the tenant a prescribed notice. The reforms in the Act prevent the application of any provisions of a lease relating to late or non-payment (e.g. additional charges such as interest) if the rent is paid within 30 days of the demand being issued. It also introduces additional restrictions on the commencement of forfeiture proceedings for breaches of covenants or conditions of a lease. It modifies section 81 of the Housing Act 1996 to prohibit the commencement of forfeiture proceedings, including the issue of a notice under section 146 of the Law of Property Act 1925, in respect of non-payment of service charges or administration charges. This is not the case if the charge has been agreed or admitted by the tenant, or a court or Leasehold Valuation Tribunal (LVT) has determined that it is reasonable and due. It also prohibits the commencement of forfeiture proceedings for other breaches unless a court or LVT has determined that a breach has occurred.

Mutual rights

In residential blocks in multiple occupation and where maisonettes are concerned, easements, both granted and reserved, will almost certainly have to be detailed in the lease. There will need to be mutual rights by way of easements and exceptions for matters such as the paths of conducting media (i.e. gas pipes, electricity cables, sewers, etc.) serving the property that have to pass across other parts of the block. Similarly, rights of access to and from the subject property will need to be detailed showing the common areas to which the lessee may have access. The reverse will also be true. There will be other lessees who may require rights over the subject property by way of express reservations detailed in the lease. The best example would be the mutual right of lessees in a multi-occupied block to access to other parts for the purposes of emergency repairs or general upkeep. Another common element required will be a mutual proviso for support and protection between flats in a block, or maisonettes. This protects the core of any multi-occupation arrangement.

16.3 **COUNCIL OF MORTGAGE LENDERS' HANDBOOK AND LEASES**

The Council of Mortgage Lenders (CML) issued *The CML Lenders' Handbook for Solicitors and Licensed Conveyancers England and Wales* in 1999. It is regularly updated to cover changes in the law and/or conveyancing practice. It provides conveyancing practitioners with comprehensive instructions on what lenders expect practitioners to do when acting for them. The handbook was issued after close consideration between The Law Society and seven of the leading UK lenders.

A lender will not, in any circumstances, accept as security for a loan a lease that contains forfeiture on bankruptcy of the lessee. In other words, if the lease allows a right of re-entry on the bankruptcy of the lessee, the lease will not be mortgageable. The reasoning is that if the lessee did become bankrupt and the lessor forfeited, the lender's security would evaporate. Additionally, where there is a property that contains several units, all on separate leases, a lender (and indeed a lessee) would not want each lessee to be responsible for the repair of his or her own section of the structure. Clearly this would lead to an inconsistent and patchy approach to repair that can be avoided if this responsibility rests with the lessor. The same argument will apply to insurance arrangements for multi-occupied property. Moreover, any absolute prohibition against an assignment or mortgage of the whole of the subject property would be unacceptable in a long residential lease. Lastly, although strictly speaking nothing to do with leases, it is worth emphasizing that flying freeholds (i.e. freehold flats or maisonettes not attached to the ground) are unlikely to be acceptable to a lender or a buyer. In particular a flying freehold will involve positive covenants that cannot be enforced. The pivotal problem arises from the current inability to enforce positive repairing covenants against a freehold covenantor's successors in title. It is this deficiency that makes a freehold flat a poor choice in the property marketplace. (There is no reason why a leaseholder should not also own a share of the freehold with other leaseholders in the same block.) In future, the position may be changed by the Contracts (Rights of Third Parties) Act 1999. It is possible that the Act will provide a method of enforceability, but this has yet to be properly tested in the courts. Many lessors expressly exclude this Act from their leases. Commonhold will also assist.

 Conduct Point Acting for the lender

- Always check the requirements of your lender in the CML handbook. Failure to carry out instructions on behalf of a client may amount to a breach of the Code of Conduct for solicitors 2007, R.1.04. You must act in the best interests of each client, R.1.05. You must provide a good standard of service to your clients.

16.4 DEFECTIVE LEASES

A residential lease will be considered defective if any of the following occurs in the lease you are considering for your client buyer if:

(a) the lease contains a forfeiture on bankruptcy provision;

(b) the lease fails to include proper repairing covenants that ensure the ongoing maintenance and renewal of the main structure, roof, foundations, and common parts. This will require the involvement of the lessor or management company;

(c) the property is in a newly-constructed block of flats where the developer is not offering an NHBC guarantee or similar guarantee scheme. Although not strictly a lease defect, many mortgagees will not lend in the absence of this protection;

(d) the lease does not include a covenant by the lessor to take action against another lessee for breach of covenant at the request of a lessee who agrees to indemnify the lessor for that action;

(e) the lease has inadequate insurance provisions, or the lessor is under no obligation to look after unlet or unsold property in a large block.

Where there are two maisonettes on lease, it has been the occasional practice also to transfer the freehold of the flats to the lessees at the time of the granting of the lease. However, in doing so the transfer is in two parts. This means that each lessee is the freeholder for the other maisonette. This sounds a simple solution that, in theory, sets up a commonality of responsibility for repairs and maintenance. However, there is one major flaw: one of the two freehold titles will be a 'flying freehold'. This is unsatisfactory conveyancing practice. In place of this arrangement the single freehold title could be vested in the joint names of the two lessees, or in a limited company jointly owned by the lessees.

16.5 LIABILITY ON COVENANTS IN LEASES: ENFORCEMENT

For many years it was the case that the original lessor and lessee were liable to each other under the covenants in their lease for the full term granted by the lease. As a consequence of the effects of privity of contract this liability remained enforceable in the courts even if the lessee had subsequently assigned the residue of the term of the lease. The practical effect of this was that a lessee could be sued for arrears of rent even though that lessee had not been the tenant in occupation for many years and where there had been various subsequent lessees liable to pay rent under the terms of the original lease. (In *Selous Street Properties Ltd v Oronel Fabrics Ltd* [1984] 1 EGLR 50 it was held that where a later tenant carries out improvements that increase the rental value, the original tenant must pay rent at that higher level even though the works were carried out after the original tenant ceased to be involved as a result of having assigned the residue of the term of the lease.)

This outdated element of landlord and tenant law has led to some very unfair situations where an original tenant has been called on to pay rent many years after assigning its interest in the subject property. A measure of reform was made by the provisions of the Landlord and Tenant (Covenants) Act 1995. Most of these provisions apply only to new leases created on or after 1 January 1996. In essence a lessee who assigns such a lease automatically enjoys a release through statute of any continuing liability under the lease covenants. However, a lessor can require the outgoing lessee to enter into a form of guarantee stipulated by the statute and known as an authorized guarantee agreement (AGA). The statute made a major change to the law—the benefit and burden of lease covenants pass automatically on assignment without any question of whether or not they touch and concern the land. The successor in title, the assignee, will take the benefit and burden of the lease covenants by reason of statute and the assignor, the original lessee, will be released from liability.

Where a buyer is purchasing a flat in a block containing many other similar flats and where all are on long leases, the doctrine of privity of contract can cause major problems where one lessee is involved in a dispute with another about the enforcement of lease covenants. To enable enforcement to take place, and for all lessees in the block to know the extent of the lease terms for all occupants of the block, the lease should state that all the leases granted for the block will or do contain the same terms as that for the subject property. Coupled with this there should be a covenant by the lessor on request by one lessee (and with that lessee agreeing to indemnify the lessor's costs) to enforce lease covenants against another lessee. Without this provision one lessee has no legal right to enforce covenants against another lessee as the covenant is not with the other lessee but with the lessor. However, the lease can be drawn up to include a covenant between the lessor, lessee, and all the other lessees in the block. If this appears, each lessee can take action against any other lessee.

 Key Points Lease contents

- In the light of the type of lease to be given or taken by your client, are the terms contained within it suitable to a lease of that kind? Try to step back and take an overview to ensure the contents are suitable.

- When instructed by buyer and lender, always remember your dual obligation to ensure that the lease to be purchased suits both your clients and their individual requirements and instructions.

- In particular, are the insurance arrangements suitable to the type of subject property? In brief, if the property is a house, the lessee should insure; if a flat, the lessor should insure; if a maisonette, either will do. The same is true for repairs.

- If your client is taking a long residential lease, reject clauses restricting alienation except if the restriction is there to ensure a direct covenant between the lessor and your client the assignee.

- When acting for a proposed lessee intending to buy a leasehold residential property with a mortgage, never agree a lease that allows forfeiture on bankruptcy as this will not be acceptable to a lender.

- Always ensure the lease to be purchased contains a lessor's covenant allowing one lessee to enforce lease covenants against another lessee through the assistance of the lessor.

16.6 GRANTING NEW LEASES

A new lease is granted by a lessor or landlord and is taken by a lessee or tenant. The lease will almost always be in two parts, the original part executed by the lessor and the counterpart executed by the lessee. Both parts will be identical; and when exchanged and dated the lease will, at the moment of exchange, come into formal and legal existence and thereby create a brand new legal estate. The lessor will be able to receive not only any premium to be paid on the grant of the new lease but thereafter any periodically recurring rent provided for in the lease.

16.6.1 LEASE-SPECIFIC CHANGES IN THE CONVEYANCING PROCESS

Before the draft contract can be prepared a draft lease must be drawn up which will form the subject of the agreement. It is perfectly possible to adopt the same contract forms, incorporating the Standard Conditions, used on a freehold sale for a leasehold disposal, whether this is to be the grant of a new lease, or an assignment or transfer of an existing lease. (SC 8 deals with leasehold property; SC 8.1 covers existing leases, and SC 8.2 new leases. If the lessor's consent is required this is covered by SC 8.3.) When the contract is drafted it should be sent to the buyer's practitioner, together with the proposed form of draft lease in duplicate. The draft contract and lease will then be approved with or without amendments. After exchange the agreed form of lease must be engrossed and executed in duplicate by the contractual parties, in readiness for completion. Where necessary the seller will have to obtain all necessary consents for the grant of the new lease from either or both the seller's mortgagee and superior title holder. At completion the buyer may be required to pay lease-specific outgoings in advance such as rent and service charges. There will possibly be Stamp Duty and Land Tax (SDLT) on the lease rental as well as the consideration, and Land Registry forms are required for any application to the registry for first registration of a registerable lease. (Section 6 of the Land Registration Act 2002 stipulates that first registration must take place within two months of the completion of a grant of a new lease for a term of more than seven years, or the assignment on sale of an existing lease where the term left to run exceeds seven years at completion.)

16.6.2 ACTING FOR THE LESSOR

The draft lease must reflect the precise wishes of the lessor and the particular nature of the property to be sold. If the lessor wishes to sell a flat within a block but retain control of that block, the lease terms must reflect these instructions. There will be times when the lessor will instruct you to proceed in a way that is unsatisfactory, e.g. the lessor may want to grant a new lease for a flat in a block, getting rid of all responsibility for the lessor who only wants to receive the rents. This may mean you will be required to draw up a lease that is unsaleable, being unacceptable to a lender as a consequence of the absence of proper repairing arrangements for the whole block. To draft such a lease would be bad conveyancing practice. If this situation does occur, you should write to your client expressing as clearly as possible your reservations about the nature of your instructions, and invite your client to reconsider. If the instructions remain the same, our advice is to stand firm and not proceed: it could amount to professional negligence to do so.

 Conduct Point Drafting a lease

- Failure to carry out appropriate proper drafting of a lease may amount to a breach of the Code of Conduct for solicitors 2007, R.1.04. You must act in the best interests of each client, R.1.05. You must provide a good standard of service to your clients.

You could suggest to the lessor that there is an alternative to simply giving each lessee their own individual repairing and insuring responsibilities, and that is to pass these responsibilities to a management company. Each lessee would be given a share in the management company and the lessor would receive the rents without any further liability for future maintenance and insurance arrangements. Furthermore, if there are freehold covenants, the lease should include a covenant on the part of the lessee to observe and perform those covenants with an indemnity against any future breach.

When drafting the contract you will need to insert in the particulars the estate and term to be offered to the buyer. You can do this by express reference or by attaching the draft lease to the contract as an annexure (SC 8.2.3 states 'The lease is to be in the form of the draft attached to the agreement'). With a new long lease, nothing more about deducing title needs be said as SC 8.2.4 stipulates that 'If the term of the new lease will exceed seven years the seller is to deduce a title which will enable the buyer to register the lease at HM Land Registry with an absolute title'. This should therefore require the seller to deduce the superior title.

16.6.3 ACTING FOR THE LESSEE

On receipt of the draft lease and contract you should check both very carefully to make sure that they describe and demise the subject property accurately. You must also be sure that your client understands the relevance of all the lease terms. To ensure that this is so, you should write to your client with a detailed report on all the terms in the lease. In this way the buyer cannot in the future allege that you did not advise him of any particular provision that may cause future problems.

The draft lease and contract, lessee concerns

Points of concern about the draft lease and contract terms that should be carefully considered include the following:

(a) The description of the subject property in the lease: are all the walls, floors, and ceilings included or excluded?

(b) Is there a garden at the front and/or rear and if so do either or both form part of the property to be purchased?

(c) Are there adequate rights of access to and from the subject property over the parts leading to the premises?

(d) Are there mutual rights of support, protection, and entry for repairs?

(e) Is the buyer aware of rental at the levels shown in the draft?

(f) Are the lessee's covenants reasonable and in particular is there any restriction on alienation; and if so is that restriction fair to a long leaseholder?

(g) Does the lease allow forfeiture on bankruptcy? If so, take steps immediately to remove this provision.

(h) Is there a covenant requiring the lessor to enforce covenants against other lessees in the block? This must be included.

(i) Does the contract make proper and exact reference to the estate and term to be sold to your client?

(j) Are there any lease-specific special conditions and if so are they acceptable in the context of your instructions for the buyer?

16.6.4 GIVING NOTICE

There is one further lease-specific task to be performed after completion where the new lessee has purchased with a mortgage. Most modern leases require notice of assignment and charge (or mortgage) to be given to the seller's solicitor. Where there is the grant of a new lease clearly only notice of charge must be given along with the payment of any fee for the registration. There is a double obligation where you also act for the lender as it is important that the lessor is aware of the lender's interest in the property should the lessee, in the future, breach any of the terms of the lease.

 Key Points New leases

- Does the new lease contain all the terms considered appropriate to the type of property to be sold or purchased?
- Does the new lease contain any terms that are unacceptable to the buyer's lender or to the buyer?
- Has the contract been drafted properly in the context of the proposed terms of the new lease, and what lease-specific special conditions are there and are they acceptable?
- On the assumption that the lease requires it, have you remembered to give notice of the buyer's charge to the lessor and have you paid the registration fee?

16.7 EXISTING LEASES

Practitioners need to be aware that in the standard contract there are just two specific Standard Conditions relating to leaseholds:

(a) SC 8.1.2 states 'The seller having provided the buyer with copies of the documents embodying the lease terms, the buyer is treated as entering into the contract knowing and fully accepting those terms'. This covers a sale where the lease terms are not all in the one document, i.e. where there has been a subsequent deed of variation of the original lease terms. It also states that there is a clear assumption that all the necessary copies have been supplied and the buyer therefore takes the property in full knowledge of the lease terms and is deemed to have accepted the transaction on that basis.

(b) SC 8.1.3 states 'the seller is to comply with any lease obligations requiring the tenant to insure the property'. This is self-explanatory and requires the incoming lessee to insure or comply with the insuring arrangements perhaps through the lessor or a management company in the manner set out in the lease. This section will only rarely apply as in most cases the lessor will covenant to insure.

16.7.1 LEASE-SPECIFIC CHANGES IN THE CONVEYANCING PROCESS

We set out below the common changes to the conveyancing process arising in leasehold transactions.

16.7.2 ACTING FOR THE SELLER—GOOD LEASEHOLD ISSUES

If the property being sold is registered at Land Registry with good leasehold title, the same provisions as to the deduction of title apply, and SC 4.1.2 stipulations also apply. The buyer must also receive a copy of the lease registered at Land Registry along with any deeds varying it or affecting it and which have been registered. However, the problem for the buyer of a good leasehold title is that the registration is such that there is no guarantee of the validity of the lease, i.e. that the lease has been validly granted. The registry will issue this class of title when the superior title, the reversionary title, has not been seen and approved by the registrar. As a consequence, a buyer faced with a good leasehold title should demand that the superior title be deduced; and because the Standard Conditions are silent on the point, an extra special condition should be inserted in the contract to that effect. (In practical terms this should be unnecessary if title is to be investigated before contracts are exchanged.) The buyer cannot persist as the law does not support this insistence. If the superior title is not available, the buyer should be advised not to proceed as a good leasehold title may not be acceptable to a lender. The seller could be asked to upgrade the title, as a good leasehold title can be upgraded to absolute so long as an applicant is able to produce to the registrar the freehold reversionary title together with any superior leasehold titles.

 Conduct Point Acting for the lender

- Always check the requirements of your lender in the CML handbook. Failure to carry out instructions on behalf of a client may amount to a breach of the Code of Conduct for solicitors 2007, R.1.04. You must act in the best interests of each client, R.1.05. You must provide a good standard of service to your clients.

16.7.3 INFORMATION REQUIRED ON A SALE

Obtain details of any rents, service charge, and insurance payments made by the client seller, as you will require these to prepare answers to preliminary enquiries or Property Information Forms. You will also need to see copies of the last three years' service charge accounts, as the buyer will inevitably ask for these prior to exchange. (In Protocol cases the seller's practitioner is required to ask the client to produce service or maintenance charge accounts for the last three years, where appropriate, and evidence of payment.) Check the lease to see what assignment preconditions there are and take steps to comply with them, such as making provision in the contract for the buyer to enter into a deed of covenant at the time of completion directly with the lessor. If necessary apply for a licence to assign supported by references from the buyer (see below) prior to exchange of contracts. SC 8.3 applies if a consent to assign or sub-let is required to enable completion to take place. SC 8.3.2(a) states that 'The seller is to apply for the consent at his expense, and to use all reasonable efforts to obtain it'. In support of this application SC 8.3.2(b) requires the buyer to 'provide all information and references reasonably required'. Either party may rescind the contract if three working days before the day for completion the lessor's consent has not been issued, or if issued it has attaching to it 'a condition to which the buyer reasonably objects'. Rescission is effected by giving written notice to the other party to the agreement; and on rescission arising in this manner, neither party is 'to be treated as in breach of contract and condition 7.2 applies' (this condition provides that the deposit is to be repaid with interest and the buyer is to return any documents and to cancel any registration of the contract, i.e. the parties are to return to the position they were in as if the contract had not existed).

If there is a management company owned by the lessees, before exchange the seller must supply copies of the memorandum and articles of association of that management company together with, where appropriate, a copy of the seller's share certificate (remember if the company is limited by guarantee there will be no share certificate).

16.7.4 ACTING FOR THE BUYER

If you are acting for a buyer, you should always check the amount of time left to run on the lease, i.e. the residue of the term granted, especially if the buyer is purchasing with the assistance of a mortgage. This is particularly so for two reasons. First, if the residue of the term is fairly limited it will be unacceptable to many lenders. Some lenders will decline to lend if the lease term has less than 60 years left to run. Secondly, the lender may have based the loan on a term of years stated to it by the buyer. If that figure turns out to be inaccurate, the lender must be told the correct details by you and you need to obtain its written approval to the amended details prior to an exchange of contracts. The same is true for any rental details.

16.7.5 LEASE-SPECIFIC ENQUIRIES AND THE CONTRACT

Where a leasehold is being purchased, lease-specific enquiries should be made covering insurance and maintenance details and should include a request for the last three years' service charge accounts along with a copy of the current insurance policy and up-to-date schedule of cover. This can be done by way of the Protocol forms, the seller's leasehold information form parts I and II.

Carefully check the contract to make sure it properly describes all the leasehold title to be purchased. Reference should be made in the contract to the property description in the lease. Look through the lease terms to make sure it contains all the necessary terms, and that it does not include any that should be avoided. Check to see if the lease plan remains accurate. Check the lease to see what obligations there are, if any, on any incoming lessee before the transfer can take place. If the lessor's consent is required for the transfer of the residue of the lease to your client, consider the need for references. Add together the amount of the current annual rent and service charges and obtain references for that amount. The references should be provided by the buyer's bankers, accountants, if any, and perhaps with one further reference as to the buyer's character. If the client is not known to you as an established client, you should decline to supply a reference for someone you do not know. If there is a management company, call for a copy of the memorandum and articles of association and a copy of the seller's share certificate. If the company is limited by guarantee, there will be no share certificate. Provide the buyer with a full and detailed written report of the terms of the lease and ask the client to confirm in writing that the terms of the lease are understood and accepted. Does the lease contain all the terms considered appropriate to the type of property to be purchased? If not you may need to approach the seller with a request that a deed of variation be obtained from the lessor to correct the position. The deed of variation can include a necessary lease term or exclude an undesirable one. Leases that are more than 15 to 20 years old tend not to include a lessor's covenant to enforce covenants by other lessees. A variation is one way in which this kind of lease can be modernized so as to include such a clause.

 Key Points Existing leases

- If the seller is seeking to sell a good leasehold title, always insist that either the title be converted to absolute, or the superior title be deduced and amend the draft contract to include a special condition to that effect.

- If you are acting for a seller of an existing lease, make sure you have details of all lease-specific outgoings as well as copies of the last three years' service charge accounts.

- If there is a management company ensure you have the details of the constitution of the management company such as the company memorandum and articles of association.

- If you are acting for a buyer, make sure the lease terms are acceptable to your client and the client's lender and supply references if needed in support of an application for licence to assign if required by the terms of the lease. The financial references should be for the total of the annual rent and the current annual service charge payments.

SELF TEST QUESTIONS

1. If a lease states that the lessor's consent is required for an assignment of the residue of the term but does not refer to reasonableness then statute adds this qualification. Is it

   (a) Landlord and Tenant Act 1954, section 40

   (b) Landlord and Tenant Act 1927, section 19(1)(a)

   (c) Law of Property (Miscellaneous Provisions) Act 1989, section 2

   (d) Landlord and Tenant Act 1987, section 4

2. Which of the following legal leases does not need to be made by deed

   (a) Lease for 5 years at a market rent

   (b) Sub-lease for 9 years (less 10 days)

   (c) Lease for 99 year at a premium of £10,000 but at a nominal rent

   (d) Lease for 3 years at a market rent

3. Alienation covenants are governed by the Landlord and Tenant Act 1927, section 19(1)(a) that says

   (a) If there is a qualified covenant, the lessor cannot unreasonably withhold his consent

   (b) If there is a qualified covenant the lessor can unreasonably withhold his consent

   (c) If there is a qualified covenant the lessor can ignore alienation applications

   (d) If there is a qualified covenant the lessee can avoid making alienation applications

4. If a lease states that the lessor's consent is required for a change of use but does not refer to reasonableness then statute adds this qualification. Is it

   (a) Landlord and Tenant Act 1927, section 19(1)(a)

   (b) Landlord and Tenant Act 1954, section 40

   (c) Landlord and Tenant Act 1987, section 4

   (d) Law of Property (Miscellaneous Provisions) Act 1989, section 2

5. A lender will not, in any circumstances, accept as security for a loan, a residential long lease that contains forfeiture on bankruptcy of the lessee. Is this statement TRUE/FALSE? Please delete the incorrect choice.

SHORT REVISION QUESTIONS

1. Your firm acts for Julia Nowell who wishes to buy a residential 99-year lease for £125,000. The draft documents have just arrived from the seller's solicitor and you have been asked by your Principal to check the draft lease to make sure it is acceptable. Please compile a checklist of the main points of concern about the draft lease and the contract terms that should be considered and checked for this purpose.

2. Your Training Partner is concerned to ensure that the fee earners handling residential long leasehold purchases are aware of elements in a residential lease that would be unacceptable to a buyer/mortgagee. She has asked you to prepare a list of such elements that you consider could be considered defects meriting concern. Please draft such a list.

3. Your Principal has mentioned to you that he needs to grant a new 10-year lease of some shop premises in York. He is aware that the Land Registry may have some requirements in relation to the format of the lease and has asked you for details. Please advise in bullet point format.

SUGGESTED ANSWERS TO SELF TEST QUESTIONS

1. The correct answer is (b). If the lease states that the lessor's consent is required but does not refer to reasonableness then statute adds this qualification (Landlord and Tenant Act 1927, section 19(1)(a)).

2. The correct answer is (d). Because the lease term is for three years it does not need to be made by deed and can be in the form of a tenancy agreement, i.e. a contract not sealed or even granted orally.

3. The correct answer is (a). Alienation covenants are governed by the Landlord and Tenant Act 1927, section 19(1)(a) that says that if there is a qualified covenant, the lessor cannot unreasonably withhold his or her consent.

4. None of these apply. There is no statutory provision that implies that the lessor's consent cannot be unreasonably withheld. However, section 19(3) of the Landlord and Tenant Act 1927 does provide that if a consent for a change of use is required, then the lessor is not allowed to demand a premium or extra rent for giving that consent.

5. This statement is true. If a lease allows a right of re-entry on the bankruptcy of the lessee, the lease will not be mortgageable. The reasoning is, of course, that if the lessee did indeed become bankrupt and the lessor forfeited the lease then the lender's security would evaporate.

SUGGESTED ANSWERS TO SHORT REVISION QUESTIONS

1. The following constitutes an appropriate checklist that covers some of the major points of concern.

   (a) The description of the subject property in the lease. Are all the walls, floors and ceilings included or excluded?

   (b) Is there a garden at the front or rear, and if so does either or both form part of the property to be purchased?

   (c) Are there adequate rights of access to and from the subject property over the parts leading to the premises?

   (d) Are there mutual rights of support, protection, and entry for repairs?

   (e) Is the buyer aware of rental at the levels shown in the draft?

   (f) Are the lessee's covenants reasonable and in particular is there any restriction on alienation and if so is that restriction fair to a long leaseholder?

   (g) Does the lease allow forfeiture on bankruptcy? If so, take steps immediately to remove this provision.

   (h) Is there a covenant requiring the lessor to enforce covenants against other lessees in the block? This must be included.

   (i) Does the contract make proper and exact reference to the estate and term to be sold to your client?

   (j) Are there any lease-specific special conditions and if so are they acceptable in the context of your instructions for the buyer?

(k) If the buyer intends to purchase with the assistance of a mortgage, we must make sure that the lease terms accord with the lender's requirements. We must therefore check the details of the mortgage offer and the CML Handbook together with any particular requirements the lender may list with the client's offer of mortgage.

2. A residential long lease will be considered defective if any of the following appear in the lease we are considering for our client buyer:

   (a) If the lease contains a forfeiture on bankruptcy provision.

   (b) If the lease fails to include proper repairing covenants that ensure the ongoing maintenance and renewal of the main structure, roof, foundations, and common parts. This will require the involvement of the lessor or a management company.

   (c) If the property is in a newly constructed block of flats where the developer is not offering an NHBC guarantee. Although not strictly a lease defect, many lenders will not lend in the absence of this protection.

   (d) If the lease does not include a covenant by the lessor to take action against another lessee for breach of covenant at the request of a lessee who agrees to indemnify the lessor for that action.

   (e) If the lease has inadequate insurance provisions, or the lessor is under no obligation to look after unlet or unsold property in a large block.

3. Land Registry has issued rules requiring certain lease contents to be in a particular position in registrable leases, i.e. new leases with a term of more than seven years. They are called prescribed clauses leases, see the Land Registration (Amendment) (No 2) Rules 2005 (SI 2005/1982). The main elements of this new set of requirements are as follows:

   - The compulsory requirements have been limited to a set number of 'prescribed clauses' with a requirement that these particular clauses must appear at the start of the lease. New Rule 58A states that '...a prescribed clauses lease must begin with the required wording or that wording must appear immediately after any front sheet'.

   - The information that must appear at the lease commencement includes:
     - lessor's title number;
     - the parties to the lease;
     - a full description of the property being leased;
     - prescribed statements (those required by statute, e.g. involving a charity or pursuant to the Leasehold Reform and Housing and Urban Development Act 1993);
     - the term for which the property is leased;
     - any premium;
     - prohibitions or restrictions on disposing of the lease;
     - rights of acquisition such as a contractual right for the tenant to renew the lease (an option to renew);
     - easements.

WIDER READING

- Chapter 10, Abbey, R, and Richards, M, *A Practical Approach to Conveyancing* (Oxford University Press, 2008)

- Abbey, R, and Richards, M, *A Practical Approach to Commercial Conveyancing and Property* (Oxford University Press, 2006)

- Sections K and L dealing with Leaseholds and Tenanted Property, Silverman, F, *Conveyancing Handbook* (The Law Society, 2006)

- Emmet on Title: Chapters 26 to 28, Leases

- For more detail on the changes introduced by the Land Registration Act 2002 see Abbey, R, and Richards, M, *Blackstone's Guide to the Land Registration Act 2002* (Oxford University Press, 2002)

- Chapter 8 (the leasehold estate); Chapter 9 (Obligations of landlord and tenant); Chapter 10 (Commonhold), MacKenzie, J-A, and Phillips, M, *Textbook on Land Law* (Oxford University Press, 2008)

- Clarke, D, *Commonhold: The New Law* (Jordans Publishing, 2002)

WEBSITES FOR FURTHER INFORMATION

- Housing Corporation, <http://www.housingcorp.gov.uk>. The Housing Corporation is a Non Departmental Public Body, sponsored by the Office of the Deputy Prime Minister. Their role is to fund and regulate housing associations in England.

- Housing Forum, <http://www.thehousingforum.org.uk/>. The Housing Forum has established itself as the only housing organization whose membership spans all sectors of housing construction.

- HM Revenue and Customs, <http://www.hmrc.gov.uk/>. This site enables you to ascertain how Revenue concerns may affect leases, especially relating to Stamp Duty Land Tax.

- Land Registry, <http://www.landreg.gov.uk/>. The registration of leases now affects all leases granted for a term of more than seven years.

- Landmark Information group, <http://www.landmark-information.co.uk/>.

- The Residential Property Tribunal Service, <http://www.rpts.gov.uk/>. The public body that can decide many rent and leasehold disputes.

- Lands Tribunal, <http://www.landstribunal.gov.uk/index.htm>. The Lands Tribunal was established by the Lands Tribunal Act 1949 to determine questions of disputed compensation arising out of the compulsory acquisition of land; to decide rating appeals; to exercise jurisdiction under section 84 of the Law of Property Act 1925 (discharge and modification of restrictive covenants); and to act as arbitrator under references by consent.

- Office for National Statistics, <http://www.ons.gov.uk/>. National statistics as they may relate to leases or leaseholders.

- Ordnance Survey, <http://www.ordnancesurvey.co.uk/home/index.html>.

- Royal Institution of Chartered Surveyors, <http://www.rics.org.uk>. Information about Chartered Surveyors.

online resource centre

ONLINE RESOURCE CENTRE CASE STUDY

COMMERCIAL TRANSACTION CASE STUDY—OCCUPATIONAL LEASES

Our client: Cambo Ltd—acquisition of 18 Clover Street London W2

Timothy Wainwright and his family have run a successful wholesale clothing business for many years. Timothy has decided to sell the business and enter the world of property investment. He has formed a company called Cambo Ltd in which he, his wife, and their three sons are all shareholders. Cambo Ltd has agreed to buy 18 Clover Street London W2 for £700,000 subject to and with the benefit of two occupational business leases.

The occupational leases are set out within the Online Resource Centre.

17 COMMONHOLD

17.1   INTRODUCTION

It has been the law for many years that positive obligations cannot be enforced in freehold land. In essence a burden of a positive covenant does not run with the land, see *Austerberry v Oldham Corporation* (1885) 29 Ch D 750. This was reiterated in the more recent case of *Rhone v Stephens* [1994] 2 AC 310. In that case the court made it very clear that the only way the law was to change was if Parliament took steps towards reform. The response was the promotion of the new concept of commonhold land. This is defined in the Commonhold and Leasehold Reform Act 2002 (CLRA 2002) as the land specified in the memorandum of association in relation to which a commonhold association exercises functions (see section 1(1)). It is in effect the name for the special way freehold land will be held by a community of freeholders entitled to participate in the association.

Commonhold has been slow to catch on with solicitors and their clients. In effect it is not very popular at present. This is probably due to a lack of education about the topic in the legal profession along with not enough confidence yet in the product. If you want to learn more about the full details of commonhold ownership we recommend you consult *Commonhold: The New Law* by DN Clarke (Jordans Publishing, 2002) as being an excellent guide to this relatively new area of Land Law and Property Law and Practice.

17.2   COMMONHOLD—A BRIEF OVERVIEW

Each separate property in a commonhold development will be termed a unit. A unit can be either residential or commercial and the owner will be the unit-holder. There will be a commonhold association that will own and manage the common parts. It will be a company limited by guarantee where all the members will be the unit-holders. Thus unit owners will have a duality of ownership. First they will own their units and, secondly, they will own a share of the commonhold association and thus indirectly the common parts.

All commonhold will be registrable at the Land Registry that will require on registration a Commonhold Community Statement (CCS) and the memorandum and articles of association. The CCS will contain the rules and regulations for the commonhold. It will be possible for owners of existing non-commonhold property to seek to convert their title to a commonhold arrangement, but 100 per cent of all owners will have to agree to the conversion. The freeholder must consent to the conversion, without which conversion cannot proceed.

In summary the unit-holder will in effect own, freehold-style, his or her flat or property instead of being a leaseholder. The unit-holder will share in the running of the common-hold-held common parts and be required to pay a management or service charge. Unlike leaseholds, the units will not be wasting assets; neither will they be at the whim of a free-holder and/or the freeholder's management policies.

17.3 IMPORTANT DEFINITIONS FOR COMMONHOLD

17.3.1 UNIT-HOLDER

A unit-holder is the person registered as proprietor, or entitled to be registered as proprietor, of a freehold estate in the unit (CLRA 2002, section 12). A sole unit-holder is a member of the commonhold association. You can also have joint unit-holders (section 13). In the case of joint unit-holders, they decide which of them is to be the member of the commonhold association. If they don't decide, then the unit-holder who is named first in the proprietor-ship register is the member. (Why can't they all be members? Presumably because it's fairer to have one vote per unit.)

17.3.2 COMMONHOLD ASSOCIATION

This is a private company limited by guarantee incorporated under the Companies Act 1985. Therefore it must have a memorandum of association setting out the objects of the company. Under section 34 of the CLRA 2002 one of the objects of the company must be to exercise the functions of a commonhold association. The commonhold land must be specified. The memorandum must fix the amount each member guarantees to contribute if the company is wound up—this is £1.

17.3.3 COMMONHOLD COMMUNITY STATEMENT

The Commonhold Community Statement (CCS) serves two purposes:

- It describes the development, the units, and the common parts.
- It sets out the rules under which it will be managed.

The CCS will set out the rights and duties of the unit-holders and the commonhold association and how management decisions are to be taken. Examples of duties are contained in section 31. They include:

- to pay money;
- to carry out works;
- to grant access;
- controlling the use of the unit e.g. residential only;
- not to cause nuisance or annoyance to neighbours.

Section 31(7) provides that a duty conferred by a commonhold community statement on a commonhold association or a unit-holder shall not require any other formality. So the duties are binding even though they are not contained in a deed. As soon as a unit-holder acquires a unit he or she is bound by the duties; there is no need for any separate deed.

Similarly the *rights* do not require to be granted by deed. They are not easements as such and do not need to satisfy the requirements of section 52 of the Law of Property Act 1925. The distinction between legal easements and equitable easements is not relevant in commonhold. Simply read the CCS to establish what rights and duties exist.

17.4 HOW COMMONHOLD IS CREATED

Land becomes commonhold land because it is registered as such.

The role of Land Registry is to ensure that:

- commonhold land is clearly defined;
- it is transferable under the general principles of land registration, subject to the variations specific to commonhold;
- all associated and necessary documents within the commonhold development are accessible to those who wish to view them.

17.5 COMMONHOLD REGISTRATION

17.5.1 REGISTRATION WITHOUT UNIT-HOLDERS

As an example, before occupation of the units a developer applies for the land to be registered as commonhold. He can do this at the same time as he applies to register a transfer of the land to him, or applies for first registration. Before he applies he must first incorporate the commonhold association and draft the CCS. Then he must lodge at Land Registry the documents set out in Schedule 1 of the CLRA 2002. These are:

- the commonhold association's certificate of incorporation as a company;
- its memorandum and articles of association;
- the CCS;
- a certificate of compliance signed by the directors of the commonhold association. This deals with such matters as confirming that the CCS complies with the Act and that the association has not traded;
- certain consents—consents are required from the registered proprietors of the freehold land, the registered proprietor of any lease for more than 21 years (not seven, interestingly) and the proprietor of any registered charge.

The registration procedure including the entries that will be made on registration are set out in rules made under section 65 of the CLRA 2002.

17.5.2 REGISTRATION WITH UNIT-HOLDERS (I.E. CONVERSIONS)

Where units are already occupied by long leaseholders an application can be made to convert to the freehold reversion to commonhold (CLRA 2002, section 9). However all leaseholders and their mortgagees must consent. You cannot mix and match commonhold and long leases.

Typically a conversion will occur where long leaseholders own a management company that controls the freehold and they want to convert to commonhold. There is no transitional period. All leases are extinguished and registration of the commonhold common parts and units then occurs.

17.6 DEALINGS WITH COMMONHOLD

17.6.1 DEALINGS BY THE UNIT-HOLDER

The unit-holder's powers to deal with his unit are set out in sections 15 to 22 of the Act.

- He may transfer the whole of his freehold unit. The new unit-holder then notifies the commonhold association of the transfer and becomes a member of the association. The outgoing unit-holder remains liable for any arrears of service charge or other previously incurred liabilities. Transfers of part are not permitted unless the commonhold association consents in writing (very unlikely I would have thought—perhaps where you agree to sell a bit of your unit to your next door neighbour). If this occurs, the CCS will need to be amended because the CCS defines the extent of the units and the extent of one at least will have changed.
- He may charge the whole of his unit (but not part).
- If he grants a lease of a residential unit, the lease must comply with conditions to be prescribed by regulations, e.g. length of lease.

17.6.2 DEALINGS BY THE COMMONHOLD ASSOCIATION

Common parts

The commonhold association may transfer land in the common parts (i.e. adding or subtracting bits). In this event, as the extent of the common parts will be changed, an amendment to the CCS will be required.

The association may also create other interests in the common parts, e.g. an easement in favour of an adjoining development.

The association's power to create charges is restricted. Essentially it can create a legal mortgage but before doing so, it must pass a unanimous resolution to create the charge.

Units

The association may decide to change the size of the units (CLRA 2002, sections 23 and 24). In this event, the CCS must be amended to redefine the extent of the unit. However, not surprisingly, the unit-holder and any mortgagee must consent in writing before any change in size is made. There will be power for the court to dispense with the unit-holder's or chargee's consent in exceptional circumstances, e.g. if the unit-holder has disappeared.

17.7 TERMINATION OF COMMONHOLD

This is covered in sections 43 to 56 of the Act. As the commonhold association is a limited company, it may be wound up. However, do remember there can be no commonhold land without a commonhold association. There are two types of winding up—voluntary, and by the court.

17.7.1 VOLUNTARY WINDING UP

Here the unit-holders simply agree to end the commonhold, e.g. because they wish to sell to a developer for redevelopment.

The commonhold association must be solvent for a voluntary winding up.

The unit-holders must agree on a termination statement. This sets out how the commonhold association intends to deal with the common parts and the units, and how it will distribute the assets.

At least 80 per cent of the members of the association must vote in favour of the termination statement and the resolution to wind up the association. If *any* member does not vote in favour of winding up, the liquidator must apply to the court to decide how the termination should proceed. This protects the interests of those who did not vote in favour.

So if 100 per cent agree on the winding up there is no need to involve the court. The liquidator simply makes a termination application directly to Land Registry.

Ultimately, with the sanction of the court if necessary, the liquidator makes a termination application to Land Registry. The land will cease to be commonhold land and it will revert to normal freehold. The procedure for such applications will be governed by rules to be made under section 65 of the Act.

17.7.2 WINDING UP BY THE COURT

Under the Insolvency Act 1986 a creditor may petition for the commonhold association which is unable to pay its debts to be wound up by the court. Of course this would be very serious for unit-holders because there can be no commonhold land without a commonhold association. So the court is given power to make a succession order allowing a newly formed commonhold association to take over. Again, rules will prescribe the procedure to be followed on applications for a successor to be registered as proprietor of the common parts.

17.8 CRITICISMS OF COMMONHOLD

Some criticisms have been levelled at commonhold. One is the somewhat restrictive requirement for the consent of all leaseholders to a conversion to commonhold. In developments that are perhaps limited in size, then the current scheme will probably be satisfactory. However, if you have a larger development, (and here we mean where there are 20 leaseholders or more) then if just one acts unreasonably and refuses to agree to a commonhold conversion, or perhaps just cannot be bothered to agree, then clearly the remaining leaseholders will be greatly frustrated by this provision. The majority are trapped with their leases and there is nothing they can do about it. Perhaps Parliament could have considered a provision requiring a small minority of leaseholders to surrender their leases and receive a freehold title in return or compensation if they prefer.

Other criticisms include not allowing the commonhold association to impose a statutory charge on a unit for arrears of service charge. There is no forfeiture allowed so the association is left with standard remedies for the recovery of debts. Money judgements and charging orders take time to obtain and will not give priority over prior mortgages and charges.

Do be aware also that commonhold is not the final answer to the problem of freehold covenants. Commonhold will solve the problem of positive obligations within a commonhold community but not in other situations. That awaits the introduction of something called land obligations, a proposed reform of covenants which has yet to receive the green light from Parliament.

 Key Points Commonhold

- A commonhold is a freehold community.
- Within the boundaries of that community are separate freeholders with their own units.
- These freeholders are called unit-holders.
- The remainder of the commonhold comprises the common parts, which are vested in a commonhold association.
- This association is a private company limited by guarantee and its only members are the freehold registered proprietors of the units within the community.
- The community is then bound together by a 'local law', which is drafted, when the community is established. This local law is known as the Commonhold Community Statement (or CCS).
- Sch 2 of the Act lists the types of registered freehold that cannot be commonhold. These are flying freeholds (e.g. no commonhold flats above a shop not forming part of the commonhold), agricultural land and where the title is contingent i.e where the estate is liable to revert by operation of law under a specified statute e.g. Places of Worship Sites Act 1873.

SELF TEST QUESTIONS

1. It is possible to change the size of a commonhold unit provided the unit-holder and any chargee consent. TRUE/FALSE. Please delete the incorrect choice.

2. To achieve a voluntary winding-up of a commonhold which of the following is NOT a requirement

   (a) The commonhold association must be solvent

   (b) The unit-holders must agree on a termination statement

   (c) At least 70 per cent of the members of the association must vote in favour of the termination statement

   (d) If not all members of the association vote in favour of the termination statement the liquidator must apply to the court to decide how the termination application should be made

3. Under the commonhold legislation a building is permitted to have commonhold flats above a shop not forming part of the commonhold. TRUE/FALSE. Please delete the incorrect choice.

4. CCS is

   (a) A statement of the rights and duties of a landlord and tenant in a commonhold

   (b) A statement produced by local estate agents

   (c) A statement of the objects of the commonhold association private limited company

   (d) A statement describing the commonhold development, the units and common parts, and the rules under which the commonhold will be managed

5. Before an application can be made to convert an existing development into commonhold, a majority of all leaseholders and their mortgages must consent. TRUE/FALSE. Please delete the incorrect choice.

SHORT REVISION QUESTIONS

1. Your firm acts for developers who have recently built a new small estate of eight light industrial workshop units on the edge of town. They want to dispose of them by sales to individual workshop owners in such a way that ensures that the maintenance of the common areas (the estate roads and pavements and surrounding garden areas) are kept to a high standard, but they do not want to get involved in making sure that this is what is done. Please advise the developers of their options.

2. Your firm acts for a local developer who has asked you for a brief overview of commonhold as he is acutely aware of the deficiencies in the leasehold arrangement where multi-occupied single sites are concerned. Your Principal has asked you to prepare some briefing notes for his use. Please provide such briefing notes.

3. Your firm's marketing department are interested in developing new area of expertise. You have suggested commonhold and the marketing department want from you a view of the potential popularity of commonhold and where it is likely to be used. Please set out your thoughts on this area.

SUGGESTED ANSWERS TO SELF TEST QUESTIONS

1. The correct selection is true, although the court can dispense with consent in exceptional circumstances, e.g. if a unit-holder has vanished.

2. The correct answer is (c)—it is 80 per cent.

3. The correct selection is false.

4. The correct answer is (d).

5. The correct selection is false—it is all of them, not a majority.

SUGGESTED ANSWERS TO SHORT REVISION QUESTIONS

1. The developers wish to sell off their development to individual workshop owners while ensuring that there is a mechanism in place to maintain the common areas of the development. This can be achieved in one of two ways: first by granting leases and then vesting the freehold in a management company where the shareholders are the eight lessees; secondly by creating a commonhold that governs this estate.

   (a) Leasehold solution. The developers will grant leases with three parties. The first will be themselves as lessors. The second will be the lessee/purchaser and the third will be a management company given the title to the common parts by a lease with the developers and with whom the lessee must covenant to pay a service charge levied by the company. They will control that company, as each owner will have a share in the company. In this way the management company will be obliged to maintain the common parts and the lessees will be obliged to pay for it.

   (b) Commonhold solution. Alternatively the developers can sell off commonhold units. Each separate property in a commonhold development will be termed a unit. A unit can be either residential or commercial and the owner will be the unit-holder. There will be a commonhold association that will own and manage the common parts. It will be a company limited by guarantee where all the members will be the unit-holders. Thus unit owners will have a duality of ownership. First they will own their units and, secondly, they will own a share of the commonhold association and thus indirectly the common parts. The unit-holder will share in the running of the commonhold-held common parts and be required to pay a management or service charge.

2. A burden of a positive covenant does not run with the land, see *Austerberry v Oldham Corporation* (1885) 29 Ch D 750. This was re-iterated in the more recent case of *Rhone v Stephens* [1994] 2 AC 310. In that case the court made it very clear that the only way the law was to change was if Parliament took steps towards reform. Their response was the concept of commonhold land. This is defined in the Commonhold and Leasehold Reform Act 2002 (CLRA) as the land specified in the memorandum of association in relation to which a commonhold association exercises functions (see section 1(1)). It is in effect the name for the special way freehold land will be held by a community of freeholders entitled to participate in the association. Each separate property in a commonhold development will be termed a unit. A unit can be either residential or commercial, and the owner will be the unit-holder. There will be a commonhold association that will own and manage the common parts. It will be a company limited by guarantee where all the members will be the unit-holders. Thus unit owners will have a duality of ownership. First they will own their units and, secondly, they will own a share of the commonhold association and thus indirectly the common parts.

   All commonhold will be registrable at the Land Registry that will require on registration a Commonhold Community Statement (CCS) and the memorandum and articles of association. The CCS will contain the rules and regulations for the commonhold. It will be possible for owners of existing non-commonhold property to seek to convert their title to a commonhold arrangement, but 100 per cent of all owners will have to agree to the conversion. The freeholder must consent to the conversion, without which conversion cannot proceed.

In summary the unit-holder will in effect own, freehold-style, his or her flat or property instead of being a leaseholder. The unit-holder will share in the running of the commonhold-held common parts and be required to pay a management or service charge. Unlike leaseholds, the units will not be wasting assets; neither will they be at the whim of a freeholder and/or the freeholder's management policies.

3. How popular will commonhold become? It appears to be a flexible solution to many of the problems in the current freehold and leasehold system. It offers titles of indefinite duration that can be freely bought and sold and mortgaged in the same way as any other freehold estate in land. Having just the one CCS for the whole development is a particularly attractive feature. It gives the assurance that the rights and obligations in the CCS will affect all unit-holders in exactly the same way. This uniformity simply does not occur in many leasehold schemes where the terms of the different leases often vary. And each time you buy a lease you are reliant on the skills of your solicitor to advise as to the adequacy of the lease drafting. So commonhold should find favour, and particularly in the following areas:

- residential flats;

- housing estates where estate rent charges would currently be employed;

- retirement villages and sheltered accommodation;

- holiday complexes offering communal facilities; and

- retail, industrial, and other commercial commonholds where there are shared facilities.

This is provided, of course, that the property market prefers the commonhold route. Commonhold will only succeed if developers can sell commonhold units for more than their leasehold counterparts. If this is not the case, developers may decide to stick with leaseholds. When you grant leases you retain a freehold interest, which has value, and once the last unit is let, you can sell your reversion to a property management company.

But if commonhold is perceived by the market to be successful for developer and occupier alike then ultimately there will be pressure from many thousands of existing leaseholders to convert.

As with any new product, its success or otherwise will depend on how the market responds. In the longer term it should become an essential feature of communal living in the 21st century.

WIDER READING

- Chapter 10, Abbey, R, and Richards, M, *A Practical Approach to Conveyancing* (Oxford University Press, 2008)

- Abbey, R, and Richards, M, *A Practical Approach to Commercial Conveyancing and Property* (Oxford University Press, 2006)

- Sections K and L dealing with Leaseholds and Tenanted Property, Silverman, F, *Conveyancing Handbook* (The Law Society, 2006)

- Emmet on Title: Chapters 26 to 28, Leases

- For more detail on the changes introduced by the Land Registration Act 2002 see Abbey, R, and Richards, M, *Blackstone's Guide to the Land Registration Act 2002* (Oxford University Press, 2002)

- Chapter 8 (the leasehold estate); Chapter 9 (Obligations of landlord and tenant); Chapter 10 (Commonhold), MacKenzie, J-A, and Phillips, M, *Textbook on Land Law* (Oxford University Press, 2008)

- Clarke, D, *Commonhold: The New Law* (Jordans Publishing, 2002)

WEBSITES FOR MORE INFORMATION

- Commonhold, **<http://>**.

- Housing Corporation, **<http://www.housingcorp.gov.uk>**. The Housing Corporation is a Non Departmental Public Body, sponsored by the Office of the Deputy Prime Minister. Its role is to fund and regulate housing associations in England.

- Housing Forum, **<http://www.thehousingforum.org.uk/>**. The Housing Forum has established itself as the only housing organization whose membership spans all sectors of housing construction.

- HM Revenue and Customs, **<http://www.hmrc.gov.uk/>**. This site enables you to ascertain how Revenue concerns may affect leases, especially relating to Stamp Duty Land Tax.

- Land Registry, **<http://www.landreg.gov.uk/>**. The registration of leases now affects all leases granted for a term of more than seven years.

- Land Registry internet register access, **<http://www.landregistrydirect.gov.uk>**. This deal with the Registry online.

- Landmark Information group, **<http://www.landmark-information.co.uk/>**.

- The Residential Property Tribunal Service, **<http://www.rpts.gov.uk/>**. This is the public body that can decide many rent and leasehold disputes.

- Licensed Conveyancers, **<http://www.conveyancer.org.uk>**. The other profession that can deal with leases.

- National Land Information Service, **<http://www.nlis.org.uk/>**. Online searches for leasehold properties.

- Office for National Statistics, **<http://www.ons.gov.uk/>**. National statistics as they may relate to leases or leaseholders.

- Ordnance Survey, **<www.ordnancesurvey.co.uk/home/index.html>**. For lease plans.

- Royal Institution of Chartered Surveyors, **<http://www.rics.org.uk>**. Information about Chartered Surveyors.

18 NEW PROPERTIES

18.1 INTRODUCTION

The sale of a new property is a more complicated transaction than the sale of an existing one for several reasons. First, a new property on an estate will comprise part of the developer's title to the whole estate, and a property lawyer must therefore think about 'sale of part' considerations such as the grant and reservation of new easements and the imposition of new covenants. There is a clear overlap here with the general topic of the draft contract, which we considered in Chapter 5. There is also some overlap with the topics of leasehold and commonhold, as the new property could of course be the grant of a lease or a new commonhold unit. You are therefore referred to Chapters 16 and 17 concerning leasehold and commonhold respectively.

The National Protocol is not normally used by a developer's solicitor, but the spirit of it is usually invoked as the solicitor will invariably be required to send out a comprehensive package of documents at the beginning of the transaction to assist the buyer's solicitor. You will need to appreciate the items that are relevant for the pre-contract package.

Where the property is in the course of construction there will also be a complication over the timing of completion because the builder/developer will not know precisely the date when the building will be physically completed. Accordingly, the builder cannot agree a fixed completion date and this can have a knock-on effect where the buyer of the new property has a related sale.

There are obvious planning considerations where a property is newly constructed and it must be remembered that as well as the dwelling itself, you must consider estate roads, drains and sewers, and their future maintenance and adoption by the local authorities. In this respect, you will appreciate the overlap with the material you covered earlier in the course when you considered town and country planning, searches, and enquiries. Remember that enquiries over and above the standard pre-contract enquiries will be appropriate where your client is buying a new property.

Some important aspects relating to new properties are now examined including: acting for a developer or buyer; road and sewer agreements; structural defects insurance; and synchronizing completion of a related sale when acting for the buyer of new property.

18.2 **ACTING FOR THE DEVELOPER**

Acting for the developer, the trainee solicitor is likely to become involved in the day-to-day running of the conveyancing files for the individual plots. Typically a partner or senior assistant will first prepare the initial documentation, e.g. standard form contract, replies to standard enquiries, relevant search results, copies of the relevant planning consents, and evidence of title. Once the legal paperwork has been set up, the trainee solicitor may handle the plot sale files. This will involve sending out to the individual buyer's solicitors the standard documentation with a covering letter or information pack, responding to any additional enquires and dealing with any suggested amendments to the contract and purchase deed. This will of course be followed by exchange and completion.

Assuming title is registered, deduction of title on the plot sales is achieved by supplying official copies and a title plan. However, very often the title plan of an estate is large and unwieldy, and in this case the seller's practitioner may apply to the Land Registry on Form OC1 for a certificate of official inspection of the title plan. This certificate on Form CI will certify that the subject property (i.e. the individual plot) to which it relates is within the seller's title. It will also indicate the entries on the title that affect the plot in question. Form CI will also assist the buyer's practitioner when carrying out the pre-completion official search; instead of having to attach a plan to Form OS2, the practitioner will simply quote the plot number specified on the Form CI.

Acting for the developer, some of the essential components of the draft contract are as follows:

- Include a full and accurate description of the property being sold by reference to a scaled plan.
- Negate any implied grant of easements in favour of the buyer under section 62 of the Law of Property Act 1925 and the rule in *Wheeldon v Burrows* (1879) 12 Ch D 31 whilst making provision for the grant and reservation of new easements and the imposition of new covenants.
- Annex to the contract the standard form of purchase deed for the plots. The purchase deed will include all relevant terms such as new restrictive covenants, easements etc.
- Provide for legal completion to take place within a certain specified period after the seller's practitioner has notified the buyer's practitioner that the property has been completed and is fit for occupation.
- Specify that the builder will provide NHBC (or similar) protection and that the NHBC documentation will be supplied to the buyer before completion.
- If the buyer is paying an additional price for 'extras' (e.g. specially designed kitchen or bathroom fittings), the contract should itemize the extras and state the additional sums being paid.
- A full 10 per cent deposit paid on exchange to be held as agent (so that it can be released to the developer client).
- The developer may wish to reserve the right to vary the method of construction or the materials used in the construction of the new properties.

In addition, do not forget other important issues of a more general nature, such as the following:

- If unusually the developer's title is unregistered, consider applying for voluntary first registration. It is easier to dispose of registered plots.
- Contact the developer's lender, if any, to make arrangements for the release of the individual plots from the lender's charge as and when they are sold.

- In conjunction with the developer client, arrange for a site inspection by a qualified surveyor and preparation of an estate layout plan for approval by the Land Registry.
- Draft the standard form of purchase deed and arrange for it to be approved by the Land Registry at the same time as the estate layout plan.
- Ensure that road and sewer agreements with supporting bonds are, or will be, in place (see below for further commentary on this).
- Check that the developer is registered with NHBC, or an alternative provider, and that all appropriate documentation is available.
- Carry out all necessary searches, copies of which are to be made available to the buyer's practitioner.
- Prepare information pack and/or covering letter.

18.3 ACTING FOR THE BUYER

It is common for the seller to refuse to negotiate any amendments on the standardized documentation. However, the buyer's practitioner should as a matter of course always consider the draft documentation carefully and seek to make amendments which properly protect the buyer's (and any lender client's) interests. Here is a reminder of the principal concerns for the buyer when approving the draft contract for the sale of a new property:

- Ensure that the buyer has all necessary easements, e.g. for access, services, and rights of entry onto adjoining plots.
- Ensure that the proposed covenants will not adversely affect the buyer's use and enjoyment of the property or the future sale or marketability of it; consider your mortgagee's instructions.
- Allow for the buyer/mortgagee's surveyor to inspect the property both before and after physical completion.
- Insist on a long stop date for completion after which your client can rescind the contract.
- The seller should be obliged to build in a good and workmanlike manner with good and substantial materials.
- Provide for the seller to rectify any snagging items, to remove all builder's rubbish before completion, to erect boundary fences, and to landscape the garden and adjoining areas.
- If the seller reserves the right to vary the methods of construction or building materials this should be qualified by a proviso that neither the value of the property nor the accommodation shall be materially diminished.
- If the property still in course of construction on exchange of contracts the risk of insurance should remain with the seller until physical and legal completion has occurred.
- Deposit to be held as stakeholder.
- Provide for NHBC protection; all relevant documentation to be supplied to the buyer on or before completion.

18.4 ROAD AND SEWER AGREEMENTS

One problem area for students is understanding the requirement for road and sewer agreements. As for estate roads, do remember that the roads and street lighting on a new estate will only become adopted by the local authority (and thus maintainable at the public expense) after the estate has been physically completed. The local authority is empowered to make up the roads and charge the house buyers for the cost of doing so, and it is for this reason that buyers require the developer to enter into an agreement with the local authority under section 38 of the Highways Act 1980. In this agreement the developer agrees to make up the roads and street lighting to an adoptable standard (i.e. to a standard acceptable to the authority) and the authority agrees to adopt them subsequently. As additional protection for the buyers in case of the developer's insolvency, the section 38 agreement should be supported by a bond or guarantee from the developer's bank or insurer which provides for the buyers to be indemnified for any costs paid to the local authority should the developer default. The developer should complete a similar agreement and supporting bond in respect of the making up and adoption of the drains and sewers on the estate. This agreement is made with the local water authority under section 104 of the Water Industry Act 1991.

Importantly, it is a standard requirement of mortgagees of properties on new large estates that section 38 and section 104 agreements with supporting bonds are in place before completion of the mortgage. This is confirmed in the Council of Mortgage Lenders' Handbook. If they are not in place the lender will usually wish to make a retention from the advance, which will be released to the borrower only as and when the agreements come into force.

18.5 STRUCTURAL DEFECTS INSURANCE

All new dwellings and conversions should be insured against structural defects, and it is a standard requirement of lending institutions that new residential properties are protected in this way. Without such insurance the property will become unmortgageable and its future marketability adversely affected. The most popular current scheme which is now in use almost universally is the NHBC Buildmark scheme. An alternative scheme known as Newbuild is offered by Zurich Municipal. The insurance cover under both schemes lasts for 10 years from completion of the construction of the property, although with Newbuild there is an option to extend cover for a further five years.

In some cases a lender may be willing to accept an architect's certificate of completion of the building instead of an NHBC or Newbuild scheme. This may apply, for instance, where the architect has supervised the construction of the building under a JCT contract (i.e. an agreement incorporating a standard set of conditions for a building contract). The insurance cover is effectively provided by the architect's professional indemnity insurers in the event of professional negligence on the part of the architect. The lender may be willing to accept the monitoring of the development by a professional consultant employed by the borrower alone or by the borrower and the builder jointly. If so, and the Lenders' Handbook is being used, the professional consultant must complete a Professional Consultant's Certificate in the required form set out in the Lenders' Handbook.

The NHBC Buildmark scheme is in two parts, comprising separate agreements in the form of warranties given by the builder and the NHBC respectively. In the first part, the builder agrees that the new dwelling will be constructed in a good and workmanlike manner and in line with the requirements of the NHBC. The builder also agrees to put right any defects in the property, notified to the builder in writing, which occur during the first two years (known as the initial guarantee period) and which occur as a result of the builder's failure to comply with the NHBC requirements. In the second part, the NHBC give separate warranties (i.e. the insurance) that will compensate the buyer against loss suffered as a result of:

(a) the builder becoming insolvent before the dwelling is finished (limited to 10 per cent of the contract sum or £10,000, whichever is the greater);

(b) the builder failing to fulfil its own warranty to correct defects arising in the initial guarantee period; and

(c) any repair works to the property the cost of which exceeds £500 which occur during the eight years following the initial guarantee period. This eight-year period is known as the structural guarantee period. Cover includes double or multiple glazing and the costs of clearing up contamination as a result of action taken by a local authority or the Environment Agency.

18.6 SYNCHRONIZING COMPLETION OF A RELATED SALE

Another problem area is the situation where a client is buying a new property and also selling an existing property at the same time. How do you synchronize completion dates when the developer/seller won't agree a fixed completion date on the new property? One way round this is to seek a condition in the sale contract regarding completion similar to that in the purchase contract, i.e. that completion shall occur a specified number of days after the seller's practitioner notifies the buyer's practitioner that the client is ready to complete. However if your client's buyer insists on a fixed completion date (e.g. because there is a chain behind), you would have to advise the client that it will not be possible to synchronize the two completions. If the client still wished to proceed, you would canvass two options. The client could either seek bridging finance to complete the purchase first (the consent of the existing lender may be required) or, more usually, complete the sale first and move into temporary accommodation until completion of the new property occurs. Whichever option the client decides upon, you must as a matter of great importance still ensure that the *act of exchange of contracts* is synchronized, so as to prevent the client ending up with two properties or none at all (see Chapter 10 generally regarding synchronization of exchange on related sale and purchase transactions).

 Key Points New properties

- The developer's solicitor should supply a full package of pre-contract documentation including replies to enquiries, standard form contract and transfer deed.
- Check the documentation for sale of part considerations, e.g. adequate description with scaled plan, grant of easements, etc.
- Check that planning consent for the development has been obtained and that there are no outstanding planning issues.
- Ensure that road and sewer agreements are in place with supporting bonds.
- If the property is in the course of construction a fixed completion date cannot normally be agreed on exchange of contracts.
- The developer will instead serve notice to complete following physical completion. Advise the client of the implications of not synchronizing completion on any related sale.
- Carry out your pre-completion Land Registry search on form OS2 quoting the plot number on Form C1.
- Ensure that NHBC protection for structural defects insurance is in place.

SELF TEST QUESTIONS

1. Your client is buying a new freehold house on an estate of 130 houses recently developed by Crest Homes Limited, who acquired the development site three years ago. The form of purchase deed that will be used to transfer the property into your client's name will be

   (a) Form TR1

   (b) Form TP1

(c) A conveyance

(d) An assignment

2. The NHBC Buildmark scheme provides insurance protection for up to 10 years against structural defects in new residential properties. Is this statement TRUE/FALSE? Please delete the incorrect choice.

3. Which of the following is NOT a requirement of the CML Lenders' Handbook

   (a) The new home warranty must be in place on or before completion

   (b) The new property must receive a satisfactory final inspection before completion

   (c) The roads and sewers immediately serving the new property must be adopted and maintained at public expense

   (d) The monitoring of a newly built property by a professional consultant may be acceptable to a lender in certain circumstances

4. Which of the following would a buyer's solicitor NOT normally expect to receive from the solicitor acting for the developer/seller of a new property on a large estate

   (a) Draft contract

   (b) Evidence of the seller's title

   (c) Draft purchase deed

   (d) Replies to standard enquiries before contract

5. A contract for sale of a new property in the course of construction will normally provide for legal completion to take place

   (a) 10 working days after exchange of contracts

   (b) 20 working days after exchange of contracts

   (c) On a fixed date agreed by the parties

   (d) Within a specified period after the seller's solicitor has notified the buyer' solicitor that the property has been physically completed and is fit for occupation

SHORT REVISION QUESTIONS

Question 1

Your firm has been instructed by Mr and Mrs Panesar to act for them in their purchase of 36 Highfields Close Winterslow, a freehold dwellinghouse which is in the course of construction by the seller/builder, Buildwell Ltd. Mr and Mrs Panesar have a property to sell, the net proceeds of which they are utilizing to help finance the purchase of 36 Highfields. Do you foresee any problem regarding synchronization of completion of their sale and purchase and, if so, how can this be overcome?

Question 2

Your firm is acting on the proposed acquisition of a leasehold industrial warehouse unit in the course of construction on a new business park on the outskirts of Reading. The proposed lease will be at a rack rent for a term of 15 years. You have received a comprehensive pre-contract package from the developer's solicitors. This includes the draft contract with draft lease annexed, official copies of the registered freehold title (which reveals a legal charge in favour of Barclays Bank plc), Form CI, copy planning consents, copy road and sewer agreements (with supporting bonds), and replies to standard pre-contract enquires. Assuming that these documents are all in order, what additional enquiries might you wish to raise of the seller's solicitors?

SUGGESTED ANSWERS TO SELF TEST QUESTIONS

1. The correct answer is (b). The developer's land will have a registered title because you are told that the developer acquired the site three years ago. Even if the land had previously been unregistered, compulsory first registration would have ensued following the developer's acquisition. Thus the current transfer of the house on the estate is a transfer of part of a registered title and Land Registry Form TP1 is the appropriate purchase deed in this case.

2. The statement is true. This question is quite straightforward and tests your basic knowledge of the NHBC structural defects insurance scheme.

3. The correct answer is (c). It is commonly the case that the estate roads and sewers are not yet adopted at the time of first occupation. In this case the lender will require suitable road and sewer agreements to be in place together with supporting bonds. If they are not in place the lender will usually wish to make a retention from the advance which will only be released to the borrower as and when the agreements come into force.

4. The correct answer is none as the seller should supply all of them. Remember that in estate conveyancing the seller's solicitor will want to standardize all legal documentation and this includes the form of purchase deed (which will be attached to the draft contract). Do not fall into the trap of choosing answer (c). Yes, the buyer prepares the draft purchase deed in most property transactions but not this one.

5. The correct answer is (d). As the property is in the course of construction the developer cannot commit itself to a fixed completion date. It serves notice on the buyer once physical completion of the new property has taken place.

SUGGESTED ANSWERS TO SHORT REVISION QUESTIONS

Question 1

As Mr and Mrs Panesar's purchase is dependent upon completion of their sale, we must ensure that each transaction is completed on the same day. In this way, the sale proceeds will be readily available to apply towards the purchase price of the clients' new property, and Mr and Mrs Panesar will be able to move out of one property and into the other on the day of completion.

As their new property is in the course of construction, the builder/seller will be unable to agree in the contract a fixed completion date. Instead, the contract will contain a provision whereby completion will take place a given number of days after the seller's solicitors have notified us that physical completion of the new property has taken place.

The property our clients are selling is not of course a new property but an existing one, and it would be customary in a contract of this nature to agree a fixed completion date. However, if that were to occur here, Mr and Mrs Panesar would have no guarantee that the completion dates on their sale and purchase would be the same.

I would therefore recommend that we do not agree a fixed completion date on the sale, but seek to agree a condition in the sale contract regarding completion similar to that in the purchase contract. That is to say, completion shall take place a specified number of days after we, as the seller's solicitors, notify the buyer's solicitors in writing that our clients are ready to complete. We would want to serve this notice once we receive the completion notice on our clients' purchase. In order to give ourselves some leeway, the notice period in the sale contract should be, say, one day less than the notice period in the purchase contract. As an example: if the purchase contract specified 14 days' notice of completion then upon receipt of the same we would prepare the sale contract notice and the following day serve it on the buyer's solicitors notifying them that completion will take place in 13 days' time, i.e. the same completion day as the purchase.

If our clients' buyer insists on a fixed completion date (for instance because there is a chain behind), we must advise Mr and Mrs Panesar that they will be unable to synchronize the two completions. If they still wanted to proceed, I would advise them that they have two options, either to seek bridging finance to complete the purchase first or, more usually, to complete the sale first and move into temporary accommodation until completion of the new property. Whatever they decide, we must still in any event make sure that the *act of exchange of contracts* is synchronized, so as to prevent Mr and Mrs Panesar ending up with two properties or none at all.

Question 2

Students should note that this is a new commercial property. It will therefore be inappropriate to raise issues regarding the NHBC Buildmark scheme. This scheme only applies to residential property and indeed structural defects insurance is rarely used in relation to commercial property. Do remember that in commercial property VAT may be chargeable and this should be clarified.

The following additional enquiries might be considered in a transaction of this nature:

- As the grant of a commercial lease is exempt from VAT but there is an option to waive the exemption, please confirm whether the seller has elected or will elect to waive the exemption for VAT in respect of the subject property.

- Please confirm that the developer will pay for all charges for construction and connection of the drainage and sewage systems and all other services of which the property will have the benefit, e.g. electricity, gas, telephone, and internet connection.

- If available, please also supply a plan showing the proposed route of all services to and from the property.

- Please confirm that the buyer will not be called upon to complete until not only the property but also all services are finished, and reasonable access to the property has been provided.

- When does the seller intend to lay the final wearing surface to the estate roads?

- Does the seller have any plans to vary the construction or dimensions of the property and can the seller confirm that any such variation will not materially diminish the accommodation to be provided or the value of the property?

- If known, please supply the postal address of the property.

- Please confirm how many industrial units will be constructed on the estate and how many of these have been let to date.

- We note that the freehold title is mortgaged. Please forward the consent of Barclays Bank to the grant of the lease.

WIDER READING

- Chapter 11 (New Properties), Abbey, R, and Richards, M, *A Practical Approach to Conveyancing* (Oxford University Press, 2008)

- Silverman, F, *Conveyancing Handbook* (The Law Society, 2006)

- Ruoff, Theodore BF and Roper, RB, *The Law and Practice of Registered Conveyancing* (Sweet & Maxwell, 2007)

- Chapter 20 (easements), MacKenzie, J-A, and Phillips, M, *Textbook on Land Law* (Oxford University Press, 2008)

- Emmet on Title: Chapter 1, part 5

WEBSITES FOR FURTHER INFORMATION

- Council of Mortgage Lenders, **<http://www.cml.org.uk>**. There is an on-line version of the CML Lenders' Handbook available at this site and should be referred to in cases of doubt about the requirements of the lender in relation to new properties.

- Land Registry, **<http://www.landreg.gov.uk/>**.

- Land Registry Internet register access, **<http://www.landregistrydirect.gov.uk>**. The location for on-line pre-completion registered land searches.

- Landmark Information group, property, and environmental risk information, **<http://www. landmark-information.co.uk/>**. Environmental searches can be obtained from the Landmark Information Group. These might shed light on former uses of the land perhaps revealed by covenants in the deeds.

- Law Society, **<http://www.lawsoc.org.uk/>**.

- NHBC, **<http://www.nhbc.co.uk>**. Full information concerning NHBC structural defects insurance.

- Ordnance Survey, **<http://www.ordnancesurvey.co.uk>**. It might be useful to consult a detailed Ordnance Survey map when considering boundary problems and to compare with title deed plans.

19 COMMERCIAL CONVEYANCING

19.1 INTRODUCTION

Property Law and Practice covers both commercial and domestic property transactions. This means that a well-rounded property lawyer will need to be aware of the requirements for both areas of practice, although a specialist will concentrate on one or other. While many areas of commercial conveyancing may resemble similar practices and procedures utilized in residential conveyancing, the nature of the subject matter has in many aspects of the process dictated a different approach. Commercial conveyancing services and supports the market in and for commercial property. As a result, this chapter will concentrate on several different topics that all relate to commercial property and which all involve specialist knowledge of commercial conveyancing. However, for most property lawyers concerned with commercial conveyancing the subject will be seen to be synonymous with commercial leases. As Legal Practice Course students you can expect to be examined in all aspects of a commercial lease. That will include the formation and negotiation of new leases as well as the renewal of existing leases. Buying and selling tenanted properties will feature strongly in the work of a commercial conveyancer, and as such a basic understanding of some elements of revenue law will also be required. These topics are all covered in this chapter.

19.2 COMMERCIAL LEASES

In commercial property the freehold will be owned as an investment by an individual or company, and that freeholder will grant such a commercial lease to an occupying lessee. The lease terms regulate the basis on which the lessee will be allowed to occupy the premises for the purposes of carrying on a business. Inevitably this has meant that there is no one common form of commercial or business lease. Practitioners will encounter a multitude of lease formats.

19.2.1 EXEMPT INFORMATION DOCUMENTS

Commercial lessors may be concerned that registered leases will be available to the public as a result of the register being open to review by anyone. The effect of this could be that lessees might find out the lease terms for adjacent or adjoining property, and this could be material to lease renewal negotiations in a large estate or could reveal concessions granted to another lessee. However, the Land Registration Rules 2003 allow for applications to remove from public view sensitive material. If the registry approves an application it will be an 'exempt information document' (EID). An application will be approved if the registry is satisfied that the document contains 'prejudicial information'. Rule 131 defines prejudicial information as:

(a) information that relates to an individual who has applied for the document to be designated an EID and if disclosed to other persons (whether to the public generally or specific persons) would, or would be likely to, cause substantial unwarranted damage or substantial unwarranted distress to the applicant or another; or

(b) information that if disclosed to other persons (whether to the public generally or specific persons) would, or would be likely to, prejudice the commercial interests of the applicant, i.e. the person who applied for the document to be designated an EID.

 Conduct Point Acting in the client's best interest

- Be very careful about how you agree a lease and subsequently apply for registration of the lease for your client. Is there sensitive information that needs to be exempt? Failure to consider this point could amount to a breach of the Code of Conduct for solicitors 2007, R.1.04. You must act in the best interests of each client, R.1.05. You must provide a good standard of service to your clients.

19.2.2 LEASE CONTENTS

A business lease should contain specific elements, and these are listed below. However, how and where they appear in any one lease will vary greatly. Some leases will use schedules, some will not. Consequently, practitioners must have in mind a basic list of necessary contents for a commercial lease as follows:

(a) heading, date, and parties;

(b) a clear parcels clause setting out a full description of the property (if necessary by reference to a lease plan), with all attaching rights;

online resource centre

(c) exceptions and reservations, i.e. a detailed list of all the rights retained by the lessor;

(d) the length of the lease term and the commencement date for that term (not always the date of the lease), known as the habendum;

(e) the rental details (known as the reddendum) including rent review clauses, frequency of payment and payment dates, and whether the rent is paid in arrears or in advance;

(f) lessee's covenants;

(g) lessor's covenants;

(h) provisos, including a forfeiture clause and other clauses regulating the mechanics of the operation of the lease terms, such as a provision for arbitration in case of dispute between the parties or a clause setting out how covenant notices are to be served (service charge details could also appear at this point);

(i) an attestation clause.

19.2.3 PAYMENT OF RENT

So far as the lessor is concerned, this is the rationale for the very existence of the lease. The lessee is allowed the use and enjoyment of the subject premises in consideration of the rental expressed in the lease. The amount to be paid must be stated in clear and definite terms. However, a lease can be granted without including a rental element or with a period of non-payment, i.e. a rent-free period. Whether there is a rent-free period or not, the lease should state a commencement date for the payment of rent and the frequency of payment. Most modern leases provide for rent to be paid quarterly in advance. Traditional quarter days are commonly used, but the more precise modern quarter days are becoming increasingly evident, e.g. the first day of January, April, July, and October. Modern leases will also include a provision referring to other payments, such as service charges, as rent. Including these payments as rent enables the lessor to use the remedies of distress and forfeit for non-payment. The remedy of distress is not available for a breach of covenant other than non-payment of rent. Modern business leases will also include a further provision allowing the lessor to collect interest on late rent.

19.2.4 **RENT REVIEWS**

Perhaps of greatest concern to the lessor is the nature and extent of the rent review provision. Rent review clauses allow the lessor to vary the rent stated in the lease so as to increase the income from the subject property. This has been especially important in times of inflation as the lessor of a long lease at a fixed rental has been at a severe disadvantage when inflation was running at high levels. Each passing year meant that the lessor in such an unfortunate position was losing even more in real terms as inflation ate into the value of the fixed rental. To combat this potential increasing loss, lessors have included in leases a provision allowing the rent to be reviewed at fixed intervals, usually only in an upward direction. (If the review mechanism permits downward reviews, as well as upward, the rent could actually be reduced on review, something that occurred in the property slump of the late 1980s and early 1990s.) Some leases simply link the annual rent to inflation, e.g. the Index of Retail Prices (see *Blumenthal v Gallery Five Ltd* (1971) 220 EG 31). Others state the amount to be paid in the future by way of fixed increases. However, most do not state the amount of the increase but try to define in the lease how the lease rental should be revalued on review.

It therefore follows that in a rent review the critical element is on what basis the rent should be reviewed. The intention of the lessor is to move the rent to the current market value for the subject premises. However, this gives rise to the all-important question of what that market value is and how it will be ascertained. Furthermore, the procedure for triggering and handling the review is critical. These valuation and procedural elements will be considered below.

Valuation

The new lease should contain a definition of a formula by which the new reviewed rent should be ascertained. If the lease terms say the intention is to fix a 'rack rent' then this is the full rent for the property (see *Corporation of London v Cusack-Smith* [1955] AC 337). Thus such a rental would reflect the changes in the property market as assessed by a valuer or surveyor. Alternatively, if the lease required the rent to be reviewed as a 'market rent', then this will be the same as for a new lease granted under the terms of the Landlord and Tenant Act 1954, but including the factors that the Act contemplates being ignored.

There is nothing to stop the lease incorporating detailed assumptions on which the review is to be based. If the lease stipulates assumptions to be made on a rent review then they will be central to the valuation process for the subject property. Typical assumptions are that the rent is to be reviewed at the renewal date, assuming the property is vacant for a term equal to that either originally granted or the residue of the term and for the permitted user stated in the lease. (As to the term, it can be argued that a higher rental will arise if the term is longer than the unexpired residue at the time of review. In the absence of any express lease term to the contrary, courts will assume the lease term on review to be the period of the unexpired term: see *Lynnthorpe Enterprises Ltd v Sidney Smith (Chelsea) Ltd* [1990] 2 EGLR 148, CA.) Modern rent review clauses will also allow the valuer to ignore any diminution in the value of the rental as a result of the lessee having failed properly to repair the subject property. Some review clauses also import assumptions with regard to improvements made by the lessee. If the lease is silent on the point, the rent review will be based on the nature of the premises at the time of review, including any improvements made by the lessee even though they were made at the lessee's cost (see *Ponsford v HMS Aerosols Ltd* [1979] AC 63). Assumptions can also cover sub-lettings to take into account any profit rental the lessee may be receiving from sub-lessees. Courts will also generally accept that the hypothetical lease will include a rent review: see *British Gas v Universities Superannuation Scheme* [1986] 1 All ER 978.

Procedure

Modern rent review clauses trigger the process by requiring the lessor to serve a notice on the lessee calling for a review of the rent at the rent review date. Some trigger notices will be required by the review procedure to state what the lessor requires as a new rental. Others may simply call for the review process to be commenced. If an amount is specified, some clauses require the lessee to agree or disagree with the stated amount within a specified period. A trap exists here for the unwary. If time is of the essence for the lessee's response then, should that time limit not be complied with, the rental stated by the lessor, no matter how exaggerated it may be, will prevail as the rent for review (exaggeration does not make the notice ineffective, see *Amalgamated Estates Ltd v Joystretch Manufacturing Ltd* (1981) 257 EG 489). In *Starmark Enterprises Limited v CPL Enterprises Ltd* [2001] EWCA Civ 1252 there was no mention of time being of the essence for service of the tenant's counter-notice. Nevertheless, an out-of-time counter-notice was deemed invalid because the parties to the lease had clearly stipulated the consequences of a party's failure to serve a notice within the time agreed by them.

Lessors can also be late calling for review by not complying with a timescale stated in the lease rent review provisions. In *United Scientific Holdings Ltd v Burnley Borough Council* [1978] AC 904 it was held that unless the clause makes it so, time is *not* of the essence for a rent review clause. If the clause makes time of the essence of part or all of the procedure then the time limits are absolute and incapable of extension. In the absence of express provision, though, delay will not defeat a lessor's claim for a rent review. Time can be of the essence even if the rent review provision does not include that actual wording. If the words of the rent review clause are such that it is possible to show that there was an intention to make time limits absolute, then the courts will infer time to be of the essence (see *Henry Smith's Charity Trustees v AWADA Trading and Promotion Services Ltd* (1984) 47 P & CR 607). Time of the essence can also arise if other wording in the lease supports this possibility. Accordingly, if the lessee can, by notice, terminate the tenancy at the review date, it has been held that this means that time is of the essence for the review (see *Al Saloom v Shirley James Travel Services Ltd* (1981) 42 P & CR 181).

Arbitration and disputes

Sensible rent review clauses will also have two further provisions. First, there will be the possibility of referring the rent to an arbitrator for a final decision should the lessor and lessee be unable to agree the level of the new rent. Secondly, there should be a clause covering what must be done in the event of a dispute between the parties. This will again sensibly entail arbitration. In both clauses, if arbitration is contemplated, it will involve provisions in the Arbitration Act 1996. Should the appointment of the arbitrator be in dispute the lease can provide that the appointment be by the President for the time being of the Royal Institute of Chartered Surveyors.

19.2.5 COVENANTS BY THE LESSEE

Repairing obligations

This is a subject area of great difficulty in two principal ways. First, deciding on what part of the subject property must be repaired by the lessee does rather depend on the extent of the definition of the lessee's property in the lease. Secondly, when the extent of the property is known the measure of the burden of the repairing liability must be clearly defined; from simple repairs necessary to deal with ordinary wear and tear, right up to the lessee being under a strict obligation virtually to replace the whole property.

Where there is a property in multiple occupation, say, an office block containing several office suites, all let to different lessees, the usual repairing arrangement is for the lessee to be required to keep in good repair the inner skin of the demised property. This would therefore require the lessee to keep properly maintained the plaster, the ceiling and flooring materials, but not much else. All structural elements of the property, including the floor and ceiling joists, the main or load-bearing walls, the roof, and foundations, should all be repairable by the lessor with all the lessees paying a service charge to reimburse the lessor for this expense (the further need for clear and appropriate service charge covenants flows from this form of repairing arrangement). The rationale for this arrangement is that there is a need for a consistent approach to the whole question of structural repairs and maintenance. On the other hand, if the lease is of the whole building, such as a lease of a shop and upper part, or indeed one office building let to one lessee, then it is common for the sole lessee to be responsible for all the repairs to the building.

The standard of repair

The precise standard of repair required was set out in *Proudfoot v Hart* (1890) 25 QBD 42 where it was held that the standard of repair is to be determined according to several factors, including the subject property's age and character and the environment in which the property is located. In effect this has meant that there is a clear difference in the expected standard of repair between a Victorian property and one that was built in the 1990s. As to the meaning of 'repair', the courts have made it clear this includes renewal (see *Lurcott v Wakeley and Wheeler* [1911] 1 KB 905). It should be remembered that a covenant requiring the lessee 'to put and keep the property in good and substantial repair' is particularly onerous. This is way above mere repair and will be interpreted as requiring the lessee to carry out all repairs and renewals, substantial or not, right from the start of the lease (see *Elite Investments Ltd v TI Bainbridge Silencers Ltd* [1986] 2 EGLR 43). This kind of covenant is, however, encountered frequently in practice. In addition, a covenant to keep in repair implies a covenant to put and keep in repair. As a result each lease repairing covenant, seen in the light of the subject property, will dictate the nature and extent of the repairs required.

Most commercial leases will also include clauses calling on the lessee to decorate internally (and externally if the lessee has the total repairing liability) at regular intervals during the term of the lease. Common repainting and redecorating intervals are every five years internally, and every three years externally. Many such covenants also call on the lessee to decorate and repaint in the final year of the term whether or not this coincides with the fixed intervals. Overall, the purpose of clauses such as these is to ensure that the nature and extent of the lessee's decorating liability is clearly defined so as to ensure the proper upkeep of the subject property.

Repair and service charges

Where the lessor is under an obligation to keep in good repair a building of which the subject property forms part, the cost of those repairs will usually be recoverable from the lessee. That cost, along with other expenses incurred by the lessor in providing services (e.g. lighting and heating of common parts) on behalf of all lessees, will form a service charge. If in the lease it is described as a rent then that enables the lessor to distrain for arrears. Normally there will be a service charge payable as a rent, with payments on account made quarterly at a level to be decided by the lessor's surveyor (whose decision shall be final, save for manifest error) at the start of each year but having regard to the expenditure during the previous year. At the end of the year accounts are prepared to reconcile the payments made and received. The lessor will usually be obliged by a covenant to carry out clearly identified obligations listed in a schedule to the lease, including repairs and renovations to the main structure and common parts, and lighting and heating the common parts. This obligation is usually made conditional on the lessees paying the service charge rental. The Commonhold and Leasehold Reform Act 2002 introduces additional restrictions on the commencement of forfeiture proceedings for breaches of covenants or conditions of a lease. It modifies section 81 of the Housing Act 1996 to prohibit the commencement of forfeiture proceedings, including the issue of a notice under section 146 of the Law of Property Act 1925, in respect of non-payment of service or administration charges.

19.2.6 USER OBLIGATIONS

It is possible for the lease to include a covenant imposing an absolute restriction on the lessee against changing the use from any stated user precisely defined by the lease. More usually, the covenant can be qualified, requiring the lessor's consent before the use can be changed, and this is more commonly seen in commercial leases. In such business leases an absolute user covenant will mean that the rental on review could be subject to a reduction in valuation. This is because a restriction on user makes the lease less attractive to tenants and it will therefore command less as a rental. However, this limitation on the rental income can be avoided by a fully qualified covenant, i.e. including wording such as 'such consent not to be unreasonably withheld'. This is because there is no statutory provision that the lessor's consent cannot be unreasonably withheld as is the case with alienation covenants. However, section 19(3) of the Landlord and Tenant Act 1927 does provide that if consent for a change of use is required then the lessor is not allowed to demand a premium or extra rent for giving that consent. The lessor can require costs to be paid by the applicant, including all legal fees. A premium or extra rent can be demanded if alterations to the structure of the property are also proposed.

19.2.7 ALTERATION RESTRICTIONS

The reversioner will want to ensure that unauthorized alterations do not take place, especially where the lease term is short in duration. Furthermore the reversioner will want to be sure that the alterations that do take place are such that the integrity of the structure will not be adversely affected. This will also be the case for additions and improvements to the subject property that are carried out by the lessee.

A covenant dealing with alterations can include an absolute bar such as: 'not to make or allow to be made any alterations additions or improvements to the demised premises'. If this is the lease covenant, the lessee cannot carry out any work whatsoever.

The lease could allow alterations to the property with the lessor's written consent. To the extent that proposed alterations amount to improvements, section 19(2) of the Landlord and Tenant Act 1927 will then apply so that consent cannot be unreasonably withheld, and the lessor cannot demand any payment beyond reasonable legal and other expenses incurred in the granting of consent for the relevant works. The statute does not stop the lessor from seeking a reasonable sum should the proposed amendments diminish the value of the premises or indeed any adjacent premises in the ownership of the same lessor. Similarly if the alteration or addition does not add to the letting value of the premises, the statute does not prevent the lessor from obtaining from the lessee a covenant to reinstate the premises to their former condition at the end or sooner determination of the lease.

What amounts to an improvement was considered in *Lambert v F W Woolworth and Co Ltd* [1938] Ch 883. In that case it was decided that an improvement will be considered as such from the lessee's viewpoint and whether it made the subject premises more useful or more valuable to the lessee.

19.2.8 **ALIENATION RESTRICTIONS**

Alienation covers covenants against assignments, underletting, mortgages, and other material dealings with the legal estate. This covenant is of great concern for business leases. The reason for this is that a business lessor will want to know who is in occupation of the property, and in particular that the financial strength of the person or company in occupation is such that the rents required by the lease will be paid. As a consequence the lessor will seek to validate intending lessees to try to be sure that they will be able to pay the rents. Once the lessor has approved the status of the incoming lessee, the lessor will normally require the proposed assignee to enter into a deed of licence. This will incorporate direct covenants between the lessor and assignee requiring the assignee to comply with the lease terms for the residue of the term of the lease. This is now subject to the terms of the Landlord and Tenant Act 1995.

There is no restriction against alienation unless there is express provision to that effect in the lease (see *Keeves v Dean* [1924] 1 KB 685 and *Leith Properties Ltd v Byrne* [1983] QB 433). Many commercial leases include a covenant whereby the lessee cannot assign the lease without the prior written consent of the lessor, such consent usually not to be unreasonably withheld. This is known as a fully qualified covenant. Some leases extend this provision to include sub-lettings and assignments. If the lease states that the lessor's consent is required but does not refer to reasonableness then statute adds this qualification (Landlord and Tenant Act 1927, section 19(1)(a)) (the Court of Appeal issued guidelines on what amounts to reasonableness in the context of section 19 in *International Drilling Fluids Ltd v Louisville Investments (Uxbridge) Ltd* [1986] Ch 513, and see below). However, if the lease includes an absolute prohibition then the lessee simply cannot assign the lease and must remain in the premises for the residue of the term. Section 19(1A) of the Landlord and Tenant Act 1927 (introduced by section 22 of the Landlord and Tenant (Covenants) Act 1995) allows the parties to a lease to agree conditions or circumstances which must be satisfied before the lessor will give consent. Section 19(1A) only relates to qualified covenants against assigning, i.e. not sub-letting or charging. If the lease requires the lessee to offer a surrender of the lease back to the lessor prior to seeking an assignment, that provision is unenforceable (see *Allnatt London Properties Ltd v Newton* [1984] 1 All ER 423) unless the provision is covered under section 38 of the Landlord and Tenant Act 1954.

19.2.9 **ALIENATION OF PART**

Many modern business leases will include an absolute covenant against dealing with part of the subject premises. There are two good reasons for including such a provision. First, good estate management practice dictates that the fewer lessees there are in a block the easier it is to manage the building as a whole. However, the second reason is far more compelling. Under the Landlord and Tenant Act 1954 business lessees in occupation at the end of a business lease are entitled by statute to renew their lease. If there have been sub-lettings of parts, the lessor is required by statute to issue new leases to all the sub-lessees in occupation and not to the original lessee who became the sub-lessor but did not remain in occupation. In this way the superior lessor could accidentally end up with several lessees where originally there was one.

19.2.10 **COVENANTS BY THE LESSOR**

Quiet enjoyment
A typical express covenant could read:

> that the lessee paying all the rents reserved by this lease and performing and observing all the covenants contained herein shall peaceably hold and enjoy the demised premises without any interruption by the lessor or any other company or person rightfully claiming under or in trust for the lessor.

The nature of the covenant is to confirm that the lessee can physically enjoy the complete benefit of the property without the lessor adversely affecting that enjoyment. It is the extent of the impact of the covenant that is open to interpretation. In *Owen v Gadd* [1956] 2 QB 99, where scaffolding was erected by the lessor outside a shop door and window and consequently affected the lessee's business, it was held that there had been a breach of covenant by the lessor.

Insurance by lessor

In modern business leases it is common practice for the lessor to insure but for the lessee to covenant to reimburse the lessor for the insurance premium. This is almost always the arrangement that prevails where there are several commercial lettings in one building. This is a desirable arrangement as it will be cost-effective to have one policy covering the whole building and will avoid inconsistencies of insurance cover that might arise if there was to be a separate policy for each letting. Where the lessee reimburses the lessor it would seem that the lessor is under no obligation to consider various insurers to find the cheapest premium (see *Havenridge Ltd v Boston Dyers Ltd* [1994] 2 EGLR 73). The insured risks should be carefully defined and should clearly include damage caused by fire, storm, flooding, subsidence, burst pipes, riot, and other usual risks covered by standard buildings insurance policies. However, terrorism needs separate specific cover, and this should be precisely stated in the lease insurance provisions.

19.2.11 FORFEITURE

All commercial leases should include a clause enabling the lessor to re-enter the subject property and terminate the lease term as a consequence of a breach of covenant by the lessee, or of the happening of a specified occurrence. The usual reasons stipulated in such a clause, giving rise to the right to forfeiture, include non-payment of rent, breach of another lease covenant, and the lessee's liquidation or bankruptcy. Each of these is considered below.

If the lessor wishes to forfeit, this can be achieved in two different ways. First, the lessor may commence court proceedings for forfeiture and seek an order for possession of the subject premises. Secondly, the lessor can simply peaceably re-enter the premises and thereby physically re-take possession. This second, apparently simple, alternative is not without its problems. Statute imposes restrictions on this remedy.

For non-payment of rent

In the absence of an express provision to the contrary the lessor must make a formal demand for the rent. Most leases will include such an express provision requiring the lessee to pay the rent usually within 14 or 21 days of the payment date (one of the quarter days), whether the rent is formally demanded or not. In the absence of payment the lessor may either commence proceedings or peaceably re-enter. The lessee may be entitled to relief from forfeiture. The lessee can apply to court for this form of relief, and if the rent arrears and costs are discharged before the court hearing for forfeiture, the lessee will be so entitled. In certain circumstances the lessee can seek relief at any time during a period of up to six months from the making of the order for forfeiture or from when the lessor peaceably re-entered. See section 210 of the Common Law Procedure Act 1852 for High Court actions and section 138 of the County Courts Act 1984 for county court proceedings and for peaceable re-entry cases (see *Thatcher v C H Pearce and Sons (Contractors) Ltd* [1968] 1 WLR 748).

For breach of another lease covenant

This area is regulated by the provisions of section 146 of the Law of Property Act 1925. Usually, no enforcement steps can be taken without a notice being prepared based on these statutory requirements and served upon the lessee. The notice must:

(a) specify the particular breach complained of;

(b) if the breach is capable of remedy, require the lessee to remedy the breach; and

(c) require the lessee to make compensation in money for the breach.

If there is non-compliance with the notice, the lessor can peaceably re-enter or obtain possession by way of a court order. The lessee can nevertheless still seek relief from forfeiture. If there has been peaceable re-entry, the relief is available even after re-entry (see *Billson v Residential Apartments Ltd* [1992] 1 AC 494). If there is a court order and the lessor has re-entered, the right to relief is no longer available to the lessee. Relief is granted on such terms as the court thinks fit (Law of Property Act 1925, section 146(2)). If the breach complained of involves a repairing covenant, the section 146 notice may also involve the terms of the Leasehold Property (Repairs) Act 1938. If the covenant is contained in a lease for a term of at least seven years, and at the date of the service of the notice there are at least three years of that term left to run, the 1938 Act will apply. In these circumstances the section 146 notice must include explicit reference to the lessee's additional right to serve a counter-notice in writing within 28 days of the receipt of the section 146 notice, claiming the benefit of the Act (Leasehold Property Repairs Act 1938, section 1(2)). If a valid counter-notice is served, the lessor cannot take proceedings to enforce any right of re-entry or forfeiture for the continuing breach without leave of the court. Indeed, the courts have proved to be reluctant to grant such an order except in cases of substantial breach by the lessee.

Liquidation or bankruptcy

Common sense dictates that an insolvent lessee is unlikely to be able to comply with lease covenants and it is probable that the covenant to pay rent is going to be breached sooner rather than later. This being so, most modern commercial leases will include the right to re-enter on the lessee being declared bankrupt or, if a company, being put into liquidation. The right is usually expressed to arise on the appointment of a receiver, a liquidator, or company administrator. The right to forfeit must be express as none is implied, and without such a clause the fact of the lessee's bankruptcy will not automatically put an end to the lease term (see *Hyde v Warden* (1877) 3 ExD 72). The lessor must serve a section 146 notice in most cases, but not where the lessee was a publican or the lease is of agricultural land (Law of Property Act 1925, section 146(9)). The bankrupt lessee, if seeking relief, must take steps to do so within the first year following the bankruptcy, failing which the right to relief is lost.

Forfeiture and the Commonhold and Leasehold Reform Act 2002

This Act introduced a new requirement that ground rent will not be payable unless it has been demanded. The demand is to be made by giving the tenant a prescribed notice. The reforms in the Act prevent the application of any provisions of a lease relating to late payment or non-payment (e.g. additional charges such as interest) if the rent is paid within 30 days of the demand being issued. The Act also introduces additional restrictions on the commencement of forfeiture proceedings for breaches of covenants or conditions of a lease. It prohibits the commencement of forfeiture proceedings, including the issue of a notice under section 146 of the Law of Property Act 1925, in respect of non-payment of service or administration charges. This is not the case if the charge has been agreed or admitted by the tenant, or a court or Leasehold Valuation Tribunal (LVT) has determined that it is reasonable and due. The Act also prohibits the commencement of forfeiture proceedings for other breaches, unless a court or LVT has determined that a breach has occurred.

 Key Points Commercial leases

- If the lease is to be registered do you need to consider applying for an EID to protect sensitive detail?

- If you are drafting a new lease incorporating a rent review mechanism, make sure that on review the rent cannot be reduced below the rental level that prevailed prior to the date of review. Furthermore avoid strict time limits that make time of the essence for the review procedure.

- If you are involved with an application for licence to assign, remember that the terms of the Landlord and Tenant Act 1988 require the application to be dealt with within a reasonable time, failing which the lessee could be entitled to a claim for damages arising from any undue delay.

- In relation to user clauses, there is no statutory provision which implies that the lessor's consent cannot be unreasonably withheld as is the case with alienation covenants. However, if there is an absolute or simple qualified covenant against changes of user it can have a deflating effect on any rental value on review. The covenant should be fully qualified, i.e. 'Not without the lessor's consent such consent not to be unreasonably withheld'.

- Practitioners acting for a lessor seeking to forfeit should advise their client about the potential dangers of waiver. If the lessor is seeking to forfeit and then demands and/or accepts rent, the courts will infer a waiver of the right to forfeit.

19.3 BUYING AND SELLING TENANTED PROPERTIES

There is a considerable commercial market in the purchase and sale of properties that are subject to the occupation of lessees with statutory security of tenure. This is particularly so in relation to property occupied by business tenants, but many of the special factors required in transactions involving commercial property will apply also to properties sold with residential tenants.

19.3.1 THE STANDARD COMMERCIAL PROPERTY CONDITIONS

online
resource
centre

The Standard Commercial Property Conditions (SCPC) were issued on 17 May 1999 for use in commercial transactions. A second edition was issued on 1 June 2004. In simple residential transactions the pre-printed contractual Standard Conditions of Sale (fourth edition) are almost universally used by conveyancing practitioners. However, if a commercial element in a proposed agreement is more complicated, and in particular if there is a lessee in occupation as a commercial tenant, then the SCPC are likely to be more appropriate.

The SCPCs are divided into two parts. Part 1 contains general conditions building on those in the first edition, while Part 2 contains new clauses, in particular detailed provisions covering VAT, capital allowances, and reversionary interests in flats. As such the emphasis is clearly on more complex commercial transactions. In general Part 1 applies unless expressly excluded, while Part 2 will only apply if expressly incorporated. Completing tick boxes on the back page of the agreement effects express incorporation, see SCPC 1.1.4 (a) and (b).

Both sets of conditions have a front page that allows practitioners to insert basic yet vital details for the agreement such as details of the seller, the buyer, the property, title information, and specified encumbrances (by SCPC 3.1.2(a) the seller sells subject to encumbrances specified in the contract, i.e. on the front page). The front page on the second edition of the SCPC now allows for the sale of chattels to be included in the purchase price. On the back page a special condition will provide for vacant possession or for a sale subject to listed tenancies. Another special condition provides for chattels to be included in the sale or to be sold separately. Finally there is a special condition on the back page that has tick boxes enabling the specific incorporation of Part 2 conditions, e.g. conditions covering VAT, capital allowances and reversionary interests in flats. See Appendix 3.

 Conduct Point Acting in the client's best interest

- Be very careful about how you draft a commercial sale contract for your client. Failure to do so properly and in the light of your client's instructions could amount to a breach of the Code of Conduct for solicitors 2007, R.1.04. You must act in the best interests of each client, R.1.05. You must provide a good standard of service to your clients.

Part 1 Conditions

Part 1 contains general conditions building on those in the first edition. It is of interest that there is no mention on the front page of the SCPC of title guarantee. There is such a provision in SCPC 6.6.2, but this is subject to any encumbrances affecting the subject property and covered by SCPC 3.1.2. Most, if not all, conveyancing practitioners will be familiar with the Standard Conditions as they are used in the vast majority of domestic conveyancing transactions. The SCPC may not be so familiar. Consequently, the following section is an examination of some of the more important features of the SCPC.

Condition 1 General

In this section there is a definition for 'direct credit'. The effect of this is that payments at exchange and completion cannot be by banker's draft and can only be by bank telegraphic CHAPS payment transfers. The purpose of this inclusion is to take account of the general commercial practice of requiring completely cleared funds at exchange or completion. SCPC defines when a party is ready, able and willing to complete, i.e. when they might be able to serve on the other party who is not so ready a notice to complete (such a notice is also defined as a notice requiring completion of the contract in accordance with SCPC 8).

SCPC 1.5.1 prohibits the transfer of the benefit of the contract. Practitioners should also be aware that SCPC 1.5.2 is a total prohibition against sub-sales in whole or in part. The buyer must be named as the transferee in the purchase deed, and no other party can be mentioned unless they are a named party in the agreement. This section is therefore close to the terms of the Standard Conditions and is there to ensure that the named buyer and only the named buyer completes with the seller.

SCPC 1.3 recognizes the use of email to deliver and serve a notice (as well as by fax). If the recipient's email is stated in the contract (on the back page within the section for details of the seller's and buyer's conveyancers), then adding the email address authorizes service by email (see SCPC 1.3.3(b)). An email is treated as being received before 4pm on the first working day after dispatch (see SCPC 1.3.7(e)).

Condition 2 Formation

As to the date of the formation of the agreement, the terms cover the moment of exchange, i.e. it will be at the time of posting or at the time of deposit in the DX or by some other procedure agreed between the parties. SCPC 2.2 regarding the deposit states that the deposit (at 10 per cent) except by auction sale must be paid by direct credit (see Condition 1 General above). In contrast to domestic conveyances, most transactions where the parties are selling and/or buying tenanted properties are unlikely to be part of a chain of transactions. Consequently, the deposit is paid to the seller's solicitor as stakeholder and is to be released to the seller on completion with accrued interest. However, where there is an auction sale the deposit is to be held by the auctioneer as agent for the seller, thus enabling the seller to get hold of the deposit prior to completion. Furthermore, if there is a deposit paid at an auction sale by cheque and all or any part of the payment is dishonoured on first presentation then the seller has on option to terminate on dishonour. The seller does not need to represent the cheque, as the provision talks of first presentation and can simply give notice to the buyer that the contract has been discharged by the buyer's breach.

Condition 3 Matters affecting the property

SCPC 3.1.2(d) has been written to put the burden on the buyer to carry out all searches and enquiries that a prudent buyer would make before entering into a contract of this type. In essence the property is sold subject to all matters that would be disclosed, e.g. a local authority search save for monetary charges. SCPC now also states that the encumbrances affecting the subject property are either specified in the contract, discoverable on inspection, or disclosable in searches or enquiries. SCPC also states that a leasehold property is sold subject to any subsisting breach of covenant regarding the condition of the property.

Condition 4 Occupational leases

The major changes in this section of the SCPC between the first and second editions are located in Condition 4 concerning leases affecting the subject property. Condition 4 covers leases and applies if any part of the property is sold subject to a lease (and a lease is defined as including a sub-lease, tenancy, and agreement for a lease or sub-lease). SCPC 4.1.3 states that the seller is not to serve a notice to end the lease or accept surrender, and is to inform the buyer without delay if the lease ends. These elements are included in the SCPC to prevent the seller from taking unilateral action that might adversely affect the value of the premises by ensuring that after exchange and before completion the seller cannot force the tenant out of the subject property or take steps towards ejecting the tenant. SCPC 4.2 is a major innovation by seeking to cover property management for the period between exchange and completion. It sets out extensive provisions for the conduct of litigation proceedings affecting leasehold premises in court or by arbitration. (However, you should note that this does not cover rent review matters that are covered by Condition 5, see below.) Furthermore, the seller is not to grant or formally withhold any licence consent or approval required by the terms of the occupational lease. This means that once contracts are exchanged the seller must always seek the buyer's permission in relation to any matters that arise from the lease terms and that need the consent or involvement of the lessor. However SCPC 4.2.7 provides that the buyer is not to withhold consent so as to place the seller in breach of a statutory duty or of an obligation to the lessee. Therefore, if the circumstances are such that the lessor should grant a licence to assign and by refusing would be in breach of a statutory duty, the buyer cannot dictate that the seller adopt this stance. SCPC 4.2.9 requires the seller to manage the property in accordance with the principles of good estate management until completion. Quite whether parties to a contract in dispute can agree as to what might amount to good estate management is open to debate.

Condition 5 Rent reviews

This is a wholly new condition included in the second edition that covers some of the details in the first edition with expanded and new items. The purpose of the condition is to explicitly cover rent review matters that will arise between exchange and completion. SCPC 5.4 imposes on both seller and buyer an obligation to cooperate promptly and effectively regarding the process of the rent review and the documentation required to facilitate the review process. Most importantly, neither can approve a rent without the written approval of the other (SCPC 5.5). The condition also covers how the cost of the rent review should be paid as between the seller and the buyer, e.g. SCPC 5.6 states that the seller and the buyer are to bear their own costs of the rent review process. More detailed time-related provisions follow relating to the payment of costs (see SCPC 5.7 and 5.8).

Condition 6 Title and Transfer

Conditions 6.1 to 6.4 are the same in both sets of conditions (requirements for both registered and unregistered titles are set out in 6.1.2 and 6.1.3). However, SCPC 6.6.4 has been drafted so that where the seller will, after completion, be bound by an obligation affecting the property, then, provided the obligation is disclosed to the buyer before exchange, the seller is entitled to an indemnity from the buyer. There must be disclosure failing which there is no binding obligation to afford any such indemnity.

If the property is registered there may be EIDs such that they may not be disclosed on or with the official copies of the registers. Accordingly, where there are any such EIDs, the buyer should make sure that the seller is obliged by a contractual term to provide the buyer with full copies. As a precautionary measure, it may be appropriate to include this in all contracts (EIDs are discussed in detail above at 19.2.1 regarding commercial leases). In the first edition old SCPC 5 allowed for circumstances in which the buyer might be permitted to go into occupation prior to completion. The second edition no longer permits this and the condition has been removed.

Condition 7 Insurance

This new clause brings together detailed arrangements for the insurance of the subject property, many of which were contained in old SCPC 5. SCPC 7.1.4 states that the seller is under no obligation to insure unless SCPC 7.1.2 applies. This provision applies where the contract terms require the seller to continue with its insurance between exchange and completion. SCPC 7.1.3 will apply if the subject property is let on terms where the seller is obliged to insure (either as lessor or lessee). Accordingly the clause, *inter alia*, requires the seller to do everything necessary to maintain the policy, including paying promptly any premium which falls due. The buyer is to pay to the seller a proportionate part of the insurance premium from the date when the contract is made to the date of actual completion. If after exchange and before completion the property is damaged by an insured risk, the seller is obliged to pay to the buyer on completion the amount of the policy monies received by the seller. If no final insurance payment has been made then the seller is to assign to the buyer all rights to monies under the insurance policy and to hold any monies received in trust for the buyer.

If SCPC 7.1.4 applies, therefore, the buyer must assume the risk from exchange and if necessary arrange insurance from that time. This replicates the position that prevailed with the National Conditions, before they were subsumed into the Standard Conditions, first and subsequent editions. Furthermore if there is double insurance, i.e. the seller and the buyer have the property insured, and the subject property is damaged by an insured risk, then the contract consideration is to be abated by any reduction in the payment made by the buyer's insurance as a result of the seller's cover.

Condition 8 Completion

In this section, being the condition regulating all matters at completion, the buyer instead of the seller is assumed to own the property from the start of the completion date. The completion date will be the actual date of completion where the whole property is sold with vacant possession, otherwise it is the date specified in the agreement. This clearly affects apportionments (see SCPC 8.3.3). These are further regulated at SCPC 8.3.4 where the detailed arrangements required for completion date apportionments are set out. Sums are to be treated as accruing from day to day throughout the period for which payment is or has to be made and at the rate applicable for that period. The SCPC also covers unquantified sums such as final year-end service charges (see SCPC 8.3.5). These are to be payable with interest on late payment, but because of the larger amounts involved in commercial property we suggest that it would be safer to set up an agreed retention with the buyer's solicitor by way of the special conditions. Alternatively, the seller's solicitor could retain the monies in a designated client deposit account pending settlement, with the interest accruing to the seller in any event. This provision should also be covered by way of a special condition in the agreement.

SCPC 8.3.6 applies where a lease affects the property being sold and there is a service charge. On completion the buyer is to pay to the seller any element of the service charge incurred by the seller but not yet due from the tenant. In the light of this provision it is vital that practitioners acting for a buyer in these circumstances raise detailed enquiries about any such expenditure. It is therefore important that proof of payment be produced along with proof that it was necessarily incurred and repayable under the terms and conditions of the lease. This is required to avoid subsequent problems with the lessee in obtaining reimbursement, and is covered by SCPC 8.3.6(a).

SCPCs 8.3.7 and 8.3.8 both seek to cover the position where there are arrears. The terms of these clauses are complicated and should be considered in detail for each subject property and amended as necessary. SCPC 8.3.7 states that SCPC 8.3.8 applies if there are arrears, there is no contractual assignment to the seller of the right to collect those arrears, and the seller is not entitled to recover any arrears from the tenant. In these circumstances SCPC

8.3.8 requires the buyer to seek to collect all the arrears in the ordinary course of management but is not obliged to commence court proceedings for their recovery. Any monies received are to be apportioned between the parties in the ratio of the sums owed to each. Leases granted post-1995 are covered by sections 3 and 23 of the Landlord and Tenant (Covenants) Act 1995 to the extent that unless specifically assigned to the buyer, the right to collect arrears remains with the seller. This is relevant in the context of these SCPCs and the conditions required activate SCPC 8.3.8. It also means that pre-1996 leases are such that the seller will not be able to recover arrears by commencing proceedings or instructing bailiffs after completion (see section 141 of the Law of Property Act 1925).

Finally in this section, SCPC 8.5 says that as soon as the buyer has performed all its obligations on completion the seller must part with the title documents. SCPC 8.7 requires payment to be by direct credit (see Condition 1 General above for the meaning of direct credit). SCPC 8.8 states that at any time on or after the completion date a party who is ready, able, and willing to complete may give to the other a notice to complete. Ten working days is the notice period excluding the day on which the notice is given. For this purpose time is of the essence, see SCPC 8.8.2.

Condition 9 Remedies

Little of this particular condition is changed from the Standard Conditions to the SCPCs, although there is one alteration of consequence for buyers. It should be noted that SCPC 9.3.1 provides that liability for interest arises only on the default of the buyer. If the seller defaults and delays completion in the absence of a special condition all that a buyer can do is sue the defaulting seller for damages. Moreover, SCPC 9.3.4 states that if completion is delayed the seller may give notice to the buyer that it will take the net income from the subject property until completion takes place together with any interest due pursuant to SCPC 9.3.1.

Condition 10 Leasehold property

As one might expect for a set of conditions designed to cover commercial transactions and especially those dealing with the selling and buying of tenanted properties, this section contains substantial provisions. There are detailed alterations from the terms of the Standard Conditions where leases are concerned and particularly in relation to the normal requirement to obtain the consent of the lessor in a commercial lease assignment or transfer.

Dealing first with new leases (i.e. a contract for the grant of a new lease), SCPC 10.2 reiterates the provisions of the Standard Conditions as to definitions and under the SCPC the lease is to be in the form of a draft attached to the agreement itself. Accordingly, it is contemplated that new leases will be part of the actual agreement by attachment. If the lease term exceeds seven years the seller is to deduce title to enable the buyer to register with absolute title. This means that a lessor will have to show the lessee its superior title. To avoid this disclosure, lessors should only grant seven-year leases or shorter.

SCPC 10.3 deals with the landlord's consent and has been substantially reworked. For example, SCPC 10.3.3(b) states that the seller is to enter into an Authorised Guarantee Agreement (AGA) if so required. Similarly the buyer is to use reasonable endeavours to provide guarantees of the performance and observance of the tenant's covenants and the conditions in the seller's lease. SCPC 10.3.1(b) defines consent as 'consent in a form which satisfies the requirement to obtain it' (see *Aubergine Enterprises Ltd v Lakewood International Ltd* [2002] 1 WLR 2149). Completion can now be postponed for up to four months if there is a delay in obtaining the consent of the lessor (SCPCs 10.3.4 and 10.3.5). The commercial conditions also require both parties to perform obligations in support of the application for the lessor's consent, and while those contractual obligations remain incomplete the party in breach cannot rescind the contract (SCPC 10.3.8).

Condition 11 Commonhold

This condition contains new requirements for commonhold transactions. It first makes it clear that the buyer having received from the seller the memorandum and articles of the commonhold association and the commonhold community statement it is treated as having accepted all their terms. If the transaction affects part of a commonhold the seller is to apply for consent to the sale of part and if the consent is not forthcoming there are provisions allowing either party, on giving notice, to rescind the agreement (see SCPC 11.4).

Condition 12 Chattels

The only change to this condition is in SCPC 12.3 where it now provides that ownership of any chattels covered by the agreement passes to the buyer at completion, but that the chattels are at the buyer's risk from exchange. This reflects the provision in the SCPC relating to the insurance risk for the subject property, where the risk also passes at the contract date. The reverse is the case for both the subject property and the chattels in the Standard Conditions (SC 9.3 states that ownership of the chattels passes to the buyer on actual completion).

Part 2 Conditions

Part 2 contains clauses and detailed provisions covering VAT, capital allowances, and reversionary interests in flats. They are completely new and there is nothing in the Standard Conditions that matches them. The main details of these three new provisions are:

A. *VAT.* The standard position in Part 1 is that the seller warrants that the sale of the property does not constitute a supply that is taxable for VAT purposes. Part 2 changes this in two possible ways. First, A1 states that the sale does constitute a supply that is taxable for VAT purposes. A1.3 requires the buyer to pay VAT on top of the purchase price in exchange for a proper VAT invoice. Secondly, Condition A2 covers a transfer of a going concern. In this case the seller warrants that it is using the property for the business of letting to produce a rental income.

B. *Capital allowances.* Condition B supports a buyer in any claims it may make pursuant to the terms of the Capital Allowances Act 2001. In doing so it requires the seller to provide copies of relevant information and cooperation and assistance as the buyer may reasonably require.

C. *Reversionary interests in flats.* C1 covers the provisions of the Landlord and Tenant Act 1987 and the tenants' rights of pre-emption on a sale. The condition requires the seller to warrant that on the facts the tenants do not have any rights arising from this statute, i.e. the relevant notice has been served but no response was forthcoming. Condition C2 covers the position where the tenants are entitled to a right of first refusal.

19.3.2 **TENANTED PROPERTIES: THE BUYER'S PERSPECTIVE**

Additional commercial enquiries

In addition to the standard enquiries that are always raised, and the additional enquiries mentioned above, it is appropriate to make further enquiries in relation to commercial lettings insofar as they may be affected or regulated by legislation. In essence a buyer will want to know how far, if at all, the lease is influenced by Part II of the Landlord and Tenant Act 1954. A buyer will want to know if there has been a court application (as if there is no clause to that effect in the lease the contracting out will be to no effect), and if so will want to see what order the court made. If the lease has been recently renewed under the terms of the Act, a prudent buyer will want details to ascertain how the length of the term eventually granted was settled along with the other terms of the lease. Perhaps of more consequence would be to see the basis on which the rental was finally settled. Valuers' reports would be of use and copies should be requested. A buyer will also want to know if the lessor originally sought to oppose the grant of the lease and why. The ground for possession would be of material interest to the buyer, especially if it related to a breach of covenant or for arrears of rent. Detailed enquiries should be directed to the seller's practitioner seeking as much information as possible about the circumstances of any recent statutory renewal. If the lease was granted after 1 January 1996 on assignment an AGA may be involved. Enquiries should be made of the terms of this agreement. If industrial premises are being purchased, detailed environmental and contamination enquiries must be made of the seller.

The Commercial Property Standard Enquiries

An attempt has been made to draft some standard enquiries for commercial properties. The outcome of this effort is the Commercial Property Standard Enquiries (CPSEs).

Details of the CPSEs can be seen at <http://www.practicallaw.com>. The enquiries in the CPSEs are intended as a standard minimum for use in any commercial property transaction.

CPSE.1 (version 2.4) is designed to cover all commercial property transactions and will (together with any additional enquiries relevant to the particular transaction) be sufficient if the transaction deals only with a freehold sold with vacant possession. The following supplemental enquiries are intended to be used in conjunction with CPSE.1. Which particular additional form or forms will be required will depend upon the individual circumstances of each transaction. The following supplemental forms are available:

- CPSE.2: where the property is sold subject to existing tenancies;
- CPSE.3: where a lease of a property is being granted;
- CPSE.4: where the property being sold is leasehold (i.e. the lease is being assigned or transferred).

19.3.3 COMPLETION MATTERS

online resource centre

On completion the seller must hand over not merely the reversionary title deeds and documents, but also the lease(s) or tenancy agreement(s) as well as rental authorities. These authorities should be completed in letter format and signed by the seller and addressed to the lessees authorizing them to pay all future rents to the buyer or as the buyer directs (standard pre-printed requisitions normally include a request that such authorities be made available on completion). Where the subject property constitutes a dwelling, section 3 of the Landlord and Tenant Act 1985 compels the buyer to give written notice of the change of ownership to the lessee or tenant in occupation within two months of completion. Where a dwelling has been sold, section 48 of the Landlord and Tenant Act 1987 compels the lessor buyer to provide the lessee in occupation with an address in England and Wales that can be used for the service of notices.

🔑 **Key Points** Selling and buying tenanted properties

- Consider whether the sale contract should be based upon the SCs or the SCPCs.

- If the sale is of a reversion subject to residential long leases the sale cannot proceed without the careful consideration of the effects of the Landlord and Tenant Act 1987 which may give the lessees in occupation a right of pre-emption. If the right exists, the contract will need to show that steps have been taken to comply with the Act.

- Where there is a substantial commercial rental income from the property the contract will need to cover the question of rent arrears and the apportionment of rent at completion. Remember that SC 3.3.2(b) requires the seller to inform the buyer of any lease or tenancy termination after exchange but before completion, and to act as the buyer reasonably directs with the buyer indemnifying the seller against any consequent loss or expense.

- Bear in mind that where the property constitutes a dwelling, s 3 of the Landlord and Tenant Act 1985 compels the buyer to give written notice of the change of ownership to the lessee or tenant in occupation within two months of completion; and s 48 of the Landlord and Tenant Act 1987 compels the lessor buyer to provide the lessee in occupation with an address within England and Wales that can be used for the service of notices.
- Do you need to make environmental enquiries and searches?
- Can you use the Commercial Property Standard Enquiries?

19.4 COMMERCIAL PROPERTY AND SOME ELEMENTS OF REVENUE LAW

In this section we will look at VAT and commercial property, as well as Stamp Duty Land Tax (SDLT), and other taxes in so far as they relate to commercial property transactions.

 Conduct Point Taxation

online
resource
centre

- Be very careful about how you advise on taxation issues. All conveyancing practitioners should be aware of the implications of the decision in *Hurlingham Estates Ltd v Wilde & Partners* (1997) 147 NLJ 453. Lightman J made it clear that a solicitor will be liable in negligence for adverse revenue implications for a client that arise from a transaction effected by the solicitor, even though the solicitor was not expressly instructed to consider the revenue implications. This is also true even if the solicitor assumed that the client had previously sought the advice of an accountant. The consequence of this decision is to make it quite clear that if a solicitor feels unable to cover the revenue implications of a commercial transaction, he or she should explain to the client, at the commencement of instructions, that this is so and that the client should separately seek professional advice on the tax implications of the proposed transaction. See Online Resource Centre, Abbey & Richards Terms and Conditions of Business

19.4.1 VAT—AN INTRODUCTION

Value added tax (VAT) is a tax that is in effect a tax on turnover. VAT payments could arise both in a commercial lease and in a commercial property purchase. HM Revenue and Customs (HMRC) deals with VAT, which is currently payable at 17.5 per cent on chargeable items. A chargeable item is called a 'supply'. In the context of commercial property, if a lease is granted, there can be the supply of a lease by the lessor to the lessee. If a commercial property is to be sold then there can be a supply of the subject property by the seller to the buyer. If a lease is assigned or transferred, there can be a supply of the residue of the term granted by the lease by the assignor/transferor to the assignee/transferee.

The general rule is that property transactions such as transfers, conveyances, assignments, or the granting of leases can all be exempt supplies, i.e. they do not attract a VAT charge. However, this can be reversed by written election (see below). On the face of it, conveyancing transactions are exempt. Nevertheless, some transactions can be compulsorily standard-rated (i.e. paying the full rate of tax), some are zero-rated (i.e. subject to VAT but at 0 per cent), and the taxpayer always has the option to elect to tax.

Parties can register as taxable persons who can pay and receive VAT. HMRC sets a threshold at which they are obliged so to register (of the value of taxable supplies, usually the business turnover figures). In the context of commercial transactions the tax can be payable either on the price paid for a commercial property, or on the rent payable by the terms of a commercial lease. Thus if the rent is £100 the VAT is added to it in the sum of £17.50, making £117.50 payable by the lessee.

Where a person or company is required to pay VAT on a purchase price or rent, they should receive an invoice (a VAT invoice) showing how much VAT has been charged. This amount of VAT is called 'input tax'. That person or company may also charge VAT to someone else; this is called 'output tax'. VAT is payable quarterly (being a 'prescribed accounting period' by section 25(1) of the Value Added Tax Act 1994). The taxpayer can, when accounting to HMRC for the output tax received, deduct input tax paid. The net balance is then actually paid, and if input tax exceeds output tax the full amount is recoverable (see section 25(3) of the 1994 Act).

The rate of VAT presently at 17.5 per cent is called the standard rate. There is another rate, called the zero rate, where there is a taxable supply but the rate of tax is zero. Otherwise a supply can be exempt, i.e. not subject to VAT at all. So, the sale of a greenfield site for development is exempt (but there is an option to tax, see below). The surrender of a lease is exempt, as is the assignment of a lease (but again, in both cases there is an option to tax). However, the charges levied by a solicitor or other professional instructed in a commercial transaction will involve fees together with standard-rate VAT. Similarly, construction services for the building of a commercial development are standard-rated.

19.4.2 **VAT AND LEASES GENERALLY**

If a commercial lease is granted, the rule is that it is generally exempt from VAT (i.e. there is an exempt supply), but it is nevertheless subject to the option to tax, i.e. to make the letting taxable. The option to tax arises when the lessor decides voluntarily to give up the exemption and to opt for VAT liability at the standard rate (see section 89 of the Value Added Tax Act 1994). Notice of the election must be given to HMRC within 30 days of its being exercised, and best practice dictates the use of customs form VAT 1614. The building or premises concerned will thereafter be a taxable supply instead of an exempt supply. If it is a taxable supply, on a lease of the subject premises VAT will be chargeable to the lessee. An election must be for the whole of the subject premises; an election in respect of part is not possible. This is also true for assignments and surrenders. It is in effect an option to waive the standard exemption. The lessor must be registered for VAT; and if there is such a registration, written notice must be given to HMRC within 30 days of the election having been made. As it will be for the lessees to pay the VAT on their rent, it is vital that at the same time they are advised of the VAT election. This election is personal to the elector. This means that if there are sub-lessees, the sub-lessor must also elect for VAT to be payable on the sub-lessees' rents.

Electing to charge VAT will only suit a lessor who wishes to recover VAT. Careful consideration should be given to the effect of charging VAT on the rent, as many prospective lessees will be put off taking the premises where they are not registered for VAT and cannot therefore recover the VAT themselves.

There should always be a covenant in all leases to require payment of VAT in addition to the rent. On the assumption that there is an existing lease and it is silent as to the payment of VAT, the lessee will nevertheless have to pay VAT on the rent should the lessor decide to opt to tax. However, there is one vital point to note where you are acting for a lessor who intends to grant a new lease and also intends to opt to tax. You must advise the lessor not to make the election before the grant of the new lease. If the election precedes the grant, HMRC will deem the new rent to be *inclusive* of VAT. This pitfall can be avoided by electing immediately *after* the grant of the lease, but including in the lease a covenant requiring the lessee to pay any VAT on all the rents. Lastly, bear in mind that HMRC views any rent-free period, or periods that are granted as an inducement to a new lessee, as subject to VAT. VAT will be payable on the unpaid rent.

If VAT is payable on a rent, it will also be payable on any service charge under the terms of the same lease by which the rent is paid. In both cases the lessor can issue mere demands (and not VAT invoices), and when the rents and service charges are actually paid receipted VAT invoices should be issued. In this way the lessor can delay accounting for VAT to HMRC until the lessor receives the actual payments. This has the benefit of delaying payment of tax, as well as ensuring that no VAT payments are made on supplies where monies have yet to reach the lessor, i.e. rent arrears.

19.4.3 VAT AND BUYING/SELLING A COMMERCIAL PROPERTY

If the commercial property to be sold or purchased is not new (i.e. not less than three years old), there is an exempt supply of the property on sale. A building is said to be VATable when the lessor has made an election and collects rent and VAT on the rent payable by the lessee(s) of the subject premises. The option to tax arises when the lessor decides voluntarily to give up the standard exemption and to opt for a VAT liability at the standard rate (see section 89 of the 1994 Act). Notice of the election must be given to HMRC within 30 days of its being exercised and best practice dictates the use of customs form VAT 1614. The building concerned will thereafter be a taxable supply instead of an exempt supply. If it is a taxable supply, on sale of the subject premises VAT will be chargeable to the buyer. An election must be for the whole of the subject premises as an election in respect of part is not possible.

When buying a commercial investment property, the buyer will want to know whether VAT will be payable on top of the proposed purchase price. Both the Standard Conditions of Sale (SC 1.4) and the Standard Commercial Property Conditions of Sale (SCPC 1.4) provide for all sums payable under the contract to be exclusive of VAT, i.e. any VAT is added to the purchase price. If the buyer wishes to avoid paying VAT, it will require a special condition to this effect. The condition will say either that the purchase price is to be inclusive of any VAT, or that the seller warrants that it has not elected to waive any exemption to VAT and will not do so on or before completion. This is especially important for buyers who make exempt supplies in the course of their businesses, e.g. banks, building societies, and insurance companies, because they are unable to recover their VAT payments.

If a new freehold building (i.e. less than three years old) is sold it is subject to the standard rate of VAT. Accordingly, if a client instructs you to sell a new commercial property, the seller will be making a supply that will be standard-rated. This being so, the consideration will attract VAT at the standard rate. However, the client will want to know whether the stated price includes or excludes the standard rate of VAT. Clearly the seller will want the VAT added to the consideration. Unless there is evidence or documentation to the contrary, there will be a presumption that the stated consideration is to *include* VAT. Practitioners acting for a seller in these circumstances should ensure that there is a clear contractual term making the consideration exclusive of VAT so that the full price is paid to the seller with VAT on top of it. To omit such a clause in these circumstances would amount to a clear act of negligence. Therefore, as a matter of course, a VAT-exclusive clause should be included in all such contracts. Both the Standard Conditions (SC 1.4) and the SCPC (SCPC 1.4) provide for all sums payable under the contract to be exclusive of VAT, i.e. any VAT is *added* to the purchase price.

19.4.4 VAT AND THE STANDARD COMMERCIAL PROPERTY CONDITIONS OF SALE

The second edition of the SCPC is divided into two parts. Part 1 contains general conditions building on those in the first edition, while Part 2 contains new clauses and in particular detailed provisions covering VAT, capital allowances and reversionary interests in flats. In general Part 1 applies unless specifically excluded, while Part 2 will only apply if expressly incorporated. Completing tick boxes on the back page of the agreement effects explicit incorporation (see SCPC 1.1.4 (a) and (b)).

The standard position in Part 1 is that the seller warrants that the sale of the property does not constitute a supply that is taxable for VAT purposes. Part 2 changes this in two possible ways. First, A1 states that the sale does constitute a supply that is taxable for VAT purposes. A1.3 requires the buyer to pay VAT on top of the purchase price in exchange for a proper VAT invoice. Secondly, Condition A2 covers a transfer of a going concern. In this case the seller warrants that it is using the property for the business of letting to produce a rental income. See Appendix 3.

 Key Points VAT And Commercial Conveyancing

- If a commercial lease is granted, the rule is that it is generally exempt from VAT but is nevertheless subject to the option to tax, i.e. to make the letting VATable.

- In a commercial lease, where VAT is to be charged on the rent the lessor must be registered for VAT; and if there is such a registration, written notice must be given to the HMRC within 30 days of the election having been made.

- If the election precedes the grant of a new commercial lease, the HMRC will deem the new rent to be *inclusive* of VAT. If acting for the lessor, to avoid this problem, make sure the lease contains a covenant by the lessee to pay VAT in addition to the rent.

- The election to tax is personal to the elector and is in respect of individual properties, i.e. on a property-by-property basis.

- On the assumption that there is an existing lease and it is silent as to the payment of VAT, the lessee will nevertheless have to pay VAT on the rent should the lessor decide to opt to tax. For certainty, always ensure that there is a covenant requiring the lessee to pay VAT on rent if required.

- If a commercial property that is not new (not less than three years old) is to be sold or purchased, there is an exempt supply of the property on sale and VAT will not be payable unless the seller opts to tax.

- If a new freehold building is to be sold it will be subject to the standard rate of VAT. Accordingly, if a client instructs you to sell a new commercial property the seller will be making a supply that will be standard rated.

- Practitioners acting for sellers should always draft contracts so as to make all sums exclusive of VAT.

- The HMRC national advice service can be contacted on 0845 010 9000 where they will deal with general VAT enquiries.

19.4.5 STAMP DUTY LAND TAX

Stamp Duty Land Tax (SDLT) is based on the taxation of transactions in place of deeds or documents that was the case for the old stamp duty regime. It is assessed directly against the buyer rather than the property being purchased.

The SDLT regime came into force on 1 December 2003. Leasehold transactions are caught by SDLT as to the consideration paid and the rent in the lease. The starting threshold for the payment of SDLT is £125,000 for non-residential and £150,000 for commercial properties. Practitioners should note that there is guidance on the HMRC website at <http://www. hmrc.gov.uk/so> regarding SDLT.

Transactions under the threshold will be taxed at 0 per cent but will still require a land transaction return to be completed for these transactions. SDLT will be at 1 per cent on a consideration up to the value of £250,000; 3 per cent for £250,001 to £500,000; and 4 per cent from £500,001 upwards.

The land transaction return, form SDLT1 replaces the existing 'Stamps L(A)451' (the 'Particulars Delivered' for m). SDLT2 and 3 and 4 supplement SDLT1. SDLT2 is used where there are more than two sellers and/or two buyers. SDLT3 is used where land is involved and further space is required in addition to the space provided on SDLT1. Perhaps of greater importance in commercial property is form SDLT4 that should be used for complex commercial transactions and leases.

SDLT includes a regime for the rental element of commercial leases. The charge will be at a rate of 1 per cent on the net present value (NPV) of the total rent payable over the term of the lease. Future rents will be discounted at 3.5 per cent per annum in order to arrive at the NPV. Leases where the NPV of the rent over the term of the lease does not exceed £150,000 will be exempt. HMRC has suggested that change in the regime could mean that some 60 per cent of all commercial leases could avoid any SDLT on the rental element. On the HMRC website there is a facility to work out the SDLT liability for leasehold transactions.

Once HMRC have received and processed a proper SDLT return and, where required, payment, they will issue a certificate of payment. The certificate, the SDLT5, is issued under section 79 of the Finance Act 2003 and evidences that SDLT has been accounted on the particular transaction notified to HMRC. This must be sent to Land Registry to enable an application to register to proceed.

19.4.6 **OTHER TAXES**

If the lessor charges and receives a premium for the granting of a commercial lease, that premium will be potentially liable to tax as a capital gain. As premiums are uncommon in the context of commercial leases, this tax liability is unlikely to be of any real consequence. However, the lessor's profit rental income will be liable either to income tax or, if a company, corporation tax. HMRC also deems a premium paid on a lease for a term of less than 50 years to be partly taxable as income. There is no double charge to tax, as the element deemed to be income will be excluded from capital gains tax. A premium paid on assignment will, potentially, attract capital gains tax as it is of course a 'disposal' which attracts this tax liability.

SELF TEST QUESTIONS

1. Where you are granting a commercial lease and the client requires it to be an 'FRI' lease, does this mean

   (a) Full rates involved

   (b) Fully repaired internally

   (c) Full repairing and insuring

   (d) Fully but reasonably insured

2. Your client is the tenant of a 12-year lease of a lock up shop used as a newsagent. The lease term expired last Monday. Your client wishes to continue trading in the property. Your advice is

   (a) To leave the premises as the lease term has ended

   (b) To remain and to continue to pay rent and await a notice to quit

   (c) To write to the court immediately asking to renew the lease

   (d) To write to the local authority claiming the property

3. You are acting for a lessee taking a new 7-year lease of offices with an option to renew. You should remember to register a lease option by a notice or restriction on the lessor's unregistered title. Is this statement TRUE/FALSE? Please delete the incorrect choice.

4. Your client is a tenant taking a new lease where you are instructed to agree an alienation clause that gives the lessee the widest possible rights. Which of the following is to be preferred

   (a) Not to assign without the lessor's consent which cannot be unreasonably withheld or delayed

    (b) Not to assign without the lessor's consent and without offering to enter into an authorized guarantee agreement

    (c) Not to assign without first offering a surrender to the lessor

    (d) Not to assign the residue of the term granted by the lease

5. A lessee can claim the benefits of Part II of the Landlord and Tenant Act 1954 only if three conditions can be fulfilled, which of the following does *not* apply

    (a) There is a lease or tenancy within the terms of the Act

    (b) The lessee must be a limited company only

    (c) The lessee is in occupation of the property

    (d) The lessee so occupies the property for the purposes of the lessee's business

SHORT REVISION QUESTIONS

1. CA&C Services Ltd ('CA&C') was granted a 15-year business lease in January 1998 and Mr Trevor Gray, a director of CA&C, guaranteed the tenant's liabilities under the lease. Explain whether or not Mr Gray is liable for the liabilities of the current tenant, Sunwalk Supplies Ltd, to whom CA&C assigned the residue of the lease last month.

2. On a lease renewal explain with authority whether an institutional landlord is likely to succeed in persuading a court to include terms that are more onerous on the tenant than those contained in the original lease that was granted prior to 1996.

3. On a lease renewal a lessor has succeeded in opposing your client's application to renew its five-year business tenancy of an office because the lessor wishes to occupy the premises. The lessee must move out next week even though it has been in occupation for the full five-year period. What other advice can you give your client in relation to its failed claim?

SUGGESTED ANSWERS TO SELF TEST QUESTIONS

1. The correct answer is (c). In many cases the lease may be referred to as an 'FRI' lease, i.e., a full repairing and insuring lease. The phrase has come to signify a lease that makes the tenant wholly responsible for maintaining the structure of the subject property.

2. The correct answer is (b). The tenant should remain in the premises and must continue to pay rent and await a notice to quit. This is because Part II of the Landlord and Tenant Act 1954 gives the tenant of business premises security of tenure.

3. This statement is false. Although the option needs to be protected the lessor's title is unregistered. Therefore the option needs to registered as a Class C(iv) land charge as the lessor's title is unregistered. If the option is not protected in this way, the lessee could have difficulty in exercising the option against a purchaser of the reversionary interest.

4. The correct answer is (a). The tenant has the widest rights from this clause that enables the lessee to deal with assignments in the knowledge that the lessor cannot withhold consent to a change of tenant unreasonably. All the other clauses have potential problems or conditions that provide more restrictive terms than the first one in (a).

5. The correct answer is (b). A lessee can claim the benefits of this statute if there is a lease or tenancy within the terms of the Act, the lessee is in occupation of the property, and the lessee occupies the property for the purposes of the lessee's business. The lessee can be a company or an individual and provided the previous three conditions apply then the Act will come into play.

SUGGESTED ANSWERS TO SHORT REVISION QUESTIONS

1. This is a 'new' lease. Under the Landlord and Tenant (Covenants) Act 1995, section 24(2): where a tenant is released from liability on an assignment, so is his guarantor. Any attempt to extend the liability of the guarantor beyond this is void (section 25) unless the original guarantee extended to any Authorised Guarantee Agreement given by CA&C. So, what needs to be ascertained is whether or not this is the case and whether or not CA&C has given an Authorised Guarantee Agreement.

2. Any change must be fair and reasonable taking into account the comparatively weak negotiating position of a sitting tenant requiring renewal. (In the case of *O'May v City of London Real Property Co. Ltd* [1983] 2 AC 726 it was held that the new lease would be on the same terms as the old lease unless one of the parties to the proceedings could show that a desired variation was fair and reasonable. Moreover, the court must have regard to the comparatively weak bargaining position of the lessee on renewal). However a 'new' lease means that the tenant will no longer be liable for the whole term if he or she assigns so the terms of an alienation covenant may be modernized to reflect this.

3. Compensation may be payable as a result of the lessor succeeding at court in opposing the renewal application. Compensation may be payable if the lessor is successful in opposing the grant of a new tenancy on the ground that the lessor intends to actually occupy the subject property. The appropriate level of compensation is related to the rateable value for the property and is dictated by the Landlord and Tenant Act 1954 (Appropriate Multiplier) Order 1990 (SI 1990/363) and in this case the appropriate multiplier is one times the rateable value (the multiplier can be two times the rateable value when the lessee or the lessee and the lessee's predecessors in title for the same business have been in occupation of the subject premises for at least 14 years prior to the date of termination). See also the recent changes made by The Regulatory Reform (Business Tenancies) (England and Wales) Order 2003, SI 2003/3096.

WIDER READING

- Abbey, R, and Richards, M, *A Practical Approach to Commercial Conveyancing and Property* (Oxford University Press, 2006)

- Chapters 12 and 13, Abbey, R, and Richards, M, *A Practical Approach to Conveyancing* (Oxford University Press, 2008)

- Sections K and L dealing with Leaseholds and Tenanted Property, Silverman, F, *Conveyancing Handbook* (The Law Society, 2006)

- Emmet on Title: Chapters 26 to 28, Leases

- For more detail on the changes introduced by the Land Registration Act 2002 see Abbey, R, and Richards, M, *Blackstone's Guide to the Land Registration Act 2002* (Oxford University Press, 2002)

- Chapter 8 (the leasehold estate); Chapter 9 (Obligations of landlord and tenant), MacKenzie, J-A, and Phillips, M, *Textbook on Land Law* (Oxford University Press, 2008)

WEBSITES FOR FURTHER INFORMATION

The following websites may assist in the process of Commercial Conveyancing:

- British Property Federation, **<http://www.bpf.org.uk>**.

- Companies House, **<http://www.companieshouse.gov.uk/>**.

- Confederation of British Industry, **<http://www.cbi.org.uk/>**.

- Office of Public Sector Information including the Her Majesty's Stationary Office, **<http://www.opsi.gov.uk/>**.

- Health and Safety Executive, **<http://www.open.gov.uk/hse/hsehome.htm>**.

- Highways Agency, **<http://www.highways.gov.uk/>**.

- Land Registry, **<http://www.landreg.gov.uk/>**.

- Land Registry internet register access, **<http://www.landregistrydirect.gov.uk>**.

- Inland Revenue, **<http://www.inlandrevenue.gov.uk/home.htm>**.

- Landmark Information group, **<http://www.landmark-information.co.uk/>**.

- Residential Property Tribunal Service, **<http://www.rpts.gov.uk/>**. This is the public body that can decide many rent and leasehold disputes.

- National Association of Estate Agents, **<http://www.naea.co.uk>**.

- National House Building Council, **<http://www.nhbc.co.uk>**.

- National Housing Federation, **<http://www.housing.org.uk/>**.

- National Land Information Service, **<http://www.nlis.org.uk/>**.

- Ordnance Survey, **<http://www.ordnancesurvey.co.uk/oswebsite/>**.

The following websites may assist in the process of granting or renewing business leases:

- Association of British Insurers, **<http://www.abi.org.uk/>**.

- Bank of England, **<http://www.bankofengland.co.uk/>**.

- British Bankers Association, **<http://www.bba.org.uk/>**.

- Council of Mortgage Lenders, **<http://www.cml.org.uk>**.

- Financial Services Authority, **<http://www.fsa.gov.uk>**.

- HM Treasury, **<http://www.hm-treasury.gov.uk>**.

- Housing Corporation, **<http://www.housingcorp.gov.uk/lcd>**.

- Housing Forum, **<http://www.thehousingforum.org.uk/>**.

- Law Commission, **<http://www.lawcom.gov.uk/review.htm>**.

- Royal Town Planning Institute, **<http://www.rtpi.org.uk>**.

- Society of Construction Law, **<http://www.scl.org.uk/>**.

online
resource
centre

ONLINE RESOURCE CENTRE CASE STUDY

COMMERCIAL TRANSACTION CASE STUDY—THE CONVEYANCING TRANSACTION

Our client: Cambo Ltd—acquisition of 18 Clover Street London W2

Timothy Wainwright and his family have run a successful wholesale clothing business for many years. Timothy has decided to sell the business and enter the world of property investment. He has formed a company called Cambo Ltd in which he, his wife, and their three sons are all shareholders. Cambo Ltd has agreed to buy 18 Clover Street London W2 for £700,000 subject to and with the benefit of two occupational business leases. Consider materials featured on the Online Resource Centre which cover aspects of this commercial transaction.

20 LANDLORD AND TENANT ACT 1954, PART II

20.1 INTRODUCTION

The Landlord and Tenant Act 1954, part II (the Act) provides security of tenure for the majority of business tenants by giving to those tenants a statutory right to renew their lease or tenancy. The court will order a new lease but will require the tenant to pay a market rent prevailing at the time of renewal. In general terms, provided the tenant occupies the subject property for business purposes, that tenant can remain in the property at the end of the contractual lease and can seek to renew the letting. The landlord is obliged by statute to agree a renewal unless he can establish one or more of the grounds for eviction under section 30(1) of the Act.

 Conduct Point

- There are strict time limits for service of the various notices under the Act and for the tenant's application to the court for a new tenancy. Failure to adhere to these time limits represents one of the most common examples of solicitors' negligence. Attention to detail and a fail-safe diary or computer entry system are therefore essential when dealing with business tenancy renewals.

The Act applies to 'any tenancy where the property comprised in the tenancy is or includes premises which are occupied by the tenant and are so occupied for the purposes of a business carried on by him or for those and other purposes' (section 23(1)). Thus to qualify for protection under the Act *a tenant must be occupying premises for the purposes of a business*. This wording is now considered.

20.2 **NEED FOR 'TENANCY'**

Only tenancies of business premises are protected under the Act. The key factor in determining whether an arrangement is a tenancy is whether the occupier has been granted exclusive possession of the property (*Street v Mountford* [1985] 2 All ER 289, HL). Exclusive possession by the occupier will connote a tenancy, and this has been confirmed in several cases involving commercial property. In *Esso Petroleum Ltd v Fumegrange Ltd* [1994] 2 EGLR 90, the Court of Appeal held that exclusive possession of a petrol station had not been granted because the licensor had reserved extensive rights over the property. These included control over the way in which the occupier's business was to be operated as well as the physical layout of the site. It should be noted that a reservation of a simple right of entry or access onto the occupier's premises will be insufficient to negate exclusive possession (see *Addiscombe Garden Estates Ltd v Crabbe* [1957] 3 All ER 563, CA). In *National Car Parks Ltd v Trinity Development Company (Banbury) Ltd* [2000] EGCS 128, the court held that an agreement to occupy premises as a car park did not constitute a tenancy and was a mere licence. Here the fact that the agreement allowed the licensor potentially to use the premises itself to park cars, and also laid down regulations as to the conduct of the licensee's business, was sufficient to deny exclusive possession.

A licence cannot be protected by the Act because it is not a tenancy. However, there are dangers for landlords who seek to avoid the Act by purporting to grant a licence to occupiers of their premises. The courts have construed many so-called licences to be mere fabrications, and have held them instead to be tenancies. If the agreement has the hallmarks of a tenancy (exclusive possession, for a term, and at a rent) then the courts will generally construe it as such, notwithstanding that the parties may call it a licence (see *Bruton v London & Quadrant Housing Trust Ltd* [1999] 3 WLR 150, HL).

20.2.1 TENANCIES EXCLUDED FROM STATUTORY PROTECTION

Fixed-term tenancies not exceeding six months (section 43(3))
Although generally excluded, it should be noted that these short fixed-term tenancies will be protected under the Act in two situations:

(a) if they contain provisions for renewing the term or extending it beyond six months (section 43(3)(a)), or

(b) if the tenant (including any predecessor in the same business) has already been in occupation for a period exceeding 12 months (section 43(3)(b)). For the tenant to have protection, such occupation must be under either a fixed-term or a periodic tenancy, i.e. not as licensee, tenant at will, or trespasser. Note that any predecessor in the tenant's business need not necessarily have been a tenant and may have been occupying as a mere licensee, or even as freeholder (see *Cricket Ltd v Shaftesbury plc* [1999] 3 All ER 283).

The exception under section 43(3)(b) allows a tenant starting up in business to be granted up to three successive tenancies of less than six months each. This is because by the time the third tenancy is granted, the tenant will not have been in occupation for 12 months.

Contracted out tenancies
Under section 38A of the Act, the prospective landlord and tenant may agree to exclude from the lease the security of tenure provisions of the Act (sections 24–28). Importantly, the agreement must satisfy three statutory requirements, failing which the agreement will be void with the consequence that the tenancy will be protected under the Act. For landlords, it is therefore vital that these requirements are observed. They are:

(a) Landlord's health warning. Before the tenant enters into the tenancy (or, if earlier, before the tenant is contractually bound to do so) the landlord must serve on the tenant a 'health warning' notice. The notice should be served 14 days before the tenant commits itself to the lease.

After receiving the health warning notice the tenant (or someone authorized by the tenant, e.g. his solicitor) must take the following action before entering into the tenancy (or, if earlier, becoming contractually bound to do so). The tenant (or authorized person) must sign a declaration that the tenant has received the health warning and accepts the consequences of contracting out of the Act. Provided the tenant receives the health warning at least 14 days before committing himself to the lease, the tenant (or authorized person) merely signs a simple declaration (not requiring a witness), stating that the tenant has received the notice and accepts the consequences of contracting out of the Act.

(b) Tenant's declaration. However, the landlord is permitted to serve the health warning notice less than 14 days before the tenant enters into the tenancy (or, if earlier, becomes contractually bound to do so). In this case, the tenant must sign a more formal statutory declaration in front of an independent solicitor (or someone else empowered to administer oaths). Thus the parties can effectively waive the 14-day period. Notwithstanding this, it is important to appreciate that however late the health warning is served, it must always be served before the tenant actually enters into the tenancy (or becomes contractually bound to do so). Failure to do so will make the agreement to contract out of the Act void.

(c) Reference in the lease. The third requirement is that the lease must contain reference to (a) the health warning, (b) the tenant's declaration or statutory declaration and (c) the agreement to contract out. Typically this will all be contained in a separate clause in the lease. Alternatively, a separate endorsement to this effect can be attached to the lease.

Other excluded tenancies

Examples of other excluded tenancies include tenancies at will (i.e. where someone occupies property with the permission of the owner but does not pay rent) and service tenancies (those granted to persons in connection with their office or employment).

20.3 NEED FOR 'OCCUPATION'

In most cases it will be fairly clear whether the tenant is in occupation of the premises. The courts have held that the important factors to be taken into account are the tenant's physical occupation or presence, and the measure of control the tenant exercises over those who use the premises.

20.3.1 SUB-LETTING

Generally, if the tenant sub-lets or parts with possession of the premises it can no longer be said to be in occupation of the part (or whole) that has been sub-let. It would therefore not qualify for statutory protection in respect of the part (or whole) of the premises occupied by the sub-tenant.

20.4 NEED FOR 'THE PURPOSES OF A BUSINESS'

To qualify for protection under the Act, the tenant is required to occupy the premises for the purposes of a business. The fact that they are occupied for business purposes does not necessarily mean that the tenant must carry on the business there. What is important is that the premises must be occupied for that purpose (see *Bracey v Read* [1962] 3 All ER 472 and *Methodist Secondary Schools Trust Deed Trustees v O'Leary* [1993] 1 EGLR 105, CA). A business carried on by one member of a group of companies of which the tenant company is a member is treated as a business of the tenant (section 42(2)(a)). Similarly, where a tenancy is held on trust, the carrying on of a business by the beneficiaries under the trust is treated as being the business of the tenant (section 41(1)).

20.4.1 MEANING OF 'BUSINESS'

The definition of 'business' in section 23(2) includes a 'trade, profession or employment and includes any activity carried on by a body of persons, whether corporate or unincorporate'. It can be seen that the definition is narrower for an individual ('trade, profession or employment') than it is for a body of persons ('any activity'). Thus a body of persons running a tennis club was held to be a business (*Addiscombe Garden Estates v Crabbe* [1958] 1 QB 513, CA), as was the administration of a hospital by a board of governors (*Hills (Patents) Ltd v University College Hospital Board of Governors* [1956] 1 QB 90, CA). Similarly, a local authority's maintenance of a park was classified as a business activity under the Act (*Wandsworth LBC v Singh* (1991) 62 P & CR 219, CA). However, an individual running a Sunday school has been held not to be within the definition of 'trade, profession or employment'. The provision of residential accommodation by way of a business venture has been classified as a business activity (*Lee-Verhulst (Investments) Ltd v Harwood Trust* [1973] QB 204).

20.4.2 MIXED USE

If the premises are used partly for business and partly for residential purposes (e.g. a flat above a shop), the test is whether the business activity is a significant purpose of the occupation, or whether it is merely incidental to the occupation as a residence. It is a question of degree in each case. For example, an office block might have sleeping accommodation for staff on the top floor. Although residential in nature, the sleeping accommodation would only be incidental to the building's principal use as business premises. Conversely, one room in a dwellinghouse set aside exclusively for business purposes (e.g. a doctor's private consultation room at home) would not alter the fact that the significant purpose of the occupation of the property was residential. This occurred in *Royal Life Savings Society v Page* [1978] 1 WLR 1329. In *Gurton v Parrot* [1991] 1 EGLR 98, a residential tenant's conversion of outbuildings into dog kennels was held to be merely incidental to the property's use as a dwellinghouse. Similarly in *Wright v Mortimer* (1996) 28 HLR 719, CA, an art historian's use of his flat for writing was held to be merely incidental to his residential use. On the other hand, a seafood importer who received business visitors and kept files, a telephone, and typewriter in his flat, and had no other business premises, was held to occupy the flat for business purposes (*Cheryl Investments Ltd v Saldanha* [1979] 1 All ER 5, CA).

If the lease prohibits business use generally (e.g. 'not to use the premises for business purposes'), the tenant cannot obtain protection from the Act simply by carrying on a business in breach of the covenant (section 23(4)).

20.5 KEY METHODS OF TERMINATION UNDER THE ACT

A business tenancy protected by the Act can be terminated only in one of the ways prescribed by the Act. Until that occurs the tenancy simply continues on the same terms as the original tenancy (except for the termination provisions). The landlord or the tenant can seek an increased rent by applying to the court for an interim rent under section 24A of the Act (see 20.9).

The most widely used methods of termination are the landlord's section 25 notice and the tenant's section 26 request, which are considered below.

The other methods of termination are:

(a) a tenant's notice under section 27(1) or section 27(2) of the Act where the tenancy is for a fixed term (these notices are used where the tenant does not wish the lease to continue or be renewed);

(b) a tenant's notice to quit in a periodic tenancy (provided the tenant has been in occupation for at least one month);

(c) surrender;

(d) forfeiture;

(e) forfeiture of a superior lease;

(f) notice to quit served by a mesne landlord on the superior landlord; and

(g) an agreement between the parties for a future tenancy under section 28 of the Act.

20.5.1 **TENANT'S NOTICES UNDER SECTION 27**

If the tenant has a fixed-term tenancy and does not wish it to continue, the tenant can terminate the lease by serving on the immediate landlord a statutory notice under section 27 of the 1954 Act. There are two types of notice. A notice under section 27(1) is served before the end of the contractual term; whereas a notice under section 27(2) is served after the end of the contractual term where the tenant is holding over.

Before the end of the contractual term—tenant's notice under section 27(1)

A tenant who has been in occupation under a business tenancy for at least one month and who does not wish to renew its fixed-term tenancy can serve a notice in writing on its immediate landlord under section 27(1). This notice must be served not later than three months before the end of the fixed term. The tenancy will then come to an end on the expiry of the contractual term. Section 27(1) applies only to 'a term of years certain', i.e. a fixed term. This would exclude periodic tenancies, but would include a fixed term of less than one year (see *Re Land and Premises at Liss, Hants* [1971] 3 All ER 380). It has been held that 'a term of years certain' would not include a term of 12 months and thereafter from year to year determinable on the landlord giving 12 months' notice (*Nicholls v Kinsey* [1994] 2 WLR 622, CA).

There is no prescribed form, but a typical notice might read as follows:

To [name of landlord]

of [address of landlord]

From [name of tenant]

of [address of tenant]

1. I am the tenant of [address of property] under a lease dated [date of lease] ('the Lease') made between [original parties to lease].

2. The Lease expires on [contractual expiry date].

3. I hereby give you notice under section 27(1) of the Landlord and Tenant Act 1954 ('the Act') that I do not wish my tenancy to be continued under the provisions of Part II of the Act.

Dated:

Signed:

[signature of tenant, or on behalf of tenant]

A tenant who has served a section 27(1) notice is not permitted to serve a section 26 request (section 26(4)). A section 27(1) notice will not affect any sub-tenancy protected by the Act.

What is the position if the tenant vacates the premises before the contractual expiry date? Is a section 27(1) notice needed? In *Esselte AB v Pearl Assurance plc* [1997] 02 EG 124, it was held that a section 27(1) notice is strictly not necessary if the tenant has ceased to occupy the premises for business purposes on or before the contractual expiry date. This is because the tenancy is no longer one to which the 1954 Act applies (i.e. not in occupation for the purposes of a business) and so cannot be continued under section 24.

The 2004 reforms amend the Act to reflect the decision in *Esselte AB v Pearl Assurance plc* [1997] 02 EG 124. Section 27(1A) provides, in effect, that a fixed term tenancy will not continue under the Act if the tenant was not in occupation at the contractual expiry date. However, in cases of doubt as to whether the tenant has fully quit the premises, it is still best practice for the tenant to serve a section 27(1) notice.

After the end of the contractual term—tenant's notice under section 27(2)

A notice under section 27(2) differs slightly from a section 27(1) notice. It is served by a tenant who is holding over after the contractual expiry date has passed and who does not wish to renew the tenancy. As with a section 27(1) notice, the tenant must have been in occupation for at least one month. It is served on the immediate landlord, who must be given at least three months' notice expiring on any day. This is a change from the position before 1 June 2004 where the three months' notice had to expire on a quarter day.

There is no prescribed form, but a typical notice might read as follows:

To [name of landlord]

of [address of landlord]

From [name of tenant]

of [address of tenant]

1. I am the tenant of [address of property] under a lease dated [date of lease] ('the Lease') made between [original parties to lease].

2. The Lease expired on [contractual expiry date] and my tenancy continues under s 24 of the Landlord and Tenant Act 1954 ('the Act').

3. I hereby give you notice under section 27(2) of the Act that my tenancy will come to an end on [date tenancy to end] by virtue of this notice.

Dated:

Signed:

[signature of tenant, or on behalf of tenant]

A tenant who has served a section 27(2) notice is not permitted to serve a section 26 request (section 26(4)). A section 27(2) notice will not affect any sub-tenancy protected by the Act. If the tenant vacates the premises after the end of the contractual term, it cannot rely on the effect of *Esselte AB v Pearl Assurance plc* [1997] 02 EG 124 and the new section 27(1A) (see 20.5.1 above). This is because section 27(2) provides that where a fixed term continues under section 24 the tenancy will not end merely because the tenant ceases to occupy the premises. The tenant must therefore serve a section 27(2) notice to bring the tenancy to an end.

Under a new section 27(3), provision is made for the appropriate apportionment of rent to be made in the tenant's favour as at the expiry of a section 27(2) notice. The tenant may therefore recover any overpayment of rent.

20.5.2 LANDLORD'S NOTICE UNDER SECTION 25

If the tenant is protected under the Act and the landlord requires the premises back at the end of the lease, the landlord must serve a section 25 notice on the tenant specifying the grounds on which the landlord is claiming possession. This is known as a 'hostile notice'. The specified grounds for possession are contained in section 30(1) of the Act. Even if the landlord is content for the tenant to remain in possession under a negotiated new lease, the landlord must still serve a section 25 notice to end the existing lease. This is known as a 'non-hostile notice'. The landlord cannot serve a section 25 notice if the tenant has already served a section 26 request or a section 27 notice.

The section 25 notice is effective only if it is in a prescribed form. Moreover, there are strict time limits for service in that the notice must be given not less than six months, or more than 12 months, before the termination date specified in the notice. As will be seen, the termination date cannot be earlier than the contractual expiry date, and may well be later. If the time limits are not observed the notice will be invalid and of no effect. If the landlord client suffers loss as a result of an invalid notice, a negligence claim against the solicitors is likely to ensue.

Prescribed form and content of section 25 notice

The current prescribed form for a section 25 notice is set out in the Online Resource Centre. A form 'substantially to the like effect' can be used, but this is not to be recommended. To ensure that the most current form is used, the safest practice is to use a printed form from law stationers or a computer software form. If firms use their own word-processed forms there is always a danger that errors or omissions could occur, leading to possible negligence claims. The section 25 notice must:

(a) specify the date at which the tenancy is to end (section 25(1)). This termination date must not be earlier than the date on which the tenancy could have been terminated at common law. Thus for a normal fixed term without a break clause, the specified termination date cannot be earlier than the last day of the contractual term. And for a fixed-term lease with a break clause (as well as a periodic tenancy), the specified termination date cannot be earlier than the date on which the landlord could have ended the tenancy by common law notice;

(b) state whether the landlord would oppose the tenant's application to the court for a new tenancy, and if so on which statutory grounds (section 25(6) and (7)). Thus the landlord must decide whether the notice is 'hostile' or 'non-hostile'. The statutory grounds of opposition are considered at 20.10. The notice cannot be amended once it has been served, so the landlord should specify all the grounds on which it wishes to rely (*Hutchinson v Lamberth* [1984] 1 EGLR 75, CA);

(c) if the section 25 notice states that the landlord would not oppose the tenant's application for a new tenancy, it must set out the landlord's proposals as to (i) the property to be comprised in the new tenancy (either the whole or part of the property comprised in the current tenancy); (ii) the new rent; and (iii) the other terms of the new tenancy (section 25(8)). This is a new provision introduced by the 2004 reforms;

(d) be given and signed by, or on behalf of, the landlord. If there is more than one landlord, all their names must be given (*Pearson v Alyo* [1990] 1 EGLR 114). If there are joint tenants, the notice must be served on all of them unless the joint tenancy is held by a partnership. In this case, section 41A of the Act permits the landlord to serve only those tenants who are partners involved in running the business;

(e) relate to the whole of the demised premises not part only (*Southport Old Links Ltd v Naylor* [1985] 1 EGLR 129). This applies even where the tenant has sub-let part of the premises. Where, after the grant of the tenancy, the reversion becomes vested in different landlords, the landlords should either serve a notice jointly, or serve separate notices which can be read together (see *M & P Enterprises (London) Ltd v Norfolk Square Hotels Ltd* [1994] 1 EGLR 129);

(f) be served on any sub-tenant where the tenant has sub-let the whole of the premises. This is provided the sub-tenancy satisfies section 23 (see also 20.8 regarding section 40).

Omission of prescribed information

If the prescribed information is omitted from the section 25 notice, is it still valid? The test, as laid down by Barry J in *Barclays Bank Ltd v Ascott* [1961] 1 WLR 717, is whether the notice gives 'the proper information to the tenant which will enable the tenant to deal in a proper way with the situation, whatever it may be, referred to in the statement of the notice'. Accordingly, if the form is not materially different from the prescribed form then it will generally be considered valid (*Sun Alliance and London Assurance Co Ltd v Hayman* [1975] 1 WLR 177).

Error or defect in section 25 notice

If the notice contains an error or is incorrectly completed, is it still valid? The test was laid down by the House of Lords in *Mannai Investment Co Ltd v Eagle Star Life Assurance Ltd* [1997] 3 All ER 352. Essentially, the court has to decide, first, whether the error in the notice is obvious or evident and, secondly, whether, despite the error, the notice read in its context is sufficiently clear to leave a reasonable recipient in no reasonable doubt as to the terms of the notice. Although each case will turn on its own facts, it may be useful to consider examples of where defects have and have not invalidated a notice.

Examples of defects which have invalidated a section 25 notice include:

- failure to name all joint landlords in the notice (*Smith v Draper* [1990] 2 EGLR 69, CA; Pearson v Alyo [1990] 1 EGLR 261);
- naming the wrong person as landlord (*Morrow v Nadeem* [1986] 1 WLR 1381, CA);
- an assignor serving a notice after the reversion had been assigned (*Yamaha-Kemble Music (UK) Ltd v ARC Properties* [1990] 1 EGLR 261).

Examples of defects which have not invalidated a section 25 notice include:

- the notice was not signed but the covering letter made it apparent that the notice was served on behalf of the landlord (*Stidolph v American School in London Educational Trust* (1969) 20 P & CR 802, CA);
- the notice stated the wrong termination date but the covering letter made it apparent what date was intended (*Germax Securities Ltd v Spiegal* (1978) 37 P & CR 204);
- failure to date the notice (*Falcon Pipes Ltd v Stanhope Gate Property Co Ltd* (1967) 204 EG 1243);
- failure to refer to a tiny part of the premises (*Safeway Food Stores Ltd v Morris* [1980] 1 EGLR 59).

If the landlord discovers that a section 25 notice it has served is defective in some way (e.g. it contains an error or has been incorrectly served), best practice is to serve a fresh notice without prejudice to the validity of the original notice. Then if the original notice is subsequently held to be invalid, the second notice will become effective (*Smith v Draper* [1990] 2 EGLR 69, CA; see also *Barclays Bank v Bee* [2001] EWCA Civ 1126, concerning a third notice held to be valid).

Time limits for service of section 25 notice

The notice must be given not more than 12 months or less than six months, before the date of termination specified in the notice (section 25(2)). Moreover, this date of termination cannot be earlier than the date on which the tenancy can be terminated at common law. There are thus different considerations for a normal fixed term, a fixed term with a break clause, and a periodic tenancy. These are considered below. In computing time limits under the Act the corresponding date rule is used, and 'month' means calendar month (Interpretation Act 1975, sections 5 and 22(1) and Schedule 2, paragraph 4(1)). This means that the relevant period will end on the corresponding date in the appropriate subsequent month. So, for example, two months starting on 2 May will end on 2 July; but two months starting on 31 July will end on 30 September, and two months starting on 31 December will end on 28 (or 29) February (see Lord Diplock's judgment in *Dodds v Walker* [1981] 1 WLR 1027, HL, at page 1029). These time limits are strictly enforced by the courts and it is therefore vitally important for practitioners to abide by them.

Fixed-term tenancies without a break clause

In the usual case of a fixed-term lease, the earliest time a landlord can serve the notice is one year before the end of the contractual term. For example, if the lease is due to end on 30 September 2009, the landlord cannot serve the notice earlier than 30 September 2008 (and for the avoidance of doubt it is probably safer to wait until the next day, 1 October 2008).

If the landlord delays serving notice until less than six months remain of the fixed term, it must still give the tenant at least six months' notice. In this situation the landlord would have to specify a termination date in the notice later than the contractual expiry date. In the example above, the lease is due to expire on 30 September 2009. If the landlord delays giving notice until after 30 March 2009, the termination date he specifies in the notice will inevitably need to be later than the contractual expiry date (30 September 2009). Even if the landlord delays serving notice until after the contractual expiry date has passed (i.e. when the lease is continuing under section 24), the tenant must still be given a minimum of six months' notice.

Periodic tenancies

The notice required to end a periodic tenancy at common law is at least one full period of the lease expiring on the last day of a completed period of the tenancy (i.e. on a rent day). The landlord serving a section 25 notice must ensure that the date of termination specified in the notice is not earlier than the date at which the tenancy could have been terminated by notice to quit (*Commercial Properties Ltd v Wood* [1968] 1 QB 15, CA). However, the section 25 notice must be given not more than 12 months, or less than six months, before the date of termination specified in the notice (section 25(2)).

Tenant's and landlord's applications to the court for a new tenancy

Section 24(1) of the Act, as amended, enables either the tenant or the landlord to apply to the court for an order for the grant of a new tenancy. The application can be made only after the service of a landlord's section 25 notice or a tenant's section 26 request (the latter is considered at 20.5.3) and must be made within the time limits referred to below. Neither party may make an application if the other has already made an application under section 24(1) and the application has been served. Nor can either party make an application under section 24(1) if the landlord has already made an application under the new section 29(2) for an order for the termination of the current tenancy and the application has been served.

Time limits

Section 29A provides that an application to the court by either party under section 24(1) must be made on or before the date specified in the landlord's section 25 notice or immediately before the date specified in the tenant's section 26 request. These are the latest dates by which the application can be made (unless there is an agreement to extend, see below). The deadline is strictly enforced and so, for example, if the tenant fails to apply within the required time the tenancy will come to an end on the date specified in the section 25 notice or immediately before the date specified in the section 26 request, as the case may be. As such the tenant's right to apply for a new tenancy will be lost and the tenant's solicitor is likely to be sued in negligence. A fail-safe diary system is therefore essential.

Even if the landlord has indicated that he is willing to grant a new tenancy and terms are nearly agreed, the tenant must still apply to the court as a 'fallback'. Without the back-up of the court application, the landlord could simply change his mind and there would be nothing the tenant could do about it (save possibly a claim in estoppel (see *Bristol Cars Ltd v*

RKH Hotels Ltd (1979) 38 P & CR 411) or that the landlord has waived its rights (see *Kammins Ballrooms Co Ltd v Zenith Investments* (Torquay) *Ltd* [1971] AC 850)).

Where the tenant has made a section 26 request, the landlord or the tenant may not apply to the court until the landlord has served the required counter-notice, or the two-month period for service of the counter-notice has expired, whichever occurs first (section 29A(3)). Without this provision, a court application might be made at a time when it was not known whether the landlord opposed renewal and, if so, on what grounds. Once the landlord's counter-notice has been served, either party may apply to the court without waiting for the two months to elapse. The position in respect of a section 25 notice is much simpler. If the landlord has served a section 25 notice, there is no two-month waiting period and either party may apply to the court immediately.

Agreement to extend time limit

Section 29B allows the parties to agree to extend the latest time for applying to the court, provided they do so before the current time limit expires. The agreement must be made in writing. The parties may agree further postponements from time to time provided the agreement is made before the end of the period of postponement specified in the current agreement (section 29B(2)). The effect of such an agreement is that the section 25 notice or section 26 request is treated as terminating the tenancy at the end of the period specified in the agreement (section 29B(4)). This provision, introduced in the 2004 reforms, has assisted in reducing the number of court applications.

20.5.3 TENANT'S REQUEST UNDER SECTION 26

This method of termination is not available to periodic tenants and those with fixed terms of one year or less. However, such tenants still have security of tenure and can apply for a new tenancy if the landlord has served them with a section 25 notice. Accordingly, to be able to serve a section 26 request the tenant must have been granted a term of years certain exceeding one year (whether or not continued by section 24), or a term of years certain and thereafter from year to year (section 26(1)).

A section 26 request must be served on the tenant's 'competent' landlord, or its agent, otherwise it will be invalid (*Railtrack plc v Gojra* [1998] 1 EGLR 63, CA). The tenant's competent landlord may not necessarily be the same as the tenant's immediate landlord (see 20.7 for a discussion of competent landlord). A section 26 request cannot be served if the landlord has already served a section 25 notice, or the tenant has already served a section 27 notice (see 20.5.1 above). Once the tenant has served a valid section 26 request it cannot later withdraw it and serve another amended one (*Polyviou v Seeley* [1980] 1 WLR 55).

Situations in which a tenant would be advised to serve a section 26 request

If a tenant has security of tenure then the tenancy will continue under section 24 until it is terminated by one of the ways under the Act. This gives rise to the question, why, if the tenant can continue in occupation under section 24, paying the existing rent, should it want to end the lease by serving a section 26 request? Why not wait until the landlord serves a section 25 notice and in the meantime carry on paying rent that is probably less than the market rent under any new lease? The following are situations in which a tenant would be advised to serve a section 26 request:

(a) Tenant's tactical pre-emptive strike. In a normal rising market, the tenant will wish to pay the current rent as long as possible because it will be lower than the market rent. In these circumstances, a prudent landlord would end the lease as early as possible by serving a section 25 notice one year before the expiry date (the termination date in the notice would be the expiry date of the contractual term, i.e. 12 months hence). However, if the landlord is dilatory and forgets to serve a section 25 notice, the tenant could serve a section 26 request, say, six months before the expiry date, in which the tenant specifies a date 12 months ahead as the termination date. In this way the tenant would get six months longer paying the old rent. As an example, assume a lease has a contractual expiry date of 31 December. If by the middle of the previous June the landlord has not served a section 25 notice, the tenant could serve a section 26 request specifying a termination date 12 months ahead, i.e. in June of the following year. That would be six months after the earliest date the landlord could have ended the lease.

(b) Proposed improvements. If the tenant intends to spend money improving the premises, it may prefer the certainty of a new fixed-term lease before doing so.

(c) Proposed sale. If the tenant intends to assign the lease, a prospective buyer will probably want the certainty of a new fixed-term lease being in place.

(d) Fall in market rent. If the market rent has fallen (e.g. during a recession) and is less than the existing rent under the lease, the tenant will want a new lease with a lower market rent in place as soon as possible. The landlord, of course, will be happy for the old (higher) rent to continue.

Interim rent

As a consequence of the 2004 reforms, tenants should be aware that interim rent is now payable from the earliest date that could have been specified for commencement of the new tenancy in the section 26 request. Thus a tenant who serves a section 26 request but states a commencement date for the new tenancy 12 months after service when the contractual termination date is only six months away (and so he could have served six months' notice) will find that the interim rent will be payable from the earliest date that he could have specified. In a rising market, a well-advised landlord could therefore reduce the effectiveness of the tenant's pre-emptive strike by applying for an interim rent payable from this earlier date.

Prescribed form and content of section 26 request

The current prescribed form for a section 26 request is set out in Online Resource Centre. A form 'substantially to the like effect' can be used, but this is not to be recommended. The section 26 request must:

online resource centre

(a) specify a date for the commencement of the new tenancy (the existing tenancy will end immediately before this date). This commencement date must not be more than 12 months or less than six months after the making of the request. Nor must it be earlier than the date on which the tenancy could have been terminated at common law. Thus for a normal fixed term without a break clause, the specified termination date cannot be earlier than the last day of the contractual term. And for a fixed-term lease with a break clause, the specified termination date cannot be earlier than the date upon which the tenant could have ended the tenancy by common law notice. In *Garston v Scottish Widows Fund and Life Assurance Society* [1998] 3 All ER 596, CA, the tenant effectively tried to engineer a downwards rent review by serving a break notice as permitted by the lease, and at the same time serving a section 26 request. The court disallowed this practice as being contrary to the spirit and purpose of the Act;

(b) set out the tenant's proposals for the new lease, namely:

(i) the property to be comprised in the new tenancy. This can be either the whole or part of the property in the current tenancy (compare this with a section 25 notice in which the whole of the property must be specified),

(ii) the new rent (valuation advice should be taken before doing so),

(iii) the other terms of the new tenancy.

These proposals must be genuine and the tenant must have a real intention of taking up the new tenancy. Thus a request served merely as a precautionary measure will be invalid (*Sun Life Assurance plc v Racal Tracs Ltd* [2000] 1 EGLR 138);

(c) be given and signed by, or on behalf of, the tenant. If there is more than one tenant, all their names must be given (*Jacobs v Chaudhuri* [1968] 1 QB 470, CA) unless the joint tenancy is held by a partnership. In this case, section 41A of the Act allows only those tenants who are partners carrying on the business to be named in the request. If there are joint landlords the notice must be served on all of them.

Time limits for service of section 26 request

As mentioned above, the date specified in the section 26 request as the date for the commencement of the new tenancy must not be more than 12 months or less than six months after the request is served on the landlord. Accordingly, the earliest time a tenant can serve a request is one year before the contractual expiry date. In the case of a 'tenant's pre-emptive strike' (see 20.5.3 above) the tenant will often specify a commencement date 12 months ahead, having given the request between 12 and six months before the contractual expiry date.

The landlord's counter-notice

Upon receiving a tenant's section 26 request the landlord has two months in which to notify the tenant if he intends to oppose the tenant's application to the court for a new tenancy (section 26(6)). There is no prescribed form of 'counter-notice' so a clear letter will suffice, but the landlord must state on which grounds in section 30 of the Act the landlord opposes the application (see 20.10 below). The landlord should be certain of his grounds because they cannot be amended later. If the landlord fails to serve a counter-notice within the two months he will lose his right to oppose the new tenancy. If the reversion is assigned after the counter-notice has been given, the incoming landlord steps into the shoes of the outgoing landlord and can rely on the grounds specified in the counter-notice (*Morris Marks v British Waterways Board* [1963] 1 WLR 1008). Needless to say, there have been many cases of negligence against landlord's solicitors who have overlooked this two-month deadline.

A typical form of counter-notice might read as follows:

To [name of tenant]

of [address of tenant]

I [name of landlord] of [address of landlord] received on [date of receipt] your request under section 26 of the Landlord and Tenant Act 1954 Part II ('the Act') for a new tenancy of [description of property] ('the Property').

I hereby give you notice that I will oppose your application to the court for a new tenancy of the Property on the following ground(s) contained in section 30(1) of the Act, namely paragraph(s) [insert paragraph letter(s)].

Dated:

Signed:

[signature of landlord, or on behalf of landlord]

20.6 'THE HOLDING'

On an application for a renewal of the lease the tenant will only be entitled to a renewal of 'the holding' as defined by the Act in section 23(3). The holding is defined as:

...the property comprised in the tenancy, there being excluded any part thereof which is occupied neither by the tenant nor by a person employed by the tenant and so employed for the purposes of a business by reason of which the tenancy is one to which this Part of this Act applies.

It follows that the holding will not include the following, in respect of which the tenant cannot claim a new lease:

(a) any part of the premises presently sub-let by the tenant will generally not form part of the holding unless the tenant can show that it remains in occupation of that part for business purposes;

(b) any part of the premises occupied by a third party;

(c) any part of the premises that is unoccupied;

(d) any part of the premises occupied by the tenant's employees in connection with another of the tenant's businesses.

20.7 'COMPETENT LANDLORD'

A tenant's request for a new tenancy under section 26 must be served on the 'competent landlord' as defined by section 44(1) of the Act. Similarly, the 'competent landlord' must serve a landlord's section 25 notice. There can only be one competent landlord at any given time, and his identity may change during the course of the renewal procedure. If this occurs, the new competent landlord must be a made a party to any proceedings under the Act (*Piper v Muggleton* [1956] 2 All ER 875, CA). The time for determining the competent landlord is the date of service of the section 25 notice or section 26 request.

20.7.1 SUB-LEASES

Where the tenant's immediate landlord is the freeholder, establishing the identity of the competent landlord will be easy (as it will obviously be the freeholder). However, in the case of sub-leases it is necessary to consider section 44(1) of the Act. This provides that where a landlord is a tenant himself, he will be the competent landlord to his immediate tenant only if his own tenancy will not come to an end within 14 months. If it will end within 14 months, the competent landlord will be the next landlord up the chain of tenancies whose tenancy satisfies this criterion (or the freeholder if you reach the top). This may be illustrated by Examples 1 and 2 in Figure 20.1 involving a sub-lease. In each case, consider who is the sub-tenant's competent landlord.

FIGURE 20.1 SUBLEASES: ESTABLISHING THE COMPETENT LANDLORD

EXAMPLE 1	EXAMPLE 2
L	L
Fixed-term headlease	Fixed-term headlease
T	T
Sub-lease of whole	Sub-lease of part
ST	ST
Example 1: L (freeholder) lets premises to T on fixed term; T sub-lets whole of premises to ST.	Example 2: L (freeholder) lets premises to T on fixed term; T sub-lets part of premises to ST.

In Example 1, because T has sub-let the whole, T is not 'in occupation', will not have the protection of the Act, and T's lease will not continue under section 24 (i.e. it ends on the contractual expiry date). Thus, once T's lease (L–T) has less than 14 months to run, it will certainly come to an end within 14 months. ST's competent landlord will be L (freeholder) in any event.

In Example 2, T occupies that part of the premises he has not sub-let to ST. Accordingly, T is protected by the Act ('in occupation') and T's lease (L-T) will continue under the Act (section 24). Thus, even during the last 14 months of T's lease, it will not come to an end within 14 months because it continues under the Act (see *Bowes-Lyon v Green* [1963] AC 420). ST's competent landlord will be T.

Importantly, however, the situation in Example 2 is reversed if L serves T with a section 25 notice, or T serves L with a section 26 request or section 27 notice. In this case T's lease will come to an end within 14 months because it is being terminated by one of the ways prescribed by the Act. In this case, ST's competent landlord will be L (freeholder).

In Example 2, for ST of part where T remains in occupation of the remainder, it is crucial for ST to know, in respect of T's lease (L–T), whether T has been served with a section 25 notice (by L), or whether T has himself served a section 27 notice or section 26 request (on L). To establish the position, ST can serve a notice on T under section 40 of the Act. Section 40 notices are considered below (see 20.8).

The following should also be considered where there is a sub-lease or sub-leases. If the immediate landlord is the competent landlord and the immediate landlord's own lease has less than 16 months to run from the date of service or receipt, he is obliged to send a copy of the section 25 notice or section 26 request to his own landlord (1954 Act, Schedule 6, paragraph 7). The superior landlord, if he becomes the competent landlord within two months of service of the section 25 notice, may serve notice withdrawing the section 25 notice (1954 Act, Schedule 6, paragraph 6). The superior landlord may then choose whether to serve his own section 25 notice on the sub-tenant.

Similarly, where the superior landlord is not himself the freeholder, he must send a copy to his landlord who has the same rights as described above. The superior/competent landlord will bind the intermediate landlord(s) in relation to section 25 notices that he gives to the sub-tenant. Moreover, the terms of any new tenancy that the superior/competent landlord agrees with the sub-tenant are binding on the intermediate landlord(s). However, the latter must give its/their consent (such consent not to be unreasonably withheld), failing which the superior/competent landlord will be liable to pay compensation for any loss arising from the making of the agreement (1954 Act, Schedule 6, paragraph 4).

20.8 SECTION 40 NOTICES

The identity of the competent landlord can change more than once during the course of the litigation and renewal procedure. In Example 2 in Figure 20.1 above, the identity of the competent landlord will depend on whether notices or requests have been given to terminate T's lease (L–T) under the Act. To request information about superior leases and sub-leases, and whether notices or requests have been given, landlords and tenants can serve on each other a notice under section 40 of the Act. Ideally, the section 40 notice should be served before or simultaneously with the notices or requests under sections 25, 26, and 27. For the consequences of a tenant serving the wrong person, see *Re 55 and 57 Holmes Road, Kentish Town, Beardmore Motors Ltd v Birch Bros (Properties) Ltd* [1959] Ch 298. A tenant can also serve a section 40 notice on any person being a mortgagee in possession. A section 40 notice may not be served earlier than two years before the date on which, apart from the Act, the tenancy would end by effluxion of time, or could be brought to an end by notice to quit given by the landlord (section 40(6)).

FIGURE 20.2 LEASE RENEWAL FLOW CHART

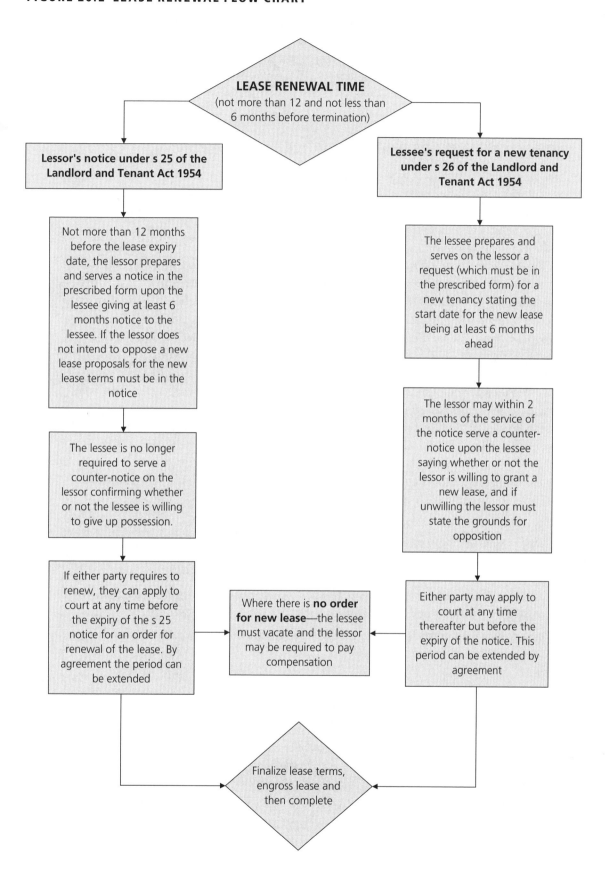

20.8.1 GOOD PRACTICE

As a matter of good practice, the only time one can safely dispense with a section 40 notice is where one is certain that the landlord is the freeholder and the tenant occupies the whole of the premises (perhaps a tenant should also resist serving a section 40 notice where he intends to serve a section 26 request and does not wish to prompt his landlord into serving a section 25 notice). Only a tenant who is entitled to serve a section 26 request may serve a section 40 notice; thus a periodic tenant cannot serve one.

20.8.2 ACTION BY RECIPIENT OF SECTION 40 NOTICE

A tenant who receives a section 40 notice must indicate within one month whether he occupies the premises or any part of them wholly or partly for business purposes. The tenant must also indicate whether he has sub-let; and, if so, must provide information about the sub-letting, including whether there has been a contracting-out and whether a section 25 notice has been served or a section 26 request made. The tenant must state the identity of any known reversioner. Conversely, a landlord who receives a section 40 notice must indicate within one month whether he owns the freehold; and if not, must give the identity of his immediate landlord and when his own tenancy will expire. A landlord must also state whether there is a mortgagee in possession and, if so, its name and address. Where there is a superior lease the landlord must state whether a section 25 notice has been served or a section 26 request has been made. The landlord must also state the identity of any known reversioner. There is a statutory duty on both landlord and tenant to update the information given for a period of six months from the date of service of the section 40 notice, where it ceases to be correct (section 40(5)).

A landlord may learn from a tenant in response to a section 40 notice that the premises have been sub-let. If the landlord has served a section 25 notice on the tenant, the landlord will now be the competent landlord of the sub-tenant. In these circumstances, generally it will be good practice for the landlord to serve a section 25 notice on the sub-tenant to prevent the sub-tenant making a section 26 request.

 Key Points Section 25 notices and section 26 requests

Landlord

If you want the tenant to leave at the end of the lease, serve a hostile section 25 notice and be sure of your statutory grounds for opposing a new lease.

- Be sure you are the 'competent' landlord for the tenant in question. It may be necessary to serve a notice under section 40 to be sure.

- The section 25 notice must be given not more than 12 months or less than six months before the date of termination specified in the notice; this termination date must not be earlier than the date on which the tenancy could have been terminated at common law (e.g. the contractual expiry date of a fixed term).

- If you are happy for the tenant to continue in occupation under a new lease and wish the new lease to be in place as soon as possible, serve a non-hostile section 25 notice one year before the contractual expiry date specifying the contractual expiry date as the termination date in the notice.

- Ensure that any section 25 notice is in the prescribed form and contains the prescribed content.

- If you receive a tenant's section 26 request and you want the tenant to leave, you must serve a counter-notice within two months specifying your statutory grounds for opposing a new lease.

- Serve by registered post or recorded delivery (in which case service is deemed to be the date of postage).

Tenant

- If you receive a landlord's section 25 notice and you want to renew your lease, ensure that you apply to the court for a new lease on or before the date specified in the section 25 notice.

- If you have not received a section 25 notice by the time there is less than 12 months to go on the lease, consider a 'pre-emptive strike' by serving a section 26 request and specifying a commencement date for the new lease 12 months hence.

- Serve the section 26 notice on your 'competent' landlord. It may be necessary to serve a notice under section 40 to be sure.

- Ensure that your section 26 request is in the prescribed form and contains the prescribed content.

- If you serve a section 26 request, be sure to apply to the court for a new lease before the date specified in the section 26 request.

- Serve by registered post or recorded delivery (in which case service is deemed to be the date of postage).

20.9 INTERIM RENT APPLICATIONS

20.9.1 LANDLORD'S APPLICATION

After an application to the court for a new lease, the current tenancy continues at the old contractual rent until three months after the conclusion of the proceedings (section 64). This is clearly disadvantageous to a landlord seeking a higher market rent under the new lease, and it is also an incentive for the tenant to extend the proceedings for as long as possible. To remedy this unreasonable state of affairs the Law of Property Act 1969 inserted a new section 24A into the Act to allow the competent landlord to apply to the court for an interim rent to be fixed until the current tenancy comes to an end. In the case of a sub-tenancy where the head tenancy is also being continued under section 24, the competent landlord will be the head landlord. Thus, rather curiously, the head landlord will be applying for an interim rent which is payable to the intermediate landlord.

20.9.2 TENANT'S APPLICATION

Under the 2004 reforms both landlords and tenants now have the right to make applications for interim rent. The reason for allowing the tenant to apply as well is because there may be market conditions under which rents are falling and, in this situation, it is only fair to allow tenants to benefit from such market conditions.

A new section 24A was introduced on 1 June 2004. It states that provided either a section 25 notice has been served or a section 26 request has been made, both landlords and tenants may apply for an interim rent while the tenancy is continuing under section 24. However, no application may be made later than six months after the termination of the contractual tenancy. To avoid duplication of proceedings, neither party may apply if the other party has already done so, unless that application has been withdrawn.

Under section 24B the interim rent is payable from:

(a) the earliest date that could have been specified for termination of the tenancy, where a section 25 notice has been served (section 24B(2)), or

(b) the earliest date that could have been specified for commencement of the new tenancy, where a section 26 request has been made (section 24B(3)).

This is intended to rule out the tactical use of section 25 notices and section 26 requests (e.g. the tenant's pre-emptive strike: see 20.5.3 above).

20.9.3 GOOD PRACTICE ON INTERIM RENT

In a normal rising market the landlord will generally apply for an interim rent as early as possible, namely as soon as the section 25 notice or section 26 request has been given or received. Conversely, in a falling market the landlord will have no need for an interim rent if the contractual rent is higher than the prevailing market rent. Here, it is the tenant who would be advised to apply for an interim rent. Another instance when it should be unnecessary for a landlord to apply for an interim rent will be where the rent was reviewed immediately before the contractual expiry date (a 'penultimate day rent review'); in this case the tenant should already be paying the market rent.

The tenant will be required to start paying interim rent as soon as the court determines it. Interest will also be payable from this date, unless the lease provides that interest will be payable from a period after the rent becomes due, e.g. 14 days. Interim rent continues to be payable until the date on which the current tenancy comes to an end.

20.10 LANDLORD'S STATUTORY GROUNDS OF OPPOSITION

There are seven statutory grounds in section 30(1) of the 1954 Act which entitle a landlord to resist a tenant's application for a new lease. If the landlord is successful in proving one or more of those grounds then the tenant's application should fail. It should be noted that some grounds are subject to the court's discretion. The landlord must state the relevant ground(s) in its section 25 notice or counter-notice to the tenant's section 26 request. No later amendments or additions to the grounds are allowed, so it is important that the landlord specifies the correct grounds at this early stage. However, the landlord's stated grounds must be genuine; if the grounds are false and made fraudulently, the notice may be rendered invalid and unenforceable (see *Rous v Mitchell* [1991] 1 All ER 676, CA). A subsequent purchaser of the landlord's interest will also be bound by the original landlord's choice of ground(s) (*Morris Marks v British Waterways Board* [1963] 3 All ER 28, CA).

In summary, the grounds of opposition are:

(a) tenant's failure to carry out repairing obligations;

(b) tenant's persistent delay in paying rent;

(c) tenant's substantial breaches of other obligations;

(d) suitable alternative accommodation is available for the tenant;

(e) on sub-letting of part, the landlord requires the whole property for subsequent letting;

(f) the landlord intends to demolish or reconstruct the premises;

(g) the landlord intends to occupy the holding.

20.10.1 DISCRETIONARY GROUNDS

Grounds (a), (b), (c), and (e) are discretionary. Thus even if the landlord establishes the ground, the court may decide to order a new tenancy in any event, e.g. because of the tenant's good conduct. Examples of situations where the court may decide to use its discretion are considered below under the individual grounds. The remaining grounds—(d), (f), and (g)—are mandatory, so that if the landlord establishes the ground the court must refuse to order a new tenancy.

The specific grounds are now considered; and to assist in interpretation, the precise wording of the grounds is set out followed by commentary and reference to cases.

Ground (a): tenant's failure to carry out repairing obligations

(a) where under the current tenancy the tenant has any obligations as respects the repair and maintenance of the holding, that the tenant ought not to be granted a new tenancy in view of the state
of repair of the holding, being a state resulting from the tenant's failure to comply with the said
obligations...

Ground (a) only applies to failure to repair the tenant's 'holding' as defined by the Act (see
20.6 above). Thus it would not apply to a part of the demised premises in disrepair which is
occupied by a sub-tenant. Moreover, a substantial breach of covenant on the tenant's part
may on its own be insufficient to establish the ground. The landlord must go further and
show that the breach is serious enough that the 'tenant ought not to be granted a new tenancy'. Because of the ground's discretionary nature, the court may grant a new tenancy despite the breach (see *Nihad v Chain* (1956) 167 EG 139). The grant could be on the basis of an
undertaking by the tenant to remedy the breach (see *Lyons v Central Commercial Properties
Ltd* [1958] 2 All ER 767, CA at p 775; although a grant was actually refused in this case). In
exercising its discretion the court will consider whether a new tenancy would be unfair to
the landlord, having regard to the tenant's past performances and conduct. It will also consider the reasons for the tenant's breach of covenant to repair (see generally *Lyons v Central
Commercial Properties Ltd*, above, applied subsequently in *Eichner v Midland Bank Executor &
Trustee Co Ltd* [1970] 2 All ER 597, CA).

   If the landlord intends to rely on this ground, it (or its surveyor) should first serve on
the tenant a schedule of dilapidations with a request that the repairs be carried out (on the
assumption that there is a lease repairing covenant). The landlord may also consider forfeiture of the lease as an alternative to ground (a). A tenant faced with opposition under ground
(a) should consider giving the landlord an undertaking to carry out the repairs within a set
time. A court may take such an undertaking into account when exercising its discretion,
but may also seek evidence that the tenant has sufficient funds to carry out the works. If the
tenant is refused a new lease under ground (a), the tenant is not entitled to compensation.

Ground (b): tenant's persistent delay in paying rent

(b) that the tenant ought not to be granted a new tenancy in view of his persistent delay in paying
rent which has become due...

The word 'persistent' is significant as it clearly means more than one incident of delay. The
court will consider the frequency and extent of the delays (*Hopcutt v Carver* (1969) 209 EG
1069, CA), the steps the landlord had to take to secure payment, and how the landlord may
be protected against delay in any future tenancy (*Rawashdeh v Lane* [1988] 2 EGLR 109, CA).
The ground is discretionary, so that even if persistent delay is proven the court may decide
to order a new tenancy if the tenant can offer a satisfactory explanation for the delay. The
word 'rent' may include other payments due under the lease if these are reserved as rent, e.g.
service charges. The tenant seeking to resist an opposition under ground (b) should ensure
that no further arrears accrue and, if appropriate, suggest means of guaranteeing future payments (e.g. a rent deposit or guarantor). If the tenant is refused a new lease under ground (b),
the tenant is not entitled to compensation.

Ground (c): tenant's substantial breaches of other obligations

(c) that the tenant ought not to be granted a new tenancy in view of other substantial breaches by him
of his obligations under the current tenancy, or for any other reason connected with the tenant's
use or management of the holding...

This is another discretionary ground. It concerns the tenant's substantial breaches (note
the use of the word 'substantial') of other obligations in the lease (i.e. other than repair or
rent), and it also extends to reasons linked generally with the tenant's use or management
of the holding. Thus a court can refuse to grant a new lease if the tenant is at fault in some
way even though the tenant has performed all his obligations under the lease. The court

must have regard to all relevant circumstances, including whether the landlord's interest has been prejudiced, the general conduct of the tenant, and any proposals for remedying the breach (see *Eichner v Midland Bank Executor and Trustee Co Ltd* [1970] 2 All ER 597, and *Beard v Williams* [1986] 1 EGLR 148).

Whether a breach is 'substantial' is a question of fact in each case. It is not necessary for the breaches to relate to 'the holding' and so substantial breaches relating to any sub-let part of the premises may be included. If the tenant is refused a new lease under ground (c), the tenant is not entitled to compensation.

Ground (d): suitable alternative accommodation is available for tenant

(d) that the landlord has offered and is willing to provide or secure the provision of alternative accommodation for the tenant, that the terms on which the alternative accommodation is available are reasonable having regard to the terms of the current tenancy and to all other relevant circumstances, and that the accommodation and the time at which it will be available are suitable for the tenant's requirements (including the requirement to preserve goodwill) having regard to the nature and class of his business and to the situation and extent of, and facilities afforded by, the holding . . .

This ground is not discretionary, so if the landlord can provide suitable alternative accommodation based on the above criteria the court must dismiss the tenant's application for a new tenancy (*Betty's Cafes Ltd v Phillips Furnishing Stores Ltd* [1957] Ch 67 at p 84). The relevant date to assess the reasonableness of the terms and the suitability of the alternative accommodation is the date of the hearing. Alternative accommodation in the future may also be sufficient for the landlord. If he can establish that it will be available at a later date (i.e. even after the termination date in the section 25 notice or section 26 request), he may still be able to succeed on ground (d) (see section 31(2) of the Act; see also 'near miss' cases at 20.10.8 below). If the tenant is refused a new lease under ground (d), the tenant is not entitled to compensation.

Ground (e): on sub-letting of part, landlord requires the whole property for subsequent letting

(e) where the current tenancy was created by the sub-letting of part only of the property comprised in a superior tenancy and the landlord is the owner of an interest in reversion expectant on the termination of that superior tenancy, that the aggregate of the rents reasonably obtainable on separate lettings of the holding and the remainder of that property would be substantially less than the rent reasonably obtainable on a letting of that property as a whole, that on the termination of the current tenancy the landlord requires possession of the holding for the purpose of letting or otherwise disposing of the said property as a whole, and that in view there of the tenant ought not to be granted a new tenancy . . .

Ground (e) is another discretionary ground and is the least used of all the grounds (indeed, there are no reported cases on how the discretion is to be exercised). It applies only where there is a sub-letting of part and the 'competent' landlord of the sub-tenant is the superior landlord, i.e. not the sub-tenant's immediate landlord. As previously explained the intermediate lease will in these circumstances have less than 14 months to run.

The landlord must show two things:

(a) the rent obtainable on separate lettings of the whole building would be substantially less than the rent obtainable on a letting of the whole. It should be noted that the rent has to be substantially less, not merely less (see *Greaves Organisation Ltd v Stanhope Gate Property Co Ltd* (1973) 228 EG 725); and

(b) on the termination of the sub-tenancy the landlord requires possession of the sub-let part to let or otherwise dispose of the property as a whole. The landlord may have difficulty in establishing this unless the intermediate lease is due to end before the sub-tenancy is terminated (on the basis that he cannot re-let the whole if the intermediate tenant is still in occupation).

In exercising its discretion a court would have regard to whether the landlord originally consented to the sub-letting. Section 31(2) of the Act also applies to ground (e), i.e. if the landlord can establish the ground at a later date (see 'near miss' cases at 20.10.8 below). If the tenant is refused a new lease under ground (e), the tenant is entitled to compensation (see 20.11).

Ground (f): the landlord intends to demolish or reconstruct premises

> (f) that on the termination of the current tenancy the landlord intends to demolish or reconstruct the premises comprised in the holding or a substantial part of those premises or to carry out substantial work of construction on the holding or part thereof and that he could not reasonably do so without obtaining possession of the holding . . .

This is the most frequently used ground. To rely on it the landlord must show on the termination of the tenancy the following three elements:

(a) the landlord's intention;

(b) to demolish or reconstruct the premises in the holding (or a substantial part thereof), or to carry out substantial work of construction on the holding (or part thereof); and

(c) that he could not reasonably do so without obtaining possession of the holding.

Each of these three elements is now considered.

Landlord's intention

The landlord's intention to carry out the work must be more than a simple desire to bring it about. The intention must be firm and settled. It must have 'moved out of the zone of contemplation—out of the sphere of the tentative, the provisional and the exploratory—into the valley of decision' (per Asquith LJ in *Cunliffe v Goodman* [1950] 2 KB 237, and subsequently approved by Viscount Simonds in *Betty's Cafes Ltd v Phillips Furnishing Stores Ltd* [1959] AC 20, HL). Further, as a question of fact, there must be a reasonable prospect that the landlord's plan will succeed, although he does not need to prove that it will be a commercial success (*Dolgellau Golf Club v Hett* [1998] 2 EGLR 75, CA).

The time when the landlord's intention must be established is the date of the court hearing (*Betty's Cafes Ltd v Phillips Furnishing Stores Ltd*, above). The fact that the landlord (or his predecessor) had no such intention at the time of serving the section 25 notice (or counternotice to section 26 request) is irrelevant (see *Marks v British Waterways Board* [1963] 3 All ER 28). Provided the landlord can prove the ground as a matter of fact, the court will not examine the landlord's motives for using the ground. Thus in *Fisher v Taylors Furnishing Stores Ltd* [1956] 2 QB 78, it did not matter that the landlord's primary object was to occupy the reconstructed premises himself.

The necessary intention is a question of fact in each case, but the landlord's position will be strengthened if, by the time of the hearing, he has taken appropriate steps. These would include: instructing professionals, obtaining quotations, preparing plans and drawings, securing any necessary planning permissions, arranging finance, and, for a company landlord, passing a board resolution. The less the landlord has to do by the time he gets to court, the better (see *Gregson v Cyril Lord* [1962] 3 All ER 907). Where planning permission has been applied for but not obtained by the date of the hearing, the test the court will use is whether there is a reasonable prospect that permission will be granted (*Westminster City Council v British Waterways Board* [1984] 3 WLR 1047, HL).

The works must be carried out 'on the termination of the current tenancy'. The Court of Appeal has held this to include within a reasonable time from the date of the termination of the tenancy (*London Hilton Jewellers Ltd v Hilton International Hotels Ltd* [1990] 1 EGLR 112). For practical purposes, 'termination of the current tenancy' would include any continuation tenancy under section 64 of the Act, as the landlord would clearly be entitled to possession before the works were carried out. A reasonable time will, of course, be a question of fact in each case.

Demolish, reconstruct, or carry out substantial work of construction

In addition to establishing an intention, the landlord must also show that the proposed works fall within the express wording of ground (f). This will depend on the nature and extent of the works and is a question of fact in each case. The key words used are 'demolish', 'reconstruct', and 'substantial work of construction'. 'Demolish' is easily understood and there must be some property on the holding which is capable of being demolished, e.g. a building or wall (see *Housleys Ltd v Bloomer-Holt Ltd* [1966] 2 All ER 966, CA, involving a wall and garage). If part of the premises are to be demolished then they must be 'substantial', which is a question of fact (see *Atkinson v Bettison* [1953] 3 All ER 340, CA). 'Reconstruct' has been held to involve rebuilding and a substantial interference with the structure of the building. The work need not be confined necessarily to the outside of the premises or to load-bearing walls (see *Percy E Cadle & Co Ltd v Jacmarch Properties Ltd* [1957] 1 QB 323, CA, and *Romulus Trading Co Ltd v Henry Smith's Charity Trustees* [1990] 2 EGLR 75, CA).

'Substantial work of construction' implies a new building or adding to what was already there (see per Ormerod LJ in *Cook v Mott* (1961) 178 EG 637). It connotes more than mere refurbishment or improvement. In *Barth v Pritchard* [1990] 1 EGLR 109, CA, an intention to rewire, re-roof, redecorate, install central heating, and reposition a staircase was held to be insufficient. Yet in *Joel v Swaddle* [1957] 1 WLR 1094, a proposal to convert a shop with two storage rooms into part of a large amusement arcade came within the ground. Other successful works of 'construction' have been the laying of pipes, wires, cables, and drains, and the laying of a road (see *Housleys v Bloomer-Holt Ltd*, above).

On the question of what amounts to a reconstruction of a substantial part of the holding, the court in *Joel v Swaddle* (above) said the proper approach was to look at the position as a whole. One should compare the result after carrying out the proposed work with the condition and state of the premises before the work was begun.

Landlord could not reasonably carry out the work without obtaining possession of the holding

The landlord must show that he needs legal possession of the holding, not merely physical possession. In other words, he must show that he needs to terminate the tenancy in order to carry out the work. If the landlord can do the work simply by exercising his right of entry under the terms of the lease, ground (f) will not be established (this right is often reserved by landlords to enable them to execute improvements and alterations; see *Heath v Drown* [1973] AC 496, HL).

20.10.2 **TENANT'S DEFENCES UNDER SECTION 31A**

Even if the landlord can show that he requires possession to carry out work, the tenant may be assisted by section 31A of the Act (inserted by section 7(1) of the Law of Property Act 1969). This effectively prevents the landlord from using ground (f) in circumstances where the proposed work would be over quickly, or where the work will affect only part of the premises. Section 31A provides that a court cannot hold that the landlord could not reasonably carry out the demolition or other work without obtaining possession if either of the following occurs:

(a) The tenant agrees to the inclusion in the terms of the new tenancy of terms giving the landlord access and other facilities for carrying out the work intended and, given that access and those facilities, the landlord could reasonably carry out the work without obtaining possession of the holding and without interfering to a substantial extent or for a substantial time with the use of the holding for the purposes of the business carried on by the tenant.

The tenant may decide to rely on this defence where the landlord has failed to reserve adequate rights in the lease to allow him to carry out the work (*Heath v Drown* [1973] AC 496, HL). The word 'interfering' refers to interference with the tenant's use of the holding for its business purposes, not the business itself or the goodwill. Thus a tenant intending to leave while the works are being carried out and then return with its goodwill unaffected cannot use section 31A (*Redfern v Reeves* [1978] 2 EGLR 52, CA).

(b) The tenant is willing to accept a tenancy of an economically separable part of the holding and either paragraph (a) above is satisfied with respect to that part, or possession of the remainder of the holding would be reasonably sufficient to enable the landlord to carry out the intended work.

Here, a part of the holding will be an economically separable part if, and only if, the aggregate of the rents which, after completion of the intended work, would be reasonably obtainable on separate lettings of that part and the remainder of the premises affected by or resulting from the work would not be substantially less than the rent which would then be reasonably obtainable on a letting of those premises as a whole (section 31A(2)). If the tenant establishes defence (b), the order for the new tenancy will be only of the economically separable part (section 32(1A)).

Section 31(2) of the Act applies to ground (f), i.e. the landlord has a second chance if he can establish the ground at a later date (see 'near miss' cases at 20.10.8 below). However, ground (f) must be established within one year of the termination date specified in the section 25 notice or section 26 request. If the tenant is refused a new lease under ground (f), the tenant is entitled to compensation (see 20.11).

Ground (g): the landlord intends to occupy the holding

(g) ...that on the termination of the current tenancy the landlord intends to occupy the holding for the purposes, or partly for the purposes, of a business to be carried on by him therein, or as his residence.

This is another frequently used ground which has three important elements: the five-year rule; the landlord's intention; and the occupation of the holding. These are now considered.

20.10.3 THE FIVE-YEAR RULE

The five-year rule is an integral part of ground (g) and is set out in section 30(2) of the Act. It provides that the landlord cannot rely on ground (g) if the landlord's interest 'was purchased or created after the beginning of the period of five years which ends with the termination of the current tenancy'. So to rely on ground (g) the landlord effectively must have owned the reversion for at least five years before the termination date specified in the section 25 notice or section 26 request. The word 'purchased' means 'bought for money', and the time at which the purchase occurs is the date of exchange of contracts (*HL Bolton (Engineering) Co Ltd v TJ Graham & Sons Ltd* [1957] 1 QB 159, CA).

20.10.4 PURPOSE OF RULE

The purpose of this rule is to prevent persons from buying the landlord's interest towards the end of the tenancy simply in order to gain possession for themselves. The rule applies only where the premises have been let on a tenancy or series of tenancies within the Act's protection throughout the five-year period. So, for example, if three years before the end of a tenancy a purchaser buys the reversion (subject to the tenancy), the five-year restriction would prevent him from using ground (g). However, if the same purchaser bought the freehold with vacant possession and then subsequently granted a lease, the five-year restriction would not apply.

20.10.5 CIRCUMVENTING THE RULE

A landlord requiring possession can circumvent the five-year rule if he can prove ground (f) instead, i.e. an intention to demolish or reconstruct the premises).

The court will not examine the landlord's motives for using ground (f), so he could lawfully move in after the construction works have been completed. In addition, the future application of the five-year rule can be avoided if the current landlord is a company. Here, if the purchaser acquires the company by share acquisition it will not be purchasing the 'landlord's interest' (see *Wates Estate Agency Services Ltd v Bartleys Ltd* [1989] 2 EGLR 87).

20.10.6 **LANDLORD'S INTENTION**

The landlord must intend to occupy the premises either for business purposes, or as his residence. As with ground (f), the landlord must be able to show by the date of the hearing a firm and settled intention. The matters considered above are therefore equally applicable here. One relevant factor will be the likely prospect of the landlord succeeding in his plans to occupy. For example, if planning permission were to be refused for the landlord's intended business use, this could make the necessary intention harder to establish (see *Westminster City Council v Bristol Waterways Board* [1985] AC 676, HL, and *Gatwick Parking Service Ltd v Sargent* [2000] 25 EG 141, CA). However, the likely failure of the landlord's proposed business is not a relevant consideration (see *Cox v Binfield* [1989] 1 EGLR 97, CA).

20.10.7 **THE OCCUPATION OF THE HOLDING**

The landlord must intend to occupy the holding for the purposes, or partly for the purposes, of a business to be carried on by him in the premises, or as his residence. Section 42(3) enables a landlord which is a company in a group of companies to rely on ground (g) where another member of the group is to occupy the premises. Section 41(2) enables a landlord who is a trustee to rely on ground (g) where there is an intention to occupy by a beneficiary under the trust. Under the 2004 reforms, ground (g) is extended to a wider category of landlords. Section 30(1A) provides that where a landlord has a controlling interest in a company, then a reference in ground (g) to the landlord is a reference either to the landlord or to the company. Similarly section 30(1B) provides that where the landlord is a company, and a person has a controlling interest in that company, then a reference in ground (g) to the landlord is a reference either to the landlord or that person.

If the tenant is refused a new lease under ground (g), the tenant is entitled to compensation (see 20.11).

20.10.8 **'NEAR MISS' CASES**

If the landlord fails to establish grounds (d), (e), or (f) (alternative accommodation, uneconomic sub-lease, or intention to demolish or reconstruct) at the date of the hearing, he may still be saved by section 31(2) of the Act. If the landlord can show that he would have been able to establish one of these grounds had the termination date in the section 25 notice or section 26 request been up to 12 months later, the court must refuse the tenant's application for a new tenancy. In this case the tenant can ask the court to substitute that later date for the original termination date in the section 25 notice or section 26 request and the tenancy will continue until the later date. For a case involving the application of section 31(2), see *Accountancy Personnel Ltd v Worshipful Co of Salters* (1972) 222 EG 1589, CA.

FIGURE 20.3 LANDLORD'S STATUTORY GROUNDS FOR OPPOSING NEW LEASE

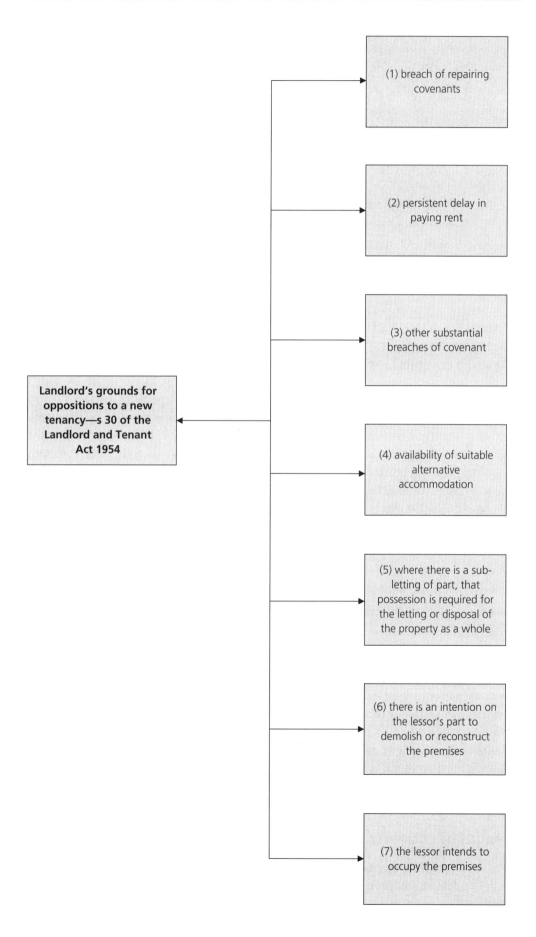

Key Points Statutory grounds under section 30(1)

Four of the seven grounds are discretionary. They are the tenant's 'fault' grounds—(a) tenant's failure to repair; (b) tenant's delay in paying rent; and (c) tenant's breaches of other obligations—and ground (e) on sub-letting of part, where the superior landlord requires the whole property for subsequent letting.

- You cannot amend your grounds at a later date, so be sure of them when the notices are served.

- Grounds (f) (demolish/reconstruct) and (g) (landlord's occupation) are the most frequently used grounds. They require a firm and settled intention on the landlord's part, to be established at the date of the hearing.

- Ground (f) (demolish/reconstruct) will not be established if the tenant is willing to accept a new tenancy of part of the holding, or under the new lease the landlord is allowed access to carry out the works.

- Ground (g) (landlord's occupation) will not be established if the landlord acquired the reversion less than five years before the end of the current tenancy.

- Grounds (d), (e), or (f) may be proven under the 'near miss' rule if the landlord can show he could have established them within 12 months.

20.11 TENANT'S RIGHT TO COMPENSATION

The tenant can claim financial compensation from the landlord if the landlord succeeds in establishing one or more of the 'non-fault' grounds (e), (f), or (g). This is often referred to as 'compensation for disturbance'. The tenant's right to compensation on quitting the premises is contained in section 37(1) of the Act. The basis for compensation is that the tenant is being denied a new tenancy through no fault of its own. Conversely, if one of the 'fault' grounds (a), (b), or (c) is established then the tenant properly will have no right to compensation. Similarly, there will be no right to compensation if the landlord can provide suitable alternative accommodation under ground (d) (on the basis that the tenant has suffered no loss).

It should be noted that section 37(1) allows the tenant compensation on quitting the holding where the landlord in his section 25 notice (or counter-notice to a section 26 request) has specified grounds (e), (f), or (g) in the notice and the tenant has either:

(a) not applied to the court for a new tenancy (see *Re 14 Grafton Street London W1, De Havilland (Antiques) Ltd v Centrovincial Estates (Mayfair) Ltd* [1971] 2 All ER 1); or

(b) made and then withdrawn an application for a new tenancy; or

(c) applied to the court for a new tenancy but has been defeated on one or more of grounds (e), (f), or (g).

Where the landlord has opposed on both fault and non-fault grounds and has been successful, the tenant must, in order to claim compensation, apply to the court for a certificate confirming that the landlord was successful only on grounds (e), (f), or (g) and on no other ground (section 37(4)). This is normally done at the hearing of the application for the new lease and the certificate is then incorporated into the court order. The landlord's stated grounds must be genuine; if the grounds are false and made fraudulently, e.g. by stating a fault ground in an attempt to avoid paying compensation, the notice may be rendered invalid and unenforceable (see *Rous v Mitchell* [1991] 1 All ER 676, CA).

20.11.1 AMOUNT OF COMPENSATION

The amount of compensation is calculated by multiplying the rateable value of the holding (as at the date of service of the section 25 notice or section 26 request) by the 'appropriate multiplier' set from time to time by the Secretary of State. The current multiplier at the time of writing is 1, as prescribed by the Landlord and Tenant Act 1954 (Appropriate Multiplier) Order 1990 (SI 1990/363) which came into force on 1 April 1990 (before that date the multiplier was 3). The rateable value to be used is taken from the valuation list in force at the date of service of the landlord's section 25 notice or section 26(6) counter-notice (section 37(5)(a); *Plessey & Co Ltd v Eagle Pension Funds Ltd* [1989] EGCS 149).

20.11.2 **DOUBLE COMPENSATION**

Double compensation is payable where the tenant or his predecessors in the same business have been in occupation for at least 14 years prior to the termination of the current tenancy (section 37(3)). The date of termination is either the date of termination specified in the section 25 notice, or the date specified in the section 26 request as being the date from which the new tenancy is to start (section 37(7)). In these circumstances, double compensation is calculated by multiplying twice the rateable value by the appropriate multiplier (presently 1). Where the tenant has occupied for nearly 14 years, the timing of a section 26 request or section 25 notice may be crucial in determining whether double compensation is payable.

20.11.3 **EXCLUDING COMPENSATION BY AGREEMENT**

The landlord and tenant may agree (e.g. in the lease) to exclude or modify the tenant's right to compensation for failure to obtain a new tenancy (section 38(3)). However, section 38(2) provides that such agreement will be void where the tenant or his predecessors in the same business have been in occupation for five years or more prior to the date the tenant quits the premises. A prospective tenant would be wise to resist attempts by the landlord to 'contract out' of compensation, as such a provision may adversely affect the marketability of the lease during the last five years of the term.

Compensation is also available in special circumstances, e.g. a failure to be granted a new tenancy on the grounds of public interest or national security (see ss 57–60 of the Act).

20.12 **THE TERMS OF THE NEW TENANCY**

If the tenant properly applies to the court after following all the correct procedures, the court will order a new lease where, (i) the landlord fails to establish an opposition ground under section 30, or (ii) the landlord has not opposed the tenant's application. In (ii), it is rare for the matter to get to court, as the parties' solicitors, after a period of negotiation, will normally be able to agree on the terms of the new lease. The tenant's application in this situation is simply a back-up in case the negotiations break down, and if the parties reach agreement on the terms of the new lease the tenant can simply instruct the court to close its file on the matter.

When conducting negotiations it is important to know the powers of the court, and in particular the lease terms that the court would be likely to impose. You are clearly in a far stronger position if you can argue for the inclusion of a particular clause on the basis that the court would order it. Accordingly, this section will concentrate on the terms a court would be likely to impose in a renewed tenancy. If the parties agree some terms but not others, the court will rule on the unresolved matters, leaving the agreed terms to stand.

20.12.1 **PREMISES**

Generally the new lease will be of 'the holding' (section 32), which is all the property comprised in the existing tenancy, excluding any part not occupied by the tenant (e.g. a sub-let part). The parties may agree as to the extent of the premises to be comprised in the new lease.

20.12.2 **DURATION**

The parties are free to agree whatever length of term they like, but in default of agreement, the maximum fixed term that the court can order is 15 years (section 33). The court has a wide discretion and may order such term as it considers reasonable in all the circumstances (subject to the 15-year maximum). The court also has the power to order a periodic tenancy (although this is rare). In the absence of agreement between the parties the new tenancy will commence when the current tenancy ends under section 64, i.e. three months after the application has finally been disposed of. The court should also specify an end date for the new tenancy.

The court will consider such matters as:

- duration of current tenancy (see *Betty's Cafes Ltd v Phillips Furnishing Stores Ltd* [1959] AC 20);
- length of time tenant has held over under the current tenancy (see *London and Provincial Millinery Stores Ltd v Barclays Bank Ltd* [1962] 2 All ER 163);
- comparative hardship caused to either party (see *Amika Motors Ltd v Colebrook Holdings Ltd* (1981) 259 EG 243);
- landlord's future plans for the property. The court may decide to order a short term where, although the landlord at the date of the hearing is unable to show sufficient intention under ground (f) (demolition/reconstruction), the court is satisfied that he will do so in the near future (see *Roehorn v Barry Corporation* [1956] 2 All ER 742, CA). The court may include a break clause in the lease, which would allow the landlord to end the lease early to carry out future development plans (see *National Car Parks Ltd v The Paternoster Consortium Ltd* [1990] 2 EGLR 99);
- any other factors relevant to the particular case (see *Becker v Hill Street Properties Ltd* [1990] 2 EGLR 78).

20.12.3 **RENT**

Rent is usually the most contentious matter between the parties. Section 34(1) provides that the rent shall be that at which '. . . having regard to the terms of the tenancy (other than those relating to rent), the holding might reasonably be expected to be let in the open market by a willing lessor'. In assessing the rent, the court will usually hear evidence from surveyors or valuers and consider comparable rents in the area ('comparables'). If relevant comparables are not available, the court will consider generally any increases of rent in the locality (*National Car Parks Ltd v Colebrook Estates Ltd* [1983] 1 EGLR 78).

As the other terms of the tenancy will have a bearing on the rent, such other terms are normally agreed before the rent. The courts have approved this as being the most sensible approach (see *Cardshops Ltd v Davies* [1971] 2 All ER 721, CA). The tenant's user covenant in the new lease will be especially relevant when determining the new rent. Landlords often seek a wider use clause so as to command a higher rent (on the basis that a wider use is more attractive to a tenant, thus increasing the rent a tenant in the open market would be willing to pay). In general the courts have been reluctant to permit a relaxation of the user covenant for this purpose (see *Charles Clements (London) Ltd v Rank City Wall Ltd* [1978] 1 EGLR 47).

20.12.4 **DISREGARDS WHEN ASSESSING RENT**

Under section 34(1), the court when assessing the rent must disregard certain factors which would otherwise work against the tenant. These 'disregards' are similar to those found in a typical rent review clause in a business lease. For further reference on rent review and cases interpreting these disregards, see Chapter 2 of *A Practical Approach to Commercial Conveyancing and Property* (Oxford University Press).

The 'disregards' in section 34(1) are:

(a) occupation: '...any effect on rent of the fact that the tenant has or his predecessors in title have been in occupation of the holding'. Thus the landlord cannot argue for a higher rent on the basis that a tenant in occupation would pay more rent to avoid the expense of moving elsewhere;

(b) goodwill: '...any goodwill attached to the holding by reason of the carrying on threat of the business of the tenant (whether by him or by a predecessor of his in that business)'. If the tenant has through his own efforts generated goodwill in his business then he should not be penalized for it by having to pay a higher rent;

(c) improvements: '...any effect on rent of an improvement...carried out by a person who at the time it was carried out was the tenant...otherwise than in pursuance of an obligation to his immediate landlord'. This effectively avoids the tenant paying for the improvements twice over; once when the tenant carries them out and again through a consequential uplift in the rent. The words 'otherwise than in pursuance of an obligation to his immediate landlord' (section 34(2)) mean that improvements to the premises that the tenant was obliged to carry out (e.g. under the terms of the lease) will not be disregarded. In other words, such obligatory improvements will be taken into account when assessing the rent.

20.12.5 RENT REVIEW IN NEW TENANCY

The court is permitted, if it thinks fit, to include a provision in the new lease for varying the rent, i.e. a rent review clause (section 34(3)). This applies irrespective of whether a rent review clause was included in the current lease. However, a court will normally include a review clause if one is present in the current lease. The scope and frequency of the rent review is entirely at the court's discretion. Upward only reviews are common, but tenants have successfully argued for the inclusion of downward reviews if market rents have fallen (see *Forbouys plc v Newport Borough Council* [1994] 1 EGLR 138).

20.12.6 OTHER TERMS OF THE NEW TENANCY

In default of agreement the other terms of the lease 'may be determined by the court; and in determining those terms the court shall have regard to the terms of the current tenancy and to all relevant circumstances' (section 35(1)). This includes the operation of the provisions of the Landlord and Tenant (Covenants) Act 1995 (see 20.12.9 below). Accordingly, if either party wishes to introduce terms that were not included in the current lease, they must justify this by showing that it is fair and reasonable in all the circumstances.

20.12.7 HELP FOR TENANT IN THE CASE OF *O'MAY*

It is usually the landlord who seeks to introduce new terms under the guise of 'modernizing' the lease. Predictably, these new terms are usually more onerous on the tenant. Such modernization provisions should be resisted by the tenant, who is assisted by the House of Lords decision in *O'May v City of London Real Property Co Ltd* [1983] 2 AC 726. In *O'May* Lord Hailsham gave the following guidance:

> ...the court must begin by considering the terms of the current tenancy, that the burden of persuading the court to impose a change in those terms against the will of either party must rest on the party proposing the change and the change proposed must in the circumstances of the case be fair and reasonable and should take into account, amongst other things, the comparatively weak negotiating position of a sitting tenant requiring renewal, particularly in conditions of scarcity, and the general pur-

pose of the Act which is to protect the business interests of the tenant so far as they are affected by the approaching termination of the current lease, in particular as regards his security of tenure.

The landlord in *O'May* failed to show that a proposed new term requiring the tenant to pay a service charge was reasonable, even though the tenant was offered a reduction in rent. The court could see that the landlord's true intention was to shift the burden of maintenance and repair of the building onto the tenant, and this was unjustified.

20.12.8 GUARANTORS

The court is able to require the tenant to provide guarantors for the new tenancy (see *Cairnplace Ltd v CBL (Property Investment) Co Ltd* [1984] 1 All ER 315). This is likely to occur where the tenant has a poor record of paying rent or performing other covenants, or where the tenant is a recent assignee or newly-formed company.

20.12.9 EFFECT OF THE LANDLORD AND TENANT (COVENANTS) ACT 1995

20.12.9.1 Alienation Covenant in New Lease

One area in which the courts may be sympathetic to a landlord seeking to introduce new terms is with regard to the tenant's alienation covenant. If the current lease was granted before 1 January 1996, the old privity of contract rules meant that the original tenant was bound for the entire duration of the lease even after he had assigned it. The change to the privity of contract rule introduced by the Landlord and Tenant (Covenants) Act 1995 (the 1995 Act) benefited tenants, in that for leases granted on or after 1 January 1996 the tenant was released from liability after assignment. A renewed lease today is therefore a 'new lease' under the 1995 Act, and the landlord's position will be worse than it was under the current lease (assuming the current lease was granted before 1 January 1996).

To reflect the changes introduced by the 1995 Act, new leases generally contain more restrictive alienation obligations on the tenant, e.g. pre-conditions to be satisfied before assignment and the use of AGAs. Accordingly, to counteract the landlord's loss of privity, the courts will generally permit a modernization of the alienation covenant in the renewed lease to reflect current practice on the grant of new leases. This is reinforced by Schedule 1, paragraph 4 to the 1995 Act, which amends section 35 of the 1954 Act to provide that the reference to 'all relevant circumstances' includes the operation of the provisions of the 1995 Act (section 35(2)). In *Wallis Fashion Group Ltd v CGU Life Assurance Ltd* [2000] 27 EG 145, the landlord argued that the renewal lease should entitle the landlord to an automatic AGA from the assigning tenant. However, Neuberger J held that although there could be an AGA condition, it should be qualified by the words 'where reasonable'. This decision is important for tenants, who can now properly resist any claim by the landlord for an automatic AGA. An AGA is appropriate only if it is reasonable in all the circumstances.

Alternatively, the landlord's loss of privity under the 1995 Act may be counter-balanced by changes to other terms in the lease, including the level of rent. To underline the point, the 1995 Act amends section 34 of the 1954 Act by inserting a new section 34(4) as follows:

> It is hereby declared that the matters which are to be taken into account by the court in determining the rent include any effect on rent of the operation of the provisions of the Landlord and Tenant (Covenants) Act 1995.

20.12.11 COSTS OF THE NEW TENANCY

The question of whether the tenant agrees to pay the landlord's costs in connection with the new lease will depend on the parties' relative bargaining strengths. However, the tenant should endeavour to resist this as it is highly unlikely that the tenant will be forced to do so by the court (see *Cairnplace Ltd v CBL (Property Investment) Co Ltd* [1984] 1 All ER 315). The Costs of Leases Act 1958, section 1, provides that, unless the parties otherwise agree in writing, each party should be responsible for its own costs.

20.12.12 COURT ORDER FOR NEW TENANCY

If the court orders a new tenancy it will not commence until three months after the proceedings are 'finally disposed of' (section 64). The landlord and tenant should execute a lease and counterpart lease respectively (section 36(1)).

 Key Points Terms of the new tenancy

The parties' advisers should appreciate the terms a court is likely to order in the lease. This puts them in a stronger negotiating position. In particular:

- The court will order a new lease of 'the holding' which generally excludes sub-let parts.

- The maximum fixed term the court can order is 15 years. The duration of the current tenancy will be an important consideration, but there are other factors too.

- In assessing the rent the court will consider comparable rents in the area and disregard the matters in section 34 of the 1954 Act.

- The court will take into account the effect of the Landlord and Tenant (Covenants) Act 1995 (i.e. landlord's loss of privity) when fixing the rent and other terms (e.g. alienation provisions).

- Tenants are within their rights to resist a landlord's demand for an automatic AGA; accept an AGA only 'where reasonable'.

SELF TEST QUESTIONS

1. Your client is the tenant of a 12-year lease of a lock up shop used as a newsagent. The lease term expired last Monday. Your client wishes to continue trading in the property. Your advice is to

   (a) Leave the premises as the lease term has ended

   (b) Remain and continue to pay rent and await a notice to quit

   (c) Write to the court immediately asking to renew the lease

   (d) Write to the local authority claiming the property

2. A lessee can claim the benefits of Part II of the Landlord and Tenant Act 1954 only if three conditions can be fulfilled. Which of the following does *not* apply

   (a) There is a lease or tenancy within the terms of the Act

   (b) The lessee must be a limited company only

   (c) The lessee is in occupation of the property

   (d) The lessee occupies the property for the purposes of the lessee's business

3. Which of the following will benefit from the provisions of Part II of the Landlord and Tenant Act 1954

   (a) A tenancy at will of a shop

   (b) A mere licence of a workshop

   (c) A letting for a fixed term of one year of a member's tennis club

   (d) A letting of a factory for a fixed term of six months

4. If a lessor wishes to serve a termination notice under the 1954 Act and wishes to oppose the grant of a new tenancy, which of the following is *not* one of the grounds for opposition under section 30(1)

   (a) A permitted sub-lessee is in occupation of the whole of the property

   (b) Availability of suitable alternative accommodation

   (c) Persistent delay in paying rent

   (d) Breach of repairing covenants

5. Your client is a lessee in the process of renewing a business lease which was originally granted for 25 years. Your client wants the longest term possible for the renewal lease. If the matter proceeded to court what is the maximum length of term the court could order

   (a) 25 years

   (b) 20 years

   (c) 15 years

   (d) 14 years

SHORT REVISION QUESTIONS

Question 1

INTERNAL MEMO

To   Trainee solicitor

From   Commercial Property partner

Re Foxton Investments Ltd

We act for Foxton Investments Ltd, a property investment company. Our client purchased the freehold of 30 Red House Lane Oxford in January 2005. The property is subject to an occupational lease in favour of an architect, Mr Richard Sykulu. Mr Sykulu has always paid his rent on time and is not in breach of any lease covenants. The lease expires on 29 September 2009 and our client is keen to secure vacant possession of the property as soon as possible to carry out various improvements and alterations prior to using the premises as its own local office. Mr Sykulu has indicated informally to the client that he does not wish to give up possession.

Please prepare a memorandum of the legal advice we should give our client and the procedure for recovering possession.

Question 2

Your firm acts for Charlotte Enterprises Ltd ('Charlotte'), a public relations company that occupies 20a Broad Street Oxford ('the Premises'), a suite of offices on the first and second floors of 20 Broad Street, a three storey building in the centre of Oxford. Charlotte has a lease of the Premises from the present landlord Stiletto Shoes Ltd ('Stiletto'). The lease expires in six months time.

Stiletto has a lease of the whole of 20 Broad Street from the present freehold reversioner, Aragon Investments Ltd ('Aragon'). This lease was granted for a term of 25 years and expires in 6 months and 10 days. Stiletto occupies and trades from the ground floor shop premises.

(i)   Your commercial property partner has asked you to prepare a memo that provides advice for Charlotte.

(ii) Would your advice be different if Charlotte's lease was for the whole of 20 Broad Street?

SUGGESTED ANSWERS TO SELF TEST QUESTIONS

1. The correct answer is (b). The tenant should remain in the premises and must continue to pay rent and await a notice to quit. This is because Part II of the Landlord and Tenant Act 1954 gives the tenant of business premises security of tenure.

2. The correct answer is (b). A lessee can claim the benefits of this statute if there is a lease or tenancy within the terms of the Act, the lessee is in occupation of the property, and the lessee occupies the property for the purposes of the lessee's business. The lessee can be a company or an individual and provided the previous three conditions apply then the Act will come into play.

3. The correct answer is (c). Business purposes include a trade, profession, or employment, and any activity carried out by a body of persons whether corporate or not. The courts have been fairly liberal in their interpretation of this requirement and have therefore included a members' tennis club (*Addiscombe Garden Estates Ltd v Crabbe* [1958] 1 QB 513). The term must exceed six months. The Act does not apply to mere licences or to tenancies at will.

4. The correct answer is (a). All the other choices listed come with section 30. The first one is not a reason to oppose renewal, as the occupant is a permitted sub-lessee in occupation of the whole of the property with consent. The sub-lessee will be the person upon whom the notice will be served.

5. The correct answer is (c). Since 1 June 2004, 15 years is the maximum term that a court can order on the renewal of a business lease (before that date it was 14 years).

SUGGESTED ANSWERS TO SHORT REVISION QUESTIONS

Question 1

INTERNAL MEMO

From   Trainee solicitor

To   Commercial Property partner

Re Foxton Investments Ltd

You have asked me for a memorandum of the legal advice we should give our above mentioned client and the procedure for recovering possession of 30 Red House Lane Oxford from the tenant Mr Richard Sykulu when the current lease expires on 29 September 2009. I therefore set out below the relevant points of law and advice required by the client as follows:

Legal Advice

The tenant Mr Sykulu appears to be a protected tenant by reason of the terms of Part II of the Landlord and Tenant Act 1954. This is because he would seem to be occupying premises for the purpose of a business. Consequently our client can only terminate the lease occupancy by one of the ways prescribed by the 1954 Act.

On the facts presented to me it would seem that there is no question of forfeiture or even of a negotiated surrender. As a result we will need to serve a section 25 notice and in that notice we will have to establish one or more of the grounds for possession under section 30 (1) of the Act.

The fault grounds, e.g. breach of repairing covenants or persistent delay in paying rent or other substantial breaches of covenant do not, on the facts, appear to apply. Indeed, nor does ground (e)—where there is a sub-letting of part, that possession is required for the letting or disposal of the property as a whole. In these circumstances the lessor must consider other grounds such as (i) the possibility of alternative accommodation, (ii) redevelopment, or (iii) own-use grounds.

I appreciate that our client is keen to secure vacant possession of the property as soon as possible to carry out various improvements and alterations prior to using the premises as its own local office. However, the own-use ground cannot be used at present because the client purchased the reversion only three years ago and as a result the five-year rule applies. To rely upon the own-use ground the lessor must show that it intends to occupy the premises for business purposes. This ground is not available to a lessor who has acquired the reversionary interest within five years of the termination of the old tenancy (section 30(2)). The lessor's intention to occupy must be capable of being put into effect within a reasonable time after the full court hearing. So, if the occupation would require a prior planning application and consent, the court would need to be shown that the application had been made and be convinced that there was a reasonable chance that consent would be forthcoming (*Gregson v Cyril Lord Ltd* [1963] 1 WLR 41, CA).

Bearing in mind the time limits set out above it would be possible to allow Mr Sykulu to hold over and then serve the section 25 notice in January 2010. This would satisfy the five-year rule for ground (g). However, it would also mean that the lessee would pay rent at the current level for an extended period and this rent might be well below the market value. Furthermore, the tenant might pre-empt us and serve a section 26 request for a new tenancy earlier. The effect of this would be to deny us the ability to use ground (g).

There is one final alternative ground, that of possible redevelopment. However, on the facts this ground is only a mere possibility. The courts will need to see redevelopment that amounts to substantial reconstruction etc. The lessor must show at the time of the hearing that the lessor intends to demolish or reconstruct the whole or a substantial part of the subject property, or carry out some considerable work of construction, and that the lessor cannot reasonably carry out these proposed works with the lessee still in possession. This would seem unlikely on the facts, although we would need to get further details of the proposed works from the client.

Procedure

The correct procedure is that we should on behalf of the lessor serve a section 25 notice on the lessee on 29 September 2009 specifying a termination date between 6 and 12 months hence. A prescribed form of notice is required. It should be noted that the termination date cannot be earlier than 29 September 2009 being the contractual expiry date.

Immediately thereafter the lessor can apply without delay for an order that the old lease terminate and that there be no new tenancy for the reason(s) set out in the termination notice If the ground(s) for possession can be proved the court will not order a tenancy renewal. If the lessor fails in this application the court can make an order for a new lease without the lessee making a fresh application.

If no such application to deny a new tenancy is made then at any time before the expiry of the termination notice either party can apply to court to renew. This period can be extended by agreement.

Question 2

INTERNAL MEMO

From   Trainee solicitor

To   Commercial property partner

Re Charlotte Enterprises Ltd and 20/20a Broad Street Oxford

(i) My advice for Charlotte Enterprises Limited ('C') is set out below. To clarify, the parties involved in this matter are Aragon Investments Limited ('A'), the freeholder, Stiletto Shoes Limited ('S'), the head tenant and C, the subtenant and our client.

1. Making the first move: The tenant could consider making the first move on the lease renewal procedure. However, the lessee should only do so if certain conditions prevail in the local lettings market. If it is apparent that market rents in the locality of the subject property have risen then the lessee could make an application to the lessor for a new tenancy as a pre-emptive strike stating 12 months hence as the end date. If the lessee does so then that way the lessee will get 6 months at

the existing or old rent but for a period extending beyond and after the contractual lease expiry date. Indeed if market rents have actually fallen C will want the new lease in place as soon as possible to take advantage of a lower rent. In the circumstances our advice to C is to serve a section 26 request stating 6 months hence as the lease end date.

2. Who is the competent landlord? S's lease has less than 14 months to run but S is 'in occupation' and so S's lease continues under the Act until terminated in accordance with the Act (e.g. A serves on S a section 25 notice or S serves on A a section 26 request, in either case terminating S's lease within 14 months). C can find out whether S's lease has been terminated in accordance with the Act by serving on S a section 40 notice. The identity of the competent landlord can change more than once during the course of any litigation and renewal procedure. To request information about superior leases, sub-leases, and whether notices or requests have been given, landlords and tenants can serve on each other a notice under section 40 of the Act. Ideally, the section 40 notice should be served before or simultaneously with the notices or requests under sections 25, 26, and 27. When acting for a tenant serving a section 40 notice on a landlord, we should request in the covering letter a copy of any section 25 notice received by the landlord terminating its tenancy. We can then serve section 40 notices and similar covering letters on the superior landlord(s) until we reach the competent landlord for our anticipated renewal period.

(ii) My advice will be different if C's lease was for the whole of 20 Broad Street. S would then not occupy the premises and thus would have no security of tenure under the Act. S's lease would therefore come to an end within 14 months and C's competent landlord would be A. C's section 26 request should therefore be served on A.

WIDER READING

- Abbey, R, and Richards, M, *A Practical Approach to Commercial Conveyancing and Property* (Oxford University Press, 2006)
- Chapters 12 and 13, Abbey, R, and Richards, M, *A Practical Approach to Conveyancing* (Oxford University Press, 2008)
- Sections K and L dealing with Leaseholds and Tenanted Property, Silverman, F, Conveyancing Handbook (The Law Society, 2006)
- Emmet on Title:—Chapters 26 to 28, Leases
- For more detail on the changes introduced by the Land Registration Act 2002 see Abbey, R, and Richards, M, *Blackstone's Guide to the Land Registration Act 2002* (Oxford University Press, 2002)
- Chapter 8 (the leasehold estate) chapter 9 (Obligations of landlord and tenant), MacKenzie, J-A, and Phillips, M, *Textbook on Land Law* (Oxford University Press, 2008)

WEBSITES FOR FURTHER INFORMATION

- Chartered Institute of Arbitrators, **<http://www.arbitrators.org/Index.htm>**.
- Estates Gazette, **<http://www.egi.co.uk/>**.
- Royal Institute of British Architects, **<http://www.ribafind.org.uk/>**.
- Royal Institution of Chartered Surveyors, **<http://www.rics.org.uk>**.
- Law Society, **<http://www.lawsoc.org.uk/>**.
- Law Society's Gazette, **<http://www.lawgazette.co.uk/>**.
- Street maps of the UK, **<http://www.streetmap.co.uk/>**.

- UK Parliament, **<http://www.parliament.uk>**.

- Valuation Office, **<http://www.voa.gov.uk>**.

online
resource
centre

ONLINE RESOURCE CENTRE CASE STUDY

COMMERCIAL TRANSACTION CASE STUDY—THE OCCUPATIONAL LEASES

Our client: Cambo Ltd—acquisition of 18 Clover Street

We act for Cambo Ltd acquiring the freehold reversion of 18 Clover Street London W2 for £700,000 subject to and with the benefit of two occupational business leases. Completion has recently taken place and our client is anxious to renew one of the occupational business leases (Ground Floor Lease) as soon as possible in order to secure a higher market rent than is currently being received (the last rent review was 4 years ago). Ground Floor Lease will expire in 13 months' time. (29 September 2009)

With regard to the other business lease (Lease of First and Second Floors) the business tenant has a history of late payment and is in breach of its repairing obligations. Our client would like to evict the tenant as soon as possible and let to another interested tenant with a better covenant. Lease of First and Second Floors ends in 6 months' time. (25 March 2009)

Our advice re Ground Floor Lease: Our client should serve a non-hostile section 25 notice on the tenant specifying the last day of the contractual term as the termination date in the notice. However the section 25 notice must be served between 6 and 12 months before the termination date specified in the notice so our client cannot serve the notice until 12 months before the contractual expiry date, i.e. in one months' time. We should prepare the section 25 notice in readiness for service at the appropriate time.

See the Online Resource Centre for a specimen draft section 25 notice.

Our advice re Lease of First and Second Floors: Our client should serve a hostile section 25 notice on the tenant specifying the last day of the contractual term as the termination date in the notice. This can be served immediately as the lease only has 6 months to run. The grounds of opposition will be ground (b) (persistent delay in paying rent) and ground (a) (breach of repairing obligations). Our client should be advised that both grounds are discretionary and so the court may allow the tenant to renew in any event, e.g. if the tenant can convince the court that it will mend its ways. In respect of the repairs the court may accept an undertaking from the tenant to carry out the repairs within a reasonable period. If our client is successful in obtaining possession based on grounds (b) or (a) then our client will have no liability to pay compensation to the tenant for disturbance.

See the Online Resource Centre for a specimen draft section 25 notice.

As an alternative to the above our client could consider seeking forfeiture of the lease for breach of the tenant's covenants. In respect of the repairs breach, a notice under section 146 of the Law of Property Act 1925 will be required to be served on the tenant accompanied by a schedule of dilapidations.

ASSESSMENT GUIDANCE

21.1 SUBJECT ASSESSMENT/EXAMINATION TECHNIQUE GENERALLY

Now that you understand what will be expected of you in a Property Law and Practice subject assessment or examination it is appropriate to consider how you should approach the method. We will now consider the method by which you are required to show your abilities, the subject assessment or examination itself. To help you we set out below some hints and tips to enhance and improve your examination technique.

21.1.1 FIRST OF ALL REMEMBER THE MNEMONIC PAT, PAUSE AND THINK

It is our experience that too often students see a question that triggers off a line of thought and immediately they are away and writing. Always give yourself time to think about the answer that is required. This is why exams may have dedicated reading time at the beginning, to allow you time to read, inwardly digest, and then think through your proposed answer before putting pen to paper. Even if there is no express reading time, the examiners will have made notional time allowances when constructing the form of assessment.

Sometimes examiners will make questions look deceptively simple when in fact they are really quite demanding. Another examiner's trick is to set a question that is apparently about a particular topic when really a good answer requires you to consider more than one area. Therefore, never rush ahead without careful reflection. If it means writing less, then so be it. Students are sometimes misled into thinking that the length of their answer will earn them more marks. This is simply not so and could militate against you when an examiner has to hunt through a lot of superfluous information to find what is actually relevant.

21.1.2 KNOW YOUR TUTOR

Wherever possible, it is always a good move to try to detect the areas of interest shown by the tutors who will be responsible for your examination paper. Clearly for some of you this will be almost impossible as some professional examinations are of course prepared by other examiners that have not taught you. This predicament will be considered subsequently. For those that can identify their tutor's areas of interest they would be well advised to reflect upon the likelihood of just those areas appearing as a topic for the exam.

21.1.3 WHAT IS TOPICAL?

By this we mean has there been a change in the law during the time of your Property Law and Practice course? If so, this could very well end up as a topic for a question in your subject assessment. Think for a moment that you are your tutor who is about to write your examination paper. You have had this responsibility for the last six years and in that time have had to write at least 12 such papers, when resits are taken into account. Each time your tutor must produce something different and yet sufficiently demanding so as to be a satisfactory test of your knowledge and ability to apply it to the question. Accordingly it is hoped that you will appreciate that if the law has changed it is one way your tutor can come up with a novel question arising from a virgin topic that is going to really test your knowledge. It will also show whether or not you were paying attention in class as, of course, the change in the law will be declared by your teachers and will be so new as to be missing from all your textbooks.

An example from current changes must be the Home Information Packs or Prescribed Clauses Leases. Similarly, a couple of important fairly recent examples were the changes caused by the Land Registration Act 2002 and the changes brought about by the introduction of Stamp Duty Land Tax in the Finance Act 2003. Questions after the introduction of these reforms looked as if they were asking about the old law, whereas of course the examiner wanted to see if students were aware of the conspicuous changes caused by these two statutes.

21.1.4 MATTERS FOR YOU TO CONSIDER BEFORE THE ACTUAL SUBJECT ASSESSMENT/EXAM

Be sure you know when and where the subject assessment/examination is to be held. It is awful to see candidates arriving late, all flustered and confused simply because they did not check on the time and place for the examination. Go to revision classes. It is not unknown for 'hints' to be given as to examination or revision topics. Do not miss the opportunity of asking your tutor to explain again any area that you are really not quite sure about. Claim your entitlements. Many institutions will give extra time to students with special needs. If you are so entitled please note this extra time will only be granted on request, so do ask. Seek help when necessary. Many students experience pre-exam nerves. This is an expected response to the stress of the impending examination but if it becomes so strong that it interferes with your revision seek help. Many institutions have support services that can help and that will get you back to the task in hand. Ignore others. Your other student colleagues will not, as a matter of student honour, ever admit to actually doing any revision or indeed any work at all! Of course it is all bravado and bluster. Do not be fazed by it as the bragging is all that it is. You will have a revision plan and you must stick with it right up to your examination. Finally, bear in mind what was last taught on the course. It is the case that the topic that was last taught can often form the basis for a question in the examination. The preparation of the examination paper could coincide with the preparation of the materials for the topic and as a result it could subsequently appear in a question.

21.1.5 KNOW YOUR SUBJECT ASSESSMENT/EXAMINATION TYPE

Not all examinations are the same. The current vogue is for open book exams, but what exactly do your tutors mean by 'open'. Before getting anywhere near the time for the exam make sure that you know exactly what you can and what you cannot take in with you. Also, exercise some discretion about what you choose to accompany you in the examination room. You only have a finite amount of time to write the exam so you do not want to be shuffling through too many textbooks for your own good. A core text plus your own notes should in most circumstances be sufficient; a wheelbarrow full of the practitioner texts will only delay and confuse you. If you can take in books please be aware that this does not mean you can give up on acquiring your own memory store of knowledge. You will not have the time to continually look up the answer to the question. Examiners will be aware that the books are available and will adjust the style of the question to take this fact into account. Use you textbook and indeed your notes to confirm your knowledge when you may be a little unsure. The book and notes should serve as a source of confirmation of your knowledge and not as the source of your knowledge. There is a more detailed and specific section containing guidance on open book exams at 21.2.2 below. Finally, be aware that many institutions now use two-part subject assessments. Be prepared for these by making sure you know when and where they are to take place and what the constituent elements of each part will be. For example, will you be completing answers to multiple-choice questions in the first part and transactional questions in the second or will the order be reversed? In which part will short answer questions occur? Is one part open book and the other closed? The moral is to always be sure of the nature and format of each part of a two-part subject assessment. They are in two parts for a reason; try to be sure you know what that is.

21.1.6 APPRECIATE THE IMPORTANCE OF GOOD TIMING

All examinations are finite and will contain questions or parts of questions that have to be dealt with separately during the examination. This being the case, if you know the number of questions to be answered, always work out in advance the time you can allow to each. This may sound simple but it is of critical importance. You will be tempted to go on writing on one question when you should really be concluding your effort so that you can devote sufficient time to all the questions. Some exams have extra reading time, some do not. Always allow for reading time if there is none allotted. Use the reading time properly by actually reading the questions and all supporting material as carefully as possible and by thinking about the question. Remember PAT.

21.1.7 WHAT TO DO ON SITTING DOWN AT YOUR EXAMINATION DESK

As the *Hitchhiker's Guide to the Galaxy* rightly expounds, 'Don't Panic!' If you have completed your preparation properly you should be quietly confident, but if not, now is too late and panicking will not help. Once again remember PAT, and when confronted with the examination paper give yourself time to consider all aspects of the several points concerned. Look to see if there are marks shown for the various sections of the paper. If there are, this is a great help to you in deciding which parts require greater effort than others earning fewer marks. The marks apportionment should therefore reflect the time apportionment wherever possible. Read the preliminary instructions on the examination paper twice. This way you should take in some of the most important information, all of which is there for a reason. For example, a part or parts of the examination may be compulsory; you should take note and complete your work accordingly. Always read these instructions before launching yourself into the body of the paper. As to the questions, read all of the paper from start to finish, so that you can then decide where your preferences lie. Finally, remember to read all the accompanying documents with the examination paper. Property Law and Practice exams will typically rely upon specimen deeds and documents, all of which must be closely reviewed by you so that you will appreciate how they relate to the question concerned.

21.1.8 ANSWER STYLE

It is probably the case that in most of your previous exams an essay would be an appropriate way of answering almost all the questions encountered. Well, this is where that practice ends. Examiners will in many cases have a marking scheme that will include style marks for your answer. You should therefore understand that if the question is in the style of, say, an office memorandum, that your answer should follow the same format. Similarly if the question asks you for a note of your advice, somehow your answer must be constructed to provide exactly that. Style marks are very easy to pick up if you just use PAT to allow you to prepare your answer in the format sought by the examiner. Do not resort to mere essay answers for all your questions; you will lose easy marks by doing so. So if the question asks you to raise requisitions on title (questions about title problems), and to give reasons for them, then do precisely that. First set out the proposed requisition and then set out your reason for posing this question. One last hint in this section, remember this is a practical subject where answers may need to be seen to replicate office procedures. In the office, time is money and so if you are recording, say, a meeting with the client, put in an estimated time record at the end. This will show the examiner you understand how an office functions and the marker should be suitably impressed.

21.1.9 ANSWER STRUCTURE

What is an answer? Answer—something with a beginning, a middle, and an end. This may seem trite but if you can noticeably structure your answers in this way the examiner will begin to note and appreciate your approach. The last thing an examiner will want to encounter is a long and indeterminate rambling answer. When a well-structured answer is encountered, it is a refreshing experience for the marker who will respond positively to your effort as a result. Get the marker on your side with this important element in your examination technique. This tripartite structure can be further considered.

- The beginning. This perhaps is the fundamental part of your answer. It is where you should grab the marker's attention by a tight, yet logical introduction to the answer. Try at the very outset to show to your marker that you know what is expected of you and that you will be answering the question in full in the body of your answer. Try to indicate your answer by signposts just like we did at the start of this chapter.
- The middle. This must be where you demonstrate your knowledge and your application of it to the facts of the transactional problem. Elements of this process will be considered subsequently.
- The ending is almost as important as the beginning. Try to leave your marker with a final impression of structure by ending with a paragraph or at least a sentence summing up and concluding the flow of your answer. Do not leave your marker with the impression that you stopped where you did simply because you ran out of time or things to say!

21.1.10 TRANSACTIONAL QUESTIONS

When dealing with Property Law and Practice questions it is clear that, in the main, problem-type questions based on a transaction for a client will be the norm. This being so, when using the structure outlined above you could extend that approach in your answer by opening with a clear identification of the area of law involved, followed by a more detailed statement of that area. You should then apply the law to the particular circumstances of the question and complete your answer with a conclusion that sums up your advice to the client.

21.1.11 THINGS TO REMEMBER WHEN IN 'THE MIDDLE', SEE 21.1.9 ABOVE

Always cite your authorities. In Property Law and Practice statute plays an increasingly pre-eminent role. Cases will always be relevant but you will need to be aware of the major statutes involved. You should all be aware at least of section 1 of the Law of Property Act 1925 and the core elements of the Land Registration Act 2002! Recent practice changes can arise from recent case decisions. For this reason, always keep an eye on reported cases in the press. However, there is another reason for keeping up to date on recent decisions and that is because they can form the basis of questions in your subject assessment/examination. As has been noted before, examiners will need to find original scenarios for their questions. This being the case, a recent decision is a heaven sent opportunity for your examiner to adopt those facts for your question. Remember, if you cannot recall the name of a case do not ignore it, simply refer to it as 'in a reported case' or 'in a recent case' if you know it to be novel. Your time in the exam is limited and you may need to repeat long and awkward statute names in your answer. Try writing the Leasehold Reform and Housing and Urban Development Act 1993 a few times and you will understand the problem! To limit the time wasted in this way, if you know you will have to repeat the title after the first instance, insert a short form thus (the LHUDA) and use it subsequently.

21.1.12 CHECK DATES

In many cases dates are in an examination question for a significant reason. Has a time limit expired, is the application out of time, or has a priority period any time remaining? Always consider the chronology of the answer carefully as it may be the key element of the whole question. This is particularly the case for searches and the submission of registration applications to the Land Registry. Dates are also of importance in abstracts of title in unregistered land. Is the root of title at least 15 years old? Similarly, in a commercial lease renewal have the strict time limits set out in Part II of the Landlord and Tenant Act 1954 been complied with? Accordingly, never overlook the importance of dates in the question.

21.1.13 DECIPHERABILITY

Write clearly. There is nothing more annoying to a marker than having to spend too much time on a script trying to read an answer, let alone understand it. Leave lines between sections; it highlights the structure in your answer. Underline headings for the same reason. Start each question on a fresh page and remember to number your answers. It all helps to get the marker on your side.

21.1.14 OTHER KINDS OF EXAM QUESTIONS

We set out in the previous chapters examples of multiple-choice questions that you might encounter in a subject assessment. You will also find some typical short answer questions that can also feature in a subject assessment and which cover matters that are relevant to the chapter topic(s). Answers to both are also set out in each chapter. Remember one crucial piece of guidance concerning multiple-choice questions. Never leave multiple-choice answers with a blank multiple-choice. If there are four possibilities and you are not sure of the answer, select the one you think might be right; after all you have a one in four chance of getting it right! Also look at the instructions on the paper. If it says select the right answer on the paper by circling the correct choice then do just that. Do not make a tick or underline your selection, as the strict response would be to fail you even though the selection may be correct. Also, it is possible that none of the answers given are right. In these circumstances follow the rubric in the question paper and explain in the relevant way why none of the listed answers apply.

21.1.15 LAST BUT NOT LEAST, SPECIAL CIRCUMSTANCES

If there are special circumstances that may have adversely affected your performance make sure the institution has some evidence to explain your difficulties. If you were unwell a doctor's certificate is vital. Indeed, if you were aware of the circumstances before the exam make sure the institution knows as well. Always supply reliable evidence to back up your assertions. Simply your statement that you had a head cold will not do; third party support with written evidence is required.

21.2 PROPERTY LAW AND PRACTICE AND SUBJECT ASSESSMENTS/EXAMINATIONS

We have tried to show you good examination practice and where necessary we have highlighted this with reference to certain elements from within Property Law and Practice. In this section we want to reinforce this with one or two further comments relevant specifically to Property Law and Practice and open book assessments.

You will now appreciate from your own course how broad a subject Property Law and Practice is and how widespread the potential is for the content of the likely questions in your examination. Your first problem is therefore to make sure you remain relevant at all times during the writing of your answer. Keep focused on the problem and the requirements of a structured answer. It could be of use, if you can exercise this form of self-discipline, to just look again at the question half way through your answer to make sure that you are keeping to wholly relevant material. Always bear in mind you need to answer the question set by the examiner and not the question you had hoped might come up and for which you may have misguidedly strategically revised. Furthermore, it is worth repeating that markers are not impressed by length; they are impressed by relevance and organization.

21.2.1 BE UP TO DATE

Make sure you adopt a modern approach to the subject. The Law Society's National Conveyancing Protocol has, for good or ill, been around now long enough for it to appear in all your textbooks. Accordingly, be aware of the nature of the scheme and how it differs from the traditional system. Little things can count a lot towards showing your grasp of the material and this is just as true for the Protocol. Use 'buyer' in place of 'purchaser' and 'seller' for 'vendor', even if some of your older tutors still find it difficult to adopt the modern idiom. (No doubt there will be instances of this in this volume for which we readily apologise!) Adopt the vocabulary of the Protocol wherever possible and use it in your answers. Of course that is not to say you should blandly accept the Protocol as a system without flaws; be ready to criticize the system, with examples and explanations, if you think this is justified. Also bear in mind the Home Information Pack and how it has a limited yet potentially costly impact upon the process of domestic conveyancing.

Remember that many of your tutors will teach across several subjects and that as a consequence you should expect questions that mix several topics. Co-ownership is a classic example of this where a question will arise in Property Law and Practice but where there will be valid information from Family law, land law, and indeed equity and trusts. Combine all your knowledge and use it in the context of the Property Law answer. Obviously you will not earn many marks by dwelling too long on the family law aspects or other aspects not seen as directly involved as Property Law and Practice. Therefore your task is to balance the information from other topics to show sufficient understanding of the need sometimes to integrate your knowledge whilst still being able to clearly show to the examiner your proficiency in Property Law and Practice. The point is in practice your client will not turn up with a simple conveyancing problem all neatly placed in its own compartment. The client is far more likely to present to you a set of facts that could well stretch across several parts of the law, all of which could well lead to litigation and advocacy.

Specifically, what kind of question can you expect in a Property Law and Practice subject assessment. Well of course you will know that the subject itself is an intensely practical one. It will therefore come as no surprise that most questions you will encounter are going to be transactional. This means that you must solve theoretical but practical problems for a 'client' by using your own Property Law/conveyancing knowledge. However, there will also be multiple-choice type questions as well as short answer questions. Examples of all three types of assessment questions are contained within all the previous chapters.

21.2.2 OPEN BOOK ASSESSMENTS AND PROPERTY LAW AND PRACTICE

Legal Practice Course providers have adopted the open book format because in practice you would be able to consider several sources of materials and the teaching teams wish to replicate the position in practice for problem solving. However, there are dangers for the unwary LPC student. You should all therefore note the following points for guidance:

- You must learn the material from each course compulsory subject including pervasive areas. You cannot simply rely on books during the exam. You will not have time constantly to refer to the texts. Your books should only be used sparingly, for very technical points or to confirm your memory recall. Over the years the LPC tutors have noted that candidates who refer constantly to their books in the exams seem to perform less well than those who do not.

- Open book exams are more complex than degree examinations and this course is at post-graduate level. You must think and analyse to formulate an answer to the problem at hand; you must be discriminating in your answer. A 'put down everything' or 'copying out of the book' approach regardless of relevance is usually penalized. It is for you to show to the examiners that you understand the difficulties posed by the questions and can provide a solution.

- Do not spend excessive amounts of time trying to find answers in your books. There is a fundamental core of knowledge that all solicitors should have if they practice within a particular area and they do not need to check in books. You should know a substantial part of this core before going into the examination room.

- The LPC contains many forms of assessment. You might be tempted to direct your efforts solely from assessment to assessment. This would be a learning method that your LPC staff would not support. You need to assimilate the detail each week as the course unfolds. Do not wait until the ends of the blocks to learn the materials; do it on a continual basis and you should be able to approach your subject assessments with confidence.

- We recommend that you take into the exams no more than two A4 binders of materials and notes contained within lever-arch files, along with one or more textbooks specified by the area leader. The Course or Subject Leader for exams may specifically prohibit some books and this prohibition will be stated in your examination instructions. The information on which to base your answers to the examination questions will be found within the issued materials, handouts, exercises and notes, or the recommended textbooks.

21.3 **AND FINALLY; A FEW CONCLUDING WORDS**

First of all, remember the answers we have provided are not model answers but are our attempts to provide suggestions of what we consider to be commendation or distinction level answers. If you feel you could have presented the material in a more efficient manner for any particular question, have the courage of your convictions and write the answer in your own style.

PAT, Pause And Think remains our key piece of advice for all of your time in the examination hall. Remember, a moment or two of careful reflection can be all that is necessary to allow you to integrate all the random thoughts and recollections running around in your mind that will come together as your answer. Give yourself the time to put together a coherent and structured answer; it will make all the difference to your performance generally.

Try to emulate our start to this chapter by listing at the start of your answer the bare bones of your structure. It immediately grabs the attention of your marker and, on the assumption that you are on the right lines, the marker will be on your side for the rest of the marking session. The use of these early signposts will be a refreshing change and will help your attempt to stand out from all the others in the marker's looming tower of scripts.

Be aware of the importance of time management. If marks are shown on the paper for each section of it, immediately work out the amount of time you need to apportion in the same proportions as the marks are allocated. If marks are mentioned, allocate the time in proportion to the number of questions on the paper. Stick closely to your timetable and try not to overshoot your time limits. Remember the next question you write may turn out to be a rich source of marks for you but if you run out of time for your answer you may be limiting the possibility of further marks.

Finally, good luck with all your examinations but, frankly, if you prepare properly luck will not be an important factor in your success.

APPENDIX 1

SPECIMEN LAND REGISTRY OFFICIAL COPY ENTRIES AND THE TITLE PLAN

Official copy of register of title

Title number DN649563   Edition date 28.02.2007

— This official copy shows the entries in the register of title on 28 February 2007 at 11:50:13.
— This date must be quoted as the "search from date" in any official search application based on this copy.
— The date at the beginning of an entry is the date on which the entry was made in the register.
— Issued on 4 June 2007.
— Under s.67 of the Land Registration Act 2002, this copy is admissible in evidence to the same extent as the original.
— For information about the register of title see Land Registry website www.landregistry.gov.uk or Land Registry Public Guide1 - *A guide to the information we keep and how you can obtain it.*
— This title is dealt with by Land Registry Plymouth Office.

A: Property register
This register describes the land and estate comprised in the title.

DEVON : SOUTH HAMS
DEVON : EXETER
CITY OF PLYMOUTH

1   (28.02.2007) The Freehold land shown edged with red on the plan of the above Title filed at the Registry and being 14 Heather Close, Waverley (WY15 9PB).

B: Proprietorship register
This register specifies the class of title and identifies the owner. It contains any entries that affect the right of disposal.

Title absolute

1   (28.02.2007) PROPRIETOR: Christopher Hunt of 14 Heather Close, Waverley (WY15 9PB).

2   (12.02.2007) The price stated to have been paid on 1 February 2007 was £125,000.

3   (28.02.2007) RESTRICTION: No disposition of the registered estate by the proprietor of the registered estate is to be registered without a written consent signed by the proprietor for the time being of the Charge dated 12 February 2007 in favour of Limitless Mortgages UK Ltd referred to in the Charges Register.

Title number DN649563

C: Charges register
This register contains any charges and other matters that affect the land.

1   (28.02.2007) REGISTERED CHARGE dated 12 February 2007.

2   (28.02.2007) Proprietor: LIMITLESS MORTGAGES UK LTD (Co. Regn. No. 7654321) of Poplar House, 104 Barge Street, Leatherhead, Surrey KT23 8BZ.

End of register

Land Registry
Current title plan

Title number **DN649563**
Ordnance Survey map reference **TL2426SW**
Scale **1:1250**
Administrative area **Devon: South Hams**

© Crown Copyright. Produced by Land Registry. Reproduction in whole or in part is prohibited without the prior written permission of Ordnance Survey. Licence Number 100026316.

This official copy issued on 4 June 2007 shows the state of this title plan, on 28 February 2007 at 11:50:13
admissible in evidence to the same extent as the original (s.67 Land Registration Act 2002).
This title plan shows the general position, not the exact line, of the boundaries. It may be subject to distortions in scale.
Measurements scaled from this plan may not match measurements between the same points on the ground. See Land
Registry Public Guide 7 – Title Plans.

This title is dealt with by Land Registry Plymouth Office

APPENDIX 2

STANDARD CONDITIONS OF SALE (4TH EDITION) (NATIONAL CONDITIONS OF SALE, 24TH EDITION, LAW SOCIETY'S CONDITIONS OF SALE 2003)

1. GENERAL

1.1 DEFINITIONS

1.1.1 In these conditions:

(a) 'accrued interest' means:

(i) if money has been placed on deposit or in a building society share account, the interest actually earned

(ii) otherwise, the interest which might reasonably have been earned by depositing the money at interest on seven days' notice of withdrawal with a clearing bank less, in either case, any proper charges for handling the money

(b) 'chattels price' means any separate amount payable for chattels included in the contract

(c) 'clearing bank' means a bank which is a shareholder in CHAPS Clearing Co. Limited

(d) 'completion date' has the meaning given in condition 6.1.1

(e) 'contract rate' means the Law Society's interest rate from time to time in force

(f) 'conveyancer' means a solicitor, barrister, duly certified notary public, licensed conveyancer or recognised body under ss 9 or 23 of the Administration of Justice Act 1985

(g) 'direct credit' means a direct transfer of cleared funds to an account nominated by the seller's conveyancer and maintained by a clearing bank

(h) 'lease' includes sub-lease, tenancy and agreement for a lease or sub-lease

(i) 'notice to complete' means a notice requiring completion of the contract in accordance with condition 6

(j) 'public requirement' means any notice, order or proposal given or made (whether before or after the date of the contract) by a body acting on statutory authority

(k) 'requisition' includes objection

(l) 'transfer' includes conveyance and assignment

(m) 'working day' means any day from Monday to Friday (inclusive) which is not Christmas Day, Good Friday or a statutory Bank Holiday.

1.1.2 In these conditions the terms 'absolute title' and 'official copies' have the special meanings given to them by the Land Registration Act 2002.

1.1.3 A party is ready, able and willing to complete:

(a) if he could be, but for the default of the other party, and

(b) in the case of the seller, even though the property remains subject to a mortgage, if the amount to be paid on completion enables the property to be transferred freed of all mortgages (except any to which the sale is expressly subject).

1.1.4 These conditions apply except as varied or excluded by the contract.

1.2 JOINT PARTIES

If there is more than one seller or more than one buyer, the obligations which they undertake can be enforced against them all jointly or against each individually.

1.3   NOTICES AND DOCUMENTS

1.3.1   A notice required or authorised by the contract must be in writing.

1.3.2   Giving a notice or delivering a document to a party's conveyancer has the same effect as giving or delivering it to that party.

1.3.3   Where delivery of the original document is not essential, a notice or document is validly given or sent if it is sent:

(a) by fax, or

(b) by e-mail to an e-mail address for the intended recipient given in the contract.

1.3.4   Subject to conditions 1.3.5 to 1.3.7, a notice is given and a document is delivered when it is received.

1.3.5

(a) A notice or document sent through a document exchange is received when it is available for collection

(b) A notice or document which is received after 4 pm on a working day, or on a day which is not a working day, is to be treated as having been received on the next working day

(c) An automated response to a notice or document sent by e-mail that the intended recipient is out of the office is to be treated as proof that the notice or document was not received.

1.3.6   Condition 1.3.7 applies unless there is proof:

(a) that a notice or document has not been received, or

(b) of when it was received.

1.3.7   A notice or document sent by the following means is treated as having been received as follows:

(a) by first-class post:	before 4 pm on the second working day after posting
(b) by second-class post:	before 4 pm on the third working day after posting
(c) through a document exchange:	before 4 pm on the first working day after the day on which it would normally be available for collection by the addressee.
(d) by fax:	one hour after despatch
(e) by e-mail:	before 4 pm on the first working day after despatch.

1.4   VAT

1.4.1   An obligation to pay money includes an obligation to pay any value added tax chargeable in respect of that payment.

1.4.2   All sums made payable by the contract are exclusive of value added tax.

1.5   ASSIGNMENT

The buyer is not entitled to transfer the benefit of the contract.

2.   FORMATION

2.1   DATE

2.1.1   If the parties intend to make a contract by exchanging duplicate copies by post or through a document exchange, the contract is made when the last copy is posted or deposited at the document exchange.

2.1.2   If the parties' conveyancers agree to treat exchange as taking place before duplicate copies are actually exchanged, the contract is made as so agreed.

2.2   DEPOSIT

2.2.1   The buyer is to pay or send a deposit of 10 per cent of the total of the purchase price and the chattels price no later than the date of the contract.

2.2.2   If a cheque tendered in payment of all or part of the deposit is dishonoured when first presented, the seller may, within seven working days of being notified that the cheque has been dishonoured, give notice to the buyer that the contract is discharged by the buyer's breach.

2.2.3 Conditions 2.2.4 to 2.2.6 do not apply on a sale by auction.

2.2.4 The deposit is to be paid by direct credit or to the seller's conveyancer by a cheque drawn on a solicitor's or licensed conveyancer's client account.

2.2.5 If before completion date the seller agrees to buy another property in England and Wales for his residence, he may use all or any part of the deposit as a deposit in that transaction to be held on terms to the same effect as this condition and condition 2.2.6.

2.2.6 Any deposit or part of a deposit not being used in accordance with condition 2.2.5 is to be held by the seller's conveyancer as stakeholder on terms that on completion it is paid to the seller with accrued interest.

2.3 AUCTIONS

2.3.1 On a sale by auction the following conditions apply to the property and, if it is sold in lots, to each lot.

2.3.2 The sale is subject to a reserve price.

2.3.3 The seller, or a person on his behalf, may bid up to the reserve price.

2.3.4 The auctioneer may refuse any bid.

2.3.5 If there is a dispute about a bid, the auctioneer may resolve the dispute or restart the auction at the last undisputed bid.

2.3.6 The deposit is to be paid to the auctioneer as agent for the seller.

3. MATTERS AFFECTING THE PROPERTY

3.1 FREEDOM FROM INCUMBRANCES

3.1.1 The seller is selling the property free from incumbrances, other than those mentioned in condition 3.1.2.

3.1.2 The incumbrances subject to which the property is sold are:

(a) those specified in the contract

(b) those discoverable by inspection of the property before the contract

(c) those the seller does not and could not know about

(d) entries made before the date of the contract in any public register except those maintained by HM Land Registry or its Land Charges Department or by Companies House

(e) public requirements.

3.1.3 After the contract is made, the seller is to give the buyer written details without delay of any new public requirement and of anything in writing which he learns about concerning a matter covered by condition 3.1.2.

3.1.4 The buyer is to bear the cost of complying with any outstanding public requirement and is to indemnify the seller against any liability resulting from a public requirement.

3.2 PHYSICAL STATE

3.2.1 The buyer accepts the property in the physical state it is in at the date of the contract unless the seller is building or converting it.

3.2.2 A leasehold property is sold subject to any subsisting breach of a condition or tenant's obligation relating to the physical state of the property which renders the lease liable to forfeiture.

3.2.3 A sub-lease is granted subject to any subsisting breach of a condition or tenant's obligation relating to the physical state of the property which renders the seller's own lease liable to forfeiture.

3.3 LEASES AFFECTING THE PROPERTY

3.3.1 The following provisions apply if any part of the property is sold subject to a lease.

3.3.2

(a) The seller having provided the buyer with full details of each lease or copies of the documents embodying the lease terms, the buyer is treated as entering into the contract knowing and fully accepting those terms.

(b) The seller is to inform the buyer without delay if the lease ends or if the seller learns of any application by the tenant in connection with the lease; the seller is then to act as the buyer reasonably directs, and the buyer is to indemnify him against all consequent loss and expense.

(c) Except with the buyer's consent, the seller is not to agree to any proposal to change the lease terms nor to take any step to end the lease.

(d) The seller is to inform the buyer without delay of any change to the lease terms which may be proposed or agreed.

(e) The buyer is to indemnify the seller against all claims arising from the lease after actual completion; this includes claims which are unenforceable against a buyer for want of registration.

(f) The seller takes no responsibility for what rent is lawfully recoverable, nor for whether or how any legislation affects the lease.

(g) If the let land is not wholly within the property, the seller may apportion the rent.

3.4 RETAINED LAND

Where after the transfer the seller will be retaining land near the property.

(a) the buyer will have no right of light or air over the retained land, but

(b) in other respects the seller and the buyer will each have the rights over the land of the other which they would have had if they were two separate buyers to whom the seller had made simultaneous transfers of the property and the retained land. The transfer is to contain appropriate express terms.

4. TITLE AND TRANSFER

4.1 PROOF OF TITLE

4.1.1 Without cost to the buyer, the seller is to provide the buyer with proof of the title to the property and of his ability to transfer it, or to procure its transfer.

4.1.2 Where the property has a registered title the proof is to include official copies of the items referred to in rules 134(1)(a) and (b) and 135(1)(a) of the Land Registration Rules 2003, so far as they are not to be discharged or overridden at or before completion.

4.1.3 Where the property has an unregistered title, the proof is to include:

(a) an abstract of title or an epitome of title with photocopies of the documents, and

(b) production of every document or an abstract, epitome or copy of it with an original marking by a conveyancer either against the original or an examined abstract or an examined copy.

4.2 REQUISITIONS

4.2.1 The buyer may not raise requisitions:

(a) on the title shown by the seller taking the steps described in condition 4.1.1 before the contract was made

(b) in relation to the matters covered by condition 3.1.2.

4.2.2 Notwithstanding condition 4.2.1, the buyer may, within six working days of a matter coming to his attention after the contract was made, raise written requisitions on that matter. In that event, steps 3 and 4 in condition 4.3.1 apply.

4.2.3 On the expiry of the relevant time limit under condition 4.2.2 or condition 4.3.1, the buyer loses his right to raise requisitions or to make observations.

4.3 TIMETABLE

4.3.1 Subject to condition 4.2 and to the extent that the seller did not take the steps described in condition 4.1.1 before the contract was made, the following are the steps for deducing and investigating the title to the property to be taken within the following time limits:

Step	Time Limit
1. The seller is to comply with condition 4.1.1	Immediately after making the contract
2. The buyer may raise written requisitions	Six working days after either the date of the contract or the date of delivery of the seller's proof of title on which the requisitions are raised, whichever is the later

Step	Time Limit
3. The seller is to reply in writing to any requisitions raised	Four working days after receiving the requisitions
4. The buyer may make written observations on the seller's replies	Three working days after receiving the replies

The time limit on the buyer's right to raise requisitions applies even where the seller supplies incomplete evidence of his title, but the buyer may, within six working days from delivery of any further evidence, raise further requisitions resulting from that evidence.

4.3.2 The parties are to take the following steps to prepare and agree the transfer of the property within the following time limits:

Step	Time Limit
A. The buyer is to send the seller a draft transfer	At least twelve working days before completion date
B. The seller is to approve or revise that draft and either return it or retain it for use as the actual transfer	Four working days after delivery of the draft transfer
C. If the draft is returned the buyer is to send an engrossment to the seller	At least five working days before completion date

4.3.3 Periods of time under conditions 4.3.1 and 4.3.2 may run concurrently.

4.3.4 If the period between the date of the contract and completion date is less than 15 working days, the time limits in conditions 4.2.2, 4.3.1 and 4.3.2 are to be reduced by the same proportion as that period bears to the period of 15 working days. Fractions of a working day are to be rounded down except that the time limit to perform any step is not to be less than one working day.

4.4   DEFINING THE PROPERTY

4.4.1 The seller need not:

(a) prove the exact boundaries of the property

(b) prove who owns fences, ditches, hedges, or walls

(c) separately identify parts of the property with different titles further than he may be able to do from information in his possession.

4.4.2 The buyer may, if it is reasonable, require the seller to make or obtain, pay for and hand over a statutory declaration about facts relevant to the matters mentioned in condition 4.4.1. The form of the declaration is to be agreed by the buyer, who must not unreasonably withhold his agreement.

4.5   RENTS AND RENTCHARGES

The fact that a rent or rentcharge, whether payable or receivable by the owner of the property, has been, or will on completion be, informally apportioned is not to be regarded as a defect in title.

4.6   TRANSFER

4.6.1 The buyer does not prejudice his right to raise requisitions, or to require replies to any raised, by taking any steps in relation preparing or agreeing to the transfer.

4.6.2 Subject to condition 4.6.3, the seller is to transfer the property with full title guarantee.

4.6.3 The transfer is to have effect as if the disposition is expressly made subject to all matters covered by condition 3.1.2.

4.6.4 If after completion the seller will remain bound by any obligation affecting the property which was disclosed to the buyer before the contract was made, but the law does not imply any covenant by the buyer to indemnify the seller against liability for future breaches of it:

(a) the buyer is to covenant in the transfer to indemnify the seller against liability for any future breach of the obligation and to perform it from then on, and

(b) if required by the seller, the buyer is to execute and deliver to the seller on completion a duplicate transfer prepared by the buyer.

4.6.5 The seller is to arrange at his expense that, in relation to every document of title which the buyer does not receive on completion, the buyer is to have the benefit of:

    (a) a written acknowledgement of his right to its production, and

    (b) a written undertaking for its safe custody (except while it is held by a mortgagee or by someone in a fiduciary capacity).

5. PENDING COMPLETION

5.1 RESPONSIBILITY FOR PROPERTY

5.1.1 The seller will transfer the property in the same physical state as it was at the date of the contract (except for fair wear and tear), which means that the seller retains the risk until completion.

5.1.2 If at any time before completion the physical state of the property makes it unusable for its purpose at the date of the contract:

    (a) the buyer may rescind the contract

    (b) the seller may rescind the contract where the property has become unusable for that purpose as a result of damage against which the seller could not reasonably have insured, or which it is not legally possible for the seller to make good.

5.1.3 The seller is under no obligation to the buyer to insure the property.

5.1.4 Section 47 of the Law of Property Act 1925 does not apply.

5.2 OCCUPATION BY BUYER

5.2.1 If the buyer is not already lawfully in the property, and the seller agrees to let him into occupation, the buyer occupies on the following terms.

5.2.2 The buyer is a licensee and not a tenant. The terms of the licence are that the buyer:

    (a) cannot transfer it

    (b) may permit members of his household to occupy the property

    (c) is to pay or indemnify the seller against all outgoings and other expenses in respect of the property

    (d) is to pay the seller a fee calculated at the contract rate on a sum equal to the purchase price and the chattels price (less any deposit paid) for the period of the licence

    (e) is entitled to any rents and profits from any part of the property which he does not occupy

    (f) is to keep the property in as good a state of repair as it was in when he went into occupation (except for fair wear and tear) and is not to alter it

    (g) is to insure the property in a sum which is not less than the purchase price against all risks in respect of which comparable premises are normally insured

    (h) is to quit the property when the licence ends.

5.2.3 On the creation of the buyer's licence, condition 5.1 ceases to apply, which means that the buyer then assumes the risk until completion.

5.2.4 The buyer is not in occupation for the purposes of this condition if he merely exercises rights of access given solely to do work agreed by the seller.

5.2.5 The buyer's licence ends on the earliest of: completion date, rescission of the contract or when five working days' notice given by one party to the other takes effect.

5.2.6 If the buyer is in occupation of the property after his licence has come to an end and the contract is subsequently completed he is to pay the seller compensation for his continued occupation calculated at the same rate as the fee mentioned in condition 5.2.2(d).

5.2.7 The buyer's right to raise requisitions is unaffected.

6. COMPLETION

6.1 DATE

6.1.1 Completion date is 20 working days after the date of the contract but time is not of the essence of the contract unless a notice to complete has been served.

6.1.2 If the money due on completion is received after 2.00 p.m. completion is to be treated, for the purposes only of conditions 6.3 and 7.3, as taking place on the next working day as a result of the buyer's default.

6.1.3 Condition 6.1.2 does not apply and the seller is treated as in default if:

(i) the sale is with vacant possession of the property or any part of it, and

(ii) the buyer is ready, able and willing to complete but does not pay the money due on completion until after 2.00 p.m. because the seller has not vacated the property or that part by that time.

6.2 ARRANGEMENTS AND PLACE

6.2.1 The buyer's conveyancer and the seller's conveyancer are to cooperate in agreeing arrangements for completing the contract.

6.2.2 Completion is to take place in England and Wales, either at the seller's conveyancer's office or at some other place which the seller reasonably specifies.

6.3 APPORTIONMENTS

6.3.1 Income and outgoings of the property are to be apportioned between the parties so far as the change of ownership on completion will affect entitlement to receive or liability to pay them.

6.3.2 If the whole property is sold with vacant possession or the seller exercises his option in condition 7.3.4, apportionment is to be made with effect from the date of actual completion; otherwise, it is to be made from completion date.

6.3.3 In apportioning any sum, it is to be assumed that the seller owns the property until the end of the day from which apportionment is made and that the sum accrues from day to day at the rate at which it is payable on that day.

6.3.4 For the purpose of apportioning income and outgoings, it is to be assumed that they accrue at an equal daily rate throughout the year.

6.3.5 When a sum to be apportioned is not known or easily ascertainable at completion, a provisional apportionment is to be made according to the best estimate available. As soon as the amount is known, a final apportionment is to be made and notified to the other party. Any resulting balance is to be paid no more than 10 working days later, and if not then paid the balance is to bear interest at the contract rate from then until payment.

6.3.6 Compensation payable under condition 5.2.6 is not to be apportioned.

6.4 AMOUNT PAYABLE

The amount payable by the buyer on completion is the purchase price and the chattels price (less any deposit already paid to the seller or his agent) adjusted to take account of:

(a) apportionments made under condition 6.3

(b) any compensation to be paid or allowed under condition 7.3.

6.5 TITLE DEEDS

6.5.1 As soon as the buyer has complied with all his obligations on completion the seller must hand over the documents of title.

6.5.2 Condition 6.5.1 does not apply to any documents of title relating to land being retained by the seller after completion.

6.6 RENT RECEIPTS

The buyer is to assume that whoever gave any receipt for a payment of rent or service charge which the seller produces was the person or the agent of the person then entitled to that rent or service charge.

6.7 MEANS OF PAYMENT

The buyer is to pay the money due on completion by direct credit and, if appropriate, an unconditional release of a deposit held by a stakeholder.

6.8 NOTICE TO COMPLETE

6.8.1 At any time on or after completion date, a party who is ready, able and willing to complete may give the other a notice to complete.

6.8.2 The parties are to complete the contract within ten working days of giving a notice to complete, excluding the day on which the notice is given. For this purpose, time is of the essence of the contract.

6.8.3 On receipt of a notice to complete:

(a) if the buyer paid no deposit, he is forthwith to pay a deposit of 10 per cent

(b) if the buyer paid a deposit of less than 10 per cent, he is forthwith to pay a further deposit equal to the balance of that 10 per cent.

7. REMEDIES

7.1 ERRORS AND OMISSIONS

7.1.1 If any plan or statement in the contract, or in the negotiations leading to it, is or was misleading or inaccurate due to an error or omission, the remedies available are as follows.

7.1.2 When there is a material difference between the description or value of the property, or of any of the chattels included in the contract, as represented and as it is, the buyer is entitled to damages.

7.1.3 An error or omission only entitles the buyer to rescind the contract:

(a) where it results from fraud or recklessness, or

(b) where he would be obliged, to his prejudice, to accept property differing substantially (in quantity, quality or tenure) from what the error or omission had led him to expect.

7.2 RESCISSION

If either party rescinds the contract:

(a) unless the rescission is a result of the buyer's breach of contract the deposit is to be repaid to the buyer with accrued interest

(b) the buyer is to return any documents he received from the seller and is to cancel any registration of the contract.

7.3 LATE COMPLETION

7.3.1 If there is default by either or both of the parties in performing their obligations under the contract and completion is delayed, the party whose total period of default is the greater is to pay compensation to the other party.

7.3.2 Compensation is calculated at the contract rate on an amount equal to the purchase price and the chattels price, less (where the buyer is the paying party) any deposit paid, for the period by which the paying party's default exceeds that of the receiving party, or, if shorter, the period between completion date and actual completion.

7.3.3 Any claim for loss resulting from delayed completion is to be reduced by any compensation paid under this contract.

7.3.4 Where the buyer holds the property as tenant of the seller and completion is delayed, the seller may give notice to the buyer, before the date of actual completion, that he intends to take the net income from the property until completion. If he does so, he cannot claim compensation under condition 7.3.1 as well.

7.4 AFTER COMPLETION

Completion does not cancel liability to perform any outstanding obligation under this contract.

7.5 BUYER'S FAILURE TO COMPLY WITH NOTICE TO COMPLETE

7.5.1 If the buyer fails to complete in accordance with a notice to complete, the following terms apply.

7.5.2 The seller may rescind the contract, and if he does so:

(a) he may

(i) forfeit and keep any deposit and accrued interest

(ii) resell the property and any chattels included in the contract

(iii) claim damages

(b) the buyer is to return any documents he received from the seller and is to cancel any registration of the contract.

7.5.3   The seller retains his other rights and remedies.

7.6   SELLER'S FAILURE TO COMPLY WITH NOTICE TO COMPLETE

7.6.1   If the seller fails to complete in accordance with a notice to complete, the following terms apply.

7.6.2   The buyer may rescind the contract, and if he does so:

    (a) the deposit is to be repaid to the buyer with accrued interest

    (b) the buyer is to return any documents he received from the seller and is, at the seller's expense, to cancel any registration of the contract.

7.6.3   The buyer retains his other rights and remedies.

8.   LEASEHOLD PROPERTY

8.1   EXISTING LEASES

8.1.1   The following provisions apply to a sale of leasehold land.

8.1.2   The seller having provided the buyer with copies of the documents embodying the lease terms, the buyer is treated as entering into the contract knowing and fully accepting those terms.

8.1.3   The seller is to comply with any lease obligations requiring the tenant to insure the property.

8.2   NEW LEASES

8.2.1   The following provisions apply to a contract to grant a new lease.

The conditions apply so that:

'seller' means the proposed landlord

'buyer' means the proposed tenant

'purchase price' means the premium to be paid on the grant of a lease.

8.2.3   The lease is to be in the form of the draft attached to the contract.

8.2.4   If the term of the new lease will exceed seven years, the seller is to deduce a title which will enable the buyer to register the lease at HM Land Registry with an absolute title.

8.2.5   The seller is to engross the lease and a counterpart of it and is to send the counterpart to the buyer at least five working days before completion date.

8.2.6   The buyer is to execute the counterpart and deliver it to the seller on completion.

8.3   CONSENT

8.3.1

(a) The following provisions apply if a consent to let, assign or sub-let is required to complete the contract.

(b) In this condition 'consent' means consent in the form which satisfies the requirement to obtain it.

8.3.2

    (a) The seller is to apply for the consent at his expense, and to use all reasonable efforts to obtain it

    (b) The buyer is to provide all information and references reasonably required.

8.3.3   Unless he is in breach of his obligation under condition 8.3.2, either party may rescind the contract by notice to the other party if three working days before completion date (or before a later date on which the parties have agreed to complete the contract):

    (a) the consent has not been given, or

    (b) the consent has been given subject to a condition to which a party reasonably objects. In that case, neither party is to be treated as in breach of contract and condition 7.2 applies.

9.   COMMONHOLD LAND

9.1   Terms used in this condition have the special meanings given to them in Part 1 of the Commonhold and Leasehold Reform Act 2002.

9.2   This condition applies to a disposition of commonhold land.

9.3   The seller having provided the buyer with copies of the current versions of the memorandum and articles of the commonhold association and of the commonhold community statement, the buyer is treated as entering into the contract knowing and fully accepting their terms.

9.4   If the contract is for the sale of property which is or includes part only of a commonhold unit:

    (a) the seller is to apply for the written consent of the commonhold association at his expense and is to use all reasonable efforts to obtain it

    (b) either the seller, unless he is in breach of his obligation under paragraph (a), or the buyer may rescind the contract by notice to the other party if three working days before completion date (or before a later date on which the parties have agreed to complete the contract) the consent has not been given. In that case, neither party is to be treated as in breach of contract and condition 7.2 applies.

10.   CHATTELS

10.1   The following provisions apply to any chattels which are included in the contract, whether or not a separate price is to be paid for them.

10.2   The contract takes effect as a contract for sale of goods.

10.3   The buyer takes the chattels in the physical state they are in at the date of the contract.

10.4   Ownership of the chattels passes to the buyer on actual completion.

APPENDIX 3

STANDARD COMMERCIAL PROPERTY
CONDITIONS (2ND EDN)

CONTRACT
Incorporating the Standard Commercial Property Conditions (Second Edition)

Date :

Seller :

Buyer :

Property :
(freehold/leasehold)

Title Number/Root of title :

Specified incumbrances :

Completion date :

Contract rate :

Purchase price :

Deposit :

The seller will sell and the buyer will buy:

(a) the property, and

(b) any chattels which, under the special conditions, are included in the sale

for the purchase price.

WARNING	**Signed**
This is a formal document, designed to create legal rights and legal obligations. Take advice before using it.	Authorised to sign on behalf of Seller/Buyer

PART 1

1.   GENERAL

1.1   DEFINITIONS

1.1.1   In these conditions:

(a)   "accrued interest" means:

(i)   if money has been placed on deposit or in a building society share account, the interest actually earned

(ii)   otherwise, the interest which might reasonably have been earned by depositing the money at interest on seven days' notice of withdrawal with a clearing bank less, in either case, any proper charges for handling the money

(b)   "apportionment day" has the meaning given in condition 8.3.2

(c)   "clearing bank" means a bank which is a shareholder in CHAPS Clearing Co. Limited

(d)   "completion date" has the meaning given in condition 8.1.1

(e)   "contract rate" is the Law Society's interest rate from time to time in force

(f)   "conveyancer" means a solicitor, barrister, duly certified notary public, licensed conveyancer or recognised body under sections 9 or 23 of the Administration of Justice Act 1985

(g)   "direct credit" means a direct transfer of cleared funds to an account nominated by the seller's conveyancer and maintained at a clearing bank

(h)   "election to waive exemption" means an election made under paragraph 2 of Schedule 10 to the Value Added Tax Act 1994

(i)   "lease" includes sub-lease, tenancy and agreement for a lease or sub-lease

(j)   "notice to complete" means a notice requiring completion of the contract in accordance with condition 8

(k)   "post" includes a service provided by a person licensed under the Postal Services Act 2000

(l)   "public requirement" means any notice, order or proposal given or made (whether before or after the date of the contract) by a body acting on statutory authority

(m)   "requisition" includes objection

(n)   "transfer" includes conveyance and assignment

(o)   "working day" means any day from Monday to Friday (inclusive) which is not Christmas Day, Good Friday or a statutory Bank Holiday.

1.1.2   In these conditions the terms "absolute title" and "official copies" have the special meanings given to them by the Land Registration Act 2002.

1.1.3   A party is ready, able and willing to complete:

(a)   if it could be, but for the default of the other party, and

(b)   in the case of the seller, even though a mortgage remains secured on the property, if the amount to be paid on completion enables the property to be transferred freed of all mortgages (except those to which the sale is expressly subject).

1.1.4   (a)   The conditions in Part 1 apply except as varied or excluded by the contract.

(b)   A condition in Part 2 only applies if expressly incorporated into the contract.

1.2   JOINT PARTIES

If there is more than one seller or more than one buyer, the obligations which they undertake can be enforced against them all jointly or against each individually.

1.3   NOTICES AND DOCUMENTS

1.3.1   A notice required or authorised by the contract must be in writing.

1.3.2   Giving a notice or delivering a document to a party's conveyancer has the same effect as giving or delivering it to that party.

1.3.3   Where delivery of the original document is not essential, a notice or document is validly given or sent if it is sent:

(a) by fax, or

(b) by e-mail to an e-mail address for the intended recipient given in the contract.

1.3.4 Subject to conditions 1.3.5 to 1.3.7, a notice is given and a document delivered when it is received.

1.3.5 (a) A notice or document sent through the document exchange is received when it is available for collection

    (b) A notice or document which is received after 4.00 p.m. on a working day, or on a day which is not a working day, is to be treated as having been received on the next working day

    (c) An automated response to a notice or document sent by e-mail that the intended recipient is out of the office is to be treated as proof that the notice or document was not received.

1.3.6 Condition 1.3.7 applies unless there is proof:

    (a) that a notice or document has not been received, or

    (b) of when it was received.

1.3.7 Unless the actual time of receipt is proved, a notice or document sent by the following means is treated as having been received as follows:

(a) by first-class post:	before 4 pm on the second working day after posting
(b) by second-class post:	before 4 pm on the third working day after posting
(c) through a document exchange:	before 4 pm on the first working day after the day on which it would normally be available for collection by the addressee.
(d) by fax:	one hour after despatch
(e) by e-mail:	before 4 pm on the first working day after despatch.

1.3.8 In condition 1.3.7, "first class post" means a postal service which seeks to deliver posted items no later than the next working day in all or the majority of cases.

1.4 VAT

1.4.1 The seller:

    (a) warrants that the sale of the property does not constitute a supply that is taxable for VAT purposes

    (b) agrees that there will be no exercise of the election to waive exemption in respect of the property, and

    (c) cannot require the buyer to pay any amount in respect of any liability to VAT arising in respect of the sale of the property, unless condition 1.4.2 applies.

1.4.2 If, solely as a result of a change in law made and coming into effect between the date of the contract and completion, the sale of the property will constitute a supply chargeable to VAT, the buyer is to pay to the seller on completion an additional amount equal to that VAT in exchange for a proper VAT invoice from the seller.

1.4.3 The amount payable for the chattels is exclusive of VAT and the buyer is to pay to the seller on completion an additional amount equal to any VAT charged on that supply in exchange for a proper VAT invoice from the seller.

1.5 ASSIGNMENT AND SUB-SALES

1.5.1 The buyer is not entitled to transfer the benefit of the contract.

1.5.2 The seller may not be required to transfer the property in parts or to any person other than the buyer.

2. FORMATION

2.1 DATE

2.1.1 If the parties intend to make a contract by exchanging duplicate copies by post or through a document exchange, the contract is made when the last copy is posted or deposited at the document exchange.

2.1.2   If the parties' conveyancers agree to treat exchange as taking place before duplicate copies are actually exchanged, the contract is made as so agreed.

2.2   DEPOSIT

2.2.1   The buyer is to pay a deposit of 10 per cent of the purchase price no later than the date of the contract.

2.2.2   Except on a sale by auction the deposit is to be paid by direct credit and is to be held by the seller's conveyancer as stakeholder on terms that on completion it is to be paid to the seller with accrued interest.

2.3   AUCTIONS

2.3.1   On a sale by auction the following conditions apply to the property and, if it is sold in lots, to each lot.

2.3.2   The sale is subject to a reserve price.

2.3.3   The seller, or a person on its behalf, may bid up to the reserve price.

2.3.4   The auctioneer may refuse any bid.

2.3.5   If there is a dispute about a bid, the auctioneer may resolve the dispute or restart the auction at the last undisputed bid.

2.3.6   The auctioneer is to hold the deposit as agent for the seller.

2.3.7   If any cheque tendered in payment of all or part of the deposit is dishonoured when first presented, the seller may, within seven working days of being notified that the cheque has been dishonoured, give notice to the buyer that the contract is discharged by the buyer's breach.

3.   MATTERS AFFECTING THE PROPERTY

3.1   FREEDOM FROM INCUMBRANCES

3.1.1.   The seller is selling the property free from incumbrances, other than those mentioned in condition 3.1.2.

3.1.2   The incumbrances subject to which the property is sold are:

(a)   those specified in the contract

(b)   those discoverable by inspection of the property before the contract

(c)   those the seller does not and could not reasonably know about

(d)   matters, other than monetary charges or incumbrances, disclosed or which would have been disclosed by the searches and enquiries which a prudent buyer would have made before entering into the contract

(e)   public requirements.

3.1.3   After the contract is made, the seller is to give the buyer written details without delay of any new public requirement and of anything in writing which he learns about concerning a matter covered by condition 3.1.2.

3.1.4   The buyer is to bear the cost of complying with any outstanding public requirement and is to indemnify the seller against any liability resulting from a public requirement.

3.2   PHYSICAL STATE

3.2.1   The buyer accepts the property in the physical state it is in at the date of the contract unless the seller is building or converting it.

3.2.2   A leasehold property is sold subject to any subsisting breach of a condition or tenant's obligation relating to the physical state of the property which renders the lease liable to forfeiture.

3.2.3   A sub-lease is granted subject to any subsisting breach of a condition or tenant's obligation relating to the physical state of the property which renders the seller's own lease liable to forfeiture.

3.3   RETAINED LAND

Where after the transfer the seller will be retaining land near the property:

(a)   the buyer will have no right of light or air over the retained land, but

(b) in other respects the seller and the buyer will each have the rights over the land of the other which they would have had if they were two separate buyers to whom the seller had made simultaneous transfers of the property and the retained land.

The transfer is to contain appropriate express terms.

4. LEASES AFFECTING THE PROPERTY

4.1 GENERAL

4.1.1 This condition applies if any part of the property is sold subject to a lease.

4.1.2 The seller having provided the buyer with full details of each lease or copies of documents embodying the lease terms, the buyer is treated as entering into the contract knowing and fully accepting those terms.

4.1.3 The seller is not to serve a notice to end the lease nor to accept a surrender.

4.1.4 The seller is to inform the buyer without delay if the lease ends.

4.1.5 The buyer is to indemnify the seller against all claims arising from the lease after actual completion; this includes claims which are unenforceable against a buyer for want of registration.

4.1.6 If the property does not include all the land let, the seller may apportion the rent and, if the lease is a new tenancy, the buyer may require the seller to apply under section 10 of the Landlord and Tenant (Covenants) Act 1995 for the apportionment to bind the tenant.

4.2 PROPERTY MANAGEMENT

4.2.1 The seller is promptly to give the buyer full particulars of:

(a) any court or arbitration proceedings in connection with the lease, and

(b) any application for a licence, consent or approval under the lease.

4.2.2 Conditions 4.2.3 to 4.2.8 do not apply to a rent review process to which condition 5 applies.

4.2.3 Subject to condition 4.2.4, the seller is to conduct any court or arbitration proceedings in accordance with written directions given by the buyer from time to time (for which the seller is to apply), unless to do so might place the seller in breach of an obligation to the tenant or a statutory duty.

4.2.4 If the seller applies for directions from the buyer in relation to a proposed step in the proceedings and the buyer does not give such directions within 10 working days, the seller may take or refrain from taking that step as it thinks fit.

4.2.5 The buyer is to indemnify the seller against all loss and expense resulting from the seller's following the buyer's directions.

4.2.6 Unless the buyer gives written consent, the seller is not to:

(a) grant or formally withhold any licence, consent or approval under the lease, or

(b) serve any notice or take any action (other than action in court or arbitration proceedings) as landlord under the lease.

4.2.7 When the seller applies for the buyer's consent under condition 4.2.6:

(a) the buyer is not to withhold its consent or attach conditions to the consent where to do so might place the seller in breach of an obligation to the tenant or a statutory duty

(b) the seller may proceed as if the buyer has consented when:

(i) in accordance with paragraph (a), the buyer is not entitled to withhold its consent, or

(ii) the buyer does not refuse its consent within 10 working days.

4.2.8 If the buyer withholds or attaches conditions to its consent, the buyer is to indemnify the seller against all loss and expense.

4.2.9 In all other respects, the seller is to manage the property in accordance with the principles of good estate management until completion.

4.3 CONTINUING LIABILITY

At the request and cost of the seller, the buyer is to support any application by the seller to be released from the landlord covenants in a lease to which the property is sold subject.

5. RENT REVIEWS

5.1 Subject to condition 5.2, this condition applies if:

(a) the rent reserved by a lease of all or part of the property is to be reviewed,

(b) the seller is either the landlord or the tenant,

(c) the rent review process starts before actual completion, and

(d) no reviewed rent has been agreed or determined at the date of the contract.

5.2 The seller is to conduct the rent review process until actual completion, after which the buyer is to conduct it.

5.3 Conditions 5.4 and 5.5 cease to apply on actual completion if the reviewed rent will only be payable in respect of a period after that date.

5.4 In the course of the rent review process, the seller and the buyer are each to:

(a) act promptly with a view to achieving the best result obtainable,

(b) consult with and have regard to the views of the other,

(c) provide the other with copies of all material correspondence and papers relating to the process,

(d) ensure that its representations take account of matters put forward by the other, and

(e) keep the other informed of the progress of the process.

5.5 Neither the seller nor the buyer is to agree a rent figure unless it has been approved in writing by the other (such approval not to be unreasonably withheld).

5.4 The seller and the buyer are each to bear their own costs of the rent review process.

5.7 Unless the rent review date precedes the apportionment day, the buyer is to pay the costs of a third party appointed to determine the rent.

5.8 Where the rent review date precedes the apportionment day, those costs are to be divided as follows:

(a) the seller is to pay the proportion that the number of days from the rent review date to the apportionment day bears to the number of days from that rent review date until either the following rent review date or, if none, the expiry of the term, and

(b) the buyer is to pay the balance.

6. TITLE AND TRANSFER

6.1 PROOF OF TITLE

6.1.1 Without cost to the buyer, the seller is to provide the buyer with proof of the title to the property and of his ability to transfer it, or to procure its transfer.

6.1.2 Where the property has a registered title the proof is to include official copies of the items referred to in rules 134(1)(a) and (b) and 135(1)(a) of the Land Registration Rules 2003, so far as they are not to be discharged or overridden at or before completion.

6.1.3 Where the property has an unregistered title, the proof is to include:

(a) an abstract of title or an epitome of title with photocopies of the documents, and

(b) production of every document or an abstract, epitome or copy of it with an original marking by a conveyancer either against the original or an examined abstract or an examined copy.

6.2 REQUISITIONS

6.2.1 The buyer may not raise requisitions:

(a) on the title shown by the seller taking the steps described in condition 6.1.1 before the contract was made

(b) in relation to the matters covered by condition 3.1.2

6.2.2 Notwithstanding condition 6.2.1, the buyer may, within six working days of a matter coming to his attention after the contract was made, raise written requisitions on that matter. In that event steps 3 and 4 in condition 6.3.1 apply.

6.2.3 On the expiry of the relevant time limit under condition 6.2.2 or condition 6.3.1, the buyer loses his right to raise requisitions or to make observations.

6.3 TIMETABLE

6.3.1 Subject to condition 6.2 and to the extent that the seller did not take the steps described in condition 6.1.1 before the contract was made, the following are the steps for deducing and investigating the title to the property to be taken within the following time limits:

Step	Time Limit
1. The seller is to comply with condition 6.1.1	Immediately after making the contract
2. The buyer may raise written requisitions	Six working days after either the date of the contract or the date of delivery of the seller's proof of title on which the requisitions are raised, whichever is the later
3. The seller is to reply in writing to any requisitions raised	Four working days after receiving the requisitions
4. The buyer may make written observations on the seller's replies	Three working days after receiving the replies

The time limit on the buyer's right to raise requisitions applies even where the seller supplies incomplete evidence of its title, but the buyer may, within six working days from delivery of any further evidence, raise further requisitions resulting from that evidence.

6.3.2 The parties are to take the following steps to prepare and agree the transfer of the property within the following time limits:

Step	Time Limit
A. The buyer is to send the seller a draft transfer	At least twelve working days before completion date
B. The seller is to approve or revise that draft and either return it or retain it for use as the actual transfer	Four working days after delivery of the draft transfer
C. If the draft is returned the buyer is to send an engrossment to the seller	At least five working days before completion date

6.3.3 Periods of time under conditions 6.3.1 and 6.3.2 may run concurrently.

6.3.4 If the period between the date of the contract and completion date is less than 15 working days, the time limits in conditions 6.2.2, 6.3.1 and 6.3.2 are to be reduced by the same proportion as that period bears to the period of 15 working days. Fractions of a working day are to be rounded down except that the time limit to perform any step is not to be less than one working day.

6.4 DEFINING THE PROPERTY

6.4.1 The seller need not, further than it may be able to do from information in its possession:

(a) prove the exact boundaries of the property

(b) prove who owns fences, ditches, hedges or walls

(c) separately identify parts of the property with different titles.

6.4.2 The buyer may, if to do so is reasonable, require the seller to make or obtain, pay for and hand over a statutory declaration about facts relevant to the matters mentioned in condition

6.4.1 The form of the declaration is to be agreed by the buyer, who must not unreasonably withhold its agreement.

6.5 RENTS AND RENTCHARGES

The fact that a rent or rentcharge, whether payable or receivable by the owner of the property, has been or will on completion be, informally apportioned is not to be regarded as a defect in title.

6.6 TRANSFER

6.1.1 The buyer does not prejudice its right to raise requisitions, or to require replies to any raised, by taking steps in relation to the preparation or agreement of the transfer.

6.6.2 Subject to condition 6.6.3, the seller is to transfer the property with full title guarantee.

6.6.3 The transfer is to have effect as if the disposition is expressly made subject to all matters covered by condition 3.1.2.

6.6.4 If after completion the seller will remain bound by any obligation affecting the property and disclosed to the buyer before the contract was made, but the law does not imply any covenant by the buyer to indemnify the seller against liability for future breaches of it:

(a) the buyer is to covenant in the transfer to indemnify the seller against liability for any future breach of the obligation and to perform it from then on, and

(b) if required by the seller, the buyer is to execute and deliver to the seller on completion a duplicate transfer prepared by the buyer.

6.6.5 The seller is to arrange at its expense that, in relation to every document of title which the buyer does not receive on completion, the buyer is to have the benefit of:

(a) a written acknowledgement of the buyer's right to its production, and

(b) a written undertaking for its safe custody (except while it is held by a mortgagee or by someone in a fiduciary capacity).

7. INSURANCE

7.1 RESPONSIBILITY FOR INSURING

7.1.1 Conditions 7.1.2 and 7.1.3 apply if:

(a) the contract provides that the policy effected by or for the seller and insuring the property or any part of it against loss or damage should continue in force after the exchange of contracts, or

(b) the property or any part of it is let on terms under which the seller (whether as landlord or as tenant) is obliged to insure against loss or damage.

7.1.2 The seller is to:

(a) do everything required to continue to maintain the policy, including the prompt payment of any premium which falls due

(b) increase the amount or extent of the cover as requested by the buyer, if the insurers agree and the buyer pays the additional premium

(c) permit the buyer to inspect the policy, or evidence of its terms, at any time

(d) obtain or consent to an endorsement on the policy of the buyer's interest, at the buyer's expense

(e) pay to the buyer immediately on receipt, any part of an additional premium which the buyer paid and which is returned by the insurers

(f) if before completion the property suffers loss or damage:

(i) pay to the buyer on completion the amount of policy moneys which the seller has received, so far as not applied in repairing or reinstating the property, and

(ii) if no final payment has then been received, assign to the buyer, at the buyer's expense, all rights to claim under the policy in such form as the buyer reasonably requires and pending execution of the assignment, hold any policy moneys received in trust for the buyer

(g) on completion:

(i) cancel the insurance policy

(ii) apply for a refund of the premium and pay the buyer, immediately on receipt, any amount received which relates to a part of the premium which was paid or reimbursed by a tenant or third party. The buyer is to hold the money paid subject to the rights of that tenant or third party.

7.1.3 The buyer is to pay the seller a proportionate part of the premium which the seller paid in respect of the period from the date when the contract is made to the date of actual completion, except so far as the seller is entitled to recover it from a tenant.

7.1.4 Unless condition 7.1.2 applies:

    (a) the seller is under no obligation to the buyer to insure the property

    (b) if payment under a policy effected by or for the buyer is reduced, because the property is covered against loss or damage by an insurance policy effected by or for the seller, the purchase price is to be abated by the amount of that reduction.

7.1.5 Section 47 of the Law of Property Act 1925 does not apply.

8. COMPLETION

8.1 DATE

8.1.1 Completion date is twenty working days after the date of the contract but time is not of the essence of the contract unless a notice to complete has been served.

8.1.2 If the money due on completion is received after 2.00 p.m., completion is to be treated, for the purposes only of conditions 8.3 and 9.3, as taking place on the next working day as a result of the buyer's default.

8.1.3 Condition 8.1.2 does not apply if:

    (a) the sale is with vacant possession of the property or a part of it, and

    (b) the buyer is ready, willing and able to complete but does not pay the money due on completion until after 2.00 p.m. because the seller has not vacated the property or that part by that time.

8.2 PLACE

Completion is to take place in England and Wales, either at the seller's conveyancer's office or at some other place which the seller reasonably specifies.

8.3 APPORTIONMENTS

8.3.1 Subject to condition 8.3.6 income and outgoings of the property are to be apportioned between the parties so far as the change of ownership on completion will affect entitlement to receive or liability to pay them.

8.3.2 The day from which the apportionment is to be made ('apportionment day') is:

    (a) if the whole property is sold with vacant possession or the seller exercises its option in condition 9.3.4, the date of actual completion, or

    (b) otherwise, completion date.

8.3.3 In apportioning any sum, it is to be assumed that the buyer owns the property from the beginning of the day on which the apportionment is to be made.

8.3.4 A sum to be apportioned is to be treated as:

    (a) payable for the period which it covers, except that if it is an instalment of an annual sum the buyer is to be attributed with an amount equal to 1/365th of the annual sum for each day from and including the apportionment day to the end of the instalment period

    (b) accruing—

        (i) from day to day, and

        (ii) at the rate applicable from time to time.

8.3.5 When a sum to be apportioned, or the rate at which it is to be treated as accruing, is not known or easily ascertainable at completion, a provisional apportionment is to be made according to the best estimate available. As soon as the amount is known, a final apportionment is to be made and notified to the other party. Subject to condition 8.3.8, any resulting balance is to be paid no more than ten working days later, and if not then paid the balance is to bear interest at the contract rate from then until payment.

8.3.6 Where a lease of the property requires the tenant to reimburse the landlord for expenditure on goods or services, on completion:

    (a) the buyer is to pay the seller the amount of any expenditure already incurred by the seller but not yet due from the tenant and in respect of which the seller provides the buyer with the information and vouchers required for its recovery from the tenant, and

    (b) the seller is to credit the buyer with payments already recovered from the tenant but not yet incurred by the seller.

8.3.7   Condition 8.3.8 applies if any part of the property is sold subject to a lease and either:

    (a) (i) on completion any rent or other sum payable under the lease is due but not paid.

        (ii) the contract does not provide that the buyer is to assign to the seller the right to collect any arrears due to the seller under the terms of the contract, and

        (iii) the seller is not entitled to recover any arrears from the tenant, or

    (b) (i) as a result of a rent review to which condition 5 applies a reviewed rent is agreed or determined after actual completion, and

        (ii) an additional sum then becomes payable in respect of a period before the apportionment day.

8.3.8   (a) The buyer is to seek to collect all sums due in the circumstances referred to in condition 8.3.7 in the ordinary course of management, but need not take legal proceedings or distrain.

    (b) A payment made on account of those sums is to be apportioned between the parties in the ratio of the amounts owed to each, notwithstanding that the tenant exercises its right to appropriate the payment in some other manner.

    (c) Any part of a payment on account received by one party but due to the other is to be paid no more than ten working days after the receipt of cash or cleared funds and, if not then paid, the sum is to bear interest at the contract rate until payment.

8.4   AMOUNT PAYABLE

The amount payable by the buyer on completion is the purchase price (less any deposit already paid to the seller or its agent) adjusted to take account of:

(a) apportionments made under condition 8.3

(b) any compensation to be paid under condition 9.3

(c) any sum payable under condition 7.1.2 or 7.1.3.

8.5   TITLE DEEDS

8.5.1   As soon as the buyer has compiled with all its obligations on completion the seller must hand over the documents of title.

8.5.2   Condition 8.5.1 does not apply to any documents of title relating to land being retained by the seller after completion.

8.6   RENT RECEIPTS

The buyer is to assume that whoever gave any receipt for a payment of rent which the seller produces was the person or the agent of the person then entitled to that rent.

8.7   MEANS OF PAYMENT

The buyer is to pay the money due on completion by direct credit and, if appropriate, by an unconditional release of a deposit held by a stakeholder.

8.8   NOTICE TO COMPLETE

8.8.1   At any time on or after completion date, a party who is ready, able and willing to complete may give the other a notice to complete.

8.8.2   The parties are to complete the contract within ten working days of giving a notice to complete, excluding the day on which the notice is given. For this purpose, time is of the essence of the contract.

9.   REMEDIES

9.1   ERRORS AND OMISSIONS

9.1.1   If any plan or statement in the contract, or in the negotiations leading to it, is or was misleading or inaccurate due to an error or omission, the remedies available are as follows.

9.1.2   When there is a material difference between the description or value of the property as represented and as it is, the buyer is entitled to damages.

9.1.3   An error or omission only entitles the buyer to rescind the contract:

    (a) where the error or omission results from fraud or recklessness, or

(b) where the buyer would be obliged, to its prejudice, to accept property differing substantially (in quantity, quality or tenure) from that which the error or omission had led it to expect.

9.2 RESCISSION

If either party rescinds the contract:

(a) unless the rescission is a result of the buyer's breach of contract the deposit is to be repaid to the buyer with accrued interest

(b) the buyer is to return any documents received from the seller and is to cancel any registration of the contract.

(c) the seller's duty to pay any returned premium under condition 7.1.2(e) (whenever received) is not affected.

9.3 LATE COMPLETION

9.3.1 If the buyer defaults in performing its obligations under the contract and completion is delayed, the buyer is to pay compensation to the seller.

9.3.2 Compensation is calculated at the contract rate on the purchase price (less any deposit paid) for the period between completion date and actual completion, but ignoring any period during which the seller was in default.

9.3.3 Any claim by the seller for loss resulting from delayed completion is to be reduced by any compensation paid under this contract.

9.3.4 Where the sale is not with vacant possession of the whole property and completion is delayed, the seller may give notice to the buyer, before the date of actual completion, that it will take the net income from the property until completion as well as compensation under condition 9.3.1

9.4 AFTER COMPLETION

Completion does not cancel liability to perform any outstanding obligation under the contract.

9.5 BUYER'S FAILURE TO COMPLY WITH NOTICE TO COMPLETE

9.5.1 If the buyer fails to complete in accordance with a notice to complete, the following terms apply.

9.5.2 The seller may rescind the contract, and if it does so:

(a) it may
   (i) forfeit and keep any deposit and accrued interest
   (ii) resell the property
   (iii) claim damages

(b) the buyer is to return any documents received from the seller and is to cancel any registration of the contract.

9.5.3 The seller retains its other rights and remedies.

9.6 SELLER'S FAILURE TO COMPLY WITH NOTICE TO COMPLETE

9.6.1 If the seller fails to complete in accordance with a notice to complete, the following terms apply:

9.6.2 The buyer may rescind the contract, and if it does so:

(a) the deposit is to be repaid to the buyer with accrued interest

(b) the buyer is to return any documents it received from the seller and is, at the seller's expense, to cancel any registration of the contract.

9.6.3 The buyer retains its other rights and remedies.

10 LEASEHOLD PROPERTY

10.1 EXISTING LEASES

10.1.1 The following provisions apply to a sale of leasehold land.

10.1.2 The seller having provided the buyer with copies of the documents embodying the lease terms, the buyer is treated as entering into the contract knowing and fully accepting those terms.

10.1.3 The seller is to comply with any lease obligations requiring the tenant to insure the property.

10.2 NEW LEASES

10.2.1 The following provisions apply to a contract to grant a new lease.

10.2.2   The conditions apply so that:

"seller" means the proposed landlord

"buyer" means the proposed tenant

"purchase price" means the premium to be paid on the grant of a lease.

10.2.3   The lease is to be in the form of the draft attached to the contract.

10.2.4   If the term of the new lease will exceed seven years, the seller is to deduce a title which will enable the buyer to register the lease at the Land Registry with an absolute title.

10.2.5   The seller is to engross the lease and a counterpart of it and is to send the counterpart to the buyer at least five working days before completion date.

10.2.6   The buyer is to execute the counterpart and deliver it to the seller on completion.

10.3 CONSENTS

10.3.1   (a) The following provisions apply if a consent to let, assign or sub-let is required to complete the contract

(b) In this condition "consent" means consent in a form which satisfies the requirement to obtain it.

10.3.2   (a) The seller is to:

(i)   apply for the consent at its expense, and to use all reasonable efforts to obtain it

(ii) give the buyer notice forthwith on obtaining the consent.

(b) The buyer is to comply with all reasonable requirements, including requirements for the provision of information and references.

10.3.3   Where the consent of a reversioner (whether or not immediate) is required to an assignment or sub-letting, then so far as the reversioner lawfully imposes such a condition:

(a) the buyer is to:

(i)   covenant directly with the reversioner to observe the tenant's covenants and the conditions in the seller's lease

(ii) use reasonable endeavours to provide guarantees of the performance and observance of the tenant's covenants and the conditions in the seller's lease

(iii) execute or procure the execution of the licence

(b) the seller, in the case of an assignment, is to enter into an authorised guarantee agreement.

10.3.4   Neither party may object to a reversioner's consent given subject to a condition:

(a) which under section 19A of the Landlord and Tenant Act 1927 is not regarded as unreasonable, and

(b) which is lawfully imposed under an express term of the lease.

10.3.5   If any required consent has not been obtained by the original completion date:

(a) the time for completion is to be postponed until five working days after the seller gives written notice to the buyer that the consent has been obtained or four months from the original completion date whichever is the earlier

(b) the postponed date is to be treated as the completion date.

10.3.6   At any time after four months from the original completion date, either party may rescind the contract by notice to the other, if:

(a) consent has still not been given, and

(b) no declaration has been obtained from the court that consent has been unreasonably withheld.

10.3.7   If the contract is rescinded under condition 10.3.6 the seller is to remain liable for any breach of condition 10.3.2(a) or 10.3.3(b) and the buyer is to remain liable for any breach of condition 10.3.2(b) or 10.3.3(a). In all other respects neither party is to be treated as in breach of contract and condition 9.2 applies.

10.3.8   A party in breach of its obligations under condition 10.3.2 or 10.3.3 cannot rescind under condition 10.3.6 for so long as its breach is a cause of the consent's being withheld.

11. COMMONHOLD

11.1 Terms used in this condition have the special meanings given to them in Part 1 of the Commonhold and Leasehold Reform Act 2002.

11.2 This condition applies to a disposition of commonhold land.

11.3 The seller having provided the buyer with copies of the current versions of the memorandum and articles of the commonhold association and of the commonhold community statement, the buyer is treated as entering into the contract knowing and fully accepting their terms.

11.4 If the contract is for the sale of property which is or includes part only of a commonhold unit:

(a) the seller is, at its expense, to apply for the written consent of the commonhold association and is to use all reasonable efforts to obtain it

(b) either the seller, unless it is in breach of its obligation under paragraph (a), or the buyer may rescind the contract by notice to the other party if three working days before completion date (or before a later date on which the parties have agreed to complete the contract) the consent has not been given. In that case, neither party is to be treated as in breach of contract and condition 9.2 applies.

12. CHATTELS

12.1 The following provisions apply to any chattels which are included in the contract.

12.2 The contract takes effect as a contract for the sale of goods.

12.3 The buyer takes the chattels in the physical state they are in at the date of the contract.

12.4 Ownership of the chattels passes to the buyer on actual completion but they are at the buyer's risk from the contract date.

PART 2[1]

A. VAT

A1 STANDARD RATED SUPPLY

A1.1 Conditions 1.4.1 and 1.4.2. do not apply.

A1.2 The seller warrants that the sale of the property will constitute a supply chargeable to VAT at the standard rate.

A1.3 The buyer is to pay to the seller on completion an additional amount equal to the VAT in exchange for a proper VAT invoice from the seller.

A2 TRANSFER OF A GOING CONCERN

A2.1 Condition 1.4 does not apply.

A2.2 In this condition "TOGC" means a transfer of a business as a going concern treated as neither a supply of goods nor a supply of services by virtue of article 5 of the Value Added Tax (Special Provisions) Order 1995.

A2.3 The seller warrants that it is using the property for the business of letting to produce rental income.

A2.4 The buyer is to make every effort to comply with the conditions to be met by a transferee under article 5(1) and 5(2) for the sale to constitute a TOGC.

A2.5 The buyer will, on or before the earlier of:

(a) completion date, and

(b) the earliest date on which a supply of the property could be treated as made by the seller under this contract if the sale does not constitute a TOGC, notify the seller that paragraph (2B) of article 5 of the VAT (Special Provisions) Order 1995 does not apply to the buyer.

---

[1] The conditions in Part 2 do not apply unless expressly incorporated. See condition 1.1.4(b).

A2.6   The parties are to treat the sale as a TOGC at completion if the buyer provides written evidence to the seller before completion that it is a taxable person and that it has made an election to waive exemption in respect of the property and has given a written notification of the making of such election in conformity with article 5(2) and has given the notification referred to in condition A2.5.

A2.7   The buyer is not to revoke its election to waive exemption in respect of the property at any time.

A2.8   If the parties treat the sale at completion as a TOGC but it is later determined that the sale was not a TOGC, then within five working days of that determination the buyer shall pay to the seller:

(a)   an amount equal to the VAT chargeable in respect of the supply of the property, in exchange for a proper VAT invoice from the seller; and

(b)   except where the sale is not a TOGC because of an act or omission of the seller, an amount equal to any interest or penalty for which the seller is liable to account to HM Customs and Excise in respect of or by reference to that VAT.

A2.9   If the seller obtains the consent of HM Customs and Excise to retain its VAT records relating to the property, it shall make them available to the buyer for inspection and copying at reasonable times on reasonable request during the six years following completion.

B.   CAPITAL ALLOWANCES

B1   TO ENABLE THE BUYER TO MAKE AND SUBSTANTIATE CLAIMS UNDER THE CAPITAL ALLOWANCES ACT 2001 IN RESPECT OF THE PROPERTY, THE SELLER IS TO USE ITS REASONABLE ENDEAVOURS TO PROVIDE, OR TO PROCURE THAT ITS AGENTS PROVIDE:

(a) copies of all relevant information in its possession or that of its agents, and

(b) such co-operation and assistance as the buyer may reasonably require.

B2.1   The buyer is only to use information provided under condition B1 for the stated purpose.

B2.2   The buyer is not to disclose, without the consent of the seller, any such information which the seller expressly provides on a confidential basis.

B3.1   On completion, the seller and the buyer are jointly to make an election under section 198 of the Capital Allowances Act 2001 which is consistent with the apportionment in the Special Conditions.

B3.2   The seller and the buyer are each to submit the amount fixed by that election to the Inland Revenue for the purposes of their respective capital allowance computations.

C.   REVERSIONARY INTERESTS IN FLATS

C1   NO TENANTS' RIGHTS

C1.1   In this condition, sections refer to sections of the Landlord and Tenant Act 1987 and expressions have the special meanings given to them in that Act.

C1.2   The seller warrants that:

(a)   it gave the notice required by section 5,

(b)   no acceptance notice was served on the landlord or no person was nominated for the purposes of section 6 during the protected period, and

(c)   that period ended less than 12 months before the date of the contract.

C2 TENANTS' RIGHT OF FIRST REFUSAL

C2.1   In this condition, sections refer to sections of the Landlord and Tenant Act 1987 and expressions have the special meanings given to them in that Act.

C2.2   The seller warrants that:

(a)   it gave the notice required by section 5, and

(b)   it has given the buyer a copy of:

(i) any acceptance notice served on the landlord and

(ii) any nomination of a person duly nominated for the purposes of section 6.

C2.3 If the sale is by auction:

(a) the seller warrants that it has given the buyer a copy of any notice served on the landlord electing that section 8B shall apply,

(b) condition 8.1.1. applies as if "thirty working days" were substituted for "twenty working days",

(c) the seller is to send a copy of the contract to the nominated person as required by section 8B(3), and

(d) if the nominated person serves notice under section 8B(4):

(i) the seller is to give the buyer a copy of the notice, and

(ii) condition 9.2 is to apply as if the contract had been rescinded.

SPECIAL CONDITIONS

1. This contract incorporates the Standard Commercial Property Conditions (Second Edition).

2. The property is sold with vacant possession.

(or) 2. The property is sold subject to the leases or tenancies set out on the attached list but otherwise with vacant possession on completion.

3. The chattels at the Property and set out on the attached list are included in the sale. [The amount of the purchase price apportioned to those chattels is £   ]

4. The conditions in Part 2 shown against the boxes ticked below are included in the contract:

☐ Condition A1 (VAT: standard rate)

[or] ☐ Condition A2 (VAT: transfer of a going concern)

☐ Condition B (capital allowances). The amount of the purchase price apportioned to plant and machinery at the property for the purposes of the Capital Allowances Act 2001 is £

☐ Condition C1 (flats: no tenants' rights of first refusal)

[or] ☐ Condition C2 (flats: with tenants' rights of first refusal)

Seller's Conveyancers*:

Buyer's Conveyancers*:

* Adding an e-mail address authorises service by e-mail: see condition 1.3.3(b)

Copyright in this form and its contents rests jointly in SLSS Limited (Oyez) and The Law Society

The Law Society
© 2004 OYEZ and The Law Society

SCPCS1   Laserform International Ltd is an Approved Law Society Supplier

APPENDIX 4

LAW SOCIETY'S CODE FOR COMPLETION BY POST (1998 EDITION)

PREAMBLE

The Code provides a procedure for postal completion which practising solicitors may adopt by reference. It may also be used by licensed conveyancers.

Before agreeing to adopt this Code, a solicitor must be satisfied that doing so will not be contrary to the interests of the client (including any mortgagee client).

When adopted, the Code applies without variation, unless agreed in writing in advance.

PROCEDURE

GENERAL

1. To adopt this Code, all the solicitors must expressly agree, preferably in writing, to use it to complete a specific transaction.

2. On completion, the seller's solicitor acts as the buyer's solicitor's agent without any fee or disbursements.

BEFORE COMPLETION

3. The seller's solicitor will specify in writing to the buyer's solicitor before completion the mortgages or charges secured on the property which, on or before completion, will be redeemed or discharged to the extent that they relate to the property.

4. The seller's solicitor *undertakes*:

    (i) to have the seller's authority to receive the purchase money on completion; and

    (ii) on completion to have the authority of the proprietor of each mortgage or charge specified under paragraph 3 to receive the sum intended to repay it, BUT if the seller's solicitor does not have all the necessary authorities then:

    (iii) to advise the buyer's solicitor no later than 4 pm on the working day before the completion date that they do not have all the authorities or immediately if any is withdrawn later; and

    (iv) not to complete until he has the buyer's solicitor's instructions.

5. Before the completion date, the buyer's solicitor will send the seller's solicitor instructions as to any of the following which apply:

    (i) documents to be examined and marked;

    (ii) memoranda to be endorsed;

    (iii) undertakings to be given;

    (iv) deeds, documents (including any relevant undertakings) and authorities relating to rents, deposits, keys, etc. to be sent to the buyer's solicitor following completion; and

    (v) other relevant matters.

    In default of instructions, the seller's solicitor is under no duty to examine, mark or endorse any document.

6. The buyer's solicitor will remit to the seller's solicitor the sum required to complete, as notified in writing on the seller's solicitor's completion statement or otherwise, or in default of notification as shown by the contract. If the funds are remitted by transfer between banks, the seller's solicitor will instruct the receiving bank to telephone to report immediately the funds have been received. Pending completion, the seller's solicitor will hold the funds to the buyer's solicitor's order.

7. If by the agreed date and time for completion the seller's solicitor has not received the authorities specified in paragraph 4, instructions under paragraph 5 and the sum specified in paragraph 6, the seller's solicitor will forthwith notify the buyer's solicitor and request further instructions.

COMPLETION

8. The seller's solicitor will complete forthwith on receiving the sum specified in paragraph 6, or at a later time agreed with the buyer's solicitor.

9. When completing, seller's solicitor *undertakes*:

   (i) to comply with the instructions given under paragraph 5; and

   (ii) to redeem or obtain discharges for every mortgage or charge so far as it relates to the property specified under paragraph 3 which has not already been redeemed or discharged.

AFTER COMPLETION

10. The seller's solicitor *undertakes*:

   (i) immediately completion has taken place to hold to the buyer's solicitor's order every item referred to in (iv) of paragraph 5 and not to exercise a lien over any such item;

   (ii) as soon as possible after completion, and in any event on the same day:

   (a) to confirm to the buyer's solicitor by telephone or fax that completion has taken place; and

   (b) to send written confirmation and, at the risk of the buyer's solicitor, the items listed in (iv) of pargraph 5 to the buyer's solicitor by first-class post or document exchange.

SUPPLEMENTARY

11. The rights and obligations of the parties, under the contract or otherwise, are not affected by this Code.

12.

   (i) References to the seller's solicitor and the buyer's solicitor apply as appropriate to solicitors acting for other parties who adopt the Code.

   (ii) When a licensed conveyancer adopts this Code, references to a solicitor include a licensed conveyancer.

13. A dispute or difference arising between solicitors who adopt this Code (whether or not subject to any variation) relating directly to its application is to be referred to a single arbitrator agreed between the solicitors. If they do not agree on the appointment within one month, the President of the Law Society may appoint the arbitrator at the request of one of the solicitors.

APPENDIX 5

Property information form

Document date [1][1]/[0][6]/[0][8]

Address of the property

1 The Street Leicester

Postcode [L][E][1][ ][2][W][E][ ]

This form should be completed and read in conjunction with the explanatory notes available separately

1 Boundaries

1.1 Looking towards the property from the road, who either owns or accepts responsibility for the boundary:

(a) on the left?

☐ the seller   [x] next door
☐ shared   ☐ not known

(b) on the right?

[x] the seller ☐ next door
☐ shared   ☐ not known

(c) across the back?

☐ the seller   ☐ next door
☐ shared   [x] not known

(d) across the front?

[x] the seller ☐ next door
☐ shared   ☐ not known

If the answer is 'not known', please give details of the boundaries that the seller has actually repaired or maintained:

The back is shared

Note: 'boundaries' mean any fence, wall, hedge or ditch which marks the edge of the property.

The Law Society

www.hips.lawsociety.org.uk

© Law Society 2007

Laserform International 8/07

1.2 Does the seller know of any boundary being moved in the last 20 years?

☐ Yes   [x] No

If Yes, please give details:

---

2   Disputes and complaints

2.1 Does the seller know of any dispute or anything which might lead to a dispute about this property or any neighbouring property?

[x] Yes   ☐ No

If Yes, please give details:

Noisy parties next door; now stopped

2.2 Has the seller made any complaint to any neighbour about what the neighbour has or has not done?

[x] Yes   ☐ No

If Yes, please give details:

see above

2.3 Has the seller received any complaint about anything the seller has, or has not done as owner?

☐ Yes   [x] No

If Yes, please give details:

---

3   Notices

3.1 Has the seller either sent or received any communication or notices which in any way affect the property or the neighbouring property (for example, from or to neighbours, the council or a government department)?

☐ Yes   [x] No   ☐ Enclosed
☐ To follow   ☐ Lost

If Yes, please supply a copy.

3.2 Has the seller had any negotiations or discussions with any neighbour or any local or other authority affecting the property in any way?

☐ Yes   [x] No

If Yes, please give details:

---

4 Guarantees

Are there any guarantees, warranties or insurance policies relating to the property?

[x] Yes   ☐ No

If Yes, please give details:

```
Damp course guarantee from 2002 with 20 yr guarantee from
Protectory Proofing Homes Ltd also for rot and infestation
(woodworm)
```

---

5 Utilities

Please indicate which of the following services are connected to or at the property:

[x] Electricity
[x] Gas
[x] Mains drainage
[x] Mains water
☐ Private drains
☐ Private water
☐ Septic tank/Cesspit
[x] Telephone

---

6 Council tax

Please state the council tax band and the amount payable.

Band A - H | d
Amount | £ 850.00 yearly

Note: Improvements that have already been made can increase the amount of council tax payable following a sale. It is the event of the sale in these circumstances that may cause the council tax banding to be increased. For further information please see the Valuation Office Agency website www.voa.gov.uk

7 Sharing with the neighbours

7.1 Is the seller aware of any responsibility to contribute to the cost of anything in joint use, such as the repair of a shared drive, boundary or drain? ☐ Yes [x] No

If Yes, please give details:

7.2 Does the seller contribute to the cost of repair of anything used by the neighbours, such as the maintenance of a private road? ☐ Yes [x] No

If Yes, please give details and state who is responsible for organising the work and collecting contributions:

8 Arrangements

8.1 Are there any formal or informal arrangements which the seller has over any neighbouring property? ☐ Yes [x] No

If Yes, please give details:

8.2 Are there any formal or informal arrangements which someone else has over the property? [x] Yes ☐ No

If Yes, please give details:

```
Selina Stott (my partner) lives with me and has helped with the
deposit and will be moving with me to the new property to be
purchased
```

9 Alterations, planning and building control

9.1 Have any of the following changes been made to the whole or any part of the property (including the garden)?

If Yes, in what year were they made?

(a) Building works (including loft conversions, extensions and conservatories) ☐ Yes [x] No [ ] Year

(b) Change of use ☐ Yes [x] No [ ] Year

(c) Sub-division ☐ Yes [x] No [ ] Year

(d) Conversion ☐ Yes [x] No [ ] Year

(e) Installation of replacement windows, roof windows, glazed doors ☐ Yes [x] No [ ] Year

(f) Installation of central heating boiler ☐ Yes [x] No [ ] Year

(g) Installation of solar panels ☐ Yes [x] No [ ] Year

9.2 If any of the changes listed in 9.1 (a) to (g) above have been made, was planning permission, building regulation approval or listed building consent obtained?

If Yes, please supply copies of the relevant permissions and, where appropriate, certificates of completion.

(a) Building works (including loft conversions, extensions and conservatories) ☐ Yes ☐ No ☐ Enclosed ☐ To follow ☐ Lost

(b) Change of use ☐ Yes ☐ No ☐ Enclosed ☐ To follow ☐ Lost

(c) Sub-division ☐ Yes ☐ No ☐ Enclosed ☐ To follow ☐ Lost

(d) Conversion ☐ Yes ☐ No ☐ Enclosed ☐ To follow ☐ Lost

(e) Installation of replacement windows, roof windows, glazed doors ☐ Yes ☐ No ☐ Enclosed ☐ To follow ☐ Lost

(f) Installation of central heating boiler ☐ Yes ☐ No ☐ Enclosed ☐ To follow ☐ Lost

(g) Installation of solar panels ☐ Yes ☐ No ☐ Enclosed ☐ To follow ☐ Lost

9.3 What consents were obtained under any restrictions in
the title registers or any other documents?

Note: The title registers of some properties include clauses which are called 'restrictive
covenants'. These may, for example, forbid the owner of the property from carrying out building
work unless someone else (often a builder of the house) gives consent.

9.4 Has the property been used other than as a private
home in the last 10 years?

☐ Yes   [x] No

If Yes, please give details:

9.5 Has the property been designated as a Listed Building?

☐ Yes   [x] No   ☐ Not known

If Yes, please state the year it was designated as a
Listed Building.

In the year

9.6 Is the property located in a Conservation Area?

☐ Yes   [x] No   ☐ Not known

If Yes, please state the year it was included in the
Conservation Area.

In the year

10 Expenses

Has the seller ever incurred any expenses for the use
of the property or any of its amenities?

[x] Yes   ☐ No

If Yes, please give details:

```
I had a problem with the drains and had to pay £435 to have
them sorted out with the man next door in number 3
```

Note: Ignore mortgage payments, council tax, water rates, and gas, electricity and telephone bills.
Disclose anything else, such as the clearance of cesspit or septic tank or drainage rates.

The information in this form has been given by:

Name   `Leslie King the seller`

The Law Society

Page 6 of 6
TA6
This form is part of the Law Society's TransAction scheme.
The Law Society is the representative body for solicitors in England and Wales.
Laserform International Ltd is an Approved Law Society Supplier

© Law Society 2007

APPENDIX 6

This 5th edition was published in 2005 and is currently under review. It contains references to The Guide to the Professional Conduct of Solicitors 1999 now replaced by the Solicitors Code of Conduct 2007.

National Conveyancing Protocol (5th edition) for Domestic Freehold and Leasehold Property

ACTING FOR THE SELLER

1. THE FIRST STEP

The seller should inform the solicitor as soon as it is intended to place the property on the market so that delay may be reduced after a prospective purchaser is found.

2. PREPARING THE PACKAGE: ASSEMBLING THE INFORMATION

On receipt of instructions, the solicitor should then immediately take the following steps, at the seller's expense:

2.1 Whenever possible instructions should be obtained from the client in person. The Consumer Protection (Distance Selling) Regulations 2000 should not then apply.

2.2 Check the client's identity if the client is not known to you. Comply with money laundering regulations and follow any guidance issued by the Law Society.

2.3 Give the client information as to costs, information relating to the name and status of the person who will be carrying out the work and, if that person is not a partner, the name of the partner who has overall responsibility for the matter. Give any other information necessary to comply with Rule 15 of the Solicitors' Practice Rules 1990 and Solicitors' Costs Information and Client Care Code 1999. If given orally this information should be confirmed in writing.

2.4 Give the seller details of whom to contact in the event of a complaint about the firm's services (Rule 15).

2.5 Consider with client whether to make local authority and other searches so that these can be supplied to the buyer's solicitor as soon as an offer is made. If thought appropriate request a payment on account in relation to disbursements.

2.6 Ascertain the whereabouts of the documents of title and, if not in the solicitor's custody, obtain them and, or if registration or a dealing has taken place after 13 October 2003, apply for an official copy of entries on the register and the title plan.

2.7 Ask the seller to complete the Seller's Property Information Form and on its return remind the seller of the need to notify you of any changes in the information supplied prior to completion.

2.8 Obtain such original guarantees with the accompanying specification, planning decisions, building regulation approvals and certificates of completion as are in the seller's possession and copies of any other planning consents that are with the title deeds or details of any highway and sewerage agreements and bonds or any other relevant certificates relating to the property (e.g. structural engineer's certificate or an indemnity policy).

2.9 Give the seller the Fixtures, Fittings and Contents Form, with a copy to retain, to complete and return prior to the submission of the draft contract.

2.10 If the title is unregistered make an index map search.

2.11 If so instructed requisition a local authority search and enquiries and any other searches (e.g. mining or commons registration searches).

2.12 Obtain details of all mortgages and other financial charges of which the seller's solicitor has notice including, where applicable, improvement grants and discounts repayable to a local authority. Redemption figures should be obtained at this stage in respect of all mortgages on the property so that cases of negative equity or penalty redemption interest can be identified at an early stage.

2.13 Ascertain the identity of all people aged 17 or over living in the dwelling and ask about any financial contribution they or anyone else may have made towards its purchase or subsequent improvement. All persons identified in this way should be asked to confirm their consent to the sale proceeding.

2.14 In leasehold cases, ask the seller to complete the Seller's Leasehold Information Form and to produce, if possible:

(1) A receipt or evidence from the landlord of the last payment of rent.

(2) The maintenance charge accounts for the last three years, where appropriate, and evidence of payment.

(3) Details of the buildings insurance policy.

If any of these are lacking, and are necessary for the transaction, the solicitor should obtain them from the landlord. At the same time investigate whether a licence to assign is required and, if so, enquire of the landlord what references or deeds of covenant are necessary and, in the case of some retirement schemes, if a charge is payable to the management company on change of ownership. On receipt of the form back from the seller, remind the seller of the need to notify you of any changes in the information supplied prior to completion.

2.15 In commonhold cases:

(1) Ask the seller to complete the Seller's Commonhold Information Form, and to produce, if possible

(i) Commonhold Association Memorandum and Articles of Association;

(ii) Commonhold Community Statement;

(iii) Details of the building insurance policy.

(2) Make a search at Companies House against the commonhold association.

(3) Obtain an official copy of commonhold title for the common parts.

(4) Obtain the account from the commonhold association for the unit and ask if there are

(i) any other claims or assessments against the unit;

(ii) details of the annual budget or estimates;

(iii) any reserve fund; and

(iv) any restricted use areas.

2.16 Check replies given by the seller on the Seller's Property Information Form and, if appropriate, the Seller's Leasehold Information Form and Seller's Commonhold Information Form from the information in your possession (see the guidance from the Law Society's Conveyancing and Land Law Committee [2003] *Gazette*, 16 October, 43).

3. PREPARING THE PACKAGE: THE DRAFT DOCUMENTS

As soon as the title documents or official copies of the registered title are available, and the seller has completed the Seller's Property Information Form and, if appropriate, the Seller's Leasehold Information Form, the Seller's Commonhold Information Form, the solicitor shall:

3.1 If the title is unregistered:

(1) Make a land charges search against the seller and any other appropriate names.

(2) Make an index map search in the Land Registry (if not already obtained—see 2.10) in order to verify that the seller's title is unregistered and ensure that there are no interests registered at the Land Registry adverse to the seller's title.

(3) Prepare an epitome of title. Mark copies or abstracts of all deeds which will not be passed to the buyer as examined against the original.

(4) Prepare and mark as examined against the originals copies of all deeds, or their abstracts, prior to the root of title containing covenants, easements, etc., affecting the property.

(5) Check that all plans on copied documents are correctly coloured.

3.2 If the title is registered, obtain office copy entries of the register, the title plan and copy documents incorporated or referred to in the register entties, if not already obtained (see 2.6).

3.3 Prepare the draft contract and complete and sign the second section of the Seller's Property Information Form and, if appropriate, the Seller's Leasehold Information Form and the Seller's Commonhold Information Form.

3.4 Check contract package is complete and ready to be sent out to the buyer's solicitor.

3.5 Deal promptly with any queries raised by the estate agent.

4. BUYER'S OFFER ACCEPTED

When made aware that a buyer has been found the solicitor shall:

4.1 Cheek with the seller agreement on the price and, if appropriate, that there has been no change in the information already supplied (Seller's Property Information Form, Seller's Leasehold Information Form, Seller's Commonhold Information Form and Fixtures, Fittings and Contents Form). Also check the seller's position on any related purchase. If any part of the purchase price is being apportioned to chattels, which will be in a separate state of severance at completion, advise the seller that apportionment must be a just and reasonable figure, and if in any doubt professional advice from a valuer should be obtained. If appropriate, supply the seller with a copy of the leaflet issued by the Inland Revenue, 'Fixtures and Chattels—Stamp Duty Land Tax'.

4.2 Inform the buyer's solicitor that the Protocol will be used.

4.3 Ascertain the buyer's position on any related sale and in the light of that reply, ask the seller for a proposed completion date.

4.4 Send to the buyer's solicitor as soon as possible the contract package to include:
   (1) Draft contract.
   (2) Office copy entries of the registered title (including office copies of all documents mentioned), the title plan or the epitome of title (including details of any prior matters referred to but not disclosed by the documents themselves) and the index map search.
   (3) The Seller's Property Information Form with copies of all relevant planning decisions, guarantees, etc.
   (4) The completed Fixtures Fittings and Contents Form. Where this is provided it will form part of the contract and should be attached to it.
   (5) In leasehold cases:
       (i) the Seller's Leasehold Information Form, with all information about maintenance charges and insurance and, if appropriate, the procedure (including references required) for obtaining the landlord's consent to the sale;
       (ii) a copy of the lease.
   (6) In commonhold cases:
       (i) Seller's Commonhold Information Form, with all information obtained under 2.15;
       (ii) a copy of the registered title for the commonhold common parts and a copy of the registered title for the seller's unit.
   (7) If available, the local authority search and enquiries and any other searches made by the seller's solicitor.

   If any of these documents are not available the remaining items should be forwarded to the buyer's solicitor as soon as they are available.

4.5 Inform the estate agent or property seller when the draft contract has been submitted to the buyer's solicitor.

4.6 Ask the buyer's solicitor if a 10 per cent deposit will be paid and, if not, what arrangements are proposed.

4.7 If and to the extent that the seller consents to the disclosure, supply information about the position on the seller's own purchase and of any other transactions in the chain above, and thereafter, of any change in circumstances.

4.8 Notify the seller of all information received in response to the above.

4.9 Inform the estate agent of any unexpected delays or difficulties likely to delay exchange of contracts.

ACTING FOR THE BUYER

5. THE FIRST STEP

On notification of the buyer's purchase the solicitor should then immediately take the following steps, at the buyer's expense.

5.1 Wherever possible instructions should be obtained from the client in person. The Consumer Protection (Distance Selling) Regulations 2000 should not then apply.

5.2 Check the client's identity if you do not know the client, comply with the Money Laundering Regulation [2003] and follow any guidance issued by the Law Society.

5.3 Give the client information as to costs, information relating to the name and status of the person who will be carrying out the work and, if that person is not a partner, the name of the partner who has overall responsibility for the matter. Give any other information necessary to comply with Rule

15 of the Solicitors' Practice Rules 1990 and Solicitors' Costs Information and Client Care Code 1999. If given orally this information should be confirmed in writing.

5.4 Give the client details of whom to contact in the event of a complaint about the firm's services (Rule 15).

5.5 Request a payment on account in relation to disbursements.

5.6 Confirm to the seller's solicitor that the Protocol will be used.

5.7 Ascertain the buyer's position on any related sale, mortgage arrangements and whether a 10 per cent deposit will be provided.

5.8 If and to the extent that the buyer consents to the disclosure, inform the seller's solicitor about the position on the buyer's own sale, if any, and of any connected transactions, the general nature of the mortgage application, the amount of deposit available and if the seller's target date for completion can be met, and thereafter, of any change in circumstances.

On receipt of the draft contract and other documents:

5.9 Notify the buyer that these documents have been received, check the price and send the client a copy of the Fixtures, Fittings and Contents Form and, if appropriate, a copy of the title plan for checking. If the purchase price is being apportioned between the property and chattels, advise the buyer what constitutes chattels for Stamp Duty Land Tax purposes, that values for the chattels must be just and reasonable, and if in any doubt, professional advice from a valuer should be obtained. If appropriate, supply the buyer with a copy of the leaflet issued by the Inland Revenue 'Fixtures and Chattels—Stamp Duty Land Tax'.

5.10 Subject to 5.20 below, make a local authority search with the usual Part 1 enquiries and any additional enquiries relevant to the property.

5.11 Make a commons registration search, if appropriate.

5.12 Make mining enquiries and drainage enquiries if appropriate and consider any other relevant searches, e.g., environmental searches.

5.13 Check the buyer's position on any related sale and check that the buyer has a satisfactory mortgage offer and all conditions of the mortgage are or can be satisfied.

5.14 Check the buyer understands the nature and effect of the mortgage offer and duty to disclose any relevant matters to the lender.

5.15 Advise the buyer of the need for a survey on the property.

5.16 Check the draft contract to ensure title is satisfactory and add any special conditions necessary to achieve this (e.g. for removal of or consents needed under any restrictions or notices revealed on the title).

5.17 Confirm approval of the draft contract and return it approved as soon as possible, having inserted the buyer's full names and address, subject to any outstanding matters.

5.18 At the same time ask only those specific additional enquiries which are required to clarify some point arising out of the documents submitted or which are relevant to the particular nature or location of the property or which the buyer has expressly requested. Any enquiry, including those about the state and condition of the building, which is capable of being ascertained by the buyer's own enquiries or survey or personal inspection should not be raised. Additional duplicated standard forms should not be submitted; if they are, the seller's solicitor is under no obligation to deal with them nor need answer any enquiry seeking opinions rather than facts.

5.19 If title has been deduced, check the seller's title to the property and raise any requisitions on the title deduced. (See Standard Conditions of Sale (Fourth Edition) 4.2.1) Matters relating to the completion arrangements should not be raised at this stage.

5.20 If a local authority search has been supplied by the seller's solicitors with the draft contract, consider the need to make a local authority search with the usual Part 1 enquiries or raise any of the optional Part 2 enquiries not included in the seller's search or any other additional enquiries relevant to the property. (The local authority search should not be more than three months old at exchange of contracts nor six months old at completion.)

5.21 Ensure that buildings insurance arrangements are in place.

5.22 Check the position over any life policies referred to in the lender's offer of mortgage.

5.23 Check with the buyer if property is being purchased in sole name or jointly with another person. If a joint purchase check whether as joint tenants or tenants in common and advise on the difference in writing.

BOTH PARTIES' SOLICITOR

6. PRIOR TO EXCHANGE OF CONTRACTS

If acting for the buyer

When all satisfactory replies received to enquiries, requisitions on title and searches:

6.1 Prepare and send to the buyer a contract report and invite the buyer to make an appointment to call to raise any queries on the contract report and to sign the contract ideally in the presence of a solicitor.

6.2 When the buyer signs the contract check:
   (1) Completion date.
   (2) That the buyer understands and can comply with all the conditions on the mortgage offer if appropriate.
   (3) That all the necessary funds will be available to complete the purchase.

If acting for the seller

6.3 Advise the seller on the effect of the contract and ask the seller to sign it, ideally in the presence of the solicitor.

6.4 Check the position on any related purchase so that there can be a simultaneous exchange of contracts on both the sale and purchase.

6.5 Check completion date.

7. RELATIONSHIP WITH THE BUYER'S LENDER

On receipt of instructions from the buyer's lender:

7.1 Check the mortgage offer complies with Practice Rule 6(3)(c) and (e) and is certified to that effect.

7.2 Check any special conditions in the mortgage offer to see if there are additional instructions or conditions not normally required by Practice Rule 6(3)(c).

7.3 Go through any special conditions in the mortgage offer with the buyer.

7.4 Notify the lender if Practice Rule 6(3)(b) or 1.13 or 1.14 of the CML Lenders' Handbook ('Lenders' Handbook') are applicable.

7.5 Consider whether there are any conflicts of interest which prevent you accepting instructions to act for the lender.

7.6 If you do not know the borrower and anyone else required to sign the mortgage, charge or other document, check evidence of identity (Practice Rule 6(3)(c)(*i*)).

7.7 Consider whether there are any circumstances covered by the Law Society's:
   (1) Green Card on property fraud
   (2) Blue Card on money laundering
   (3) Pink Card on undertakings
   (4) Money Laundering Guidance.

7.8 If you do not know the seller's solicitor/licensed conveyancer check that they appear in a legal directory or are on the record of their professional body (see Practice Rule 6(3)(c)(*i*) and the Lenders' Handbook).

7.9 Carry out any other checks required by the lender provided they comply with Practice Rule 6(3)(c).

7.10 Check the lender's requirements as to whether it requires the original mortgage deed to be lodged with it following registration.

7.11 At all times comply with the requirements of Practice Rule 6(3) and the Lenders' Handbook and ensure if a conflict of interest arises you cease to act for the lender.

8. EXCHANGE OF CONTRACTS

On exchange, the buyer's solicitor shall send or deliver to the seller's solicitor:

8.1 The signed contract with all names, dates and financial information completed.

8.2 The deposit provided in the manner prescribed in the contract. Under the Law Society's Formula C the deposit may have to be sent to another solicitor nominated by the seller's solicitor.

8.3 If contracts are exchanged by telephone the procedures laid down by the Law Society's Formulae A, B or C must be used and both solicitors must ensure (unless otherwise agreed) that the undertakings to send documents and to pay the deposit on that day are strictly observed.

8.4 The seller's solicitor shall, once the buyer's signed contract and deposit are held unconditionally, having ensured that the details of each contract are fully completed and identical, send the seller's signed contract on the day of exchange to the buyer's solicitor in compliance with the undertaking given on exchange.

8.5 Notify the client that contracts have been exchanged.

8.6 Notify the seller's estate agent or property seller of exchange of contracts and the completion date.

9. BETWEEN EXCHANGE AND THE DAY OF COMPLETION

As soon as possible after exchange and in any case within the time limits contained in the Standard Conditions of Sale:

9.1 The buyer's solicitor shall send to the seller's solicitor, in duplicate:
   (1) Completion Information Form and include any requisitions on title which are necessary and could not be raised prior to exchange of contracts, or ask seller's solicitor to confirm that there is no variation in any replies given prior to exchange.
   (2) Draft conveyance/transfer or assignment incorporating appropriate provisions for joint purchase.
   (3) Other documents, e.g. draft receipt for purchase price of fixtures, fittings and contents.

9.2 As soon as possible after receipt of these documents the seller's solicitor shall send to the buyer's solicitor:
   (1) Replies to Completion Information and Requisitions on Title Form.
   (2) Draft conveyance/transfer or assignment approved.
   (3) If appropriate, completion statement supported by photocopy receipts or evidence of payment of apportionments claimed.
   (4) Copy of licence to assign from the landlord if appropriate.

9.3 The buyer's solicitor shall then:
   (1) Engross the approved draft conveyance/transfer or assignment.
   (2) Explain the effect of that document to the buyer and obtain the buyer's signature to it (if necessary).
   (3) Send it to the seller's solicitor in time to enable the seller to sign it before completion without suffering inconvenience.
   (4) If appropriate prepare any separate declaration of trust, advise the buyer on its effect and obtain the buyer's signature to it.
   (5) Advise the buyer on the contents and effect of the mortgage deed and obtain the buyer's signature to that deed. If possible, and in all cases where the lender so requires, a solicitor should witness the buyer's signature to the mortgage deed.
   (6) Send the certificate of title (complying with Rule 6(3)(d)) to the lender.
   (7) Take any steps necessary to ensure that the amount payable on completion will be available in time for completion including sending to the buyer a completion statement to include legal costs, Land Registry fees and other disbursements and, if appropriate, Stamp Duty Land Tax.
   (8) Make the Land Registry and land charges searches and, if appropriate, a company search.
   (9) Ensure that you have by this stage obtained sufficient information from each buyer to complete the relevant land transaction return, including national insurance numbers, and prepare the return. After checking with the buyer that the information on the form is accurate, advise the buyer that an Inland Revenue enquiry is possible within the following nine months which might result in costs and penalties. Ask the buyer to sign the form in black ink and return it immediately as penalties will be charged by the Inland Revenue unless the form is lodged within 30 days of completion.
   (10) Explain and discuss with the buyer the need to disclose overriding interests in the property and complete Form D1.

9.4 The seller's solicitor shall:
   (1) Request redemption figures for all financial charges on the property revealed by the deeds/official copy entries/land charges search against the seller.
   (2) On receipt of the engrossment of the transfer or assignment, after checking the engrossment to ensure accuracy, obtain the seller's signature to it after ascertaining that the seller understands the nature and contents of the document. If the document is not to be signed in the solicitor's presence the letter sending the document for signature should contain an explanation of the nature and effect of the document and clear instructions relating to the execution of it.
   (3) On receipt of the estate agent's or property seller's commission account obtain the seller's instructions to pay the account on the seller's behalf out of the sale proceeds.

(4) Consider if the consent of any restrictioner (e.g. a managing agent or management company) who will have a continuing interest is needed and if so, take steps to ensure that such consent will be available on completion.

10. RELATIONSHIP WITH THE SELLER'S ESTATE AGENT OR PROPERTY SELLER

Where the seller has instructed estate agents or property seller, the seller's solicitor shall take the following steps:

10.1 Inform them when the draft contracts are submitted (see 4.5).

10.2 Deal promptly with any queries raised by them.

10.3 Inform them of any unexpected delays or difficulties likely to delay exchange of contracts (see 4.9).

10.4 Inform them when exchange has taken place and the date of completion (see 8.6).

10.5 On receipt of their commission account send a copy to the seller and obtain instructions as to arrangements for payment (see 9.4(3)).

10.6 Inform them of completion and, if appropriate, authorise release of any keys held by them (see 11.3(1)).

10.7 If so instructed pay the commission (see 9.4(3) and 11.6(2)).

11. COMPLETION: THE DAY OF PAYMENT AND REMOVALS

11.1 If completion is to be by post, the Law Society's Code for Completion shall be used, unless otherwise agreed.

11.2 As soon as practicable and not later than the morning of completion, the buyer's solicitor shall advise the seller's solicitor of the manner and transmission of the purchase money and of steps taken to despatch it.

11.3 On being satisfied as to the receipt of the balance of the purchase money, the seller's solicitor shall:
(1) Notify the estate agent or property seller that completion has taken place and authorise release of the keys.
(2) Notify the buyer's solicitor that completion has taken place and the keys have been released.
(3) Date and complete the transfer.
(4) Despatch the deeds including the transfer or the assignment and the licence to assign to the buyer's solicitor with any appropriate undertakings.

11.4 The seller's solicitor shall check that the seller is aware of the need to notify the local and water authorities of the change in ownership.

11.5 After completion, where appropriate, the buyer's solicitor shall give notice of assignment to the lessor.

11.6 Immediately after completion, the seller's solicitor shall:
(1) Send to the lender the amount required to release the property sold.
(2) Pay the estate agent's or property seller's commission if so authorised.
(3) Account to the seller for the balance of the sale proceeds.

11.7 Immediately after completion, the buyer's solicitor shall:
(1) Date and complete the mortgage document and, if appropriate, give notice of any second or subsequent charge to the first chargee.
(2) Confirm completion of the purchase and the mortgage to the buyer.
(3) Lodge Form SDLT with the Inland Revenue and pay any Stamp Duty Land Tax that is due. On receipt of the certificate of notification from the Inland Revenue, hold it to lodge with the Land Registry application.
(4) Consider the need to register a restriction and, if appropriate, complete Form RX1.
(5) Deal with the registration of the transfer document and mortgage with the Land Registry within the priority period of the search including lodging with the application form (AP1 or FR1) Form D1 and, if appropriate, Form RX1.
(6) If appropriate, send a notice of assignment of a life policy to the insurance company.
(7) On receipt of notification from the Land Registry that registration has been completed and a title information document has been supplied, check its contents carefully and supply a copy of that document to the buyer.
(8) Send the original mortgage deed and/or the title information document to the lender, if appropriate, and deal with any other documents in accordance with its instructions.

(9) Take the buyer's instructions as to any documents not being held by the lender, and if the documents are to be sent to the buyer or anyone else to hold on the buyer's behalf, inform the buyer of the need to keep the documents safely so that they will be available on a sale of the property.

(10) If the sale was a sale of part of the land in the registered title, then on completion of the registration of the transfer of part, the seller's solicitor shall check that the title certificate and amended registered plan are accurate and send a copy to the seller.

INDEX